LIBERTY CRUSADE

Restoring The Republic

LARRY BALLARD

PRAISE FOR THIS BOOK

Larry Ballard has once again delivered a timely and powerful message for our nation and the world. In *Restoring the Republic,* he paints a vivid picture of what lies ahead, a future where oppressive financial systems collapse, and a kingdom-based economy rises, built on longevity, reusability, shared resources, and life-changing technology.

Larry's deep insights as a speaker, author, and visionary bring clarity to our current times and hope for what's to come: a period of peace, prosperity, and spiritual awakening. Drawing from the original American economic system, an economy designed to uplift all of humanity, he shows us the path to rebuilding our nation and safeguarding our freedoms for generations to come. This book is a must-read for anyone who believes in the promise of America and desires to see our Republic restored to its founding principles.

Francine Fosdick
upfrontintheprophetic.com

If you want to be excited about the restoration of our Republic, happening now, this is a must-read! Larry Ballard, a close friend and brother in Christ, has the most insightful analysis of how the United States of America WILL become the new "Kingdom Superpower" in this new age! As a speaker at the ReAwaken America Tour Conferences, I can say this masterpiece is on point with the heartbeat of truth, with those who know!

Robert Agee
Founder, Banners 4 Freedom Ministries

Restoring the Republic, by Liberty Crusades' Larry Ballard, is a timely and fervent appeal to the conscience of a nation adrift. With clarity, conviction, and an undercurrent of moral urgency, Ballard invites readers to reconsider the founding ideals of the American experiment. A brisk yet thoughtful read, part manifesto, part mirror. It is as much a call to remembrance as it is to action.

Mel Carmine
International podcaster and entrepreneur, *carminesgold.com*

From the first time we met Larry, we knew God had anointed him to do great things and educate the masses regarding what's going on with global affairs. Not only is he a phenomenal writer and speaker, but he backs everything up with hardcore facts and research. If you really want to become educated and hear the truth, unplug from all mainstream media, dive into Larry's new book, *Restoring the Republic*, and devour and digest everything he says.

Daryn Ross and Randy Mansell
Co-hosts of the *Patriots with Grit* podcast

As the host of *The B2T Show* and head of FaithNFreedomTV and B2T Ministries, I wholeheartedly endorse Larry Ballard's book. Through our exclusive show, *Blessed Crusade*, on the FaithNFreedomTV network, I've witnessed Larry's profound knowledge, deep patriotism, and unwavering love for the Lord. His ability to weave extensive research on the globalist elite's plans with biblical insights offers readers a unique and invaluable perspective. This book is not just a source of knowledge but a wellspring of wisdom, backed by Larry's meticulous research and compelling insights.

Rick Rene
Blessed2Teach (B2T) Ministries, host of *The B2T Show*

Larry Ballard is an amazing man of God. The Lord has given him insights that he is able to demonstrate point-by-point in an easy-to-understand flow of knowledge. Also, his material is easy and enjoyable to read. Actually, you feel somewhat better even having it on the bookshelf. I highly recommend Larry Ballard; he is a Bible study partner of mine.

Trey Smith
Author, Host of *God in a Nutshell Project*

CONTENTS

INTRODUCTION

America Will Rise Like the Phoenix and Restore Order Out of Chaos

BEFORE YOU BEGIN reading, I want to point out something. There may appear to be a fair amount of redundancy in this book. When I believe it is necessary, I repeat important information and quotes that drive home a point or teaching. However, it is not redundancy, but *reinforcement*. It is an intentional effort so that by the time you finish reading this book, you will know beyond the shadow of a doubt that we are in a war that has our very existence at stake. This book covers some vital material at a very crucial time in history. God wants to encourage and empower His people, and to herald the truth, so that the truth will set you free. We are all in God's hands.

I'm not writing this to entertain you or to impress you with my writing ability. It has a singular purpose, which is to teach and inform you, because people are about to perish for lack of knowledge. Ordained by God, this book is to open people's eyes so that the truth may set the captives free. We are entering a pivotal moment in human history. A group of very evil and powerful people is very near to being able to implement a one-world government dictatorship. Should they be successful, they will kill most of humankind and relegate the survivors to being a genetically altered subspecies of subservient, enslaved people.

God has other plans. The election of Donald J. Trump as the 47th President of the United States charts a new course for the U.S. and the world. God is about to intervene in the affairs of man and lead the world into a period of unparalleled peace, prosperity, and godliness. If we wake up and stand up, God will do the heavy lifting, and He will set us, the captives, free. There is one requirement: we must wake up, stand, and submit to God so He may open the windows of heaven and pour out a blessing the likes of which we cannot imagine. The requirement is to reinforce the unabridged truth with repetition in various ways and contexts until it becomes undeniable and unforgettable.

HOW THIS BOOK CAME TO BE

This book is part two of a three-part series. The primary focus of my first book was to establish: What made America great to begin with, and the forces that have endeavored to bring America down. It laid the foundation for Book Two.

The primary focus of this book (Book 2) is to show how we learn from the past and forge a future that restores America to its former greatness. America was the world's first "Republic." A Republic is a government of the people, by the people, and for the people. It requires a public that is:

- United in purpose
- Moral
- Self-reliant
- Educated
- Informed, and
- Focused on what is in the best interest of the public rather than self-serving interest

These attributes made America the greatest nation the world has ever known. Over the last 250 years, America's founding principles have been usurped by a group of power-crazed tyrants. Drawing on 250 years of history, this book seeks to unify America as one people, one nation, under God, working towards a future liberated from past bondage. It elaborates on how, once America escapes the "debt trap" of its "puppet masters," God will empower the nation to spread freedom, prosperity, and unity globally.

The task will be to take the best from our past and present and forge a better tomorrow where America leads the world through the transition from our current debt-based slavery system into God's kingdom economy, where the wealth has been transferred from the wicked to the righteous. This book lays the foundation for that destiny to be realized. The third book (slated for release in late 2026) takes what we have learned from the first two books and takes humanity on the journey from materialism to spirituality.

In 1968, I had a near-death experience during which God showed me all the events that would shape the world from then until now. It was a profound time for me, as God revealed that His hand had saved me. He will draw upon the experiences of my life in the future to: 1) help me deeply understand world events, and 2) present valuable, personal insights into the diverse fields in which the global elite employs a strategy to enslave us all.

Restoring the Republic offers discernments that few people can see because it combines history, the Bible, economics, politics, current events, and more to provide an easy-to-understand explanation of geopolitical events from above the fray, allowing readers to discern the truth. This book will open your eyes and change your life, not because I wrote it but because God ordained it. It is His truth—His gift to the world.

THE TRUTH WILL SET YOU FREE

There is a financial elite that controls the global central banking system. With the flick of a pen, they create worthless fiat currency, which they use to buy power and influence at every stratum of society. They control the world's natural resources, manufacturing, and trade, which are the basis of all wealth. They form a global shadow government that is the actual governing power of the world. Their shadow government controls the four centers of power:

- Monetary
- Political
- Intellectual
- Religious

Virtually all our political leaders (including our presidents) are selected, groomed, financed, and placed in their positions of power and influence based on having agreed to be the puppets of these global puppet masters. This applies not only to our political leaders but also to our corporate leaders, educational leaders, and religious leaders. They control all the necessities of life and all the sources of information that make up our perception of reality.

Though it may be hard to believe, we are programmed from cradle to grave. Nearly everything we choose to believe and every action we take is influenced by these puppet masters because they control our political, economic, social, and ethical belief systems. Lacking contradictory information, we believe in their falsehoods and succumb to their manipulation and brainwashing.

God intends to end the division that is intentionally inflicted on us by our overlords. They keep us at odds with one another because it distracts us from their agenda to enslave us, and because they know a house divided cannot stand. They project the evil they do onto others as a means of deflection. They call truth tellers conspiracy theorists and blame their misdeeds on others.

Let me highlight a key point that might be hard for some to accept: Donald Trump is not an insurrectionist, and he certainly is not the would-be dictator as some portray him. God ordained him to unite the people and lead the U.S. and the world on a path to peace, prosperity, and godliness. I ask you to judge this man not by the things said about him, but to judge him by the promises he makes, the promises he keeps, and the results he produces. He has pledged to Make America:

- Greater than ever
- Prosperous
- Respected, and most importantly
- A Godly Nation

PRESIDENT TRUMP'S ACHIEVEMENTS WHILE IN OFFICE

- ✓ The stock market went from 10,000 to 30,000.
- ✓ There have been no new wars during his administration.
- ✓ He gave us access to oil and natural gas, and as a result, the cost of energy was at record lows.
- ✓ Inflation was at a record low.
- ✓ He got us out of NAFTA (North American Free Trade Agreement), which was an intentionally losing trade deal.
- ✓ He negotiated fair-trade deals with several major countries.
- ✓ He eliminated many regulations put in place, intentionally making America less competitive in the global marketplace.
- ✓ He lowered the tax on corporate funds held outside the U.S. because high taxes created disincentives to bringing that money back home to America.
- ✓ He placed tariffs on China to support U.S. manufacturers.
- ✓ Employment across all demographics was at record highs!

- ✓ He rebuilt our military's readiness after Obama had cut the nuclear force to "atrophy" and the entire military was in "desperate need of modernization and renewal," according to a 2016 NPR article.
- ✓ He built the wall and forced Mexico to house illegal immigrants in Mexico!
- ✓ Illegal border crossings are a fraction of what they were under the Biden administration!
- ✓ There have been significant reductions in tent city squatters and homeless encampments across America.
- ✓ Crime is much lower, and America is a safer place than it was under Biden!

Trump has made America prosperous. He has made it respectable. Trump is working hard to close our borders to protect America from the infiltration of gangs and criminal illegal aliens. What is it about those achievements that you find objectionable, I ask? Not one of these things was the action of a tyrannical, Hitler-like despot. The Democrats call Trump a "Hitler," when in fact their policies are the ones that threaten our freedom!

Had it not been for the false rhetoric of the media and the political class, there would be no hysteria about Trump. But he has been constantly portrayed as a threat to our democracy when, in fact, it is the policies of the Democrats, not those of Trump, that threaten what they call our democracy. They don't even know that our founding fathers referred to democracy as a *mobocracy*. They knew it represented majority rule.

The moment those least able or least willing to work realized that they could get handouts from the public coffers, it was just a matter of time before we lost our freedom. Why is that? Entitlements and handouts destroy the fabric of society because they create a race to the bottom as politicians compete to buy people's votes with promises of freebies.

America was founded as a *republic,* not a *democracy.* A republic is a government of the people, by the people, and for the people. It requires a moral, educated, informed, and self-reliant populace willing to vote for what is truly in the best interest of society, rather than for the person or party who promises the most handouts.

Take a moment to reflect on the platform Kamala Harris ran on. She promised an *opportunity economy* based on government handouts. It goes back to the often-familiar phrase:

A government big enough to give you everything you want
is big enough to take everything you have.

In truth, it is the Democrats' policies under Biden and Harris that are despotic and Hitler-like. The facts speak for themselves. What follows is an account of the Biden–Harris policies. If you put aside your biases and look at them objectively, you cannot escape the fact that their policies, not those of Trump, are based on socialism and communism and undermine our Constitution and our freedoms!

KAMALA HARRIS'S OPPORTUNITY ECONOMY

If Kamala Harris had been elected president, she would have employed her "New Way Forward," a plan that would have had devastating effects on our nation. In the plan, she and her running mate, Tim Walz, outlined what she called her "Opportunity Economy," a way for all middle-class families to have the same chance to compete and the same opportunity to succeed as others.

However, the plan was essentially a way to sway U.S. voters who were dissatisfied with the economy of her predecessor, Joe Biden, and to bring them over to her wealth redistribution theories and tactics. Here are a few essential features the Harris campaign stressed under the opportunity economy umbrella:

1. Based on handouts, not on the opportunity to have a livable wage
2. A $25,000 handout for first-time homebuyers
3. Forgiveness of debt from college tuition
4. Social security and other entitlements for illegal immigrants, etc.

BIDEN/HARRIS POLICIES AND ACCOMPLISHMENTS
THAT THREATENED YOUR FREEDOM OR FINANCES

Here is a list of policies and events from Joe Biden's term, backed by Kamala Harris, which significantly jeopardized America's freedom and economy:

- The War in Ukraine
- The debacle in Afghanistan
- Responsible for rampant inflation
- Supported mandatory gun confiscation (2nd Amendment)

- Election tampering and censorship (e.g., they pressured Zuckerberg to censor Trump during the 2020 election)
- Supported ending the filibuster to pass the climate bill
- Supported packing the Supreme Court
- Supported LGBTQ rights above those of our children
- Supported ending private insurance
- Supported a ban on fracking and offshore drilling
- Supported transgender transition operations for prison inmates
- Supported open borders
- Responsible for the surge in drug and human trafficking
- Ended the stay in Mexico
- Supported decriminalizing illegal immigration
- Supported sanctuary cities
- Supported a variety of entitlements for illegal immigrants
- Supported a path to citizenship for illegal immigrants
- Supported defunding the police and ICE
- Supported no-cash bail laws

After reviewing the facts, how is it possible to call Trump a Hitler, a warmonger, and a tyrant? The facts show that honor goes to Biden, Harris, and the Democrats.

But I must, in all fairness, say that the globalist banking cartel has infiltrated both the Democrat and Republican parties. I believe that one day soon, we will yet find out that the 2020 election was, in fact, stolen! And when that is revealed, many people from both parties will be removed from office.

As Trump says, "The swamp must be drained," so we can reestablish our republic, a government of the people, by the people, and for the people. The elite puppet masters must be removed from power if we are going to restore our republic and usher in a period of peace, prosperity, unity, and godliness.

God is about to collapse the Elite's corrupt system of slavery without chains and usher in His Harvest of Souls. The truth from this divinely inspired book offers freedom! I hope that you will be blessed and empowered as you read these pages.

Sincerely,
Larry Ballard

CHAPTER 1

GLOBAL INSIGHTS
Seeing Things How They Really Are

TOPICS COVERED IN THIS CHAPTER:

- WHY AMERICA IS GOD'S CONVENANT NATION
- THE ENEMY'S ENDGAME AGENDA
- WHAT IT TAKES TO BE A GLOBAL SUPERPOWER
- WHO THE GLOBAL ELITE ARE
- HOW THE U.S. GOVERNMENT WAS HIJACKED

FOR THOSE WHO read my first book, some parts of this book may be redundant, especially here in the first chapter. Still, a groundwork must be established to perceive today's happenings. My first book laid the foundation necessary to enable us to view current events through the prism of the global elite's endgame agenda. Based on the premise that reducing resource consumption to sustainable levels is necessary, it is imperative to reduce the human population to 500 million by any means possible. Once you know the truth, the financial elite can no longer control you with their lies, deception, and manipulation because the truth will make you immune.

Before we can understand our current social and political nightmare, we must first understand where it all began and how things have progressed over time to reach this point, where things look hopeless. That's because that is precisely how our enslavers want us to feel. They have thrown everything they can at us to make us feel so desperate that we will throw up our hands and surrender. That may be the enemy's plan, but it is not God's plan. He knows the end before the beginning, and he knows the plans of the enemy and how to thwart them.

They think they are winning, but the truth is, they lost before they even began. Like the Israelites in Egypt, we have been in the dark hour of despair for a long time. However, it is time for our Red Sea moment, which sets us free and delivers us into the Harvest of Souls that God has purposed before the foundation of time. It is essential to understand our position in the Bible scriptures. Now comes God's spotless church and the Harvest of Souls, then comes the tribulation, and finally, the millennial reign.

Our story starts with the founding of God's chosen nation: America. I know not everyone reading this book is a Christian, so I will not belabor this part of our story. The reasons for America's designation as God's chosen nation become clear by exploring history, specifically Abraham's narrative and his ordered sacrifice of Isaac, paralleling God's sacrifice of His son for mankind's transgressions.

So, Abraham had laid his son on an altar made of stone and, with a knife in hand, was about to thrust it in and take the life of his beloved son. Then, at the last second, God stopped him and showed him a ram caught in the thicket that he was to sacrifice in place of his son. Then God said to Abraham that his deeds were righteous, and so He would make a great nation of him and bless him.

> And I will make of thee a great nation, and I will bless thee,
> and make thy name great; and thou shalt be a blessing.
> Genesis 12:2 (KJV)

> The angel of the LORD called to Abraham from heaven a second time and said, "I swear
> by myself, declares the LORD, that because you have done this and have not withheld
> your son, your only son, I will surely bless you and make your descendants as
> numerous as the stars in the sky and as the sand on the seashore. Your descendants
> will take possession of the cities of their enemies, and through your offspring, all
> nations on earth will be blessed, because you have obeyed me."
> Genesis 22:15-18 (NIV)

Skipping forward, the Israelites left Egypt, and ten of the tribes came to be known as the "Lost Tribes." They migrated up the Euphrates River and ended up in England. In 1607, the Virginia Trading Company financed the settlement of the first colony in America. Their arrival at Cape Henry, now Virginia Beach, led to their being called the "First Landing." Upon landing, they took down the mast from the ship and erected a cross, dedicating America to God. Read the quote below:

> **We do hereby dedicate this land, and ourselves, to reach the people within these**
> **shores with the Gospel of Jesus Christ, and to raise up Godly generations after us, and**
> **with these generations take the Kingdom of God to all the earth.**
> **May this Covenant of Dedication remain to all generations,**
> **as long as the earth remains, and may this Land, along with England,**
> **be an Evangelist to the world.**
> **May all who see this Cross, remember what we have done here,**
> **and may those who come here to inhabit join us in this Covenant**
> **and in this most noble work that the Holy Scriptures may be fulfilled.**
> Rev. Robert Hunt, Cape Henry, Virginia - April 29, 1607

Then, in 1620, the people who were now known as the "Pilgrims" found themselves so desperate for religious freedom that they embarked from England. Bound for America, aboard the Mayflower, they landed at what is now Plymouth, Massachusetts. They immediately dedicated their colony to God in the Mayflower Compact.

Fast forward to 1789, America had won the American Revolutionary War against Britain, and the 1ˢᵗ Continental Congress was sworn in. As his first official act as President, George Washington led a delegation from Freedom Hall in New York (Washington, D.C. did not yet exist) to St. Paul's Chapel, where America once again was dedicated to God. I say again, America was and is under Abraham's Covenant.

America, more than any other nation in the world, has been blessed and has been a blessing. Now is the time of God's Harvest of Souls. Get ready. The Shadow Government of the global elite is about to fall, and the world, led by America, God's Covenant Nation, is about to experience the *Latter Day Reign*, with the greatest revival and transfer of wealth the world has ever seen.

Coincidentally, St Paul's Chapel is near the site of Ground Zero of 9/11. The Chapel, constructed in 1766, is the oldest church building in Manhattan and is less than 100 yards from the World Trade Center site. It is believed that a giant sycamore tree protected the church during the collapse of the Twin Towers.

No, that was not a coincidence. God knows the end before the beginning. 9/11 was the moment in history when the enemy's plans began to turn on him. When everything finally comes out, we will know that 9/11 was a *false flag event* orchestrated by our government. The wars that followed were part of their plans to drive America into unmanageable debt.

But there was more to their plan. When the traitor, George W. Bush Jr., announced the war on terror, he said, "This will be a generational war lasting 30 years or more." My question is: How would he know that if it wasn't planned? The plan was to create an undefined enemy that could emerge from the shadows and strike us anywhere, at any time. It was supposed to make us passive, but it had the opposite effect; it woke up the American people. Or I should say, started the process!

The next wake-up call occurred with the 2008 financial collapse, when people began to put the puzzle pieces together and realized that 9/11 was a precursor to the 2008 economic collapse. I will lay it out for those of you who haven't made the connection.

Below are the three cylinders in the economy's engine:

1. Trade
2. Stock Market, and
3. Real Estate

TRADE

The attack on trade began with Nixon and Carter. Nixon's assignment from his puppet masters was to ensure that China siphoned off a significant portion of U.S. trade, leaving the U.S. economy weakened, with one cylinder of the economy crippled. To achieve that, Nixon was to open trade with China, but being the crook that he was, he got caught trying to steal an election and was forced to step down. Enter the grinning peanut farmer, Carter. He oversaw the stagnation of the U.S. economy, where a false flag oil embargo provided the illegal FED with the excuse to intervene and see that both interest rates and inflation skyrocketed to 18 to 21% during Carter's entire term in office. This process became known as *Stagflation* because it completely stagnated the U.S. economy, giving China time to ramp up and take control of global trade from the U.S. The rise of China and the fall of the U.S. were officially underway.

Then along came the slime bag and corrupt Bill Clinton to finish the job that Nixon the Thief and Carter the Clown had started. He signed into law the intentionally losing NAFTA trade deal, which ensured America could not compete fairly in international trade. The intent was that the U.S. would be forced into intentionally losing trade deals, which would further drive the U.S. into unmanageable debt, allowing China's rise to power. If you doubt the veracity of this, then reflect on the following quote:

> The Rockefeller File is not fiction. It is a compact, powerful, and frightening presentation of what may be the most important story of our lifetime—the drive of the Rockefellers and their allies to create a one-world government combining super-capitalism and communism under the same tent, all under their control...not one has dared reveal the most vital part of the Rockefeller story: that the Rockefellers and their allies have, for at least fifty years, been carefully following a plan to use their economic power to gain political control of first America, and then the rest of the world. Do I mean conspiracy? Yes, I do. I am convinced there is such a plot, international in scope, generations old in planning, and incredibly evil in intent.
>
> Congressman Larry P. McDonald, GA, Introduction, *The Rockefeller Files*, 1976

On August 31, 1983, McDonald was killed aboard Korean Airlines Flight 007, which inadvertently strayed over Soviet airspace and was *accidentally* (my a$$) shot down. Media coverage was brief and limited, omitting McDonald's leadership in a congressional effort to reveal a "dangerous international conspiracy."

In a nutshell, the plan from the outset was to create a hybrid world government that combined elements of super-capitalism and communism. Capitalism gives the one-world government the robust economy it needs, and communism gives it the control it needs to have its global dictatorship.

THE STOCK MARKET

Immediately following the 9/11 attacks, the stock market crashed, leaving the U.S. with only one cylinder to the economic engine: real estate. The stage was set for the 2008 financial collapse, where a real estate frenzy would be created, driving prices up until the appointed time. Then, on cue, they popped the bubble, and the house of cards came tumbling down. But just like the Great Depression of 1929, there was more to the story than meets the eye. Their plot required the cooperation of a cast of characters, including the maniacal banker gangsters, our bought-and-paid-for corrupt politicians, and the assistance of greedy, corrupt companies.

REAL ESTATE

So, was there a plan to use real estate to drive the U.S. further into unmanageable debt? You bet there was. Here is what happened: This consortium of evil created what were called "collateralized debt obligations" and sold them to the world. Remember, on the surface, it may appear that the U.S. was the target of their plot, but just as in 1929, the actual target was the global economy.

The world's leading economy, the U.S., had to fall for the rest of the dominoes to topple. A collateralized debt obligation is a loan vehicle created by bundling conventional 20%-down mortgages with what came to be known as "caustic subprime zero-down mortgages." These bundles of risky loans were sold worldwide, facilitated by corrupt rating companies that gave these caustic, high-risk investments AAA ratings.

By doing this, they set a trap to drag the world into another global depression. Enter what I call the three most notorious members of *The Rogue's Gallery of Disgraced Traitors*: None other than Barack Obama, Bill Clinton, and George Bush, Jr. What actions caused these men the prestigious honor of being in the Rogue's Gallery?

Let's take them one at a time. What we are going to explore are the events leading up to the 2008 financial collapse, which could never have happened were it not for the involvement of these men.

OBAMA

The traitorous Islamic Senator, Obama, fresh out of Harvard Law School, sued Citibank for redlining, which is alleged discrimination when applying for a mortgage. He won the case, and this laid the foundation for the subprime loans, which underpinned the 2008 financial collapse. For the first time in U.S. history, it was possible to buy a home with no money down and no income verification at prevailing rates as low as 1 to 2%. Can you say, "Traitor?"

CLINTON

Bill's job was to ensure that when the real estate collapse occurred, the banks would be deemed too big to fail. To that end, he signed the repeal of the Glass-Steagall Act, which was our firewall separating commercial and investment banking, and that prevented the formation of banks that were too big to fail. As soon as Clinton signed the legislation, the largest bank merger in U.S. history could occur. Go figure. Just another convenient coincidence? Not. Can you say, "Traitor?"

BUSH, JR

In the months leading up to the 2008 collapse, the Governor of Georgia, who had a banking background, passed an anti-predatory lending bill designed to protect the residents of Georgia from the financial collapse he could see coming. Following his lead, other governors joined forces to pass similar legislation to protect their residents. The Traitor Bush immediately interceded to get the Georgia bill rescinded and made sure that no other anti-predatory lending state legislation would pass.

Then Bush did what he was instructed to do by his puppet masters; he stood by and did nothing, assuring the collapse would occur on schedule. Once again, can you say, "Traitor?"

> In 2003, during the height of the predatory lending crisis, the OCC invoked a clause from the 1863 National Bank Act to issue a formal opinion preempting all state predatory lending laws, thereby rendering them inoperative. The OCC also promulgated new rules that prevented states from enforcing any of their own consumer protection laws against national banks. The FEDeral government's actions were so egregious and so unprecedented that all 50 state attorneys general and all 50 state banking superintendents actively fought the new rules.

Governor Eliot Spitzer, NY, Washington Post Op-Ed– 2/14/2008 [Emphasis added]

ALLEGATIONS

President Bush intentionally stood by and allowed the 2008 housing collapse to occur when he had it in his power to prevent it by allowing anti-predatory lending legislation to pass. Former New York Governor Eliot Spitzer accused Bush in his February 2008 Op-ed of causing the financial collapse, saying:

> **When history tells the story of the subprime lending crisis and recounts its devastating effects on the lives of so many innocent homeowners, the Bush administration will not be judged favorably. The tale is still unfolding, but when the dust settles, it will be judged as a willing accomplice to the lenders who went to any length in their quest for profit. So, willing, in fact, that it used the power of the FEDeral government in an unprecedented assault on state legislatures, as well as on state attorneys general and anyone else on the side of consumers.**
>
> Governor Eliot Spitzer, NY, Washington Post Op-Ed–2/14/2008
>
> [Emphasis added]

WHAT IT TAKES TO BE A GLOBAL SUPERPOWER

Let's reconsider what's necessary to control trade and the world economy to be a global superpower. What you are about to read is the formula for how the Elite orchestrated the rise and fall of first Britain, then the U.S., and finally, China, which is the nation that most threatens us today. To orchestrate the rise or fall of a superpower, you need:

CONTROL OF NATURAL RESOURCES

These were provided to China by all the greedy Globalist corporations eager to get in on the wealth transfer from the U.S. to China.

CONTROL OF MANUFACTURING

This was facilitated by Nixon, Carter, and Clinton by stagnating the U.S. economy and passing the intentionally losing trade deal, NAFTA.

CONTROL OF TRADE

What assures control of trade is the ability to produce goods at a lower cost than your competitors. So, the centuries-old *British Free Trade Slavery System*, which enslaved the world for over 300 years, was reinstated. China exploited its people and put them to work under sweatshop conditions so they could undercut the labor cost of industrialized nations, especially the U.S. Then, traitorous U.S. corporations swarmed to China like bees to honey to cash in on the profits from China's inhumane labor practices.

CONTROL OF MONEY AND POWER

In the strictest sense, as the world's reserve currency, the U.S. is still in control of the global monetary system. The wealth of America was squandered thanks to the debt inflicted on the U.S. by our wars for profit and our intentionally losing trade deals. America is unofficially broke. As a result, America went from being the wealthiest nation in the world at the end of World War II to now having the distinction of being the world's largest debtor nation.

And guess who one of our largest debt holders is? It's China. So, while America has atrophied with its infrastructure rotting, China has built gleaming cities. But much more critical is what China has done with its vast riches to position itself to supersede the U.S. as the world's undisputed Superpower. But don't worry. You will soon find out that their plans will backfire on them. Like I said, we win, they lose.

In summary, China has capitalized on America's debt crisis and has modernized its cities, infrastructure, and factories. But that is only what is plainly visible. They have reached out to resource-rich but underdeveloped nations, lending them money to facilitate modernization. But in typical Communist fashion, there is always a trap that enslaves the country and allows China to take control of its natural resources so that the developing nations end up poorer and China ends up richer. China is a pariah nation, and the world is waking up to that fact, and that will be its downfall.

God says there is nothing new under the sun. What was, will be again. So, you shouldn't be surprised to find out that China's plan to steal natural resources from resource-rich nations is just a rehash of a much older plan used as far back as the colonial period. This quote from the book, *Confessions of an Economic Hitman*, should make this abundantly clear. There is nothing new under the sun.

Economic hit men (EHMs) are highly paid professionals who cheat countries around the globe out of trillions of dollars. They funnel money from the World Bank, the U.S. Agency for International Development (USAID), and other foreign aid organizations into the coffers of huge corporations and the pockets of a few wealthy families who

(cont'd next page)

control the planet's natural resources. Their tools include fraudulent financial reports, rigged elections, payoffs, extortion, sex, and murder. They play a game as old as empire, but one that has taken on new and terrifying dimensions during this time of globalization. I should know; I was an EHM.

John Perkins, in his Preface to *Confessions of an Economic Hit Man*

Turning our attention to political affairs, China has leveraged its newfound wealth to gain power and influence at every level of society. They endow universities and gain access to vitally crucial intellectual property. They buy politicians in the U.S. and around the world. They interfere in elections. And when the truth finally comes out, I believe we will find out our previous and cognitively challenged President, Mr. Biden, and his family are on their payroll. Time will tell.

Moving on. One of my favorite books is *The Art of War by Sun Tzu*. It is the story of a 5th-century BC Chinese General and military strategist who defeated an army of 300,000 men with an army of 30,000. His military strategies are renowned and taught at every military academy worldwide. You can bet that the global elite use his methods.

If you genuinely want to understand geopolitical affairs, you need to read this book. From what I know, it is one of President Trump's favorite books. Don't forget that Trump went to a military academy. The convergence of these two experiences may account for how, no matter what his enemies throw at him, he always seems to use it against them. Sun Tzu was a master of unconventional warfare. He was a master strategist who routinely used his enemies' strengths against them. Heaven knows our enemies are adept at Sun Tzu's strategies. But even so, our enemy has made some serious mistakes that may prove to be his downfall. More on this later.

I want to touch on a few key insights from *The Art of War*, as they significantly empower us to join the resistance against this global communist takeover. To defeat an enemy, especially one as wily as the global elite, we need to be master strategists.

1. **You must know your enemy as well as you know yourself** and look at things through the prism of not only your experience but his as well. Allowing you to expect your enemies' actions before they take them so that you can ensnare them in a trap of their own making.

2. **You need to have individuals in your enemy's inner circle** to keep you informed. That is why our enemy buys power and influence in all strata of society, including our government, the military, security agencies, the education system, media, and entertainment. I have a quick example of the tactics China uses in this regard. China loaned Ethiopia money to build its FEDeral building. Chinese contractors constructed the building. A few years after the building's construction was completed, it was discovered that China had installed listening devices in the walls of the building. Every night, the building's servers were transmitting all their conversations to China. To reiterate, we must know who our enemy is and what he is capable of.

3. **The ultimate victory in war is to destroy your enemy without open warfare.** For example, our enemy uses the inexhaustible supply of money they obtain from their wars for profit, their central banks, and trade to gain power and influence in every stratum of society. Remember, strength under the right circumstances can be a weapon against an enemy. More on this later.

4. **One need not destroy an enemy.** You only need to destroy his willingness to fight back. That is why our enemy is endeavoring to divide us, to feed us an unending stream of propaganda, and to control all the necessities of life. He wants to pacify us so that we will lose all hope and surrender. Reflect on these words that are claimed to have been made by former President Barack Obama, and you will understand our enemy's strategy for pacifying us. That knowledge can strip the enemy of their power.

> You just have to flood a country's public square with enough raw sewage. You just have to raise enough questions, spread enough dirt, and plant enough conspiracy theorizing that citizens no longer know what to believe.
> Once they lose trust in their leaders, in mainstream media, in political institutions, in each other, in the possibility of truth, the game's won.
> Former President Barack Obama
> Stanford University, Keynote Address, April 21, 2022

5. **In his book,** *The Art of War*, **Sun Tzu said,** "No nation has ever benefited from prolonged war. It depletes assets and affects morale, and at some point, the cost of victory is too great." That is precisely why our enemy gets us into war and drags it out as long as possible. We need to say no to their wars for profit and control.

6. **We must assess our enemies' strengths and weaknesses,** as well as our own, and measure our resolve against theirs. So, what do we know about what our enemy will do to get what he wants? His actions show he will do whatever it takes, i.e., exterminate seven billion of us *useless eaters,* poison our food, sterilize us without our consent, genetically alter us to turn us into a passive subspecies with neither the intellect nor the will to stand against them, inflict us with wars for profit, control all the necessities of life, brainwash us, etc.

Again, I say there is no limit to the atrocities our enemy will commit. As Sun Tzu would say, under these conditions, we are on *death ground.* The good news is that if we recognize we're on death ground, we realize we must unite to overcome our enemy, no matter what. We are many; they are few. They need our compliance to control us. If we stand united and say "No," it will take away their strength, and we will win.

In summary of Sun Tzu's strategies, before engaging an enemy, you must know your end game and that of your enemy. You must know the who, what, where, when, how, and why of your enemy's every action and yours as well. The war for the soul of mankind will not be determined on the battlefield in conventional warfare. The outcome hinges on unconventional warfare, which is psychological warfare. We must wake up before it is too late. We cannot allow our enemy to make us feel so hopeless that we surrender.

Remember, we are many; they are few. If we set aside the manufactured, fake differences the enemy has fostered in our minds and stand united as one nation under God, the enemy will be vanquished. As I write this, dominoes are falling that will remove from our enemy the source of his power and render him impotent. He has an Achilles' heel, and it has been exposed. But that is a topic for a little later.

With all that has happened since COVID-19 was released on us, many people have opened their eyes and seek the truth. However, this issue goes much deeper than most people realize. Therefore, I feel compelled to examine the question of precisely who our enemy is. That knowledge is vital to our winning our freedom and to our keeping it. You can rest assured that in due course of time, the enemy will regroup and come at us again.

Only with an in-depth understanding of who the enemy is and how he has managed to enslave mankind for centuries will we be able to keep him at bay. The Bible tells us he will eventually get his one-world demonic system. But the more we know about his plans and the more we cleave to God, the longer we will keep him at bay.

China, Russia, Iran, Iraq, and North Korea are all over the news these days. The bobblehead fake news anchors are telling us that World War III is at the door and doing everything they can to foster fear. Try to put their propaganda out of your mind for now, and let's focus on who our real enemy is, because it is none of these countries. They are all just puppets of the global financial elite, who are, as you might say, the head of Satan's snake from the Garden of Eden.

Cut off the head, and the body dies, so that is where we need to focus our attention. Let's explore who the global elite are and the source of their power. We'll start with a brief definition of who the global elite are, and then we'll delve into the details.

Below is an organizational chart of the United Nations (UN), or what I refer to as the *Rothschild-Inspired New World Order Command Center*. Those of you who have read my first book are familiar with this, but I need to include it here because not everyone who reads this book will have read the first one.

Without further delay…

GRAPHIC LEGEND: GLOBAL OVERSIGHT ORGANIZATIONS

1. **(BG) Bilderberg Group:** The central command center of the global cabal, composed of the wealthiest globalist families in the world (the financial elite).

2. **(NATO) North Atlantic Treaty Organization:** A military compliance organization that masquerades as peacekeepers.

3. **(IMF) International Monetary Fund, World Bank (WB), and the U.S. Agency for International Development (USAID):** All are banking organizations, which, in concert with central banks such as the FED, control the world's monetary system on behalf of the financial elite. Their job is to drive sovereign nations into unmanageable debt so they can eventually be forced to accept the New World Order.

4. **(WTO) World Trade Organization:** Controls global trade. Used to reintroduce the British Free Trade Slavery System, repackaged as the Chinese Free Trade. Its job is to collapse the free market system by driving major industrialized nations, particularly the U.S., into unmanageable debt through the creation of trade imbalances.

5. **(WHO) World Health Organization:** Is responsible for establishing global health accords favoring major corporations owned by the financial elite and is designed to reduce the population in third-world countries through vaccines, gene manipulation, disease, and starvation. And we mustn't overlook their role in inflicting mass genocide on the world through their role in COVID-19.

FEET-ON-THE-GROUND *(The foot soldiers who carry out the plans of the upper echelon)*

1. **The Council on Foreign Relations (CFR) and the Trilateral Commission (TC):** The two most important of these feet-on-the-ground organizations. I will discuss them in detail momentarily, but first, let's quickly look at the other feet-on-the-ground organizations.

2. **The FED:** The illegal Rothschild-owned central bank that drives us into debt by forcing us to pay interest for printing worthless fiat currency that they use to buy power and sway across all levels of society. The FED is also the vehicle by which they regularly orchestrate financial collapses, which they use to take our life savings and even our homes legally.

3. **Media:** The Rothschild-owned fake news outlets and entertainment outlets that are propaganda arms of the financial elite. The news media feeds us the truth, mingled with half-truths and out-and-out lies, spun in such a way that we can't tell fact from

fiction, truth from lies, or friend from foe. And what they call entertainment is subliminal brainwashing. If you doubt that, listen to the lyrics of one of the more famous rappers or watch a recent Disney movie and see the sexual perversion presented to your children.

11. **Corporations, Government, Academia, and Unions:** The Corporate CEOs, politicians, college professors, and union heads have sold out the American public to the globalist communist fronted by the UN and China.

12. **Community Organizers:** There are community organizing groups like Antifa and Black Lives Matter that are hired as agitators to create chaos and divide us.

We will get to the CFR and TC momentarily. But first, back to establishing the United Nations. It was a crucial part of establishing the control mechanisms necessary to establish a one-world dictatorship. That is why the Rothschilds attempted to initiate it three times, from 1814 to 1945, when they finally achieved their goal.

1. **First Attempt at a World Government:** The Rothschilds attempted to establish a world government in 1814 at the Congress of Vienna, but Russian Tsar Alexander I thwarted their efforts. The Rothschilds swore they would get even, and they did. During the Bolshevik Revolution in Russia, the Rothschilds saw to it that the entire Romanov royal family, including the children, was executed.

2. **Second Attempt at World Government:** The Rothschilds attempted to establish the *League of Nations* at the Versailles Conference following World War I, but not enough countries ratified it!

3. **Third Attempt at World Government:** They finally established their global governance organization with the founding of the United Nations at the end of World War II.

The disbanding of the UN is necessary if we are ever to achieve world peace. It is the head of the snake that controls and enslaves the world.

The global elite's army of traitors is not limited to what we just discussed. They have infiltrated all our three-letter agencies, and I will walk you through that momentarily. However, first, to be clear: a person does not need to be part of a formal organization to be used by the financial elite. They buy power and influence wherever they find it useful. For example, a university professor could be on their payroll and be providing them with intellectual research data. The CEO of any left-leaning international corporation could be on their payroll. Your local hospital may receive financial incentives to ensure specific COVID-19 protocols are followed, while others are not. Anywhere that useful information or influence is for sale, you will find traitors. So, their net is cast far and wide. That is why we need to cut off the head of the snake at the source of its power, which is where it gets its money. We will discuss how we do that a little later.

IS THE U.N. REALLY THE ENEMY OF MANKIND?

As the popular expression from the late 1960s states, "You bet your sweet bippy, it is." Some state that the United Nations' goal is to reduce population selectively by encouraging abortion, forced sterilization, and control of human reproduction, and regard two-thirds of the human population as excess baggage, with 350,000 people eliminated per day.

The United Nations, along with Agenda 21, will cause some of the greatest removals of personal freedom we have ever witnessed. See the graphic below for more information.

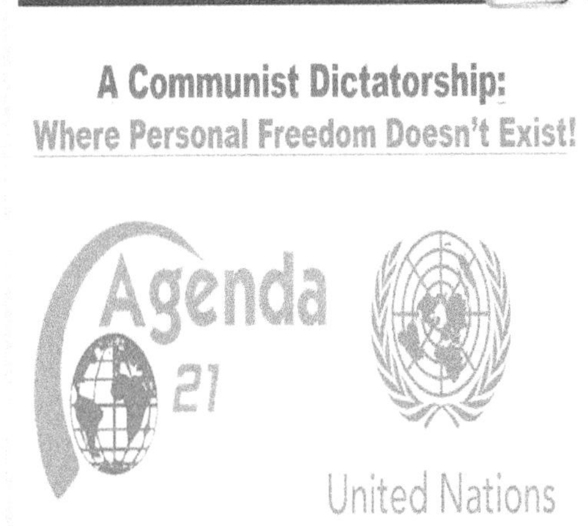

Isn't the only hope for the planet that the industrialized civilizations collapse?
Isn't it our responsibility to bring that about?
Maurice Strong, Founder of the UN Environmental Program (UNEP)
Opening Speech, Rio Earth Summit 1992

THE CFR AND TC
TWO OF THE MOST DANGEROUS ORGANIZATIONS IN THE WORLD

The Council on Foreign Relations (CFR) and the Trilateral Commission (TC) are committed to ending U.S. Sovereignty and birthing the one-world government.

COUNCIL ON FOREIGN RELATIONS (CFR)

1. "The Council on Foreign Relations is the American branch of a society that originated in England, and it believes national boundaries should be obliterated and one-world rule established." Taken from Dr. Carroll Quigley, Historian, Author, *Tragedy and Hope: A History of the World in Our Time*, 1966, Professor, Georgetown University, college mentor of President Bill Clinton.

2. "The CFR is the establishment. Not only does it have influence and power in key decision-making positions at the highest levels of government (Congress and the White House) to apply pressure from above, but it also finances and uses individuals and groups to bring pressure from below (Community Organizing Groups, Special Interest Groups, etc.) to justify the high-level decisions that convert the U.S. from a sovereign republic into a servile member of a one-world dictatorship." As taken from Congressman John R. Rarick, LA, April 28, 1972.

TRILATERAL COMMISSION (TC)

1. "The Trilateral Commission doesn't secretly run the world. The Council on Foreign Relations does that." Sir Winston Lord, Assistant Secretary of State for the Bureau of East Asian and Pacific Affairs, 1993-1997, President of the Council on Foreign Relations

2. "The Trilateral Commission is international and is intended to be the vehicle for multinational consolidation of the commercial and banking interests by seizing control of the political government of the United States...They rule the future. The real rulers in Washington are invisible and exercise power from behind the scenes."

From Supreme Court Justice Felix Frankfurter, with some portions attributed to Senator Barry Goldwater

3. "The Trilateral Commission represents a skillful, coordinated effort to seize control and consolidate the four centers of power—political, monetary, intellectual, and ecclesiastical. (Religious) What the Trilateral Commission intends is to create a worldwide economic power superior to the political governments of the nation-states involved (a dictatorship). As managers and creators of the system, they will rule the future." From Senator Barry Goldwater, AZ, *With No Apologies*, 1979

Why did I call these organizations two of the most dangerous organizations in the world? Because of the influential people who belong to these traitorous globalist organizations. As the following graphic shows, practically every person of power in Washington belongs to one or both organizations.

That means that most of our elected officials in Washington are nothing more than puppets of the financial elite, put in office to serve their interests, not the interests of the American people. That is why Washington must be swept clean, and God is orchestrating that house cleaning!

The Shadow Government!
Most Of Our Politicians Are Guilty of Treason!

LIBERTY CRUSADE

COUNCIL on FOREIGN RELATIONS

The Council on Foreign Relations (CFR) and Trilateral Commission (TC) are committed to ending US sovereignty and birthing the One-World Government

Name	Position	CFR	TC
Brzezinski	Presidential Advisor & Founding Member	CFR	TC
Colin Powell	Chairman Joint Chiefs of Staff	CFR	
George H. Bush	U.S. President	CFR	
William Clinton	U.S. President	CFR	TC
Jimmy Carter	U.S. President	CFR	
Walter Mondale	U.S. VP	CFR	
John McCain	Senator [Arizonian] Presidential Candida	CFR	
Albert Gore. Jr.	U.S. VP	CFR	
Hillary Clinton	Secretary of State Obama Admin.		TC
Condoleezza Rice	Secretary State Bush Admin.	CFR	
John Kerry	Senator & Chairman Foreign Relations	CFR	
James Woolsey	Director CIA	CFR	
Robert Gates	Sect of Defense & Former Dir. CIA	CFR	
Henry Cisneros	Sect. Housing & Urban Development	CFR	
Dick Chaney	Vice President		

"The case for government by elites is irrefutable." – William Fulbright U.S. Senator

THE ORIGIN OF OUR FBI AND CIA
AND OTHER TRAITOROUS INTELLIGENCE AGENCIES

The FBI, CIA, and all the other three-letter agencies that they spawned. As it became apparent that the U.S. would enter World War II, a spy network was needed, and it just so happened that the CFR already had one in place. It was integrated into the U.S. government, forming the nucleus of our intelligence agencies. Then, when the war ended, the FBI played a pivotal role in the formation of the traitorous UN. Go figure. Will coincidences never end?

THE ORIGIN OF THE TRAITOROUS UNITED NATIONS

The planning of the UN can be traced to the 'secret steering committee' established by Secretary of State Cordell Hull in January 1943. All of the members of this secret committee, with the exception of Hull, a Tennessee politician, were members of the Council on Foreign Relations. They saw Hull regularly to plan, select, and guide the labors of the State Department's Advisory Committee. It was, in effect, the coordinating agency for all the State Department's postwar planning.
Professors Laurence H. Shoup and William Minter, Authors,
Imperial Brain Trust: The Council on Foreign Relations and United States Foreign Policy, *Monthly Review Press*, 1977.

WHY I SAY THE UNITED STATES IS A COMMUNIST DICTATORSHIP

What is being sold to the American people today as Americanism,
if you peel off the label, you find so much similarity to what we were fighting against
when we were fighting Communism, Nazism, and Fascism...
G. Edward Griffin, Author, *The Creature from Jekyll Island*

The media controls the information a person gets. In various ways, one can ensure that the average American watching the tube and reading the newspaper will come out with a certain mindset, which states, "This is good," or "That is bad."

Let's take a step back in history. Following the Civil War, the U.S. declared bankruptcy, which gave the banker gangsters the opportunity to coerce Congress into passing the Act of 1871. The act created a separate government for the District of Columbia. In the process, it usurped our original constitutional republic and created the unconstitutional U.S. Corporation. At that moment, the U.S. ceased being a sovereign nation and instead was under the control of a Crown, the Vatican, and a Swiss Corporation.

Then, in 1933, during the Great Depression, the U.S. declared bankruptcy again. Because of these two events, an international banking cartel was able to embed an army of bureaucrats in the government to form a shadow government intended to rewrite our laws slowly, morphing the U.S. into a communist order.

DECLARATION OF BANKRUPTCY

DECLARATION OF BANKRUPTCY: All United States offices, officials, and departments are now operating within a de facto status, in name only, under Emergency War Powers. With the Constitutional Republican form of government now dissolved, the receivers of the bankruptcy have adopted a new form of government for the United States. This new form of government is known as a DEMOCRACY, being an established socialist communist order under a new government for America.
United States Congressional Record, March 17, 1933, Vol. 33, page H-1303,
Speaker/Representative James Traficant, Jr (OH)
U.S. Bankruptcy Speech [Emphasis added]

THE OBJECTIVES OF THE COMMUNIST MANIFESTO

The Communist Manifesto's objectives were implemented and inflicted on the American people through the creation of the agencies and entities listed below:

1. Impose A Central Banking System: the **FED**
2. Government-Controlled Education: **Public Schools, Project Head Start, and the LGBTQ agenda**
3. Government Control of Labor: the **DOL**
4. Government Control of Transportation: the **DOT**
5. Government Control of Communication: the **FCC**
6. Government Control of Agriculture Production and Food Processing: the **USDA**
7. Confiscation Of Private Property: **Take Rights**

Don't panic! America and the world are about to be set free. We will soon enter an unparalleled period of peace and prosperity. But that story will have to wait until we finish laying the foundation for what is to come. Hang in there; it is worth the wait.

GET READY TO BE RED-PILLED

Once you know the truth, it will set you free. The financial elite can no longer control you with their lies, deception, and manipulation because the truth will make you immune! We began this chapter with the founding of America because we were focusing on American history. But as we move on to our examination of current geopolitical affairs, we must go back even further in history.

Let's return to the story of how the money-grubbing Rothschilds joined forces with the maniacal Catholic Church, whose lineage goes back to its role in the assassination of Christ. I say "assassination" because Christ's death was a politically motivated execution. This background will be crucial in enabling you to assess the current geopolitical roles of the three most powerful countries of our time: Russia, China, and the U.S., objectively.

You might discover that things are not exactly the way our politicians and media outlets tell us. You might conclude that they are misinformed or, heaven forbid, that they are lying to us. Either way, the truth will set you free!

HISTORY OF THE FOUNDING OF THE ILLUMINATI
(THE CLIFF NOTES VERSION)

Most people believe that politicians, bankers, and powerful families, such as the Rockefellers and the descendants of European royal families, like the Windsors of the British Royal Family, control our world. And on the surface, that is true. But even these influential people are just puppets of the Illuminati. So, we need to understand who the Illuminati are and what their goal is.

1. **The Origin Story:** Our story begins in the Middle East, specifically in Canaan, with a group of people known as the Khazarians, who worshiped the deity Baal and practiced child sacrifice. Because of their inhumane practices and behavior, they were exiled and migrated to Ashkenaz, near modern-day Turkey.

2. **In 600 AD,** the Russian Tsar gave the Khazarians an ultimatum: stop practicing child sacrifice and convert to Christianity, Judaism, or Islam. They chose Judaism but in name only because, despite being warned, they continued the practice of child sacrifice.

3. **In 965 AD,** the Russian Tsar decided that the Khazarian practices could no longer be tolerated and planned to wipe them out, but they got wind of the plan and escaped with their treasure trove of gold. When they left Russia, they decided it would be advisable to change their name, becoming known thereafter as Ashkenazi Jews. They migrated across Europe, developing residences in Austria, Prussia, Portugal, France, Spain, and England. Eventually, because they continued to practice child sacrifices, they were driven out of all these countries, finally making their home in modern-day Ukraine, where they live to this day. They swore that one day, they would destroy every one of the nations that had cast them out.

4. **The year 1776** was the birth of the Illuminati and the hatching of the plan for world dominance. By now, the Ashkenazi Rothschild bankers had become incredibly wealthy and had devised a plan of revenge against all the nations that had driven them out; moreover, they had also developed a plan for world domination. They allied with the Catholic Jesuits, considered the military assassin order of the Catholic Church. Remember, it was the Sadducees and Pharisees who persuaded Rome to crucify Christ.

    Later, as the Roman Empire declined, it was succeeded by the Holy Roman Empire, an alliance between Rome and European Monarchs. The Monarchs used their armies to enforce absolute subjugation to the Catholic Church. Credited with killing over 2 million in the Crusades and millions more in their never-ending inquisitions, they brought the masses into subjugation to the Catholic Church. So, the merger of Rothschild's money and the Catholic Church's brutality formed the perfect alliance of evil to hatch a plan of world dominance.

THE ENDGAME AGENDA OF THE ILLUMINATI

The Rothschilds called on the Jesuit-trained Adam Weishaupt to formalize their plan. They provided him with a 14th-century letter called the *"Constantinople Letter,"* which was a letter soliciting advice when the king of France had put the Ashkenazi on notice that they had to convert to Christianity or face severe consequences. The following is an excerpt from that letter; as you read it, ask yourself if this isn't precisely what is occurring to enslave us today. We are seeing their plan hatched in secrecy in 1776 play out today by those we call the Illuminati, the financial elite, the Cabal, etc.

> As for what you say that the king of France obliges you to become Christians: do it, since you cannot do otherwise, but let the law of Moses be kept in your hearts.
> As for what you say about the demand to despoil you of your goods: make your sons merchants that little by little they may despoil the Christians of theirs.
> As for what you say about their making attempts on your lives: make your sons doctors and apothecaries that they may take away Christian lives. As for what you say about their destroying your synagogues: make your sons canons and clerics in order that they may destroy their churches. As for the many other vexations you complain of: arrange that your sons become advocates and lawyers and see that they always mix themselves up with the affairs of State, in order that by putting Christians under your yoke, you may dominate the world and be avenged on them.
> Do not swerve from this order that we give you, for you will find by experience that, humiliated as you are now, you will reach the actuality of power.
> Sequel to Fall of the Cabal, Constantinople, Elders of Jewry. Signed V.S.S.V.F.F., Prince of the Jews, 21st Caslu (November), 1489

THEY MADE GOOD ON THEIR THREATS

The plan was to destroy us by using trade as a weapon. Isn't that precisely what they have done with their British Free Trade Slavery System and now with the Chinese Free Trade, coupled with intentionally losing trade deals?

The plan was to use the medical system to destroy us. Isn't that what they are doing with their vaccines, their chemtrails, poisoning our food, genetic manipulation, and now COVID-19?

The plan was to take over our churches, insert false doctrine, and create division. Haven't our churches become the lukewarm church Christ talked about?

The plan was to take over the legal and political arenas and establish a legal dictatorship. Hasn't Washington become a swamp, and truth be told, aren't the vast majority of our politicians bought by the financial elite?

WAKE UP AND STAND UP—WE ARE AT WAR!
AND MOST OF US DON'T EVEN REALIZE IT!

THE JESUIT OATH

I do further promise and declare that I will have no opinion or will of my own…but will unhesitatingly obey each and every command that I may receive from my superiors in the Militia of the Pope and of Jesus Christ.

I furthermore promise and declare that I will, when opportunity present make and wage relentless war, secretly or openly, against all heretics, Protestants and Liberals, as I am directed to do, to extirpate and exterminate them from the face of the whole Earth; and that I will spare neither age, sex or condition; and that I will hang, waste, boil, flay, strangle, and bury alive these infamous heretics, rip up the stomachs and wombs of their women, and crush their infants' heads against the walls, in order to annihilate forever their execrable race. That when the same cannot be done openly, I will secretly use administer the poisoned cup, the strangling cord, the steel of the poniard or the leaden bullet, regardless of the honor, rank, dignity, or authority of the person or persons… as I at, anytime may be directed so to do by any agent of the Pope or Superior of the Brotherhood of the Holy Faith, of the Society of Jesus.

In conformation of which, I hereby dedicate my life, my soul, and all my corporal powers, and with this dagger which I now receive, I will subscribe my name written in my own blood, in testimony thereof, and should I prove false or weaken in my determination, may my brethren and fellow soldiers of the Militia of the Pope cut off my hands and my feet, and my throat from ear to ear, my belly opened, and sulfur burned therein, with all the punishment that can be inflicted upon me on earth and my soul be tortured by demons in an eternal hell forever!

Sun Tzu, the 5th-century BC military strategist, said that we must:

- Know our enemy.
- Know his endgame!
- Know how he intends to execute his plan.
- Know what he is willing to do to achieve his plan.
- Know who his allies are.

Only then can you defeat your enemy. We now know that the enemy is the Catholic Church, the Rothschilds, and all the descendants of the European Monarchies and the network of central banks. They schemed to put us in debt. It is also the UN and all of its global governance organizations that they have established to enable them to institute a legal global dictatorship.

We also know that "He who controls the money controls the world." So, our enemy has taken his ill-gotten money, notably from war and trade, and used it to buy power and influence in all the spheres of influence in society. Below you'll find the eight notable societal spheres of influence, along with the enemy's evil agenda for them.

THE EIGHT SPHERES OF INFLUENCE

1. **The Family:** It must be torn apart!
2. **The News Media:** Used to keep the truth from us!
3. **Entertainment:** Used to brainwash us subliminally!
4. **Education:** Used to indoctrinate us!
5. **Religion:** Used to divide us and dilute the true message of Christ.
6. **Politics:** Used to pass laws to impose a legal dictatorship!
7. **Military Industrial Complex:** Used to keep us in a constant state of war!
8. **Economy:** Used to control the monetary system and keep us in perpetual poverty!

We know our politicians are mostly puppets of our enemy, put in a position to knit together a web of laws that impoverish us, take away our freedom, and ultimately allow the imposition of a legal dictatorship. But the most important thing to know is that the enemy is not invincible. Let's stand together and take away our enemy's control of the monetary system. His power dissolves just like an ice cube does in warm water. Soon, our enemy will be no more. Before you finish this book, you will know how we bring our enemy to nothing. Keep the faith. All ends well!

You just read that the Rothschilds and the Catholic Church make up the Illuminati, which is the head of the empire of evil that intends to kill most of us and make those they allow to live their mindless slaves. I believe that there is sufficient information available about the Rothschilds, so what you have read is believable. But with the Catholic Church, it will be hard for many of you to accept that it is perhaps the evilest entity on the face of the earth. I want to take a moment to highlight some additional aspects you should know regarding the Catholic Church.

A short while ago, I pointed out the bloody history of the Catholic Church, with its wars and inquisitions intended to drive the people into subjugation to the power of the church. And we just discussed the Catholic Church's alliance with the Rothschilds, and you read both the plan to impose a world dictatorship and the oath to the Pope of the Jesuit assassin cult.

There is credible evidence connecting the Catholic Church to the Ashkenazi Rothschilds, who were driven out of country after country because they worshiped Baal and committed child sacrifices. Remember, it was the descendants of the Catholic Church that had Christ killed and usurped his throne. Stories came out as early as the 1960s, exposing the public to the fact that the Catholic Church is a den of pedophiles. However, over time, the stories faded away, and we forgot.

I urge you to go to Google Images and search for demonic images at the Vatican. What comes up will shock you. It seems they worship snakes and demons. Look at the trim on the Pope's robes and cross-reference what you see with pedophile symbols. You find that it indicates that the Pope is indeed a pedophile. Lastly, conduct some research and inquire about why the Pope, Bishops, and Cardinals wear red shoes. You find that it has to do with child sacrifice ceremonies. I ask you to do this because you will be more likely to believe it if you do your own research!

THE ASHKENAZI TAKE REVENGE
IN ALL THE COUNTRIES THAT OUSTED THEM

Our story of revenge begins with the French Revolution. The Rothschilds are notorious for starting wars to achieve a political objective. Consider the following:

If my sons did not want war, there would be none.
Gutle Schnapper Rothschild, wife of Mayer Amschel Rothschild

This blood-sucking crew has been the cause of untold mischief and misery in Europe during the present century, and has piled up its prodigious wealth chiefly through fomenting wars between States which ought never to have quarreled. Whenever there is trouble in Europe, wherever rumors of war circulate, and men's minds are distraught with fear of change and calamity, you may be sure that a hook-nosed Rothschild is at his games somewhere near the region of the disturbance.
From the British socialist newspaper, *Labour Leader*, 1891

The Rothschilds are said to have orchestrated the French Revolution, which fulfilled their vendetta against France for driving them out because of their child sacrifices. They then used Jesuit-trained Napoleon Bonaparte to conduct the Napoleonic Wars, which just targeted the very countries the Ashkenazi swore revenge against.

All went as planned until the Battle of Waterloo, where British forces defeated Napoleon. But the Rothschilds turned defeat on the battlefield into financial victory. Rothschild had spies monitoring the battlefield, and when it became apparent that Napoleon had lost, his spies were dispatched to bring him the news, which he received two days before receiving the official reports. Upon receiving the news, he immediately sold his English bonds, driving the market into a panic because the assumption was that the British had lost, which they had not. As soon as the bond market bottomed out, he bought all the bonds he could get his hands on, reaping a vast fortune and giving birth to these now-famous quotes!

> **I care not what puppet is placed upon the throne of England to rule the Empire upon which the sun never sets. The man who controls Britain's money supply controls the British Empire, and I control the British money supply.**
> Nathan Mayer Rothschild

> **Give me control of a nation's money, and I care not who makes the laws.**
> Mayer Amschel Rothschild

The Rothschilds now understood for sure that if they could drive nations into war and bankrupt them, they could subsequently force them to accept a central bank. That is precisely how the U.S. established its first central bank. America won the Revolutionary War, but it left the nation bankrupt. Subsequently, before Washington left office, America was forced to accept the Central Bank of England. By 1811, the bank's charter had expired, and Congress refused to renew it.

The War of 1812, also known as the Second American Revolutionary War, was thrust on America, and at the end of the war, Congress renewed the bank charter. This practice has been repeated all over the world as nation after nation has been forced into the Rothschild Central Banking System, which, as the next quote states, is the precursor to full-blown communism!

> **The establishment of a Central bank is 90% of communizing a nation.**
> Vladimir Lenin

Finally, with our historical foundation in place, we are ready to examine current geopolitical events through the lens of history. We will start our analysis with the Russian/Ukrainian War and see if the mainstream media is lying to us about what is going on over there. Later in another chapter, we will use this same deductive reasoning process to project outcomes for the rise and fall of both China and the U.S.

It has been my observation that history tends to repeat itself, and that when similar circumstances recur, they often yield similar outcomes. So, how does this apply to the war in Ukraine?

EXPLORING THE TRUTH ABOUT THE WAR IN UKRAINE

According to the nightly news on mainstream media and our politicians in both Washington and Brussels, Putin is a militaristic aggressor who attacked Ukraine with no provocation and likely has ambitions of conquest beyond Ukraine. Stopping him is essential. Putin is often compared to Hitler and his invasion of Europe, which led to World War II. We are not supposed to question the prevailing narrative in the comparison of Putin to Hitler. We are expected to support politicians unquestioningly, sending huge sums to Ukraine for border protection.

Meanwhile, our politicians are reluctant to spend money to build a wall to protect *our* border. If we don't support sending money to Ukraine, then we are seen as aiding and abetting mass murder on the part of a crazed monster.

So, the question is, does this narrative ring true? Or is there another side to the story that casts Putin in a more favorable light and provides a possible justification for the invasion? Let's examine both history and current events to see if they offer a different perspective on the events unfolding in Ukraine.

AN ALTERNATE INTERPRETATION OF THE UKRAINE WAR

Nothing ever happens without a reason, and almost always, the root cause of current events lives in history. So, with that said, I will examine the Ukraine war first from a historical perspective and then from the vantage point of current events. Perhaps this will give us a different perspective from what is being presented to us by the globalist-controlled media and our puppet politicians. Things are rarely as straightforward as they seem. As I always say, the truth will set you free.

HISTORICAL PERSPECTIVE

In 1776, the Baal-worshipping, child-sacrificing, Rothschild-Ashkenazi bankers and the Catholic Jesuit Assassin cult joined forces and formed the Illuminati and swore that they would take revenge on all the nations that had cast out the Ashkenazi, including Russia. They further devised a plan to implement a one-world government ruled by them.

Over the centuries, the Illuminati (comprised of the Rothschild Ashkenazi bankers and the Catholic Church) seems to have kept their promise of revenge. The French Revolution toppled the French Monarchy. The Napoleonic Wars toppled most of the nations that had expelled the Ashkenazi. The Bolshevik Revolution saw the (Russian) Romanov royal family exterminated.

ADDITIONAL HISTORICAL BACKGROUND

Three additional reasons the Rothschild-Ashkenazi bankers and their allies, the Catholic Church (The Rothschild-Ashkenazi bankers), have reason to want to destroy Russia:
It was the Russian Tsar who, in 1814, at the *Congress of Vienna,* foiled their first attempt at world governance. They swore revenge, which, as we have learned, they got when they later killed the Romanov Royal Family.

During the American Civil War, France and Spain were planning to aid the Con**FED**eracy, but Russia intervened, threatening them, saying that if they did, Russia would come to the aid of the North. The significance of this event stems from the fact that the global elite, headed by Britain at the time, believed that unless the U.S. were divided, it would become too powerful and threaten the European monarchies.

Russia is the only major nation in the world today that does not have a central bank controlled by the Rothschild-Ashkenazi network. Remember: this puts Russia in direct opposition to the global elite's one-world government. Bottom line: Russia is no friend of the global elite.

One might say, "Well, Russia attacked Ukraine, so they must be the bad guys! Right?"

But says who? The Rothschild-controlled media and its puppet governments around the world. That's who. But they wouldn't lie to us. No, not much, just every second of every day. The Devil is a liar.

Let's take another look at history. Every war follows a similar pattern: either the bad guys initiate a false flag event or provoke the other side into attacking them. They always want it to appear that their war for profit and control is justified.

Let's take World War II as an example: Japan didn't just wake up one day and decide to attack the U.S. No. They were baited into attacking. Roosevelt had an eight-step plan to provoke Japan into attacking. The plan included what were called 'pop-up incursions' into Japanese waters, in the hope of provoking an incident. They placed an embargo on oil and steel shipments to Japan, among other countries. All that remained was giving Japan a tempting enough target. The 7th Fleet, harbored in Hawaii, would do the trick. U.S. Secretary of War under Roosevelt, Henry L. Stimson, 1940 to 1945, made two interesting journal entries concerning this dilemma of World War II:

The question was how we should maneuver them into firing the first shot...
Journal Entry, November 25, 1941

...it was desirable to make sure the Japanese were the ones to do this so that there should remain no doubt as to who were the aggressors.
Journal Entry, December 7, 1941

WHAT POSSIBLE JUSTIFICATION COULD RUSSIA HAVE FOR ATTACKING UKRAINE?

Ukraine is to Russia what the Cuban Missile Crisis was to the U.S. There was no way on earth the U.S. was going to allow missiles deployed just minutes from the U.S. mainland. Ukraine was petitioning NATO for membership, and there were plans to put NATO missiles on the Ukrainian border with Russia. Putin warned them of the consequences if they persisted. Still, they ignored him, and the result was that Russia invaded Ukraine. Our lying media seems to have forgotten this vitally important part of the story.

Then there was the history of Russia with the Illuminati, the Rothschild-Ashkenazi bankers, and the fact that Russia is the only major country in the world not to have a Rothschild Central Bank. It just may be that the enemy was at the door, and like the Japanese in World War II and the U.S. with the Cuban Missile Crisis, Putin had no choice but to take the battle to the enemy.

FINAL THOUGHTS ON THE UKRAINE WAR

In the Bible, Russia is referred to as the "sleeping bear." To appreciate the potential significance of that name, we must understand our current context in the Bible. Russia figures in the combination beast of Revelation that brings war upon the world during the tribulation. But we are not in the Book of Revelation yet. We are at the point of fulfillment of Abraham's promise and the Harvest of Souls. First, the people awake, and the church becomes the church without spot or blemish. Then comes the Harvest of Souls. Then, and only then, do we enter the Book of Revelation, where Russia emerges as a warring nation.

God has a history of using the most unlikely people to serve His purpose. For example, He used Nebuchadnezzar to free the Jews from captivity and to rebuild the Temple. Perhaps He is using Russia now, but we don't see it. What do I mean?

Throughout this chapter, a story has been unfolding about exactly who is behind all the suffering and evil we see in the world today. Our historical account repeatedly points to the Illuminati, which is the union of the Catholic Church and the Rothschild-Ashkenazi bankers and all the people they have bought with their ill-gotten gains. And a consistent theme keeps popping up: these entities are evil beyond imagination, and they worship Lucifer and the deity Baal, and take part in pedophilia and child sacrifice.

I cannot prove what I am about to say. Still, as I mentioned a moment ago, history certainly leads one in a certain direction. Both the Catholic Church and the Ashkenazi are apparently involved in satanic rituals, including pedophilia and child sacrifice. It seems that the Rothschild-Ashkenazi ended up in Ukraine, and there is no evidence that they ever converted to Judaism or Christianity, but continue to this day, worshipping Baal. To this day, replicas of the Arch of Baal and the demon Moloch continue to appear in Washington, D.C., and other locations around the U.S. and the World. They serve as a constant reminder that the forces of evil are still among us and hold positions of power.

Finally, some claim that Ukraine is a stronghold of satanic worship and that the practice of pedophilia and child sacrifice continues in Ukraine to this very day. Some contend that Ukraine and the Vatican are both integral parts of the Rothschild's Globalist banking cartel and that Ukraine is a global center of money laundering. This claim is partly related to alleged money laundering by the Biden family.

Consider the Rothschild-Ashkenazi agenda to reduce the global population to 1 billion or fewer. Some say both China and Ukraine have bio-labs and are developing bio-weapons for mass genocide. If Putin had proof of these allegations, then the possibility of missiles on his border capable of delivering bio-weapons could have left him no choice but to attack Ukraine preemptively in self-defense.

Of course, given the Rothschilds' control of our media and our politicians, it is virtually impossible to validate what I just postulated. But history, the Bible, and recent events certainly give this postulation credibility. Sorry, but there are no certainties in a world where our leaders operate in secrecy and lie to us.

However, I can say with certainty: what our politicians and the mainstream media tell us is almost certainly based on the truth, mingled with half-truths and out-and-out lies. This is to ensure we cannot discern fact from fiction, truth from lie, or friend from foe. That is why I rely so heavily on history, the Bible, and my own experiences to ferret out as much of the truth as I can.

In closing this chapter, all I can say is don't trust those in power. They are intent on killing most of us and making slaves of those they allow to live. What I am trying to do in this book is to give you as much truth as I can, so that your eyes will be opened and you will be empowered to stand against the forces of evil, helping to usher in the Harvest of Souls and an unprecedented period of peace and prosperity on earth. Please do your research. It's time to stand and say no to our slavery.

CHAPTER 2

EXPOSING THE ENEMY WITHIN
The Truth Will Take Away His Power

TOPICS COVERED IN THIS CHAPTER:

- THE ORIGIN OF OUR SLAVE MASTERS
- HOW OUR SLAVE MASTERS CONTROL MANKIND
- WHAT MOTIVATES OUR ENEMY'S ACTIONS
- THE EXTENT TO WHICH OUR ENEMY WILL GO TO ACHIEVE HIS AGENDA

THE ORIGINAL SLAVE MASTERS:
THE EUROPEAN FEUDAL KINGS

HIERARCHY OF EUROPEAN FEUDALISM

- **King:** Monarch, and absolute ruler!
- **Nobles:** The upper class, with lands and estates granted by the king, in exchange for their service and loyalty.
- **Knights:** Aristocratic soldiers sworn in service to the king!
- **Peasants:** The commoners who had no right to own property and had no say in the government.

OUR FOREFATHERS FOUNDED America to escape European feudalism, where they had no property rights, no religious rights, and no human rights.

Feudalism is a governmental system characterized by a supreme leader, such as a king, monarch, dictator, or tyrannical ruler, who forces the population into servitude and denies them fundamental rights, including the right to life, liberty, and the pursuit of happiness. Today, we refer to this form of government as socialism and communism.

Under feudalism, *peasants* were referred to as *chattel*, which means a personal possession, such as livestock. Peasants had no rights other than those randomly bestowed upon them by the king or the ruling power structure, such as the financial elite of today. Peasants were not allowed a voice in the government. They were not allowed to own property and were under an oppressive tax system that kept them impoverished. They were subject to being conscripted into the king's army to fight his wars of conquest and financial gain. Isn't this a perfect definition of the system we suffer under today?

Feudalism is just another name for socialism, communism, fascism, dictatorship, democracy, or any system by any name that takes away people's freedom. It is the system of rule that the financial elite presently inflicts on the mass of humanity, on what they refer to as "useful idiots and useless eaters." I refer to this system as "slavery without chains," and it is the system we must defeat if we are to reclaim our nation and our liberty.

COUNTERINSURGENCY:
A PRACTICAL APPLICATION OF ANTICIPATORY THINKING

WHO IS THE ENEMY WE CALL THE FINANCIAL ELITE?

They are the descendants of the feudal monarchs of Europe who colonized the world. As their monarchies failed, they morphed into the banking moguls that today control a global network of central banks. Their central banks create an endless supply of worthless fiat currency. Currency used to enslave mankind by charging the nations interest for printing their worthless fiat currency. That money is the basis of the debt system that controls the world's countries. Our enslavers turn on their printing presses and out comes an inexcusable supply of money. That money buys authority and sway at every level of society.

There is a saying, "He who controls money controls the world." Truer words were never spoken. That money buys a seat at the table of every bank, every corporation, every governmental agency, and every institution of power and influence. It is through these institutions that the chains of our slavery are forged. Passing laws enables the formation of a legal dictatorship where we are stripped of all rights and taken back to where it all began, back to feudalism, that old system of slavery that continues enslaving mankind to this day.

WHAT IS THE ENEMY'S ENDGAME AGENDA?

The quote below says it all: the goal of our enemy is to establish a one-world dictatorship by whatever means necessary.

> We shall have world government whether or not you like it. The only question is whether world government will be by conquest or consent.
> James P. Warburg, Federal Reserve Vice Chairman
> Representing Rothschild Banking Concern to the United States Senate, 2/17/1950

There is more to the enemy's endgame agenda than just establishing a world government. As we will discuss shortly, their ultimate goal is to exterminate 7.5 billion of us. Wake up before it is too late!

WHAT IS THE SOURCE OF OUR ENEMY'S POWER?

The source of their power is money. Take away their ability to control the issuance of money, and their ability to buy power and influence evaporates, and along with it, their ability to enslave the inhabitants of the earth. Their Achilles' heel that will strip them of their power to the extent that, as we look back over the years, it will be as though they never existed.

It is essential to understand the source of their funds and how they utilize them once they receive them. Their wealth originates from:

- Controlling the world's natural resources!
- Converting those resources into finished goods.
- Converting the finished goods into money through the control of global trade routes.

Using the money acquired from trade, they establish a network of central banks, giving them the ability to print an inexhaustible supply of money backed by absolutely nothing of value. With this inexhaustible supply of money, again I say, they buy power and influence at every stratum of society. This tactic allows them to enslave mankind in a system of slavery without chains, where the masses are made dependent on a monetary system designed to make them indentured slaves: Chattel, the personal property of a moneyed elite.

WHAT MOTIVATES OUR ENEMY'S ACTIONS, AND TO WHAT EXTENT IS HE WILLING TO GO TO ACHIEVE HIS AGENDA?

With the advent of robotics, nanotechnology, and artificial intelligence, fewer and fewer of us are needed, making us expendable. To the Elite, we are consuming unacceptable amounts of *their* natural resources—the basis of all wealth. So, to achieve what the financial elite consider *sustainable levels of resource consumption,* they have to exterminate 7.5 billion of us, per the UN's Agenda 21 and Agenda 2030.

Their means of extermination include: wars, famine, abortion, and mass sterilization done without our knowledge or consent. And their current favorite methods of extermination are manmade viruses, i.e., COVID-19 and vaccines, along with genetic manipulation.

This desire of the financial elite to control what they consider to be *their* natural resources is behind the hoax of climate change. The U.S. controls the weather using electromagnetic energy. The device that controls our weather is called HAARP, and it can cause droughts, floods, hurricanes, tornadoes, earthquakes, tidal waves, and volcanic eruptions. The U.S. has had a treaty with Russia since the 1970s, agreeing not to use HAARP as a weapon of weather manipulation across borders. But that does not stop them from using it against America.

The Enemy's End-Game: Climate, as a weapon.
HAARP: High-Frequency Active Auroral Research Project

At the DOD (Department of Defense) news brief at the University of Georgia on April 27, 1977, Secretary of Defense William Cohen of the Clinton administration stated the existence of weapons systems utilizing electromagnetic energy for triggering earthquakes, volcanic eruptions, and climate alterations. Cohen cited the 1977 Treaty, in which the U.S. ratified a treaty agreeing not to use environmental manipulation as a weapon of war to create earthquakes, tidal waves, volcanic eruptions, or disturb the weather across national borders.

Do some research, and you will come to realize that the hoax of climate change is just another weapon in their arsenal of control mechanisms.

There is literally nothing that our enemy will not do to establish their vision of a one-world utopian society. We must wake up and stand united and resolve that no matter what it takes, we will win this genocidal war and take back control of our lives. If not, the day will come when most of us are dead, and those of us allowed to live will find ourselves genetically altered into compliant, submissive subspecies of sheeple. We will have lost our free will and be incapable of revolting against our masters. We will truly be a subspecies with no more rights than any other form of livestock!

> **QUESTION:** How do our puppet masters control mankind through their system of slavery without chains?
> **ANSWER:** They control us by controlling all the spheres of influence: Family, religion, education, media, entertainment, the military-industrial complex, politics, and the economy.

The Elite use their inexhaustible supply of fiat money to buy power and influence in all spheres of influence. Take the money from them, and their power evaporates. As to how we cut them off from their money supply and take their power away from them, that is the subject of an entire chapter, so we will not delve into that here. However, we will discuss how they currently control these spheres of influence, which constitute the web of deceit they use to control us. It is time for the truth to come out and for people's eyes to open. It is time to set the captives free. Once we have a thorough understanding of how our chains are forged, we will be able to stand united and reclaim our freedom. Out of chaos comes order. Soon we will walk into the light, and the kingdoms of man will fall to be replaced by God's kingdom of peace, prosperity, and brotherly love.

THE SPHERES OF INFLUENCE

The Military Industrial Complex: Here is how the web of deceit, deception, and control is woven. The global financial elite orchestrated false flag events and started wars that should not have happened. They finance both sides of the war and ensure that one or all the nations involved go bankrupt. At which point they offer to bail them out on condition of accepting their central bank, which they must agree will print their currency at interest. The debt cycle that eventually enslaves the nations in its debt trap is initiated.

**The one aim of these financiers is world control
by the creation of inextinguishable debts.**
Industrialist Henry Ford, 1957

The establishment of a Central bank is 90% of communizing a nation.
Vladimir Lenin

General and U.S. President Dwight Eisenhower warned us about the military-industrial complex when he said:

**In the councils of government, we must guard against unwarranted influence, whether
sought or unsought, by the military-industrial complex. The potential for the
disastrous rise of misplaced power exists and will persist.**
President Dwight D. Eisenhower, Farewell Address to the Nation, 1/17/1961

There is a body of historical facts that substantiates that the Vietnam, Iraq, and Afghanistan wars were all started based on false flag events. Deliberately prolonged, the U.S. was driven into massive debt, which created huge profits for the military-industrial complex.

To our young men and women, I say, don't allow yourselves to be pawns of the global elite who gladly sacrifice you in pursuit of their dream of global dominance and cast you aside once you have served your purpose. All these wars were wars for profit and control of oil, and meant to drive America deep into debt. When the next 9/11 comes along, please don't fall for their lies and become a willing lamb led to slaughter. Say "No" to their wars for profit and power.

Reflect on these eye-opening words from Henry Kissinger: "Military men are dumb, stupid animals meant to be used as pawns for foreign policy" [*i.e., cannon fodder*]. Say "No "to sacrificing your life or limbs to a corrupt government that has absolutely no regard for you and considers you as cannon fodder!

The Global Financial System: So, our puppet masters orchestrate wars to force nations to submit to a central bank that prints their money at interest and drives countries into unmanageable debt. Then gradually and covertly, the government and its institutions are subverted to where one day the public wakes up and finds they have succumbed to communism, i.e., that old system of slavery and *feudalism*!

Religion: Our forefathers came to America to escape the bondage of feudalism and to have the right to worship as they pleased. Under feudalism, only the king or the Pope could translate the Bible, and possession of an unauthorized Bible was punishable by death.

Religion is the basis and Foundation of Government.
James Madison, Virginia House of Delegates, June 20, 1785

We've staked the future of all our political institutions upon our capacity...
to sustain ourselves according to the Ten Commandments of God.
James Madison, Second Continental Congress, 1778,
to the General Assembly of the State of Virginia

That represented a serious threat to the feudal Kings of Europe and to the Catholic Church, which presided over what they called the Holy Roman Empire. They claimed that the Pope was the vicar of Christ on earth, and none could approach Christ except through the Pope. So, America, establishing a government that took that power away from the church and state, represented a serious threat to their power. Under feudalism, religion was a control mechanism utilized to its advantage. Anyone who challenged their interpretation of the Bible was branded a heretic and subject to imprisonment, torture, confiscation of property, and death. The brutal inquisitions killed millions to maintain their control.

Today, these same forces are at work, not in the form of an open inquisition, but by creating multiple competing denominations of Christianity and pitting them against one another. And by causing discord between Christianity and other religions. But Christianity is the one religion that most threatens the puppet masters and which they most vehemently come against.

That is why they removed prayer from our schools, and why Chaplains are not allowed to pray in the name of Jesus Christ. It is why globalist puppet Barack Obama said America is not a Christian nation, and why he refused to host the annual day of prayer at the White House, then hosted an Islamic prayer session instead. As it says in the Book of Matthew:

> But Jesus knew their thoughts, and said to them: "Every kingdom divided against itself is brought to desolation, and every city or house divided against itself will not stand."
> Matthew 12:25 (NKJV)

In this present age, religion is used by our puppet masters to create division because if they can keep us fighting amongst ourselves, it takes our focus off what they are doing. Religion is just one way in which they divide us. For example, Obama was elected President on the promise of bringing the nation together, but instead repeatedly played the race card to divide us. Again, I say a nation divided cannot stand, and that is why we must wake up and stand united against our enemy. We are many. They are few. If we stand united against their tyranny, they will fall.

Obama is credited with having said the following. No matter who said it, it is a declaration of what the global elite are doing to collapse America and birth their one-world dictatorship!

You just have to flood a country's public square with enough raw sewage. You have to raise enough questions, spread enough dirt, and plant enough conspiracy theorizing that citizens no longer know what to believe. Once they lose trust in their leaders, in the mainstream media, in political institutions, in each other, in the possibility of truth, the game's won!

Our would-be masters know what has made America the greatest nation in history, and they are unwavering in their resolve to destroy it. That is why it is thought to be believed that Joseph Stalin, a Russian leader and mass murderer, said, "America is like a healthy body, and its resistance is threefold: its patriotism, its morality, and its spiritual life. If we can undermine these three areas, America will collapse from within."

This book will exhaustively explain the global elite's enslavement tactics. Knowing this will empower you to join the ranks of those committed to restoring America's foundation to the principles of life, liberty, and the pursuit of happiness, based on the belief that this nation was founded on the principles of freedom of speech and freedom of religion. Now is the time. We are at a tipping point in history. As Sun Tzu would say, "America is on death ground." Either we stand united and reclaim our freedom, or we will lose it forever.

The Family: The global elite knows well that family and religion form the foundation of society. They know that from Sodom and Gomorrah to Rome, every nation that abandoned the family as the basis of society fell into homosexuality and eventually collapsed from the debauchery that ensued. That is why globalist pawn Barack Obama got behind the LGBTQ movement and saw to it that same-sex marriage became the law of the land. This is leading our society down a dangerous path where minor children are encouraged to question their sexuality and potentially undergo sex transition procedures. Our politicians, our schools, the media, and the entertainment industry are all rewarded financially for supporting the LGBTQ movement and the perversion that it inflicts on our society.

Parents, I encourage you to visit Google Images, and you will see the extent to which Disney has gone to pervert our children. You will see images from their movies of pedophile symbols, animals with their noses up the butts of other animals, drag queens, banners promoting gay pride, and much more; see for yourself. It will shock you.

Education: We supposedly have a legal system that is blind and treats the rich and the poor the same. We all know that is bunk. Neither is it true that we have an educational system that provides our children (rich or poor) with the same educational opportunities. My analysis concludes that there are three discrete educational systems. First, there is one, for the children of the financial elite, that teaches them things that we idiots are simply not allowed to learn. Because, to them, an educated person poses a threat to their system of slavery without chains. It is, as Hermann Göring, Hitler's designated successor, said, "Education is dangerous. Every educated person is a future enemy."

Give me four years to teach children, and the seed I have sown will never be uprooted.
Vladimir Lenin, Founder of the Soviet Union

This is to say that our schools are places where the state sends our children to indoctrinate them and teach them to be obedient sheep. To give you an idea of just how deep this indoctrination goes, consider this: at one point, the California Appellate Court ruled that parents do not have a Constitutional right under California law to homeschool, a decision that was later overturned. Their justification was that "a primary purpose of the education system is to train schoolchildren in good citizenship, patriotism, and loyalty to the State and the Nation as a means of protecting public welfare."

TRANSLATION: Our schools intend to indoctrinate our children in whatever most effectively makes them submissive to the end-game agenda of our globalist enemies.

The second educational system is for the middle class, where they are allowed to learn just enough to be useful in positions the Elite feel are necessary. However, they are denied access to the vital information that the children of the Elite have.

The third educational system is imposed on the children of the poor because the intention is that they are to be permanent members of the welfare class. They intentionally provide children with a subpar education, which will deny them access to good-paying jobs. They are to live lives of desperation, to become disenfranchised and perhaps turn to drugs, prostitution, or crime because this element of society is necessary. After all, it would not fit their agenda if they couldn't play the class or race card to create an adequate level of hatred and division. Remember, their agenda is to divide us and pit us against each other so we are distracted from seeing what is taking place to enslave us all.

The kingdoms of man are about to implode, and the kingdom of God is about to spring to life. The financial elite are about to lose their power as their money is stripped from them. When this happens, we will have a unified educational system that treats us all equally and finally ends the division imposed upon us as a control mechanism.

News Media: Control of the media started with the newspapers in the late nineteenth century. The Rothschilds bought the nation's twenty-five largest newspapers to control public opinion. Today, on the surface, it appears that we have six giant conglomerate news outlets. In reality, we have one fake news outlet, controlled by humanity's number one enemy, the Rothschilds. The reason I say this is that all the news feeds are syndicated through the AP and Reuters. According to my research, the Rothschilds own Reuters. At any rate, it is blatantly evident that to control our access to the truth, they censor our media.

I leave you with this to ponder: The news media have become a propaganda machine for the White House and corporations, whose primary purpose is not to report the news but to shape public opinion. They know that if they can define the perceived facts, they can control what we think, and they can largely control opposition and dissent. They feed us the truth mingled with a half-truth and out-and-out lies so that we are so confused that we can't tell truth from lie, fact from fiction, or the difference between what the Elite call conspiracy theory and what is happening to drive us into their one-world dictatorship.

Entertainment: There is not much to say about the entertainment industry. It is blatantly apparent that most of the movies and music push the LGBTQ agenda, satanism, and in one fashion or another, are intended to condition us sublimely, or play the race card, or to divide us in some way. Joseph Stalin, Russian leader and mass murderer, said, "If I could control the medium of the American motion picture, I would need nothing else to convert the entire world to communism."

Hollywood is the perfect propaganda and brainwashing platform because it bypasses all our psychological and intellectual filters. After all, it is just entertainment. Right? Wrong. It is the ultimate vehicle for mind control. I leave you to ponder this quote from Edward Bernays, the father of modern advertising:

> Those who manipulate the unseen mechanism of society constitute an invisible government which is the true ruling power of our country...In almost every act of our lives whether in the sphere of politics or business in our social conduct or our ethical thinking, we are dominated by the relatively small number of persons who understand the mental processes and social patterns of the masses. It is they who pull the wires that control the public mind.
> Edward Bernays, 1928

TRANSLATION: They brainwash us!

Politics: The way I see it, our politicians are analogous to the Gestapo. They enact and enforce the laws that their puppet masters, the financial elite, want. They impose on us a body of laws designed to inflict on us a legal dictatorship. A body of laws that rewards wrong behavior and punishes right behavior. Reflect on the quotes below.

> **Our government will soon become what it is already a long way toward becoming: an elective dictatorship.**
> Senator J. William Fulbright, AR

> **The real menace of our Republic [and the world] is the invisible government, which, like a giant octopus, sprawls its slimy legs over our cities, states, and nation. To depart from mere generalizations, let me say that at the head of this octopus are the Rockefeller–Standard Oil interests and a small group of powerful banking houses generally referred to as the international bankers.[or as I call them, "The financial elite"]. The little coterie of powerful international bankers virtually run the United States government (and the world) for their own selfish purposes. They practically control both parties [and all sovereign governments of the world]. [Emphasis added]**
> John F. Hylan, Mayor of New York 1918-1925

> **What is being sold to the American people today as Americanism, if you peel off the label, you find so much similarity to what we were fighting against when we were fighting Communism, Nazism, and Fascism... The media controls the information a person gets. In various ways, we can make sure that the average American watching the tube, reading the newspaper, is going to come out with a certain mindset: "This is good." Or "That is bad."**
> G. Edward Griffin, Author, *Creature from Jekyll Island*

So, is it possible that America is no longer a Republic but has somehow been transformed into a socialist communist order? Sadly, as the quote validates, that is the case. The American political system has been taken over; we just never got the memo. So, get ready for a jolt of the truth. It is time we learned the truth, so the truth can set us free. The time has come for us to stand united, take back our government, and reinstate our original constitution with the freedoms it confirms for We the People!

IN SUMMARY: THE TRUTH WILL SET YOU FREE!

I know the material in this book is a heavy dose of reality, but that is precisely what we need. As Sun Tzu would say, we are on death ground, and we must stand up and fight as our lives depend on it, because it does. We are in the midst of the last battle that has been going on for centuries. Although you may not think so, we are winning this battle. Sometimes it is not devising a strategy that defeats an enemy as much as it is that the enemy makes a blunder that you can exploit. Then, in an instant, the tide of the battle changes, and defeat turns to victory, which is what is happening now.

The events that have resulted in this reversal of fortunes started in 2016 when, against all odds, Donald Trump (God's Cyrus) defeated Hillary Clinton (The Jezebel) and became the 45th President of the United States. At this appointed time, God intervened in our political process to lay the groundwork for setting the captives free. Immediately, the enemy began trying to impeach Donald Trump and remove him from office. This action marked the reversal of the events outlined in the Book of Esther. You see, God knows the end before the beginning.

Immediately, the enemy began their smear campaign, accusing Trump of collusion with Russia. But unbeknownst to them, the smear campaign they were releasing would only open the people's eyes to who the real enemies are. The hounds of hell were released as global elite billionaires who called out their army of paid assassins in the form of corrupt CEOs, politicians, talking bobbleheads, Hollywood perverts, and a host of sleeper agents who professed to be truth tellers but were liars.

Lie by lie, the enemy has dug his own grave. The lies grew larger and larger, and the censorship became increasingly blatant, until it became clear that a smear campaign was in full force. Donald Trump was being railroaded. It became apparent that the enemy had released all the forces of hell against Donald Trump and, by association, the American people. It became increasingly difficult to deny what was happening. But for those of us who woke up long ago, this was a time to celebrate, not a time to despair, because we could see that the government sworn to protect and serve was in fact our enemy. We were at the point where we knew that soon the truth would set the captives free. As I mentioned earlier in this chapter, it has been stated that, "You just have to flood a country's public square with enough raw sewage...." Heed this statement.

Whether Obama spoke these words is not important; they expose the plan of the enemy for all to see. As I have said repeatedly, "The truth will set us free." Ask yourself, isn't this exactly what has been happening? Here, in a single statement, we know who the enemy is and what their strategy is, so we are empowered to stand and reclaim our freedom. We know who to remove from power to restore our freedom.

Therefore, we can see that our fellow Americans are not our foes. We can ignore the race card when played, the attacks on Christian conservatives, and different ethnic groups, etc. Because the real enemy is the government sworn to serve and protect all its bought and paid-for influencers that make up the eight spheres of influence that are the central focus of this chapter.

With this truth out in the open, we can stand united and take our country back! How we accomplish that is the subject of another chapter. For now, it is enough that we know who the enemy is and what he is doing to enslave us—more disclosures to come.

CHAPTER 3

HISTORY AT A GLANCE
Pivotal Points that Defined U.S. and World History

TOPICS COVERED IN THIS CHAPTER:

- WHAT IS THE CORPORATOCRACY AND HOW DOES IT CONTROL US?
- HOW MONEY IS USED AS A CONTROL MECHANISM
- HOW WARS ARE USED AS A CONTROL MECHANISM
- THE HARMFUL (OR HELPFUL) LEGACIES OF FORMER U.S. PRESIDENTS

WE ARE AT a pivotal moment where the fate of the world hangs in the balance, so you need to know the whole truth about how they are enslaving you. You also need to know that this truth is the most powerful weapon on earth. It surpasses the power of the enemy's lies. It will give you the faith and courage to stand in the days ahead when the enemy is going to make his last desperate moves to enslave the world.

By seeing exactly what the enemy has done to enslave us and what he has planned, we will understand that surrender is not an option. We are on death ground, and we must fight like our lives depend on us winning because they do. What the enemy has envisioned for us, that they allow to live, is not like anything mankind has ever experienced. They intend to turn us into a subhuman species of mindless zombies who exist solely to serve them. We will have no rights, and worse yet, all that defines our humanity will be bred out of us. Truly, we will no longer be human beings but simply domesticated animals who exist at the pleasure of their master. Please, please stand and join the army of God, and let's take back this nation and all the nations of the world and usher in an era of unbelievable peace, prosperity, and brotherly love. God is on our side, and He will see us through to victory, but first, we must stand. As you read what follows, think about what President Franklin D. Roosevelt said:

In politics, nothing happens by accident.
If it happened, you can bet it was planned that way.
American History at a Glance

The historical account that follows is unlike any history book you have ever read. God has told me that my assignment is to make the complex simple and to tell the people the truth that will set the captives free. What follows is a journey through American history, pausing at key tipping points to highlight how a group of powerful men who serve forces of darkness hijacked America.

This chapter will discuss the genuine history of America. The movement that will emerge from that awakening will spread across America and the world. That light will eclipse the darkness of the forces of evil, and it will be like in Egypt when the enemy of God's people vanished to be seen no more. America is going back to God. This chapter is the equivalent of a 500-page book in itself! It will open your eyes, and if you are not already red-pilled, you will be. What is coming is truly amazing.

1775-1783: THE AMERICAN REVOLUTIONARY WAR

According to Benjamin Franklin, the real reason for the Revolutionary War was that in 1773, King George III outlawed the *interest-free* currency of the American Colonies and forced them to borrow money at interest from the Central Bank of England, immediately plunging the colonies into debt.

> The inability of the colonists to get power to issue their own money permanently
> out of the hands of King George III and the international bankers
> was the prime reason for the Revolutionary War.
> Benjamin Franklin

America won its independence from England, but in the process, it became bankrupt, and the first central bank of America was established.

1776: THE BIRTH OF THE ILLUMINATI

The king of France gave the Ashkenazi (referred to as fake Jews) an ultimatum that, because of their practices regarding child sacrifices, they had to convert to Christianity or else. They sought advice regarding the ultimatum from the Catholic Jesuits (referred to as the assassin's cult), who responded by referencing a 14th-century letter called the "Constantinople letter." The letter framed the structure for what was to become the Illuminati and their master plan to establish a one-world government. The following is an excerpt from that letter. As you read it, ask yourself if this isn't exactly what is being done to enslave us today. We are seeing their plan, hatched in secrecy in 1776, play out today by those we call the "Illuminati" or the financial elite, the Cabal, etc.

> As for what you say that the king of France obliges you to become Christians: do it, since you cannot do otherwise, but let the law of Moses be kept in your hearts. As for what you say about the demand to despoil you of your goods: make your sons merchants that little by little they may despoil the Christians of theirs...As for what you say about their making attempts on your lives, make your sons doctors and apothecaries that they may take away Christian lives...As for what you say about their destroying your synagogues, make your sons clerics in order that they may destroy their churches...As for the many other vexations you complain of, arrange that your sons become advocates and lawyers, and see that they always mix themselves up with

(cont'd next page)

the affairs of state, in order that by putting Christians under your yoke you may
dominate the world and be avenged on them...Do not swerve from this order that we
give you, for you will find by experience that, humiliated as you are now,
you will reach the actuality of power.
Sequel to Fall of the Cabal

Please stop and reflect on what you just read. The financial elite are doing exactly what the letter above directed. Controlling the money supply and using it to buy power and influence in all spheres of influence. Soon, their wealth and power will be stripped away, and a transfer of wealth and power will occur. The censorship will end. Once the masses truly understand what has been done to enslave us, they will unite across America and around the world. People will stand united. Revival will break out, and freedom will spread like wildfire.

1791: INCEPTION OF THE FIRST CENTRAL BANK OF AMERICA

Following the Revolutionary War, America declared bankruptcy, forcing the acceptance of the first central bank of America. Fiat currency, issued as a loan, with assessed interest, created our national debt. The colonists were once again indentured servants of King George III.

1796: IMPOSITION OF PROPERTY TAX AND TAKE RIGHTS

President Thomas Jefferson warned: If the American people allow private banks to control the issuance of the currency, first by inflation and then by devaluation, the banks and corporations that will grow up around them will deprive the people of all their property until their children will wake up homeless on the continent their fathers conquered.

What President Jefferson warned about is happening today. Thanks to the imposition of property taxes and eminent domain, no American owns a home outright. Fall behind on your mortgage or property tax, and you soon realize that you are a Renter, and the Government is your landlord. Just as under communism, the government owns all property.

1801: WARNINGS THAT A CENTRAL BANK IS A DEBT TRAP:

The FED must be abolished!

The modern banking system manufactures money out of nothing . . . Bankers own the
earth . . . if you want to continue the slaves of bankers and pay the cost
of your own slavery, let them continue to create money and to control credit.
Sir Josiah Stamp, Director and President of the Bank of England during the 1920s

1811: LEAD UP TO THE WAR OF 1812

The charter for the Rothschild's first central bank of America expired, and Congress elected not to renew it. Nathan Mayer Rothschild threatened, "Either the application for renewal of the charter is granted, or the United States will find itself involved in a most disastrous war."

1811: THE BRITISH DECLARE WAR ON THE UNITED STATES

The plan was to drive the U.S. so deeply into debt that it would force the renewal of the bank charter. Became known as the 2nd American Revolution. Sure enough, the charter was renewed.

1814-1945: EFFORTS TO ESTABLISH GLOBAL GOVERNANCE

- **1814: Conference of Vienna:** This was the 1ˢᵗ attempt by the Rothschilds to establish a global governance organization intended to end all sovereign nations and establish their one-world government.
- **1918: League of Nations:** Following World War I, the Rothschilds made a second attempt at forming a global governance organization.
- **1945: UN Founded:** Following World War II, the Rothschilds founded the Globalist UN, dedicated to ending all sovereign governments!

1837: THE PLAN TO START THE CIVIL WAR TO DIVIDE AMERICA IN HALF

> The division of the United States into FEDerations of equal force was decided long
> before the Civil War by the high financial powers of Europe. These bankers were afraid
> that the United States, if they remained in one block and as one nation,
> would attain economic and financial independence,
> which would upset their financial domination over the world.
> The voice of the Rothschilds prevailed...Therefore, they sent their emissaries into the
> field to exploit the question of slavery
> and to open an abyss between the two sections of the Union.
> Otto von Bismarck, first Chancellor of the German Empire [Emphasis added]

At the wedding of Nathan Rothschild's eldest daughter, it was stated, "I shall divide the United States in half, half for you, Lionel, and half for you, James." An agreement was made that one brother would fund the North and the other the South, and the loser would pay reparations to the winner.

Since then, all our wars, Wars for Profit, have been orchestrated through false flag events with the financial elite funding both sides and the loser paying reparations to the winner. For example, this is exactly what happened at the end of World War I, when Germany was forced to pay reparations to the Allied countries.

1837: THE TERMINATION OF THE SECOND CENTRAL BANK OF AMERICA

**I killed the Bank [referring to the Central Bank of the United States].
The bold effort the present bank has made to control the present governments
are but premonitions of the fate that awaits the American people should they be
deluded into a perpetuation of this institution, or the establishment of any other like it.**
President Andrew Jackson [Emphasis added]

1863-1869: THE BUILDING OF THE U.S. TRANSCONTINENTAL RAILROAD

America built the transcontinental railroad to gain access to its vast storehouse of natural resources, thereby ending its dependency on the British Free Trade System.

**It, [The British System Free Trade System] is the most gigantic system of slavery the
world has yet seen, and therefore it is that freedom gradually disappears from every
country over which England (The Free Trade System) is enabled to obtain control.**
Henry C. Carey, economics adviser to Abraham Lincoln [Emphasis added]

The world embraced America's transcontinental railroad. Plans were underway to build an interconnecting network of railroads connecting North America, South America, Europe, and Africa. England's control of trade by sea was threatened, so it orchestrated plans to initiate World War I to maintain its control of global maritime trade routes.

Today, the British free trade system has morphed into the Chinese free trade system as the old system of slavery continues under a new name.

1842-1876: THE AMERICAN ECONOMIC SYSTEM AND THE 1876 CENTENNIAL CELEBRATION

For 34 years, America innovated the *American economic system,* which gave birth to the Industrial Revolution. Efforts culminated in 1876, on America's 100th anniversary, with a *Centennial Celebration* announcing that America, the youngest nation in the world, was the wealthiest. The rise of the U.S. to an economic superpower status was largely based on high tariffs on British goods, which facilitated the domestic development of the U.S. manufacturing base.

The American economic system, based on human ingenuity, shared resources, and technology, proved superior to the British Free Trade System, based on controlling natural resources and suppressing wages. The American system uplifted the condition of humankind, while the British System enslaved them.

> **Two systems are before the world . . . One is the English system;**
> **the other we may be proud to call The American System of Economics . . .**
> **the only one ever devised the tendency of which was that of elevating while equalizing**
> **the condition of man throughout the world.**
> Henry C. Carey, Conclusion in *Harmony of Interest,* 1851
> Economics Adviser to Abraham Lincoln

1861-1865: THE CIVIL WAR BEGINS AND THE GREENBACK IS ISSUED

President Lincoln approached New York Bankers to obtain loans to fund the war. Under Rothschild's thumb, the banks made him an absurd offer of 24% to 36% interest. Lincoln decided to print his own debt-free money: the *Greenback*. Upon its distribution, he said, "We gave the people of this Republic the greatest blessing they ever had, their own paper money to pay their own debts."

In response, *The Times of London* published the following:

> *If that mischievous financial policy, which had its origin in the North American Republic, should become indurated down to a fixture, then that government will furnish its own money without cost. It will pay off debts and be without a debt. It will have all the money necessary to carry on its commerce. It will become prosperous beyond precedent in the history of civilized governments of the world. The brains and the wealth of all countries will go to North America. That government must be destroyed, or it will destroy every monarchy on the globe.*

1865: LEADING UP TO LINCOLN'S ASSASSINATION

Shortly before his assassination, President Lincoln made the following statement to Congress:

> I have two great enemies, the Southern Army in front of me, and the financial
> institutions in the rear. Of the two, the one in my rear is my greatest foe.
> President Abraham Lincoln

Lincoln warned about what was to become the "corporatocracy." He said:

> I see in the near future a crisis approaching that unnerves me and causes me to tremble
> for the safety of my country . . . corporations have been enthroned, and an era of
> corruption in high places will follow, and the money power of the country will endeavor
> to prolong its reign by working upon the prejudices of the people until all wealth is
> aggregated in a few hands and the Republic is destroyed.
> President Abraham Lincoln, Nov. 21, 1864, in a letter to Col. William F. Elkins

The corporatocracy was the merger of the banking cartel with the corporations, who then solicited corrupt politicians to pass laws that force the public to pay illegal FEDeral income tax and other taxes.

APRIL 14, 1865: PRESIDENT LINCOLN IS ASSASSINATED

Subsequently, eight British spies are hanged for their part in his assassination.

> The death of Lincoln was a disaster for Christendom . . . I fear that foreign bankers with
> their craftiness and torturous tricks will entirely control the exuberant riches of
> America and use it systematically to corrupt modern civilization. They will not hesitate
> to plunge the whole of Christendom into wars and chaos in order that
> the earth should become their inheritance.
> Otto von Bismarck, first Chancellor of the German Empire

THE ACT OF 1871 AND THE BIRTH OF THE U.S. CORPORATION

The Civil War bankrupted the U.S., resulting in the formation of the illegal U.S. Corporation. Our Original Constitution Reads: The Constitution *for* the United States of America. The altered version reads: The Constitution *of* the United States of America.

The Act of 1871 meant that, under no constitutional authority, Congress created a separate form of government for the District of Columbia, which was an act of treason! This separate government status is in effect for the District of Columbia, the Vatican, and the City of London—control centers for the Corporation.

NOTE: If you are wondering why servers outside the U.S. count our votes and why foreign nations collude in our elections, it is because America is no longer a sovereign nation. It is controlled by the U.S. Corporation, owned by foreign bankers. We must take back our country and its Constitution.

The second Declaration of Independence (presented in the last chapter of this book) declares the U.S. CORP to be illegal. Therefore, all elected and appointed officials and all laws passed under the U.S. CORP are unlawful and subject to removal.

1897: THE BUYING OF THE FIRST U.S. PRESIDENT

The three wealthiest men in America, Carnegie, J.P. Morgan, and Rockefeller, backed pro-business candidate McKinley against anti-monopoly candidate Bryan and got their man elected. The Rothschilds now understand they can buy Presidents and other politicians to control democratic governments.

1912: THE PLAN TO SELECT A PRESIDENT WHO WOULD ESTABLISH THE THIRD CENTRAL BANK OF AMERICA

The candidacies of all three presidential candidates—Taft, Roosevelt, and Wilson—were financed by Paul Warburg, representing the European Banking Cartel.

> We will have a world government whether you like it or not. The only question is whether that government will be achieved by conquest or consent.
>
> Paul Walburg

1912: THE SINKING OF THE TITANIC

Three primary opponents of the FED, Benjamin Guggenheim, Isidor Straus, and John Jacob Astor, died on the Titanic. Coincidence?

1913: FEDERAL RESERVE, THE THIRD CENTRAL BANK, IS ESTABLISHED

President Wilson, put into office by J.P. Morgan, a front man for Rothschild, broke his campaign promise not to impose a central bank, the privately owned FED, on the American people. The FED is established and takes over the printing of our currency at interest. From that point, the FED and IMF control the government, and our politicians are little more than figureheads.

Some believe that in the 1960s, Senator Barry Goldwater warned that both houses of Congress were irrelevant. America's domestic policy is now being run by the Chairman of the FED and the FEDeral Reserve. The International Monetary Fund is also now running America's foreign policy. Not even the President can challenge decisions made by the FED Chairman. Remember, "He who controls the money controls the world."

1913: FORMATION OF ANTI-DEFAMATION LEAGUE

This group was formed to slander anyone who threatens the secret agenda of the global financial elite.

1913: THE PASSAGE OF THE 16TH AMENDMENT

The amendment was passed to bypass the Constitution and allow a person's labor to be taxed. The FEDeral income tax was declared illegal in six Supreme Court cases, but it was implemented anyway. Revenue from FEDeral income tax goes to the foreign bankers who own the private FED.

1913: THE 17TH AMENDMENT PASSED

The 17th Amendment changed how Senators were selected. Before the 17th Amendment, senators were appointed by State Legislature. After the 17th Amendment, they were chosen by popular vote. This took power away from the States and seeded it to a power-crazed FEDeral government!

1914: THE PLAN TO CAUSE WORLD WAR I

As the world welcomed America's transcontinental railroad, plans were underway to build an interconnected network of railroads spanning North America, South America, Europe, and Africa. This threatened England's control of trade by sea, so England orchestrated plans to start World War I to maintain its control of global trade routes by sea.

Following the war, the wreckage of the Lusitania was found, and just like the Germans claimed, it was carrying munitions, making it a legitimate war target. So, America entered World War I on a false flag event.

1915: ROTHSCHILD INTERESTS START TAKEOVER OF MEDIA OUTLETS

They purchase the 25 largest newspapers in America and appoint their editors to influence public opinion. Editors were tasked with influencing public opinion on topics such as militarism, war preparedness, and financial policies. This was to prepare for WWI and was the first step in taking over Hollywood, TV, news outlets, and the education system, and most recently, their influence is seen in rigged search results on the internet.

1917: THE U.S. ENTERS WORLD WAR I ON THE SIDE OF ROTHSCHILD-CONTROLLED ENGLAND

The war devastated Europe, halting the construction of the transcontinental railroad system and disrupting the emerging industrial revolution in Germany, whose success threatened England.

NOTE: As with most things, the Rothschilds orchestrated America's entry into the war. They wanted a homeland in Palestine for the Jews, so they made a deal. America would enter the war on the side of England, and the Jews would get a homeland, soon to be known as the Balfour Declaration. The condition for the Rothschilds' funding of both sides of the war was that the winner would pay the debts of the vanquished.

1921: THE COUNCIL ON FOREIGN RELATIONS IS BORN

It was supposed to represent U.S. interests abroad. But it represented the interests of the U.S. CORP and FED on behalf of the City of London. You can read more about the CFR in Chapter 1, as well as reflect on the quote below.

> The Council on Foreign Relations is the American branch of a society which originated
> in England ...[and]...believes national boundaries should be obliterated
> and one-world rule established.
>
> Dr. Carroll Quigley, Historian, Author of *Tragedy and Hope: A History of the World in
> Our Time*, 1966, Professor, Georgetown University
> College Mentor of President Bill Clinton

1924-1964: IMMIGRATION IS HALTED

Immigration was suspended because the number of poor people coming in constituted a financial burden, and there were too many people coming in to allow assimilation. This action reveals a national security crisis at our southern border, which is allowed to happen through unconventional warfare.

1929: THE GREAT DEPRESSION

Impeachment charges are brought against the FED for intentionally causing the Depression.

> Whoever controls the volume of money in any country is the absolute master of all industry and commerce...and when you realize that the entire system is very easily controlled, one way or another, by a few powerful men at the top, you will not have to be told how periods of inflation and depression originate.
>
> President James A. Garfield, two weeks before his assassination in 1881

1933: U.S. DECLARES BANKRUPTCY DURING THE HEART OF THE DEPRESSION

The U.S. declares bankruptcy and becomes a *democracy,* a socialist-communist order (see page 34 for the official declaration). At that moment, the Republic fell, and America was taken over from within by the Shadow Government. Both houses of Congress became irrelevant, and America was controlled by the FED and the IMF. A bank holiday was declared.

Under Executive Order of the President issued April 5, 1933: All persons are required to deliver on or before May 1, 1933, all gold coin, gold bullion, and gold certificates now owned by them to the Federal Reserve Bank, branch or agency, or any other bank of the Federal Reserve System. All safety deposit boxes have been opened, and all gold has been confiscated.

The public is ordered to surrender all gold with the penalty of 10 years in prison and/or a $10,000 fine. So, the people were forced to turn in gold in exchange for fiat dollar promissory notes that are now virtually worthless. These actions mark the Shadow Government's takeover of the U.S. Government, with an army of unelected bureaucrats being placed in the government to write regulations that undermine the Constitution and control the economic system.

The bankruptcy allowed the implementation of *the Law of the Sea, also known as Admiralty Law,* to be in effect in our courts and signified by the gold fringe on the American flag in courtrooms. With their takeover of the U.S. Government, the Rothschilds were ready to implement their plans to establish their one-world dictatorship.

THE ROTHSCHILD'S MASTER PLAN

Several key areas were part of the master plan to establish a one-world dictatorship. They included the need to:

- Gain control of America's monetary system to control the four centers of power: monetary, political, intellectual, and religious.
- Recruit men who would, for a price, support the Rothschilds' agenda, and place them in high places in the Federal government, the Congress, the Supreme Court, and all Federal agencies.
- Create racial, ethnic, and class strife to cause division and tear the country apart from within.
- Create a movement to destroy religion, patriotism, morality, and the family.
- Buy media outlets to control public opinion!
- Endow universities to control their curriculum and steer them toward socialist, progressive ideologies.
- Create "Wars for Profit" and fund both sides.

MISSION ACCOMPLISHED
DONE, DONE, DONE, DONE, DONE, AND DONE!

1936: SOCIAL SECURITY NUMBERS ARE ISSUED

The issuance made American citizens trustees under the U.S. CORP so that we could be assets of the U.S. CORP.

1939: CFR PLOTTED TO CAUSE WORLD WAR II

The CFR established a committee to address post-war problems before the end of 1939, before the war even began. In other words, the CFR orchestrated the start of the war (State Department Publication 2349, submitted by Secretary of State and CFR member Edward Stettinius). Rothschild controlled I.G. Farben, the world's leading producer of chemicals and Germany's largest steel producer, increasing production so Germany could build its military in preparation for World War II.

During the war, I.G. Farben used slave labor in the concentration camps. They created the lethal Zyklon B gas, a cyanide-based insecticide, used to exterminate the Jews. At the end of the war, reports stated that the bombing raids on Germany did not target the I.G. Farben plants. Their plants had sustained only 15% damage.

1941: PRESIDENT ROOSEVELT PLANS TO TAKE AMERICA INTO WORLD WAR II

Roosevelt had an 8-point plan intended to force Japan to attack the U.S., giving him an excuse to enter the war. As part of that plan, the U.S. refused to sell Japan scrap steel or oil. He also staged what were called "pop-ups," where U.S. Naval ships would make incursions into the war zone in hopes of inciting a conflict.

Japan needed a tempting target, so Roosevelt gave them one. Against the advice of his Admirals, he brought the Seventh Fleet into Pearl Harbor, where they were sitting ducks. Over 3,000 Americans lost their lives that day, but as planned, America entered the war under a false flag event.

1941: INCEPTION OF THE FBI, CIA, AND OTHER THREE-LETTER AGENCIES

The U.S. needed a spy network, and it just so happens that the financial elite CFR had a vast spy network. CFR's spy network resides within the U.S. Government. It became the CIA and infiltrated the Department of Justice. Have you ever wondered why top-level FBI and Department of Justice heads seem to be corrupt?

1942: PRESCOTT BUSH'S COMPANY SEIZED UNDER THE TRADING WITH THE ENEMY ACT

Prescott Bush was funding Hitler while the enemy killed American soldiers in Germany. He is the father of President George H. W. Bush and the grandfather of George W. Bush. Both Bush Presidents belonged to Yale University's *Skull and Bones* secret society, which is known for grooming people for positions of power in the government.

1945: THE UNITED NATIONS IS ESTABLISHED

This organization is wholly dedicated to establishing a one-world government. The Council on Foreign Relations is involved in establishing the United Nations. Read below what the CFR states in its handbook:

The New World Order will be built...an end-run on national sovereignty, eroding it piece by piece, will accomplish much more than the old-fashioned frontal assault.
Council on Foreign Relations Journal 1974, page 558

The UN serves as an umbrella organization for all global governance organizations, including the World Bank, the IMF, NATO, the World Trade Organization, and the World Health Organization, among others. As previously mentioned, they aim to abolish all countries and eliminate most of the population, deemed unnecessary.

1963: PRESIDENT JOHN F. KENNEDY ASSASSINATED ON NOVEMBER 22ND

JFK had issued Executive Order #11110 to end the Federal Reserve's Charter, effectively putting it out of business. He issued silver certificates to replace the FED's fiat dollar. He refused the efforts of the Rothschild-controlled military complex to commit more troops to the Vietnam War.

If the Rothschilds were to maintain control of the U.S. government, Kennedy had to die. Once Johnson became President, he reversed all three of the initiatives listed above. If Kennedy had lived, America would be debt-free, and the American people would be free.

> **It is well enough that people of the nation do not understand our banking and monetary system, for if they did, I believe there would be a revolution before tomorrow morning.**
> Henry Ford, Industrialist

1964-1975: THE VIETNAM WAR FOR PROFIT

The Vietnam War was a false flag event perpetrated by the Rothschild global shadow government. The Gulf of Tonkin event, which was President Johnson's provocation for committing troops to the Vietnam War, was proven to have never occurred. It was a hoax, a false flag event!

Pentagon Papers disclosed the Vietnam War could not be won, yet dragged out to drive the U.S. into debt. Vietnam was a *War for Profit.* Intentionally prolonged to drive the U.S. into debt and begin its long decline.

Sustaining any war without supplies is not possible. Cut off the enemy's supply lines, and the war is over. Period end of statement. So, how did the war end? Nixon mined Haiphong Harbor, leading to the end of the war.

TRANSLATION: The Vietnam War could have ended any time the U.S. wanted.

1971: NIXON TAKES THE U.S. OFF THE GOLD STANDARD

Why was this done? Because the dollar was no longer worth a dollar, the idea of walking into a bank laying a $20 bill on the counter and getting a $20 gold coin was absurd. As the dollar devalued, it became impossible for nations across the globe to demand gold in exchange for their dollars. That is why, a short time later, we entered into the Petrodollar Agreement with Saudi Arabia.

1971: U.S. SUSPENDS CONVERTIBILITY OF THE DOLLAR

This was done in preparation for using the dollar as a weapon to force compliance with U.S. (globalist) policy.

> **I have directed Secretary Connally to suspend temporarily the convertibility of the dollar into gold or other reserve assets...**
> President Richard Nixon, in his Address to the Nation, 8/15/1971

1974: BIRTH OF THE PETRO DOLLAR

It was here that the U.S. and Saudi Arabia signed the Petro Dollar agreement. Saudi Arabia will sell its oil in U.S. dollars in exchange for U.S. military protection and technological assistance. This gave the U.S. the ability to use the dollar as a weapon to force compliance with U.S. (globalist) policy.

1977-1981: PRESIDENT CARTER'S LEGACY

The U.S. economy is afflicted by 18% interest rates and inflation, coupled with an unprecedented period of corporate raiding, which saw many major corporations bought only to be broken up and sold off in pieces. This cleared the way for the reintroduction of the British free trade system, rebranded as the Chinese free trade system. It also led to the intentional loss of free trade deals, which gutted the U.S. manufacturing base and created a devastating trade imbalance for the U.S., a major contributor to our debt crisis.

Henry Kissinger said NAFTA was a stepping stone to a one-world government. NAFTA was also intended to model the U.S. after the European Union, which started as a trade agreement, then adopted a common currency, and ultimately a common socialist constitution. Today, our open borders policies have nothing to do with human rights (it is a smokescreen). It has everything to do with merging the U.S., Mexico, and Canada into a servile Socialist trading bloc modeled after the European Union.

1989-1993: PRESIDENT GEORGE H.W. BUSH'S LEGACY

Twenty days following the fall of the Berlin Wall, President Bush, a member of Skull and Bones, met with Russian leader Gorbachev and Communist Pope Paul II and announced the birth of *The New World Order.*

1992: UN PUBLISHES AGENDA 21

The plan is to end all sovereign nations and replace them with ten servile trading blocs, known as "the Beast System," where no one can buy or sell unless they submit to the demonic one-world government.

1993-2001: PRESIDENT BILL CLINTON'S LEGACY

Clinton signed the intentionally losing NAFTA trade deal into effect, leading to a massive increase in the national debt.

> **What Congress will have before it is not a conventional trade agreement but the architecture of a new international system.... a first step toward a new world order.**
> Henry Kissinger, CFR Member, and Trilateralist
> *The Los Angeles Times* concerning NAFTA, 7/18/1993

> **We practiced what I call "losing trade,"**
> **deliberately losing trade over the last 50 years...**
> Congressman Duncan Hunter (R-CA), in an interview with
> Human Events, December 4, 2006

Clinton played a central role in the 2008 financial collapse by rescinding the Glass-Steagall Act, which was America's firewall against the formation of banks that were too big to fail. As a result, the American public was on the hook for a $700 billion bailout due to the 2008 financial collapse.

1993: FORMATION OF THE EUROPEAN UNION

This step marked the birth of the first of the UN's plans to establish 10 servile trading blocs, to constitute the *Beast System* that determines who can buy and sell. To restate a previous quote, the words below shed light on the UN's intention to establish a world government.

Here is a list of the *Servile Trading Blocs* planned by the globalist UN:

1. The Amero Union comprised the USA, Canada, and Mexico
2. The E.U. – countries of the European Union, Western Europe as a whole
3. Japan
4. Australia, New Zealand, and South Africa
5. Eastern Europe, Pakistan, Afghanistan, Russia, and the former countries of the Soviet Union
6. Central and South America, Cuba, and the Caribbean Islands
7. The Middle East and North Africa
8. The rest of Africa, except South Africa.
9. South and Southeast Asia, including India
10. China and Mongolia

This is confirmed in the Bible, in Revelation 17:12 (NKJV), where it discloses the plans of the globalists to establish their beast system.

> The ten horns which you saw are ten kings who have received no kingdom as yet, but they receive authority for one hour as kings with the beast.

This Bible verse above refers to the ten trading blocs planned by the UN to control humanity by controlling what can be bought and sold, by whom, and under what conditions.

2001-2009: BUSH JUNIOR'S LEGACY

- 9/11 was on Bush.
- The Iraq War was another "War for Profit." When Bush declared war on Iraq, he said it would be a generational war lasting 20 years or more. It was another protracted war for profit, costing the U.S. over $7 trillion.

- Project for the New American Century (PNAC): The report, written in 2000, outlines three primary U.S. military objectives:
  - o The need for strategically positioned military bases worldwide.
  - o The need to bring about regime change in countries unfriendly to U.S. policy.
  - o The desire to increase military spending by upwards of a trillion dollars. Then came 9/11, and they got everything they wanted, go figure!

9/11 CRASH SITES EXPOSED

French accident investigator François Grangier said, "What is certain when one looks at the photos of the façade [the Pentagon] that remains is that it is obvious that the plane [a Boeing 757] did not go through there" on 9/11.

Wally Miller, Somerset County Coroner at the site of Flight 93, said, "It looks like there is nothing there except a hole in the ground…It looked like somebody just dropped a bunch of metal out of the sky. It looked like somebody took a scrape truck, dug a 10-foot ditch, and put trash in it…I stopped being a coroner after about 20 minutes because there were no bodies there. I have not to this day seen a single drop of blood, not a drop."

Aaron Russo (a friend of the Rockefellers) says on *InfoWars*, "9/11 was done by people in our own government, in our own banking system, to perpetuate the fear of the American people to subordinate themselves to anything the government wants them to do. That's what it's about; to create an endless war on terror…the whole war on terror is a fraud, a farce. It's very difficult to say that out loud because people are intimidated against saying it; they want to make you into a nutcase. But the truth has to come out. That's why I am doing this interview."

2005: BUSH ATTEMPTS TO FORM THE AMERO UNION

A secret meeting was held at Baylor University to discuss plans to merge the U.S., Canada, and Mexico under what is dubbed the *Security and Prosperity Partnership*. Details of the plan were leaked, and the plan was aborted. The plan would have made the U.S. a servile member of the UN's 10-nation (Beast System) trading bloc, similar to the European Union.

Bush was complicit in the 2008 financial collapse! He prevented governors from passing anti-predatory lending legislation and then sat back and waited for the economic collapse to devastate the nation—the act of a traitor. Reread the quote that I mentioned earlier on the following page:

> **When history tells the story of the subprime lending crisis and recounts its devastating effects on the lives of so many innocent homeowners, the Bush administration will not be judged favorably. The tale is still unfolding, but when the dust settles, it will be judged as a willing accomplice to the lenders who went to any length in their quest for profit. So willing in fact, that it used the power of the FEDeral government in an unprecedented assault on state legislatures, as well as on state attorneys general and anyone else on the side of consumers.**
>
> Governor Eliot Spitzer, NY, Washington Post Op-Ed–2/14/2008, [Emphasis added]

Had it not been for the actions of Presidents George W. Bush, Bill Clinton, and Barack Obama, the 2008 financial collapse would never have happened.

2009-2017: BARACK OBAMA'S LEGACY

- He taught Rules for Radicals as a strategy to cause social and economic strife.
- He sued City Bank, leading to the subprime loans that, without which, the 2008 financial collapse would never have occurred.
- He left office having created more debt than any of the 43 presidents who preceded him.
- When asked about his faith, he responded with comments about his Muslim faith.
- He recited the *Muslim Call to Prayer*, which makes us infidels and his enemy.
- He pledged to reduce the military to a level acceptable to his Muslim brothers, and he kept his promise.
- He sent pallets of cash to Iran in the cover of night, knowing they would fund terrorism.
- He said, "I will stand with the Muslims should the political winds shift in an ugly direction." (*The Audacity of Hope*, page 261)

2009: BRICS OFFICIALLY ESTABLISHED

Brazil, Russia, India, China, and South Africa formed B.R.I.C.S. (BRICS) to provide the world a gold-backed, commodity-based currency as an alternative to the U.S. fiat currency, in response to the decline in the value of the dollar and the U.S.'s use of the dollar to impose sanctions on nations whose policies did not align with those of the U.S. and its globalist allies.

2017-2021: PRESIDENT TRUMP'S FIRST TERM LEGACY

Donald Trump was the first U.S. President in decades not put into office by the financial elite. Upon taking office, he immediately initiated policies to:

- Restore access to our oil and other natural resources.
- Allow the rebuilding of our infrastructure, including the construction of factories.
- Negotiate *fair trade agreements* and helped us exit the intentionally unfavorable NAFTA trade agreement.
- Impose tariffs on China to create fair trade!

And with his actions, the U.S. economy begins a remarkable recovery. The stock market goes from 10,000 to 30,000.

2019: THE COVID-19 PANDEMIC AND GLOBAL LOCKDOWNS

There were three primary objectives of the COVID-19 pandemic:

1. Depopulation because the Elite believe we are consuming too many natural resources, which they believe are theirs.
2. Disrupt global trade, leading to deglobalization and the financial collapse of China.
3. Collapse the global monetary system and usher in the Great Reset, including the de-dollarization of the U.S.

2021-2024: PRESIDENT JOE BIDEN'S LEGACY

Joe Biden's devastating policies and strategies ravaged America. By his actions, he:

- Cut oil and gas production
- Unleashed rampant inflation
- Supported packing the Supreme Court
- Supported ending the filibuster
- Supported mandatory gun confiscation
- Pressured Facebook to censor Trump
- Supported a ban on fracking and offshore drilling
- Supported LGBTQ rights above those of our children
- Implemented many "open borders" policies
- Ended stay in Mexico
- Established numerous sanctuary cities

- Created entitlements for illegals
- Supported defunding the police and cash bonds
- Caused a surge in crime
- Unquestioningly supported the war in Ukraine
- Created a debacle in Afghanistan

JUNE 9, 2024: BRICS MOVES TO UNDERMINE THE FIAT DOLLAR

Brazil, Russia, India, China, and South Africa (BRICS nations) provide the world with a gold-backed, commodity-based currency as an alternative to the U.S. fiat currency. On this date in 2024, Saudi Arabia announced that it would not renew the Petrodollar agreement. This is intended to collapse the U.S. dollar and trigger a global financial reset.

2025-2028: THE AMERICAN COMEBACK UNDER TRUMP

We are witnessing historic changes that will bring America back to its rightful status as a global superpower under the second administration of Donald Trump. The rise of the U.S. to economic superpower status in 1876 was based on American innovation and high tariffs on British goods, which forced the domestic development of the U.S. manufacturing base. Trump will do essentially the same thing with the same results. Here is what we have seen or will watch happen over the remainder of his second term:

- A one-year celebration focused on American heritage and unity
- Drain the swamp and take back control of all the spheres of influence
- Access to oil, gas, and free energy
- Close the border and finish building the wall
- Crime will go down
- Tariffs to force "Made in America" policies
- A new medical system
- Election reform
- Deregulation to stimulate infrastructure projects
- A stronger economy
- A focus on morality and Christian values
- America will be respected again

- U.S. manufacturing will be restored (as of September 2025, Trump has received commitments for $17T for investments in the U.S.)
- Trump has negotiated peace agreements in seven conflicts

Please do not walk away from this discouraged. There is good news, not bad news. You can do nothing until you know who the enemy is and what his plan is. Now you know. You now have the power to regain your freedom and establish a better, kinder, more spiritual world filled with actual peace, happiness, and harmony. It is up to you. Stand and be counted!

GET READY TO BECOME TIRED OF WINNING!

Under Donald Trump's leadership, with the swamp drained, America will once again rise from the ashes to superstar status, and it will elevate the entire world along with it.

CHAPTER 4

HOW OUR GOVERNMENT WAS HIJACKED BY THE FINANCIAL ELITE
And How We Get It Back!

TOPICS COVERED IN THIS CHAPTER:

- HOW WE LOST CONTROL OF OUR ELECTION PROCESS
- IS THE U.S. A COUNTRY? OR A CORPORATION?
- THE REAL RULING POWER OF THE U.S. AND ALL NATIONS OF THE WORLD

DO YOU THINK your vote counts? One man, one vote. That is supposed to be the way our government is set up, right? News flash. That might have been the intent when the Constitution was written, with the separation of powers—Executive, Legislative, and Judicial—intended to prevent any one branch of government from gaining too much power. Not only did we lose control of the election process, but our entire governmental process is at risk, and we must regain control. We must return to the foundation of our nation and restore things to their original state. Only then will America once again be the land of the free and the home of the brave.

SO HOW DID WE LOSE CONTROL OF OUR GOVERNMENT?

The first thing we need to understand is that the United States began as a *republic*. It was referred to as the *"Great Experiment"* because it was the first time in history that a government served the common man instead of special interest groups.

A *republic* is defined as "a government of the people, by the people, for the people." Our republic came from the Constitution and the Declaration of Independence, which were themselves based on the Ten Commandments of God. A *republic* requires an educated population that is well-informed about the issues affecting society.

It requires a public willing to vote for what is in the best interest of society at large, rather than for vested self-interest. In other words, it was inherently against the public education system that currently indoctrinates and dumbs down our kids. It required a free and independent press, rather than what we have today, where all our news goes through the Rothschild-controlled propaganda network and is spat out the other side as fake news. They have hijacked our republic.

Let us pick up our story in 1871 with the infliction of the unconstitutional *corporation:* A corporation is a legal entity that is separate and distinct from its owners. Its sole obligation is to the financial interests of its shareholders. Let us contemplate what it means to be a *Corporation vs. a Republic.*

MIGHT THE UNITED STATES BE A *CORPORATION,* NOT A *COUNTRY,* BECAUSE OF THE 1871 ACT?

Our original Constitution reads: The Constitution *for* the United States of America. The altered version reads: The Constitution *of* the United States of America. This may not seem like a big deal. Still, it changes our entire governmental system from one dedicated to freedom to one predicated on entrenching the public's dependence on a moneyed elite.

February 21, 1871, Congress passed the Act of 1871. See Acts of the Forty-First Congress, Section 34, Session III, chapters 61 and 62. On this date, Congress passed an Act titled "An Act to Provide a Government for the District of Columbia," also known as the Act of 1871. This Act effectively created a separate form of government for the District of Columbia, with no constitutional authority to do so. It was essentially **an act of treason!**

The Act of 1871 superseded the United States Constitution
and created a new constitution:
A CORPORATE CONSTITUTION or A CHARTER

Under this *corporate charter*, we, the people, have no rights. The only obligation of the *Corporation* is to optimize the profits of its shareholders, i.e., *the financial elite,* who control the corporatocracy. The merger of the power of the banks, corporations, and big government. Consider the following quote by President Abraham Lincoln:

I see in the near future a crisis approaching that unnerves me and causes me to tremble for the safety of my country... corporations have been enthroned and an era of corruption in high places will follow, and the money power of the country will endeavor to prolong its reign by working upon the prejudices of the people until all wealth is aggregated in a few hands and the Republic is destroyed.

President Abraham Lincoln, Nov. 21, 1864, in a letter to Col. William F. Elkins

Lincoln's fears materialized just a few years later when a rogue Congress illegally imposed the corporation on the nation. As inconceivable as it seems, as of 1871, the birth certificate of every person born in the U.S. is used as collateral for the financial elites' *debt trap* that binds us in invisible chains of debt slavery. Fear not, we are about to reclaim our Republic, but that's a story for a little later.

Another important date in U.S. history is 1896, which marked the election of William McKinley as the 25th President of the United States. This event led the financial elite to realize that they had the power to circumvent the election process and install the candidates they wanted in office. The Elite could install presidents, legislators, and judges at the FEDeral, state, and local levels. Over the years, they have refined the process, but here is how it all began.

William McKinley was running for president on the Republican ticket, and William Jennings Bryan was his Democratic opponent. Ironically, this race had little to do with party affiliation. There was something much more critical driving this election. It was a question of whether the robber barons of the time, such as Rockefeller of Standard Oil, Carnegie of Carnegie Steel, and J.P. Morgan, a financier and frontman for the Rothschild banking concern, could buy a presidential election.

What was at stake was whether these three tycoons would be allowed to retain their monopolies, as McKinley wanted, or be broken up, as Bryan wanted. Our three robber barons got together and colluded to use their money, power, and influence to elect McKinley. McKinley's election was a significant tipping point in American history. At that moment, the Rothschilds knew emphatically that if they could buy an American Presidential election, they could select, groom, finance, and get elected virtually anyone they wanted and thereby control the government from the very top echelon to the very bottom. Moreover, they could buy power and influence at every level of society. They could buy influence or even control over the media, the entertainment industry, the education system, religious denominations, the military-industrial complex, the economy (including corporations and Wall Street), and, of course, politicians. Most important of all, they could maintain their grip on the banks, the ultimate source of their power. There is a formula for world dominance.

As Sun Tzu would say, they had discovered the formula for conquering entire countries and eventually the world as a whole from the safety of the shadows. By conquering nations through covert means, unconventional warfare was born.

McKinley's election was the catalyst that set things in motion that had been brewing since the beginning of the Civil War in 1861. So, let's go back to that time in history and look forward to today to see what we can learn that might help us regain control of our government. First, let's take a brief history refresher. The Civil War was about freeing the slaves. Right? No, that is fake news. The Civil War was a continuation of the ongoing battle for our freedom from British control. Britain had decided that the U.S. had to be torn in half because a United America posed a threat not only to Britain but to every Monarchy in Europe. We had to be cut down to size before we got any more powerful.

The war was about whether to stay on the British free trade slavery system or not. The agrarian South needed cheap goods from Britain, but the industrializing North wanted to break free from British oppression. The war began in 1861, and in 1862, during the conflict, Lincoln made a bold move to issue interest-free currency known as the *Greenback.* Truth be told, when Lincoln issued the *Greenback,* he unwittingly triggered the events that led to his assassination and the hanging of eight British spies.

One more leap forward in time, and this part of our story will be complete. In 1869, with the completion of the East–West Transcontinental Railroad, America had access to its vast treasure trove of natural resources, allowing it to embark on its destiny with full force. Just a few years later, in 1876, America hosted its Centennial Celebration, showcasing its technological marvels for the world to see. America, the youngest nation in the world, had become the most prosperous nation in the world, supplanting Britain, which had a 300-year head start.

I want to emphasize what I just said, because it has everything to do with how we regain control of our government. In just a few years, unfettered by British financial control, the U.S. blossomed into a superpower, and before you finish this book, you will learn how we will do it again. I am not blind. I fully realize that America is at a crucial tipping point and is on the brink of a catastrophic financial collapse. But I also see the global perspective, and from my vantage point, America will rise from the ashes like the Phoenix and be greater than ever. And it will help pull the entire world out of the impending crash. Before we can discuss how that will happen, we need a further understanding of how we lost control of our money supply and our government. Remember, history repeats itself, and it is a great teacher. So please read on.

The next stop on our journey through history takes us to 1913, which marked the apex of American power and the beginning of our slow decline. America had emerged from World War I more powerful than when it entered. But thanks to the traitorous President Woodrow Wilson, we were about to suffer a horrific economic defeat.

Like so many of our past presidents, Wilson told us what we wanted to hear. Then he did as his powerful handlers, members of the Rothschild family, instructed him to do. It had been 51 years since Lincoln gave us the greatest gift we could ever have: *our debt-free currency.* And in that time, America had become the world's undisputed #1 Superpower. We were a free, proud, prosperous, and moral nation. A nation we could truly be proud to be a part of. But all that was about to change, and we were about to enter one of the darkest times in American history.

During the 1912 election, Wilson stood before the American people and promised not to impose another central bank on the people. However, J.P. Morgan, a front man for the Rothschild banking dynasty, financed his campaign. When you take their money, you do as told. So, in 1913, Wilson imposed the current central bank, the FED, and just 16 years later, the money manipulators had orchestrated the 1929 Great Depression.

Long story short, people were allowed to buy stocks in emerging technologies, such as the radio and the automobile, with just a 10% down payment. Then, on the appointed day, they called in all the margin loans, and the market crashed instantly. Then, in 1933, in the depths of the Depression, the robber barons' dreams came true when America declared bankruptcy. As we have discussed, it became a democracy: a socialist-communist order. The real significance of that event was that a literal army of unelected bureaucrats was embedded in the government to begin quietly, subversively laying the groundwork to convert America into a legal dictatorship. Wilson later made this confession about what his betrayal had done to America. It has been said:

> *Our great industrial nation is now controlled by its system of credit. We are no longer a government by free opinion, no longer a government by conviction and the vote of the majority, but a government by the opinion and duress of a small group of dominant men…Our great industrial nation is controlled by its system of credit. Our system of credit is privately centered. The growth of the nation, therefore, and all our activities are in the hands of a few men…Who necessarily, by very reason of their own limitations, chill and check and destroy genuine economic freedom. We have become one of the worst ruled, one of the most completely controlled and dominated governments in the civilized world.*

What we are doing is going on a journey together, stopping at key tipping points in history because each of them has a lesson to teach us about how we lost control of our government, our money supply, our election process, and much more. We will summarize these events at the end of the chapter, and you will see for yourself exactly how we lost control of our election process and our government. Please stay with me, just a few more stops to make.

The following quote is not related to a specific tipping point. Still, I want to drop it in here so you can see that those in our shadow government always have a plan, and they are very patient. They will plan events years, decades, and even centuries in advance.

**Today, the path of total dictatorship in the United States can be laid by strictly legal means, unseen and unheard by the Congress, the President, or the people.
Outwardly, we have a Constitutional government.
We have operating within our government and political system,
another body representing another form of government—a bureaucratic elite.**
Senator William Jenner, 1954

Our march toward this legal dictatorship was born in 1933 when the army of unelected bureaucrats was embedded in our government following our bankruptcy, and as you will shortly see, that legal dictatorship was finally realized in 2008.

I could comment on World War II and the Vietnam War, but for the sake of time, I will jump forward to 9/11 and the War on Terror. When Bush announced the war, he said it would be a generational war. Remember, Sun Tzu said no nation ever benefited from a prolonged battle. But as a puppet of the Rothschilds, Bush was told that this was to be a protracted war. Why? Because it was a perfect way to drive the U.S. into unmanageable debt. It is as President Adams warned us:

There are two ways to conquer and enslave a nation.
One is by the sword. The other is by debt.

How lucky can you get? In the War on Terror, we got a twofer: a war and an enormous debt. We got a grand slam because the best was yet to come. You see, the war led us into the 2008 financial crash and straight into the Patriot Act, where Bush Junior was waiting to inflict us with legislation that finally laid the groundwork for the legal dictatorship, I mentioned a short while ago.

> **The interest behind the Bush administration, such as the CFR, the Trilateral-Commission, founded by Brzezinski for David Rockefeller and the Bilderberg Group have prepared for and now are moving to implement open world dictatorship.**
> Johannes B. Koeppl, Ph.D., Former German Ministry for Defense Official
> Advisor to former NATO Secretary General Manfred Wörner

What makes this quote so egregious is that it was at 3:45 a.m. on the morning the Patriot Act was to be signed. Bush pulled the version negotiated by Congress and replaced it with one written by the White House, which contained language that allowed for the implementation of a legal dictatorship. Even worse, our Puppet Congress signed it without ever reading it. Can you say, "Traitors"?

HOW WE LOST CONTROL OF OUR GOVERNMENT

The financial elite control us by merging the power of the banks, corporations, and big government to form an all-powerful corporatocracy, which gives them the money they need to literally hijack the government and put in place special interest groups to see to it that the bills they want passed are passed. It is like Rothschild said:

> **Give me control of a nation's money and I care not who makes the laws.**
> Nathan Mayer Rothschild

> **We can either have democracy in this country, or we can have great wealth concentrated in the hands of a few, but we can't have both.**
> Louis D. Brandeis, U.S. Supreme Court Justice

Let's bring the conversation back to where the chapter began. The monopolies did not dismantle. Instead, they merged their power with the banks, becoming an all-powerful corporatocracy.

INFLICTING THE FED'S FIAT CURRENCY SYSTEM

This action drives us into unmanageable debt. They take their money and control the necessities of life, so we will vote for whoever promises us the most handouts!

Until the control of the issue of currency and credit is restored to government and
recognized as its most conspicuous and sacred responsibility, all talks of the
sovereignty of Parliament and of democracy is idle and futile...
Once a nation parts with the control of its credit, it matters not who makes the laws...
Usury once in control will wreck the nation.
William Lyon Mackenzie King, former Prime Minister of Canada

INFLICTING PROLONGED WARS FOR PROFIT

To drive us into debt and force us to accept a central bank, which is 90% of converting a country to communism.

I sincerely believe... that banking establishments are more dangerous than standing
armies, and that the principle of spending money to be paid by posterity under the
name of funding is but swindling futurity on a large scale.
Thomas Jefferson to John Taylor, 1816

IMPOSING A SHADOW GOVERNMENT AS THE REAL RULING POWER

They identify individuals of interest and recruit them to represent their agenda. Whereupon they are groomed, financed, and given every assistance in obtaining the office that the financial elite is interested in controlling. You will recall that they finance both sides of wars, ensuring they will get what they want regardless of who wins the war. Similarly, they generally back one or more candidates from each party, so in reality, they stack the deck; no matter who we vote for, they win. There are notable exceptions, such as Kennedy, Reagan, and Trump. However, the reality is that they control enough of our politicians and judges to influence most major decisions made in both the political and Judicial arenas.

In other words, we effectively have a *UNI-Party*, acting not on behalf of *We the People*, but on behalf of special interest groups who want to end all sovereign nations and forcibly reduce the global population by 7.5 billion. What happens in our government is nothing but political theater. All primary outcomes are predetermined by those who put our politicians in office, and that is not the voters.

What we need to understand is that voter fraud is the Elite's weapon of last resort. In most cases, they have fed us enough false promises and lies that their candidate would win even without election tampering. Which is to say, election tampering is their insurance policy against the public seeing through their rigged elections.

BUYING POWER AND INFLUENCE AT EVERY STRATUM OF SOCIETY

That means the Media, the entertainment industry, the education system, our churches, our corporations, and all three branches of government. They control the four centers of power: intellectual, political, religious, and monetary.

TAMPERING WITH THE VOTING PROCESS

The registration rolls are intentionally inaccurate, containing deceased individuals and numerous errors. Our electronic voting machines are subject to vote tampering. Mail-in ballots with no signature verification and ballot harvesting create the opportunity to cast illegitimate votes, as they do not require photo IDs. Extending vote counting for days allows for the creation of illegal ballots if the algorithms in the voting machines are insufficient to swing the election in the desired direction. What do all these things have in common? They could all be changed in a heartbeat if our political leaders were not puppets of the Elite.

REFINING THE PROCESS OF STEALING ELECTIONS

When we think of election fraud, I think most of us think about the things that happen on election day, like rigged voting machines, dead people voting, people voting multiple times, or non-citizens voting, etc. I believe the tendency is to think things can change by altering voting laws or regulations, but that is not the case.

All these things can happen, and they can affect the outcome of an election. However, unless we delve deeper and explore how these things are possible, we will never be able to get to the root of the problem. What I am getting at is that it is not just the votes counted on Election Day that should be the focus of our attention. We must dig deeper and find out what happened behind the scenes. What happened to the fabric of our governmental system that enabled such abuse of power?

When problem-solving, we often focus on the wrong place. We see the outcome and try to solve the problem at that point, without realizing that the outcome is where things end. Therefore, focusing on the outcome can never correct the situation. We must go back to the very beginning and unravel things step by step until we reach the one thing that, if changed, would alter the outcome. That is the root cause or the least common denominator. It is only at the beginning that you can sufficiently modify the outcome to effect permanent change.

THE ONE THING THAT CONTROLS EVERYTHING
AND UPON WHICH THE FATE OF OUR NATION AND THE WORLD RESTS

So, what is that one thing that is the root cause of our corrupt voting system and virtually every problem this nation and the world faces? It is a fact that he who controls money controls the world. Therefore, they can change virtually everything.

The one question we must ask is: How do we take control of money away from the enemy? That is not a simple question to answer, but I assure you, there is an answer, and before you finish this book, you will have the answer to that all-important question. You will not only learn how to prevent stolen elections, but most importantly, you will know how to regain control of our government, our liberty, and our freedom.

The solution is not piecemeal. It is an all-or-nothing solution that must be executed militarily, so please be patient and read on. We have more foundation to lay before we can solve this most important of all questions.

CHAPTER 5

HOW BANKERS HAVE ENSLAVED
THE WORLD
And How We Strip Them of Their Power!

TOPICS COVERED IN THIS CHAPTER:

- HISTORY OF THE FED'S MONEY MANIPULATION
- HOW BANKER GANGSTERS CONTROL THE WORLD
- HOW THE 2008 FINANCIAL COLLAPSE WAS ORCHESTRATED
- THE FORMULA THAT DETERMINES THE RISE AND FALL OF NATIONS
- THE FORMULA THAT TRIGGERS BOOM/BUST ECONOMIC CYCLES
- HOW BANK FAILURES ARE ORCHESTRATED

THE BANKERS ARE OUR ENEMY

He who controls money controls the world.
Henry Kissinger, former U.S. Secretary of State and National Security Advisor

**The goal of The Financial Elite, who control central banks around the world and want
nothing less than to create a world system of financial control in private hands able to
dominate the political system of each country . . . by central banks . . .
acting in concert by secret agreements**
Carroll Quigley, member of the Trilateral Commission, mentor to Bill Clinton

HISTORY OF THE FED'S MONEY MANIPULATION:
EVERY WAR AND EVERY DEPRESSION WE HAVE HAD WAS
INFLICTED ON THE U.S. BY THE FED

HERE IS AN account of how the FED (Banker Gangsters) has hijacked the U.S. government. What they have done to the U.S., they have done to countries all around the world. They are a league of criminals who will do anything to maintain their control over the world's money supply. Reflect on this quote below by President Woodrow Wilson, who sold out to the puppet masters of the financial elite and later regretted what he had done.

**Since I entered politics, I have chiefly had men's views confided to me privately. Some
of the biggest men in the United States are in the fields of government and
manufacturing. They know there is a power somewhere, so organized, so subtle, so
watchful, so interlocked, so complete, so perverse that they better not speak above
their breath when they speak in condemnation of it.**
President Woodrow Wilson

Let's take a quick stroll through history and see just how the money manipulators have managed to hijack the U.S. economy, the government, and enslave the population in a system of slavery without chains.

Statesman Benjamin Franklin: The American Revolution was to prevent King George III of England from driving America into debt by imposing the Bank of England and charging interest to print our currency.

President George Washington: America won the Revolutionary War and its independence, but the cost of fighting the war had bankrupted the treasury. So, before Washington left office, America was forced to sign the first Central Bank Charter, imposing England's system of economic slavery on America!

President James Madison: In 1811, the central bank charter expired, and Madison refused to renew it. As a result of his refusal, America and England fought another war, known as the War of 1812, also referred to as the Second American Revolution. America retained its independence as a nation, but once again was forced to accept economic enslavement under the English central bank.

President Andrew Jackson: When President Jackson came into office, he said of the international bankers, "You are a den of vipers and thieves. I have determined to rout you out, and by the Eternal, I will rout you out. He later said: I killed the Bank, referring to the second Central Bank."

Jackson also said, "The bold effort the present bank has made to control the present governments is but premonitions of the fate that awaits the American people should they be deluded into a perpetuation of this institution, or the establishment of any other like it."

President Thomas Jefferson: Looking back on the presidency of the third president of America, he said, "The Central bank is an institution of the most deadly hostility existing against the principles and form of our Constitution…if the American people allow private banks to control the issuance of the currency, first by inflation and then by devaluation of the banks and corporations that will grow up around them will deprive the people of all their property until their children will wake up homeless on the continent their fathers conquered."

The predictions of these American Presidents are undeniable today. It is an illusion to think that any American owns a home or a piece of land. We are simply renters, and our landlord is the federal government and its enforcers, the illegal IRS. Doubt what I say? Then, try not paying your real estate tax and see what happens. They will seize your home and sell it to pay back taxes. They will make no effort to sell the house for fair market value, deduct the back taxes, and give you the balance.

For example, a person could be behind on property taxes in the amount of, say $10,000 on a $500,000 home. The government takes the home lock, stock, and barrel. How is that anything but out-and-out theft? Not always, but most of the time, the entities that buy those tax liens are insiders at banks or federally owned Fannie Mae and Freddie Mac. How can this be described as anything but theft?

President Abraham Lincoln: We've been led to believe that the Civil War was about setting the slaves free, but it wasn't. It was about the British efforts to prevent the U.S. from becoming too powerful. The agrarian South wanted to stay under the British free trade slavery system because it depended on the cheap goods. However, the industrial North sought to break free from England's central banking system. During the war, Lincoln issued the debt-free *Greenback*, severing the country's dependency on the English Central Bank. For that, they assassinated him, and eight British spies were hanged for treason.

President Woodrow Wilson: Wilson is the traitor who inflicted America with the third central bank of England (the FED). J. P. Morgan, the Rothschilds' front man in America, heavily financed Wilson's campaign. Wilson campaigned on the pledge that under his presidency, there would be no central bank. He lied.

A year after being elected, he inflicted America with the private Federal Reserve Bank (FED), which is responsible for inflicting America with our almost $39 trillion national debt, thrust on us by an illegal IRS. Our constitution prohibits taxing a person's labor, so the FEDeral income system and the IRS are illegal. They were illegally imposed on us by Wilson, the financial elite's puppet. Six Supreme Court cases upheld the decision that they are illegal, but the elite ignored the ruling. Any illusion that our legal system treats the rich and the poor the same is utter nonsense.

As we covered in the previous chapter, with the exceptions of Reagan, Kennedy, and Trump, all our presidents since McKinley in 1897 have been puppets of the financial elite. Their goal is to end all sovereign nations and impose a one-world dictatorship. Then exterminate 7.5 billion of us, and those they allow to live will be as *chattel*, personal property, or beasts of burden.

President Franklin Roosevelt warned us: "The real truth of the matter is that a financial element in the large centers has owned the government since the days of Andrew Jackson."

JUMPING FORWARD TO MORE CURRENT TIMES

President George W. Bush said, "The Constitution is just a God da## piece of paper." (November 2005, *Capitol Hill Blue*).

Secretary of State Henry Kissinger, a member of the traitorous CFR, said, "The illegal we do immediately. The unconstitutional takes a little longer."

Most of our politicians in Washington serve themselves and the special interest groups that buy their loyalty, and not We the People. What we have in Washington is, for all practical purposes, a politically controlled mafia. America is effectively a uniparty dictatorship. We must sweep Washington clean of all those who have sold out to the financial elite, which is unfortunately the vast majority of our politicians and judges!

Truer words were never spoken than those you are about to read. They've hijacked our government, and our politicians are little more than bought and paid for figureheads. Puppets of the financial elite. Further validation of the fact that the FED and not Congress runs the U.S. government is in the response made by then FED Chairman Alan Greenspan when asked on PBS's *The Lehrer Report*:

> **What is the proper relationship between the Chairman of the Federal Reserve and the President of the United States? He responded: Well, first of all, the Federal Reserve is an independent agency, and that means basically that, uh, there is no other agency of government which can overrule actions that we take. In so long as that is in place . . . what that relationship is, uh, doesn't frankly matter.**

TRANSLATION: Neither the President nor Congress can tell the FED what to do. In other words, the banker gangsters are running things. And our government is just a figurehead of the financial elite who want to exterminate us.

There is a quote that is often cited as being stated by President John F. Kennedy. What would he have been referring to when he said, "There is a plot in this country to enslave every man, woman, and child. Before I leave this high and noble office, I intend to expose that plot."

The following quote tells us what that plot is. Appearing before Congress, President John F. Kennedy referred to the Federal Reserve as, "This establishment that virtually controls the monetary system; That is subject to no one; That no Congressional Committee can oversee; and that not only issues the currency, but loans it to the Government at interest."

This belief led Kennedy to shut down the FED by replacing the dollar with silver certificates, which he had printed. You don't threaten the power of the global elite and live. So, a short while later, Kennedy was assassinated, and the records relating to his death were sealed so we would not be able to find out the truth about who killed him. But of this much I am certain, it wasn't the patsy, Lee Harvey Oswald.

THE BANKER GANGSTERS AND NOT CONGRESS RUN THE NATION
AND WE NEED TO UNDERSTAND EXACTLY HOW THEY CONTROL US

PROPERTY TAKE RIGHTS

We discussed that with their underlying ability to take property rights, they have taken away our property rights and made every one of us nothing but renters, with them as our landlords. This imposes on us the same system of slavery we fled from in Europe under Feudalism, where the kings considered us as chattel.

ILLEGAL PROGRESSIVE INCOME TAX

We also discussed how they have inflicted upon us an *illegal progressive income tax* that indentures us to their system of slavery without chains. It just so happens that this tax system is one tenet of communism.

WARS FOR PROFIT

We also discussed the fact that they inflict wars on us for profit, which are intentionally dragged out for years as yet another means to drive us into unmanageable debt.

USURY AND PROGRESSIVE CREDIT CARD INTEREST

At one time, all but six states had usury laws to protect consumers. However, the banker gangsters circumvented this encumbrance by incorporating in those six states, which enabled them to establish a presence in all 50 states. Not only can these crooks charge excessively high rates, but thanks to the assistance of our bought-and-paid-for politicians, they can also charge interest on the unpaid balance month after month, year after year. For example, this means that if you had a straightforward, honest 10% loan on, say, $10,000, the loan would be considered paid in full when you had paid back the original loan amount plus 10%, which calculates to $1,000.

However, credit card companies are permitted to charge exorbitant rates of 18% or more, not on the loan amount, but on the unpaid balance. So, if a person paid only the minimum payment, it could take years to pay off the debt, and every month, they would be charged 18% or more on the unpaid balance, which could come to many thousands. To make matters even worse, the credit card companies target those least able to pay, i.e., single moms, students, seniors, and low-income individuals, because they know they will fall victim to their debt trap.

HOME MORTGAGES

Here again, you are charged interest on the unpaid balance. Still, there are notable differences from what the credit card industry does to enslave you. The mortgage companies front-load the interest payments, so it takes 26 years to reach the 50% mark on a 30-year loan. That way, they will get the most out of you. Just imagine that half of your principal has been paid off in the last four years of a 30-year loan. What a scam.

But wait, that isn't the end of it—it isn't even the *worst* of it. They want you on the hook for your entire life, so if you move or refinance, your amortization table starts over at month one. Given that the average American moves seven times or more in their lifetime, many Americans retire and are still responsible for mortgage payments. I don't know about you, but I blame our bought and paid-for politicians who pass the laws that allow the banks to bleed us to death. It doesn't have to be that way.

There is absolutely no reason, other than greed, that requires your amortization table to start over if you buy a new home or refinance your existing one. Here is how it could and should work. Say you buy a new home, and it costs $10,000 more than your current mortgage. The bank could offer you a second mortgage for $10,000 with an amortization table starting from month one. Your original mortgage would remain in place at your current interest rate and in the same position on the amortization table. But that would give people a chance to get out from under the thumb of the banker gangsters, and they can't allow that, can they?

Virtually everything I have just described is unethical, and need I say, it is downright criminal. And when it comes to blame, both the banks and our politicians share equally. One final comment: When you buy a house, regardless of the contract price, the actual cost at the end of a 30-year mortgage will be two and one-half times or more the contract price. Again, which is criminal!

THE WORST IS YET TO COME

Our politicians collude with bankers to ensure that even the most frugal and responsible among us are not immune to their white-collar crimes. So, what they do is devise boom and bust cycles to ensure you are never financially secure, because at any time they can pull the rug out from under you and steal your hard-earned savings or your home.

The first such calculated theft occurred just a few years after our politicians inflicted us with the FED in 1913. By 1929, they had concocted a scheme to rape and pillage the masses financially. The Great Depression was the event, and it was no accident. Congressman McFadden said of the crash and subsequent depression:

> **It was a carefully contrived occurrence. International bankers sought to bring about a condition of despair so that they might emerge as the rulers of us all.**
> Congressman Louis T. McFadden, PA

Let's walk you through the details of both the 1929 Great Depression and the 2008 financial collapse to prepare you for what is to come. It will be the most significant financial crash in history.

THE 1929 GREAT DEPRESSION

The world was experiencing the industrial revolution, and people were anxious to invest in the stock market to capitalize on the profits to be made from emerging technologies like the radio and the automobile. The banker gangsters took full advantage of the situation. They allowed people to buy stocks on margin with just 10% down, and then, on the appointed day, the banker gangsters called in all the margin loans. On cue, the stock market had a colossal collapse. At that time, there were no 401(k)s, so the number of people heavily invested in the stock market was relatively small. Given this fact, one would expect that the crash would be relatively minor and limited to the U.S.. However, the financial elite had plans in place to maximize the damage and bring the people of the world into submission.

Remember, I have said several times that to understand geopolitical events, you need the perspective of history because these kinds of events are planned and plotted over years and decades. To truly understand what was in the making, we first must go back to 1914 and the beginning of World War I. During the war, the U.S. loaned money to the allies, notably Britain and France. After the war, the United States loaned money to Germany to pay war reparations to Britain and France. Here is how this played into the crime that was the Great Depression.

In 1918, when the war ended, Europe was decimated, and countries were rebuilding, so they needed money. America had emerged from the war richer than ever, so we were effectively the source of funds to rebuild Europe. But that wasn't the end of the story. On cue, the U.S. stock market crashed, and right on cue, the banks dried up all credit. Now, Germany couldn't pay war reparations to Britain and France. They, in turn, couldn't pay their war loans to the U.S. So, what initially appeared to be a minor collapse was calculated to be the most significant financial collapse in history.

However, there was still more to this story, and to truly appreciate the grandeur of their criminal endeavor, we must go all the way back to 1775 and the start of the American Revolutionary War. Britain wanted to keep America as an indentured colony under the oppression of its central bank. America was a threat to Britain, and from its inception, it had plotted ways to take it over once and for all. No sooner had we won our independence than we declared bankruptcy and had to submit to the Bank of England.

Then, in 1933, amid the Great Depression that was orchestrated immediately following the Fed's takeover, America declared bankruptcy again. The receivers of the bankruptcy, the British Central Bank, established a new government for America (refer to page 33 for the official declaration).

The ultimate agenda of the 1929 Great Depression was to create a global depression and force the U.S. into bankruptcy. Then they could embed an army of unelected bureaucrats into the U.S. government to covertly collapse America a little at a time, no matter how long it takes. The 1929 Great Depression effectively placed the U.S. under a socialist-communist government. It embedded an army of bureaucrats in the government to pass laws to create a legal dictatorship.

Moving on to the financial collapse of 2008, it didn't just happen either. It was planned years in advance and meant to be part of a cascade of events orchestrated to allow the rise of China and the decline of America. That cascade of events included: 9/11, the Iraq war that Bush said would be a generational war, the 2008 financial collapse, and culminating with the release of COVID-19. All designed to trigger the Great Reset, which would ultimately usher in the New World Order Dictatorship under a Hillary Clinton Presidency. But thank goodness God had other plans.

HOW DID THE FINANCIAL ELITE ORCHESTRATE THE 2008 FINANCIAL COLLAPSE?

Step 1: Utilize President Carter to initiate trade with China and then stall the U.S. economy. Use President Clinton to impose the intentionally losing trade deal, NAFTA, to orchestrate the further decline of America and the rise of China by creating events that led to a massive U.S. trade deficit, with manufacturing fleeing the U.S. and relocating to China. Effectively, the first engine of the economy—trade—was destroyed.

Step 2: Use President George W. Bush to devastate the second engine of the economy by orchestrating the events of 9/11, intended to crash the U.S. stock market.

Step 3: Also use Bush to harm the one remaining cylinder of the economy: real estate. 9/11 marked the beginning of the assault on the real estate market. Every crash starts with a carrot and ends with a thud. And they always play on our greed. In the instance of the 2008 financial collapse, here is how they orchestrated it. Because of "Senator" Obama, you could get a home for the first time with no money down, no income check, and 1-2% interest. With the trap set, all they needed now was a trigger for the market to collapse.

No problem! They figured it out well in advance. Conventional 20% down mortgages are almost always fixed-rate mortgages. But that was not the case with the zero-down subprime mortgages. They were variable-rate mortgages, which had trigger dates at which the interest rates would increase. All the banker gangsters had to do was flood the market with variable-rate mortgages and then sit back and wait for the defaults to crash the market.

All the while claiming not to understand how such a catastrophe could have ever happened. If you have forgotten about the role of Bush, Clinton, and Obama, go back to Chapter 1. It will remind you that they were all in on this crime of the century from the very start. They are all three criminals.

Step 4: Create collateralized debt obligations by combining 20% down conventional mortgages with 0% down subprime mortgages and selling them to unsuspecting investors worldwide.

Step 5: Solicit the aid of rating companies to give these caustic investments AAA ratings and wait for the suckers to get sucked in. Then just wait for all those ticking time bomb variable-rate mortgages to trigger their rate hikes, which in turn trigger an avalanche of defaults and an instant financial collapse. However, as with 1929, our story is not yet over.

Step 6: The execution of the endgame was to lay the groundwork for the imposition of a legal dictatorship. As discussed in Chapter 1, this honor fell to George W. Bush. He ensured that the Patriot Act stipulated that, in the event of a state of emergency declared by the then-president, the government could assume control of all essential services and confiscate the assets of those deemed unnecessary.

Then comes the implementation of the long-dreamed-of New World Order Dictatorship. History often repeats itself, so it should come as no surprise that there are parallels in history. Hitler orchestrated the burning of the German Parliament building, the Reichstag. He blamed it on the communists and used it as an excuse to declare a national emergency that allowed him to become Führer, Supreme Leader-Dictator. Our story doesn't end here. There is one more step to the Elite's endgame agenda, but that is a story for a little later. HINT: *It has to do with COVID-19.*

You may be thinking, "Now I understand what they have done to us, and I am empowered to stand up and join the ranks of those who are endeavoring to take power from the financial elite and restore America." You are getting close, but you still have a way to go before you know the entire story of our enslavement.

For example, in the context of this chapter, we now know who the enemy is. We are aware of his ultimate agenda. And we have a practical understanding of how he has executed the events up to this point. But we lack the all-important knowledge that enables these events to occur. There are simple repeatable formulas for how the Elite orchestrate the rise and Fall of Nations and the triggering of boom-and-bust cycles. We touched on the rise and fall of nations earlier, but it is worth repeating here as we conclude this chapter.

THE FORMULA THAT DETERMINES THE RISE AND FALL OF NATIONS

It is remarkable that something as straightforward as a five-step formula can help predict the rise and fall of nations. But failure to control even one of these crucial ingredients will prevent a nation from being a global superpower. The basis of all wealth goes like this:

- Natural resources that convert into,
- Manufactured goods, which are
- The basis of international trade, which,
- In turn, is converted into money,
- Which is used to buy power and influence at all strata of society.

The source of the financial elite's power is money, used to buy influence and power. So, if we are to defeat the financial elite, we must deny them control of the money supply. That means that no one nation or group can be allowed to control natural resources, manufacturing, or trade, which is the genesis of all wealth. Meaning, in turn, that the world must reverse the process of Globalization and move toward a Deglobalization World Model. That will be discussed in an upcoming chapter. While it might seem impossible, you might be shocked to learn the reversal is underway.

THE FORMULA THAT TRIGGERS BOOM AND BUST ECONOMIC CYCLES

On the surface, the events that drove the 1929 crash and the 2008 crash, or any crash in history, are all driven by the same simple formula. Understanding what that formula is and how it is executed will enable you to protect your assets. However, the real goal is to deny the financial elite the ability to control money and, therefore, to deny them the ability to manipulate the global economy. The formula for creating a boom-and-bust cycle is as simple as the one for determining which country(ies) become global superpowers. Here it is:

1. It begins by focusing people on a specific investment, e.g., in 1929, it was stocks, in the 1990s, it was the dot-com bubble, and in 2008, it was real estate. The idea is to funnel as much money as possible into one place.
2. Expand the money supply to ensure a sufficient amount of money is available for borrowing.
3. Then you lower the interest rate, making it cheaper to borrow, which encourages people to invest.
4. You create a buying frenzy by driving the prices up and allowing people to make a return on their investment.
5. Then, at the appointed time, you pull the plug, causing a market crash.

6. Then the last step in the theft is to dry up credit, so people are trapped in their overextended stock positions, their now upside-down mortgages, and so on.

7. After all of this, the vultures sit back and wait for the panic to set in. Then they buy back for pennies the very assets they sold at a profit as markets rose. The Financial elite make money at both ends of their Ponzi scheme.

This process works every time. At least until the people figure out how they are being taken to the cleaners, and then wise up. But better yet, let's deny the crooks the ability to run their shell game. Let's fix it so they don't have the power to manipulate the markets, thereby denying them the ability to run their scams. But how do we do that?

The formula that determines the rise and fall of nations and the formula that determines how to create a boom-and-bust cycle are intricately interconnected. You can't have one without the other because the common denominator between the two is control of the international money supply. So, it all goes back to one simple thing. The enemy's greatest strength is his weakness. The root source of the enemy's power is his control of the money supply. Conversely, deny him that control and you deny him all control. He is rendered powerless. That is literally what we are going to do, but how we are going to do that will have to wait until we have all the facts and know all the players.

HOW BANK FAILURES ARE ORCHESTRATED

Do you mean to tell me that the banker gangsters orchestrate the failure of their banks? Yep. In their minds, they have nothing to lose and everything to gain. After all, they fully expect that when push comes to shove, their buddies in Washington will bail them out, leaving the public stuck with the mess. And after all, they have a license to print as much money as they want. All they have to do is turn on their printing presses. At least that is how it works for the FED banks, and as for those smaller banks that go under, they get absorbed into the spider web we call the Central Banking System, and the spider just gets bigger.

At least, that is how it has worked in the past. But surprise: that is not how it is going to work this time! This time, the collapse is going to take down the entire banking system and put an end to the counterfeit printing racket. The world is implementing a new banking system backed by the value of God's natural resources. As to exactly how that will occur is the topic of another chapter. But first, we must understand how they orchestrated the soon-to-occur mother of all bank runs and all those that preceded it. Let's call this the 2024 bank collapse because I think it is already underway and will likely culminate in 2026.

The collapse started with Silicon Valley Bank (SVB). They tried to tell us that what happened at SVB was an isolated event, but we soon discovered that was not the case. The entire banking system is teetering on the brink of a catastrophic collapse. Let's unravel their web of lies and learn the disturbing truth. Here we go!

HOW THE FED IS INTENTIONALLY CREATING THE MOTHER OF ALL FINANCIAL COLLAPSES:
THE SOON-TO-COME COLLAPSE

- Banks invested in long term, low-yield treasury notes and mortgage securities because the FED had led them to believe interest rates were going to stay low. The FED knew better.
- The FED knew that the money printing it initiated during the COVID-19 pandemic (aka the plan-demic) would cause inflation and serve as a justification for rate hikes.
- The FED knew when inflation hit, which was guaranteed, banks would have to sell their low-yield, long-term investments at a loss.
- The FED knew that when (not if) the banks were forced to sell those investments before they reached maturity, they would be sold at a loss, causing an insolvency crisis.
- The FED knew that with banks locked into a portfolio of low-yield investments, when interest rates went up, as they knew they would, depositors would withdraw their money and put it somewhere they could earn higher interest rates.
- The FED knew that these sudden withdrawals would cause a liquidity crisis and trigger bank failures.
- Remember that in every planned financial collapse, when the FED (and the banker gangsters) are ready to collapse the economy, they first raise interest rates and second, they freeze credit. Instant financial collapse. It works every time.

Don't be fooled. The people at the FED are not stupid. They knew in advance that all the things I just laid out would happen, guaranteed. Claiming to be caught off guard doesn't pass the smell test. In plain and simple language, the FED orchestrated all these events with full knowledge of the outcome. They had planned what was to come.

HOW THE FED ORCHESTRATED THE CURRENT GLOBAL FINANCIAL CRISIS

- COVID-19 (the plan-demic) was the excuse to drive the world into unmanageable debt. During the COVID-19 pandemic, more U.S. dollars were printed than in the entire history of the U.S. This insane money printing wasn't limited to the U.S. It was a worldwide phenomenon.
- The FED knew that the world was in such a debt crisis that the only way nations could manage that debt burden was at zero % interest rates. They knew that when they raised interest rates on the pretext of curbing inflation, it would cause a global financial crisis.
- The FED knew that, since the U.S. is the world's reserve currency, rate hikes in the U.S. would hurt nations worldwide. The reason is that foreign nations must buy U.S. dollars to purchase oil and other internationally traded commodities. News flash: that is about to change. More on this later. But for now, a rate hike in the U.S. affects all nations. Countries around the world got a double whammy. They were suffering from domestic inflation, and they also had to buy U.S. dollars at a higher exchange rate. They had accumulated so much national debt that it led to a liquidity crisis in many countries. For example, Britain and Japan had such a severe liquidity crisis that they had to sell massive amounts of Treasury Bonds at a loss.
- The FED used COVID-19 as an excuse to ensure that when the planned withdrawals occurred, the banks would be insolvent. Under the fractional reserve banking system, banks are allowed to lend 90% of their deposits, holding only 10% in reserve to cover withdrawals. However, the FED, a puppet of the financial elite, used COVID-19 as an excuse to remove the 10% reserve requirement, leaving banks extremely vulnerable to the inevitable withdrawals they knew were coming. As of the writing of this book, that policy has not been rescinded.

HOW THE FED HAS INSURED THAT THIS COLLAPSE WILL BE BIBLICAL IN MAGNITUDE

The intent is to create such a devastating financial collapse that we will have no choice except to surrender to the financial elite and accept their one-world dictatorship. But don't panic. God will not let that happen. Soon, I will explain why I am certain our enemies' plans will backfire on them, leaving them destitute and ushering in God's financial system, along with a period of peace and prosperity.

God never does anything without giving us a foreshadowing of things to come. You will be pleasantly surprised to discover that there is precedent in U.S. history for the economic system God has in store for mankind. Captives will be set free from the bondage of the current financial system, which has been inflicted on us by the financial elite. But it is not the time for that story, but soon.

- The Dodd-Frank Act, passed in 2010 after the 2008 financial collapse, promised that in the event of another financial crisis, the banks would not be bailed out, leaving the American people holding the bag for the mismanagement of the corrupt banker gangsters. But that has already proven to be just another lie. When Silicon Valley Bank (SVB) got in trouble, Biden bailed it out!
- Provisions have been made to allow banks to do "bail-ins." What that means is that in the event of a banking crisis, banks may take depositors' assets. This was done in Greece several years ago. Here is how it is supposed to work. Supposedly, your deposits will be covered by the FDIC up to $250,000 per account coverage limit. The bank can take any amount you have in a bank account above that amount and use it to cover losses. How this legal theft is accomplished is that when you deposit your money in the bank, it is no longer yours. It becomes the property of the bank.
- The FDIC is insufficiently funded. That is why I said that you are supposedly protected up to $250,000. They have approximately 1% of the assets they insure in reserve to cover bank failures. That is why in 2008, we, the taxpayers, were inflicted with the Stimulus Bill under threat of martial law if it was not passed. It covered the FDIC's insolvency to the tune of $700 billion of taxpayers' money.

> **As a reminder, when the financial industry imploded in 2008, Congress had to pass a special law to fund a $700 billion bailout...The Federal Deposit Insurance Corp. had nowhere near enough resources to fund its resolution.**
> Thomas Hoenig, Los Angeles Times, December 18, 2014

I leave you to ponder this: The most powerful clique in these (CFR) groups has one objective in common: they want to bring about the surrender of the sovereignty and the national independence of the U.S. They want to end national boundaries and racial and ethnic loyalties, supposedly to increase business and ensure world peace. What they strive for would inevitably lead to dictatorship and loss of freedoms by the people. The CFR was founded for the purpose of promoting disarmament and submergence of U.S. sovereignty and national independence into an all-powerful one-world government. (*Harper's Magazine*, July, 1958)

In essence, *Harper's* is saying that the CFR is our enemy. Therefore, anyone who belongs to the CFR is, by association, our enemy. Given that most of the power brokers in Washington belong to the CFR, they are our enemy. Therefore, most politicians in Washington should be removed from their positions. The quote also implies that the surrender of our sovereignty would result in a dictatorship, and given that the UN is the entity behind ending national sovereignty, they are also our enemy.

The UN, along with its various global governance organizations, must go. That means the World Bank, the IMF, the global network of central banks, the World Trade Organization, the World Health Organization, and all UN-controlled entities must go. Remove the money, and all these entities lose their power to control us. This quote tells us one last thing. The endgame agenda of the financial elite is Globalization, i.e., a one-world Dictatorship.

As you will soon learn, the world is already moving toward deglobalization. As this occurs, no single nation or entity will be able to control the levers of power that enable global dominance. A new era of peace and prosperity is on the horizon. Before you finish this book, you will know how that miracle is going to be bestowed on mankind.

However, for that to happen, the financial elite must be stripped of their most powerful weapon: control of the global monetary system. We will never be free until we break free from the central banking system's fiat currency system and adopt a currency based on natural resources, the foundation of all wealth. God's wealth transfer is coming sooner than you think!

CHAPTER 6

HOW AND WHY WARS ARE IMPOSED ON US
And How We Put an End to Them!

TOPICS COVERED IN THIS CHAPTER:

- WHAT WAR MEANS TO THE ELITE
- MEASURES USED TO IMPOSE A LEGAL DICTATORSHIP
- HOW AND WHY THE ELITE HAVE ORCHESTRATED THE RISE OF CHINA AND DECLINE OF THE U.S.
- THE TRUTH ABOUT 9/11
- THE ELITE HAVE GONE TOO FAR; IT WILL CAUSE THEIR DOWNFALL

THIS CHAPTER ISN'T easy for me to write. On the one hand, the truth that will be exposed has the potential to save lives when the next war for profit is imposed on us. But on the other hand, I am not sure how those whose lives were forever changed by the trauma of war will feel when they come to realize that they were lied to about the wars they fought in. I pray the truth will save lives in the future, and that knowing the truth may, in some way, be healing. My heart goes out to all those whose lives have been impacted by war, and I hope that the truth I am about to tell will save lives, future anguish, and torment. God bless you all.

It is my sincere hope that the next time we turn on our TV or go on Twitter and hear about some horrific attack, we will not fall victim to the lies of the talking heads paid to stir up patriotic fervor.

WAR IS NOTHING BUT BUSINESS TO THE ELITE

Remember: The endgame agenda of the financial elite is to end all sovereign nations and kill billions of us. The lives of our loved ones mean nothing to them. Say "no" to war! To those who would be our enslavers, war is just a business, and it serves their agenda in many ways, including those listed below:

1. They loan money to both sides of the conflict.
2. Their military-industrial complex makes billions, trillions off arms contracts.
3. Nations must rebuild after every war. That's how the financial elite makes trillions by doing just that.
4. The endgame agenda of the financial elite is to reduce the global population to 1 billion or less. War kills tens of millions.
5. Their goal is to create so much social instability and despair that we lose hope, become passive, and submit. The strategy is: *Order out of Chaos.*
6. They want drug addiction, homelessness, overwhelming debt, and despair because it allows them to step in and offer to fix the very problems that they have ruthlessly orchestrated to birth their one-world dictatorship. War is an integral part of their strategy of genocide and enslavement.

WORDS OF WISDOM FROM THE PAST

While testifying at the Nuremberg War Trials, Hermann Göring, Hitler's right-hand man, told us exactly how you get peace-seeking people to go to war:

> Naturally, the common people don't want war: Neither in Russia, nor in England, nor for that matter in Germany. That is understood. But, after all, it is the leaders of the country who determine the policy, and it is always a simple matter to drag the people along, whether it is a democracy, or a fascist dictatorship, or a parliament, or a communist dictatorship. Voice or no voice, the people can always be brought to the bidding of the leaders. That is easy. All you have to do is tell them they are being attacked, and denounce the peacemakers for lack of patriotism and exposing the country to danger. It works the same in any country.

Then we have these words of wisdom from Julius Caesar:

> Beware of the leader who bangs the drums of war to whip the citizenry into patriotic fervor, for patriotism is indeed a double-edged sword. It both emboldens the blood, just as it narrows the mind. And when the drums of war have reached a fever pitch and the blood boils with hate and the mind has closed, the leader will have no need in seizing the rights of the citizenry, (who) infused with fear and blinded by patriotism, will offer up all of their rights unto the leader and gladly so. How well I know?
> For this I have done. And I am Julius Caesar.

The notion that ruthless men would inflict wars on nations solely to gain power dates back centuries. It is time we woke up and stopped letting them manipulate and enslave us. The Rothschilds are credited with funding the Nazis in World War II, being commissioned by the Royal Family to put down the American Revolution, financing the Communist Revolution in Russia, destroying Palestine to create Israel, and being behind 9/11 and the resulting wars. It is time for man's kingdoms to fall, ushering in an era of peace and prosperity. The truth will set us free. Stand up and say "No" to war.

The balance of this chapter is dedicated to exposing the false flag events and the resulting wars America has endured. Before we dive into this subject, we need to define exactly what a false flag event is and why it is staged. It is believed that David Cole, a professor of Law at Georgetown University, defines a false flag event as "A horrific staged event blamed on a political enemy and used as a pretext to start a war or enact draconian laws in the name of national security."

This statement suggests that anyone who criticizes the act is unpatriotic and a traitor. And speaking of draconian laws, reflect on this quote about the events surrounding 9/11 and the Drums of War, also attributed to Professor Cole. "The real purpose of the name ("Patriot Act") was to suggest that anyone who criticizes the Act is unpatriotic, is a traitor."

Let's take a stroll down memory lane and see what they forced on us because of 9/11. They passed laws that laid the groundwork for the imposition of a legal dictatorship. Globalist traitor George Bush used 9/11 to lay the foundation for the imposition of a legal dictatorship at the opportune time. A bipartisan version of the Patriot Act was negotiated and ready for signature. But at 3:45 AM, Bush had it pulled and replaced by a version written by the White House staff. Our bought-and-paid-for puppet Congressmen and Senators signed it without ever reading it.

You see, these bills are written by an army of bureaucrats representing the financial elite. The role of our politicians is to put on a show, pretending to negotiate bills they had no part in drafting. Washington is just a political theater staged for our benefit. Congress is irrelevant. The actual power is thrust on us from the shadows. As they say, you cannot ever fail to take advantage of a crisis.

I refer once again to the warning by Senator Barry Goldwater in the 1960s: "…both houses of Congress are irrelevant. America's domestic policy is now being run by… (the Chairman of the Federal Reserve) and the Federal Reserve. America's foreign policy is now being run by the International Monetary Fund."

TRANSLATION: The banker gangsters rule the U.S. and the world,
and they want a one-world dictatorship, whether by consent or conquest,
no matter how many lives it costs and how much carnage it causes.

Read their plans and then tell me our enemies aren't ruling America to steal our rights and make us slaves. The time is now. We must stand united and take back our nation. As I have said before, they are few; we are many. As the global financial system implodes, they will lose control of the printing of our currency, and their power over all the spheres of influence will evaporate as though it never existed. They will have no money with which to buy power and influence. In the closing chapters of this book, we will discuss in detail exactly what we need to do to regain our freedom and maintain it.

However, it is not the time for that conversation now. But for now, here is what the financial elite hope to do. But rest assured, their plans will fail, and soon you will have the details as to why they will fail.

MEASURES IMPLEMENTED TO IMPOSE A LEGAL DICTATORSHIP

Executive Order 51 grants the President authority to declare an undefined national emergency and impose martial law without the approval of Congress. Grants the president the power to assume all "National Essential Functions" for continuity of government, including directing all Federal, state, local, and tribal governments, as well as private sector organizations.

FEMA, under a National Emergency, is given the authority to develop plans to establish control over the mechanisms of production, distribution, of energy sources, wages, salaries, credit, and the flow of money in U.S. financial institutions. Including the power to seize all financial instruments, currency, gold, silver, and any other assets if they deem an emergency exists.

TRANSLATION: They create an emergency as an excuse to enslave us.

Executive Order 11921 states that when the President declares a state of emergency, *Congress cannot review the action for six months.* If this isn't the definition of a dictatorship, I don't know what would be. Wake up, stand up, and be counted. I have one more truth bomb to drop on you before we move on. If one looks at the tenets of communism, one will realize that our corrupt shadow government has created and integrated three-letter agencies into our legal system. America has been co-opted and is, in fact, a communist dictatorship operating from the shadows.

THE TENETS OF COMMUNISM

- Imposition of a central banking system, i.e., the FED
- Government-controlled education system, i.e., the public schools, Project Head Start, and the LGBTQ Agenda)
- Government Control of Labor, i.e., the DOL
- Government Control of Transportation, i.e., the DOT

- Government Control of Communication, i.e., the FCC
- Government Control of Agriculture Production and Food Processing, i.e., the USDA
- Confiscation of private property, i.e., take rights

There you have it. America is a de facto communist dictatorship operating in the shadows—one last thing.

BUSH SIGNS THE MILITARY COMMISSIONS ACT AND SUSPENDS HABEAS CORPUS

U.S. citizens can be declared enemy combatants and secretly arrested, without
charges, a lawyer, or a trial, stripped of citizenship, flown to offshore prison camps,
indefinitely detained, and even tortured.
By Jerry Markon, Washington Post, Saturday, September 10, 2006, page A10

Isn't this what the people who were at the White House on January 6, 2020, went through?

Section 802 of the Patriot Act classifies any criminal act, even a misdemeanor, as a terrorist act. Just think about January 6 and the poor people who have been locked up all this time with no rights. Isn't this what legal dictatorship looks like?

In the long history of the world, only a few generations have been granted the role of
defending freedom in its hour of maximum danger.
I do not shrink from this responsibility; I welcome it.
President John F. Kennedy, Inaugural Address, 1/20/1961

Please join the fight to restore our freedom. Those of us who stand for freedom are not terrorists or traitors. We are Patriots.

The Constitution is not an instrument to restrain the people; it is an instrument for the
people to restrain the government, lest it come to dominate our lives and interests.
Patrick Henry, Founding Father, Governor of Virginia

The Declaration of Independence guarantees our unalienable rights of life, liberty, and the pursuit of happiness…(and) when any form of government becomes destructive to these ends, it is the right of the people to alter or to abolish it, and to institute new government, laying its foundation on such principles and organizing its power in such form, as to them shall seem most likely to affect their safety and happiness.

It is time to learn the truth about America's long history of war and how our would-be masters have used war as a tool of control and oppression.

THE REAL CAUSE OF THE AMERICAN REVOLUTIONARY WAR

According to Benjamin Franklin, the real reason for the Revolutionary War was that in 1773, King George III outlawed the *interest-free* currency of the American Colonies. He coerced them into getting a loan with interest from the Central Bank of England, instantly plunging the colonies into financial straits and making them indentured slaves of King George III.

America won the Revolutionary War and became the United States of America. But fighting the war bankrupted the nation, so before Washington was out of office, we were forced to accept the first central bank, and thus began our financial slavery.

THE REAL CAUSE OF THE SECOND AMERICAN REVOLUTIONARY WAR

The first Central Bank Charter had expired, and President Madison refused to renew it. England responded that unless we signed the charter, they would take us back to a colonial status, and the result was the War of 1812. Otherwise known as the second American Revolution. In the end, America retained its independence but was forced to renew the Central Bank Charter, making America once again the indentured slave of England.

THE REAL CAUSE OF THE CIVIL WAR

Abraham Lincoln had no intention of banning slavery. British free trade was the culprit. The industrialized North favored the high tariffs of the American Economic System, while the agrarian South sought the low tariffs of the British free trade system.

During the Civil War, Lincoln printed debt-free currency called the *Greenback*. Upon its distribution, he said, "We gave the people of this Republic the greatest blessing they ever had, their own paper money to pay their own debts."

By printing the *Greenback*, Lincoln threatened Britain's global control of its free trade slavery system and central banking system. For that, he had to die. Because of his assassination, eight British spies were hanged.

THE REAL CAUSE OF WORLD WAR I

England conspired to cause WWI by assassinating the heir to the Austrian throne, Archduke Ferdinand. As to the motivation for the assassination, the Industrial Revolution and the transcontinental railroad threatened England's control of trade by sea. England was committed to destroying all of Europe to destroy its industrial rival, Germany.

They were also committed to protecting their control of trade by sea by ending the threat posed by a transcontinental railroad that would connect Europe, North America, South America, and Africa. To that end, they sacrificed 17 million people.

THE FALSE FLAG EVENT THAT TOOK AMERICA INTO WORLD WAR I

America baited Germany into sinking the passenger ship, the Lusitania. German spies claimed the Lusitania was carrying munitions, and if it entered the war zone, they would sink. They went so far as to print a warning in New York papers, but the warning was ignored. As it turns out, they found wreckage of the Lusitania, and it was indeed carrying munitions and was therefore a legitimate military target. One thousand one hundred ninety-eight innocent people sacrificed as an excuse for America to enter the war.

As to America's motivation for such an act, the Military Industrial Complex and the American Government had substantial monetary motivation. They knew the war would be in Europe, not on U.S. soil. America could supply munitions and loan money to the allies. After the war, the interest paid to the U.S. could rebuild war-torn Europe. All it cost was eight million lives and twenty-one million wounded. War is business, and the financial elite are pure evil.

It sounds wild to think that England would inflict war on Europe, given that they knew they would be a part of the war. But it is not as wild as you might think. England had it all worked out to the last detail. They were more than willing to see Europe decimated because they knew the battle would be on the mainland, and given that England is an island, it would withstand any attempts to destroy it. They also knew that Europe would be economically decimated, but not them. After all, their wealth came from their colonies, which were in the far corners of the world.

British soldiers would indeed lose their lives, but after all, the Elite consider the mass of humanity as useless idiots and cannon fodder. Their lives were of no significant loss. The sad truth is that seventeen million people died so that England could keep control of trade by sea. A people who would orchestrate the deaths of seventeen million people would not hesitate to kill billions more. To them, we are only decimal points.

Now, the financial elites are faced with an even larger threat to their dreams of world domination than they faced in World War I. They view the world's natural resources as belonging to them, and we are consuming too many of their precious natural resources. So, they must exterminate us like the cockroaches that we are. They have decided that, with the present level of technology, it is a good idea to commit mass genocide in the name of achieving what they consider "resource sustainability." Wake up and stand up before it is too late!

THE FALSE FLAG EVENT THAT TOOK AMERICA INTO WORLD WAR II

The Seventh Fleet at Pearl Harbor was the bait to get Japan to attack America, so we had an excuse to enter World War II.

> **The question was how we should maneuver them (Japan) into firing the first shot... it was desirable to make sure the Japanese be the ones to do this so that there should remain no doubt as to who were the aggressors.**
> Henry Stimson, U.S. Secretary of War, prior to World War II, Nov. 25, 1941
> [Emphasis added]

Japan didn't decide to attack the U.S. out of the blue. No. They were baited into attacking. Roosevelt had an 8-step plan to get Japan to attack. The plan included what were called "*pop-up incursions*" into Japanese waters, in the hope of provoking an incident. An embargo was placed on oil and steel shipments to Japan. All that remained was to give Japan a tempting enough target. The 7th Fleet, which harbored in Hawaii, would do the trick. Roosevelt had to go through three Admirals before he found one willing to do such a stupid and reckless thing as harbor our ships within striking range of a potential enemy in time of war.

Before the Pearl Harbor attack, we had cracked the Japanese code, allowing us to monitor their transmissions. IBM developed a decoding machine and shipped it to all areas near the war zone. But an interesting coincidence occurred. The one designated for Pearl Harbor got lost and never arrived. Wait a minute!

Roosevelt himself said, "In politics, there is no such thing as a coincidence. If it happened, it was planned that way." That means *they planned* for the U.S. to enter World War II. All we needed was to bait Japan into attacking us. As to why the U.S. would enter World War II, there was a financial incentive similar to what motivated Britain to start World War I. The U.S. knew the war would be in Europe and that it would destroy Europe, leaving the U.S. as the manufacturing superpower of the world. All it cost was the lives of 1,500 servicemen as the excuse to enter the war, with an additional 70 to 85 million lives because of the war. No big deal. Right?

WHAT AMERICA STOOD TO GAIN FROM ENTERING WORLD WAR II

Remember, the key to being the world's undisputed superpower rested on the:

1. Control of Natural Resources: The U.S. controlled mineral rights worldwide.
2. Control of Manufacturing: With Europe decimated and China still a third-world country, the U.S. would emerge from World War II as the world's undisputed manufacturing superpower.
3. Control of Trade: The U.S. had virtually no competition. The rest of the world would be in shambles.

CONTROL OF THE GLOBAL MONETARY SYSTEM

It so happened that at the end of the war, the global economy was in shambles. The only major country with significant financial resources was the U.S., which at the time held approximately 70% of the world's gold. So, go figure that they had a little meeting at a place called Bretton Woods, and when they adjourned, the U.S. emerged as the world's reserve currency. That meant that, effectively, the U.S. could print as much money as it liked.

They could also control the monetary system to force nations into compliance with their policies, or face sanctions and have their assets frozen, effectively barring them from international trade. The emergence of the BRICS movement is about to take that power away from the U.S. More on this later. But first, reflect on this:

> **America's Permanent War Economy . . . has endured since the end of World War II . . .**
> **Since then, the U.S. has been at war, somewhere, every year, in Korea, Nicaragua,**
> **Vietnam, the Balkans, Afghanistan—all this to the accompaniment of shorter military**
> **forays in Africa, Chile, Grenada, Panama, and increasingly at home against its people.**
> Seymour Melman, author of several books, from the article *In the Grip of a*
> *Permanent War Economy,* counterpunch.org, March 15, 2003

THE TRUTH ABOUT WHY JFK WAS ASSASSINATED

Kennedy was opposed to sending more troops to Vietnam, getting rid of the FED, and limiting the power of the CIA. The financial elite had him assassinated, plain and simple.

THE TRUTH ABOUT THE VIETNAM WAR

The Bay of Tonkin incident never happened. The incident was another pretext for war. Vietnam was a war for profit, plain and simple. Meant to last for years, it drove the U.S. into debt. Classified documents, *The Pentagon Papers*, obtained from a whistleblower, disclosed that Eisenhower, Kennedy, and Johnson knew we couldn't win the Vietnam War, yet under Johnson, it escalated. Over 100,000 of our sons and daughters were sent there to be maimed and killed for nothing.

Once *The Pentagon Papers* came out, anti-war protests heated up to such an extent that the war had to end. President Nixon cut off the enemy's supply chain by mining Haiphong Harbor. Pretty simple; no supplies, no war. The truth is that the war could have ended at any time the powers that be wanted it to. Again, I say, war is a business, and the lives of our sons and daughters are of no consequence. To the Elite, they are just dumb animals led to slaughter.

Switching topic, here is a question for you. If the financial elite saw to it that the U.S. emerged from World War II as the undisputed economic superpower of the world, why would they now want to drive it into insurmountable debt? Remember, their ultimate goal is to eliminate all sovereign nations and establish their one-world dictatorship. The operative word here is "dictatorship." Communist China aligns better with its long-term strategy than the Capitalist U.S. So, America was getting too strong, and a new pawn was required. America had to fall so that China could rise.

To grasp the financial elite's strategy, you must be able to look back ten, twenty, or even thirty years or more. The Vietnam War was laying the groundwork for their plan to strip the U.S. of control of global trade and shift it to Communist China. But why? Refer to the quote in Chapter 1 by Larry P. McDonald, which will help you understand their long-term strategy.

And of course, as described earlier, McDonald's life was cut short in a plane crash involving "accidental" circumstances. There was no mention in the media about McDonald's work to expose a dangerous international conspiracy. Remember, there are no coincidences. In politics, nothing happens by accident!

So, in summary, the financial elite's plan was to:

- Gain control of America and use its wealth and power to control the world!
- Transition into a hybrid super-capitalist, communist economy because it gave them the economic engine of capitalism and the control of communism.

By the time Carter's Presidency began, this strategy was in the open. Under Carter, the U.S. economy was brought to a screeching halt, with interest rates and inflation at 18 to 21%. Then along came slick Willie Clinton, who signed the intentionally losing trade deal NAFTA, and magically, China was positioned to take over control of global trade from the U.S. At that time, after over 200 years as a nation, the U.S. debt was a scant $600 billion. As soon as NAFTA was signed, our debt began to skyrocket. As of today, it stands at an unsustainable $38 trillion. Go figure! This was planned, and most of our politicians are puppets of the global elite!

THE TRUTH ABOUT 9/11

9/11 was another false flag event perpetrated by our government. A pretext planned for the invasion of Iraq, the collapse of the stock market, and eventually the '08 housing collapse. The combined cost of these events was over $16 trillion, which is nearly half of our total national debt. A document titled "Project for the New American Century" (PNAC), written in 2000, exposes the government's treasonous acts. It called for:

- A need for strategically positioned military bases around the world.
- The need to bring about regime change in countries unfriendly to U.S. policy. For example, Iraq was offered an oil deal similar to the Saudi Petro Dollar Deal, and Saddam turned it down. And go figure, Saddam ended up dead, and Iraq ended up in rubble!
- The desire to increase military spending by upwards of a trillion dollars.

Within a year, all three objectives of PNAC had been realized. In politics, nothing happens by accident. It just so happens that PNAC also specified the invasion strategy for the Iraq War a year before the invasion.

There was a fourth motive behind 9/11 and 2008 that went far beyond the objectives of PNAC. That was to lay the foundation for a legal dictatorship. That task fell to Bush Jr., alias "The Rat."

THE PATRIOT ACT LAID THE FOUNDATION
FOR LEGALIZED DICTATORSHIP

Our swamp-dwelling Washington politicians would have us believe they never saw the 2008 financial collapse coming. If that is the case, how do you account for the fact that they had a 2,000-page stimulus bill written and ready to be signed?

At 3:45 a.m. on the day the Patriot Act was to be signed, President Bush pulled the bipartisan version and replaced it with one written by his handlers and designed to take away your liberties.

THE PRESIDENT CAN, AT HIS DISCRETION, DECLARE A NATIONAL EMERGENCY

Executive Order 51: The President may declare an unspecified national emergency, without conferring with Congress, and assume all functions necessary for the Continuity of Government, including directing all federal, state, local, and tribal governments, as well as private sector organizations.

Under National Emergency, FEMA is given the authority to develop plans to establish control over the mechanisms of production, distribution, of energy sources, wages, salaries, credit, and the flow of money in U.S. financial institutions, including the power to seize all financial instruments, currency, gold, silver, and anything else if they deem an emergency exists.

As mentioned previously, I believe Bush is a traitor. Ponder the comments made by filmmaker and once-political candidate, Aaron Russo, on Alex Jones' *InfoWars*. Rockefeller told Russo:

> 9/11 was done by people in our own government, in our own banking system, to perpetuate the fear of the American people to subordinate themselves into anything the government wants them to do. That's what it's about: to create an endless war on terror...Look, this whole war on terror is a fraud, a farce...

So Russo asked Rockefeller, "What's the point of all this?"

Rockefeller responded:

> The end goal is...to control the whole society, to have the banks and the elite people and some government controlling the whole world.

Then there is this from FBI Agent Ted Gunderson, in charge of the Los Angeles Bureau, who says, "The CIA is behind most of our terrorist attacks. What the CIA has done to this country is unbelievable. The CIA is behind most, if not all, of our terrorist attacks: We had Pan Am 103, we had the USS Cole, we had Oklahoma City!"

We have reached the point where the truth becomes undeniable. The photos in the following graphics are absolute proof that the Twin Towers came down by controlled demolition. Shanksville was a staged crash site. There was no wreckage. Something other than a 757 hit the Pentagon.

Again, there was no wreckage, and the 757's wingspan was too large to have fit through the opening we see in the photo. Then there is Building 7, which was not hit by a plane and had minimal damage, yet it also came down in free-fall fashion. Use your own eyes; don't let the Elite tell you what truth is and what lies are. They are master liars.

CONTROLLED DEMOLITION BROUGHT DOWN THE TOWERS

Remember, the planes hit the upper floors. So, how do you account for the cut support columns in the basement? No fire in the world could have done what you see in the photos below. The only thing capable of doing what you see is a shape charge using thermite, which burns at 4,500 degrees and cuts through steel like a knife through butter. The only plausible explanation for how the towers came down is controlled demolition, likely involving the use of shape charges and thermite.

Given the size of the hole in the façade of the Pentagon and the lack of wreckage or bodies, the only explanation for what you see in the photos on the next page is that a missile, not a plane, hit the Pentagon.

It Is A Scientific Fact That Jet Fuel DOES NOT Burn Hot Enough To Melt Metal…

But Thermite Used In Controlled Demolition Does!

To take down a building by controlled demolition you cut the support beams in the basement on a 45-degree angle just like in these photos. No fire from jet fuel can do that, but a SHAPE CHARGE can! Also remember the air-plane hit on the 73rd floor, so how do you account for the beams in the basement being cut?

Experts Say: NO Commercial Airliner Hit The Pentagon!

French Accident Investigator Francois Grangier said: "*What is certain when one looks at the photos of the facade that remains is that it is obvious that the plane [the 757] did not go through there.*"

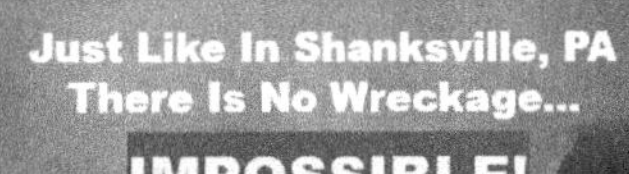

Seriously, Where Is The Wreckage? There Should Be Wreckage!

THE DAMAGE TO BUILDING 7:
NOT EXTENSIVE ENOUGH TO BRING IT DOWN

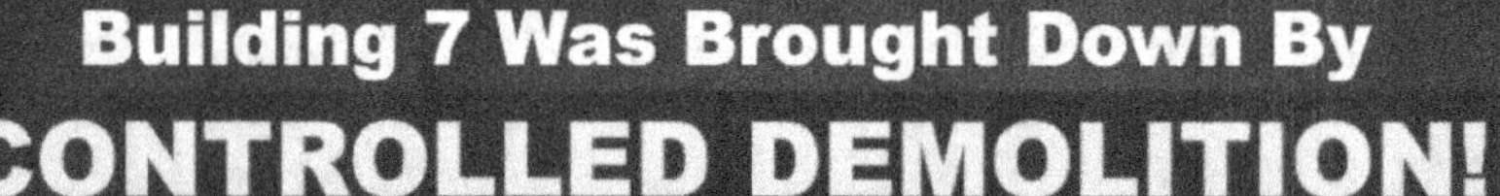

Think about this. It takes days to wire a building for controlled demolition, so this was an admission that 9/11 was planned and executed in advance. That means there had to be an inside man, but who could it be? It just so happens that George Bush had a younger brother, Marvin, who had a financial interest in a security company named "Securacom." Go figure!

And Securacom held the security contracts for the Twin Towers, Dulles Airport, and United Airlines. What a coincidence. But wait—there's more!

Just days before 9/11, the towers were shut down, and all security cameras were shut off, supposedly for an upgrade to the fiber optics system. What a perfect opportunity to wire the building for controlled demolition. But don't worry; I am sure that was just another coincidence. Lastly, Larry Silverstein customarily had breakfast with his daughter on the 95th floor of the towers, but not on 9/11? Just another coincidence.

HOW DO YOU HAVE A PLANE CRASH BUT NO WRECKAGE OR BODIES?
SIMPLE ANSWER: THAT IS IMPOSSIBLE

Yet on 9/11, there were three plane crashes, and there was no wreckage and no bodies. Impossible. Yet the photos don't lie. Something smells rotten.

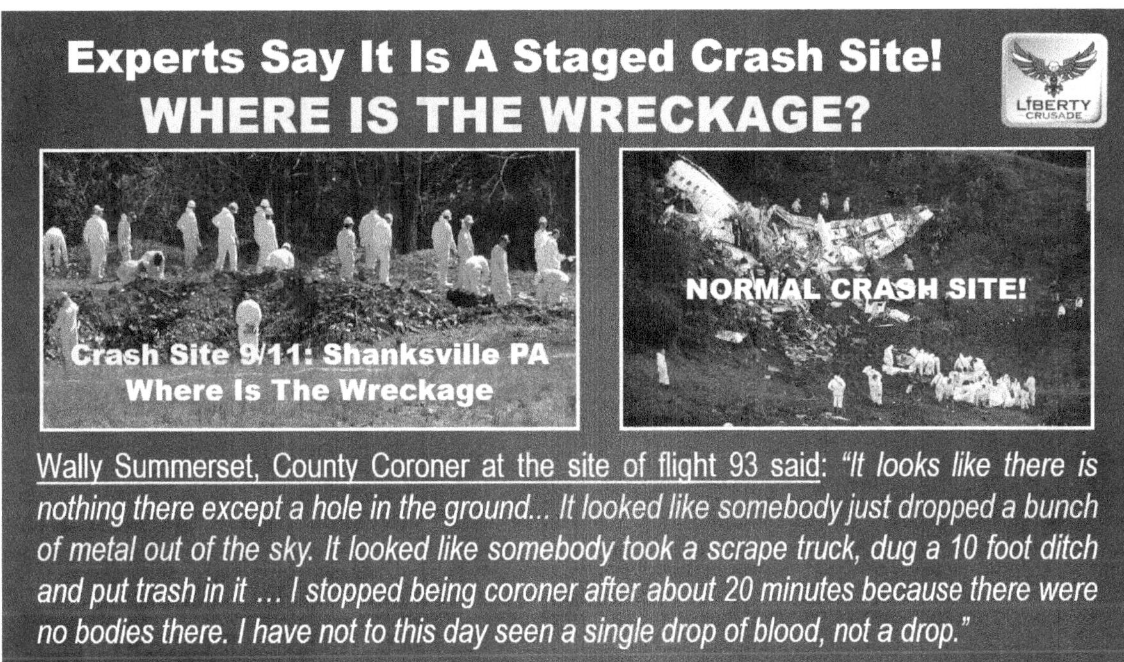

Photo from the Crash of Flight #93

I have one last image about 9/11 to share, and it raises a very interesting question. How is it possible that back in 1945, the Empire State Building was hit by a B-25 bomber, a plane as large as the ones that hit the towers, and it did not come crashing down? In fact, it was open for business only 48 hours after the accident!

IN SUMMARY

For centuries, the Monarchs of Europe and their descendants have ruled the world. As monarchs, they ruled from their thrones as kings with absolute power. As their power waned, they merged it with the Catholic Church, becoming the Holy Roman Empire. Under the Holy Roman Empire, the church instructed the kings on what they wanted done, and the Kings saw to it. As the monarchies fell, they morphed into a network of central banks and used money and war to enslave the nations of the world.

Today, they have overplayed their hand and are on the verge of losing their tyrannical grip on humanity. They are orchestrating the current financial crisis, thinking that their banks will be bailed out, like always. But this time, they will not be bailed out. When they released COVID-19, the world was locked down, and massive financial distress was inflicted.

This went too far. The sheeple woke up, and today people are standing up in countries all over the world and saying, "No more! No more will you enslave us. We are many; they are few."

Remember, India got its independence from both England and the financial elite by doing exactly what people all over the world are now doing. The people of India stood up and said "No" to going along with slavery without chains. They also boycotted the British economic system, and finally, they knuckled under, and India gained its independence.

The only power someone has is the power we give them by our compliance. They need *us* more than we need *them*. The truth will set us free. If we stand up and say "No," their power will dissolve. The global financial system is on the brink of utter collapse. When they lose their money, they will lose control over all the spheres of influence because they will not have the money that they need to buy the power and influence that they need to enslave us.

In a few years, it will be as though they never existed. We have ultimate control, not them; our power rests in us, but even more in God. Now is the time of the reversal promised in the Book of Esther. That meant to destroy us, will destroy our enemy.

God is going to release peace and prosperity upon the earth. He is going to take the wealth of the wicked and give it to the righteous, who will use it for good, not evil. God's Harvest of Souls is about to be released. Just open your eyes. The empire of evil is crumbling before your eyes. The truth is about to set you free!

CHAPTER 7

WHY ILLEGAL IMMIGRATION IS A COVERT WAR
And How America Is Under Attack From Our Own Government!

TOPICS COVERED IN THIS CHAPTER:

- WHY LEGAL IMMIGRATION WAS STOPPED IN THE U.S. FROM 1924-1964
- THE HIDDEN AGENDA BEHIND ILLEGAL IMMIGRATION
- THE ORGANIZATIONS THAT ARE FUNDING ILLEGAL IMMIGRATION
- HOW ILLEGAL IMMIGRATION IS BEING USED TO COLLAPSE THE U.S. AND EUROPE
- THERE IS A SIMPLE WAY TO STOP ILLEGAL IMMIGRATION, BUT OUR CORRUPT POLITICIANS DON'T WANT IT STOPPED

THE ELITE TELL us it is unethical not to let the hordes of illegal immigrants at our Southern border into our country. The Globalist UN, which wants to end all sovereign nations, is drafting a resolution saying migration is a human right. Our politicians say they are for closing our border and building a wall. At least that is what they said until Donald Trump was elected and started building the wall that they said they wanted.

Then, suddenly, a wall became immoral. And suddenly, the left changed its rhetoric, and the truth came out. Do you think maybe our bought-and-paid-for politicians tell us what we want to hear when they are running for office? Once elected, they carry out the wishes of their puppet masters, which are never beneficial to America or its true citizens.

Our corrupt politicians care more about illegal immigrants than they do those who served in the military and now need our help. They have no problem letting our ex-military sleep in the streets, while they put the illegal immigrants (who have done nothing for this country) up in hotels, feed them, and give them all manner of entitlements. What does that say about our politicians? It says to me that they are on the take. They know that many, if not most, of these illegal immigrants represent a financial burden to hard-working citizens already stretched to their financial limits.

But wait, I spoke too soon. These people do have something very valuable to offer the financial elite, whose goal is to collapse America to birth their one-world order dictatorship. They want to drive America into unmanageable debt. Ask yourself if opening our doors to millions of people who don't speak English, have no visible source of income, or hold religious and cultural values that often are not in line with those of most Americans, isn't a pretty good way to divide and impoverish a nation and tear it apart from within?

Contemplate the following quotes, and you will come to realize that illegal immigration furthers the agenda of the financial elite to collapse America and every sovereign nation and impose a one-world dictatorship.

The New World Order cannot happen without U.S. participation,
as we are the most significant single component. Yes, there will be a New World Order,
and it will force the United States to change its perceptions.
Henry Kissinger, April 19, 1994, World Affairs Council Press Conference,
Regent Beverly Wilshire Hotel, April 19, 1994

Here is the truth about the role immigration played in American History. America is often referred to as the melting pot of the world because, in the early years of our history, people fleeing oppression in other parts of the world (notably Europe and China) came to America, the land of freedom and opportunity. God had a plan for mankind. He wanted to bring together people who had been pitted against one another and demonstrate to the world that it was possible to live in peace and harmony. Soon, God will use America a second time to show the world that it is possible to live together in peace and harmony.

However, that won't happen until the people of America learn the truth about what has been done to divide us. People who speak another language are not our enemy. Neither are people of a different race our enemy, nor are people of different religions our enemy. So, with that said, the people coming into America are, mostly, not our enemy. They are pawns of the global elite who want to divide America and drive it into unmanageable debt. So, with this said, why am I against immigration? I am not against immigration. I am against illegal immigration because it serves the hidden agenda of the global elite to end U.S. sovereignty.

History repeatedly tells us that a nation without a border has no nation to be sovereign over. Ask yourself why China built the Great Wall, why Israel has a wall, and why Jericho had a wall, as did every city in biblical times. A wall or a closed border policy protects a nation in many ways. So I say again. I am not against immigration. But I am against illegal immigration because it is a covert war of incursion intended to collapse nations without firing a shot.

Sun Tzu, the world-famous military strategist, said, "The supreme art of war is to destroy the enemy without fighting". That is exactly what illegal immigration will do. Collapse us without a fight. So, let's step back in history and find out the truth about the role of immigration in American history.

IMMIGRATION COMPLETELY STOPPED IN AMERICA FROM 1924 TO 1965

Why? Not because we hated immigrants, but because America's labor-intensive infrastructure projects were complete. Long since completed was the transcontinental railroad, which President Lincoln signed into law. We built our bridges, our sewers were laid, our factories were constructed, and Eisenhower's interstate highway system was complete. Automation was also taking over a significant amount of manual labor. So, we didn't need as many laborers as we did when America was being built. These were important factors, but they were not the primary reason immigration stopped. Immigration stopped for two reasons:

- **Debt**: Because we couldn't afford to take in all the poor people. It was a drain on our economy.
- **Assimilation:** There were so many people coming to America that they couldn't assimilate into the existing culture. That threatened national sovereignty and unity. America is the greatest nation in the world, mainly because it has taken people from different backgrounds and assimilated them, thereby unifying its people. We became the United States of America, and that made us virtually invincible in all that we did.

We became one nation under God with liberty and justice for all. We were one people with one unified set of values, and that made America the shining light on the hill, the inspiration for all of mankind. America was the great hope for a better world.

It also made America the greatest threat the financial elite had ever faced. So America had to be destroyed, torn apart from the inside, and illegal immigration was (and still is) one of the primary ways they used to destroy America.

> **The Council on Foreign Relations [A subversive organization to which most of our politicians belong] is the American branch of a society, which originated in England...**
> **[and]...believes national boundaries should be obliterated**
> **and one-world rule established.**
> Dr. Carroll Quigley, Historian, Author
> *Tragedy and Hope: A History of the World in Our Time, 1966*
> Professor, Georgetown University, College Mentor of President Bill Clinton
> (Emphasis added)

Trump knows what made America great, and that is in part why he built the wall (at least part of a wall) and attempted to close the border. Our Washington turncoats know the truth. But despite that, they want open borders because they are puppets of the financial elite who want to collapse America from the inside.

> The New World Order will be built...an end run on national sovereignty, eroding it
> piece by piece, will accomplish much more than the old-fashioned frontal assault.
> *Council on Foreign Relations Journal,* 1974, page 558

Today, there are three very important reasons why the borders must be closed that did not exist from 1924 to 1965. They are:

1. **Drug Trafficking:** The Caucasian Europeans inflicted China with opium to pacify the nation. Two Opium Wars were fought to free China from this devastating man-made epidemic. And now the puppet masters are using Opium and Fentanyl to pacify America and collapse it from within. They are also using the open border as a conduit for sex trafficking. All of this is part of a strategy to destroy the family because our enemy knows that the family represents the heart and soul of America. Even though it is not related to illegal immigration, the LGBTQ+ movement is part of the attack on the family.

> America is like a healthy body, and its resistance is its patriotism, its morality,
> and its spiritual life. If we can undermine these three areas,
> America will collapse from within.
> Joseph Stalin, Russian Leader

2. **Terrorist Attacks:** We are not just looking at families seeking a better life. We are seeing countries that consider America their enemy, releasing criminals from their jails and sending them to America as a means of destabilizing our society. We are also witnessing military-age males coming from countries that we know are enemies of America. What better way to covertly invade a nation than to embed military terrorists with a horde of illegal immigrants?

3. **Crime:** Drugs and poverty breed crime. We have been infiltrated by gang members whose way of life is to take what they want and kill whom they please. They run Mexico and many other Latin American countries, and they are being imported to America by the financial elite with the aid of our corrupt politicians, with the explicit purpose of destroying America. They get an all-expenses-paid trip to America, the land of opportunity, with the expectation that they will turn it into a hellhole.

No, illegal immigration is not a humanitarian right. In the instance of America, it is a carefully planned and financially funded covert military invasion masquerading as a human right. I say again, history has shown us that a nation without a border has no nation to be sovereign over. It is a nation on the path to internal collapse.

EUROPE: A LESSON FROM THE PAST

Are there ways other than illegal immigration that the financial elite uses to end the national sovereignty of nations? Of course, and we have discussed several of them. However, one we haven't discussed deals with Europe and how the countries of Europe lost their sovereignty and became the servile trading bloc that we today call the European Union. It is essential to understand what was done to Europe because the globalists are trying to do the same thing to the U.S. and the rest of the world. The surrender of Europe's sovereignty began with the signing of trade agreements. However, the final act of their story is related to immigration, or more specifically, the Syrian refugee crisis. A refugee crisis is just another name for an orchestrated immigration incursion intended to collapse a nation.

So, let's examine Europe's metamorphosis into a servile trading bloc. Then we will explore the similarities to what is being done to the U.S. to achieve the same outcome.

The European Union started as:

- A trade agreement, just like NAFTA.
- Then, a common currency, called the "Euro," was issued.
- Then, the constitutions of individual countries were replaced by a socialist constitution.
- Then, non-elected bureaucrats in Brussels set about passing laws and writing regulations, which constituted a shadow government, the real ruling power in Europe.

You will recall that when the U.S. declared bankruptcy in 1933, an army of non-elected bureaucrats was embedded in the government to perform precisely the same functions as those in Brussels. This realization is what is behind the *Brexit* moment in England. The British want their freedom and their Constitution back. I am not the only one who sees what is happening.

A meeting was held in March 2005:

> **Baylor University welcomes President George W. Bush, Mexican President Vicente Fox, and Canadian Prime Minister Paul Martin on March 23 for meetings the leaders said provided a framework for the next generation of trilateral relations between the North American Countries.**
>
> Reported by Lori Scott Fogelman, March 23, 2005

Here is what Stan Jones, U.S. Senate Candidate for the Libertarian Party, had to say at the 2006 CSPN Debate:

> **... What I am about to say is fact. The secret organizations of the world power elite are no longer secret... They have planned and are now leading us into the One World Communist Government. This combining of National governments began with the European Union. That union started with trade agreements, then a common currency, the Euro, and now a European Parliament...Now it is North America's Turn. Building with...NAFTA... the Commerce Department is busy drafting laws and regulations for a North American Union, a union of Canada, America, and Mexico. The President (Former President Bush) has attended secret meetings and signed at least two agreements under the 'Security and Prosperity Partnership Program.' Information leaked out about the meetings, and now it is in the open...**

Suppose the secret meetings referenced in the above quotes were not exposed. In that case, the U.S. would most likely be part of the Amero Union, our currency would be the Amero, and our constitution would have long since been shredded. Or has it already been shredded? I say this because our politicians often act with impunity, disregarding the Constitution.

> **The Constitution is just a God da## piece of paper.**
>
> George W. Bush, Nov. 2005, Capitol Hill Blue [Emphasis added]

The Elite are nothing if not persistent. Biden (the usurper) also tried to merge Mexico, Canada, and the United States. Why is it so important to merge these three nations?

The ultimate goal is to establish ten servile trading blocs that will form the *Beast System*. That system, overseen by the Globalist UN, is intended to supersede the laws of all nations, effectively establishing the Globalists' one-world dictatorship. The globalists believe that with Europe already under their control, if they can get control of America, the rest of the world will be easy prey.

But don't get worried. We are not in the Book of Revelation yet, where it describes the empire of evil. We are in the time of the Harvest of Souls, where God keeps his covenant with Abraham when he says:

> Then He brought him outside and said, "Look now toward heaven, and count the stars if you are able to number them." He said to him, "So shall your descendants be."
> Genesis 15:5 (NKJV)

We are also in the time when God tells us He is coming back for a spotless church.

> That He might present her to Himself a glorious church, not having spot or wrinkle or any such thing, but that she should be holy and without blemish.
> Ephesians 5:27 (NKJV)

Nothing in God's universe happens by accident. The things we are experiencing now are not to punish us but to refine us and turn us into the church without blemish.

> But may the God of all grace, who called us into his eternal glory by Christ Jesus, after you have suffered a while, make you perfect, establish, strengthen, and settle you.
> 1 Peter 5.10 (NKJV)

> For whom the LORD loves He chastens, and scourges every son whom He receives.
> Hebrews 12:6 (NKJV)

What we are seeing now is the downfall of the kingdoms of man and the establishment of the kingdom of God. The financial elite have gotten ahead of themselves. They thought that Hillary, the witch, would be elected President following Obama, the Evil One. But God surprised the world when He put Donald Trump, the bull in the China shop, in place to disrupt their plans. If we examine the Bible, we see that Trump is the archetype of King Cyrus of Persia, who freed the Israelites and helped them rebuild the temple. This fact has not escaped the Israelis, who have had a temple coin minted depicting the silhouettes of Donald Trump and King Cyrus.

AFTER THE HARVEST OF SOULS COMES THE TRIBULATION, FOLLOWED BY CHRIST'S MILLENNIAL REIGN

For now, let's get back to our discussion of how the surrender of Europe's sovereignty began with trade agreements. The final act of their story revolves around immigration, specifically the Syrian refugee crisis. A refugee crisis is just another name for an orchestrated immigration incursion intended to collapse a nation.

It wasn't enough to create the European Union and establish a shadow government, as they did in the U.S. in 1933. For the global elite to achieve their dream of establishing their one-world dictatorship, Europe, and for that matter, all sovereign nations, must be driven into total submission. What the globalists are orchestrating between America and China is not unlike what they are orchestrating between Europe and Islam.

As we have discussed, they want to collapse America and cede its power to China and create a super-capitalist, communist hybrid economy with the industrial might of capitalism and the control of communism. The following is an excerpt from the introduction of the book *The Rockefeller Files* by Garry Allen:

> The Rockefeller File is not fiction. It is a compact, powerful, and frightening presentation of what may be the most important story of our lifetime, the drive of the Rockefellers and their allies to create a one-world government combining super-capitalism and communism under the same tent, all under their control. . . not one has dared reveal the most vital part of the Rockefeller story: that the Rockefellers and their allies have, for at least fifty years, been carefully following a plan to use their economic power to gain political control of first America, and then the rest of the world. Do I mean conspiracy? Yes, I do. I am convinced there is such a plot, international in scope, generations old in planning, and incredibly evil in intent.
>
> Congressman Larry P. McDonald, GA, Introduction, *The Rockefeller Files*, 1976

They want to do the same thing with Europe and Islam. They want the technological might of Europe controlled by an extremist, oppressive Islamic regime that imposes Sharia law and a totalitarian dictatorship. This is the model for their subservient ten-nation trading bloc, with ten kings upon whose heads crowns are placed for one hour, alongside the beast.

Time for another history lesson. Christianity and Islam have been at war for 1,400 years. Christianity under the power-crazed Holy Roman Empire tried to conquer Islam, and Islam, under clerical extremists, tried to conquer Europe. But neither conquered the other for more than a brief time. But the concept of war has changed, and a covert war is underway that few people even realize is going on, and takes us back to the parallels between illegal immigration in the U.S. and the Syrian refugee crisis in Europe.

Modern-day Christianity practices monogamy, one husband or wife, while Islam practices polygamy, more than one husband or wife. The significance of this is related to the declining birth rates, particularly in Europe. The strategy for the Islamic conquest of Europe combines the effects of the Syrian refugee crisis with demographics. The conquest of Europe was to seed Europe with Islamic refugees, composed of family units with multiple wives, each having multiple children. The estimate is that this strategy will result in Europe being a Muslim-majority nation under Sharia Law within one generation. At that point, Islam will have accomplished through covert means what it could not do through conventional warfare in 1,400 years. I remind you again, it is as Sun Tzu said, "*The supreme art of war is to destroy the enemy without fighting!*"

That is precisely what is happening in both the U.S. and Europe. Both nations are being conquered covertly through demographics as the catalyst to overthrow the existing form of government to be replaced by one controlled by the globalists, whose goal is to exterminate 7.5 billion of us! As Sun Tzu said: *We are on death ground*. It is time to reveal the truth, so God can set the captives free.

Putting myself in the mindset of the reader, I immediately say: Wait a minute, you mean to tell me that Islam was willing to be decimated in a war to insert their people in Europe so they can conquer it by out-birthing the Europeans? That is exactly what I mean. It is similar to the story of how the Greeks used a Trojan Horse to gain entrance to the city of Troy and achieve victory. It is like what England did when it orchestrated World War I, even though they knew it would destroy Europe. Our enemy does not value human life. Any number of deaths is acceptable if they get the desired victory.

So, how was the Syrian refugee crisis orchestrated? Enter the tag team of Hillary, the witch, and Obama, the Evil One. They orchestrated what has come to be known as the Arab Spring, a CIA-orchestrated covert operation intended to destabilize the entirety of the Middle East and North Africa. Nation after nation fell through internal conflict. But what was the source of that conflict? During modern times, ethnic and religious hatred has been kept in check by strong men like Muammar Gaddafi of Libya, Hosni Mubarak of Egypt, Saddam Hussein of Iraq, Bashar al-Assad of Syria, etc. The globalist puppet masters knew that with a bit of help from Obama and Hillary, they could destabilize the Middle East and North Africa by taking out the military strong men who kept a lid on ancient hatreds.

Besides that, they wanted Gaddafi out of power because he was trying to orchestrate an African gold-backed currency. That couldn't be allowed, so he had to die. The United States offered an oil deal to Hussein similar to the one we had up until June 9, 2024, but he turned it down. So, he had to die.

Since 2011, 13 million Syrians have been displaced either within Syria or to other countries. The number of European refugees is difficult to tally accurately, but estimates are around six million. Two factors attributed to why there are so many refugees from Syria and Libya: 1) a large volume of migrant workers, and 2) unlike many Arab nations, Syria and Libya degenerated into a full-blown civil war.

In any event, the illegal immigration in the U.S. and the refugee crisis in Europe both serve the globalist puppet masters' agenda to collapse the U.S. and Europe from within through debt and internal chaos!

I must mention Obama before I conclude, the one who advises Biden and Harris. Upon leaving the presidency, Obama was asked in an interview if he would like a third term. He responded, "No," but said he wouldn't mind calling the shots from the sidelines.

Even though his primary residence is on Martha's Vineyard, he still maintains a residence in Washington, D.C., near the White House, where Valerie Jarrett, someone who is thought to follow Muslim beliefs, holds down the fort. There is plenty of evidence that Obama is a Muslim and not a Christian, including the following:

- In his book *The Audacity of Hope*, on page 261, he said that he would stand with the Muslims should the political winds shift in an ugly direction.
- Obama recited the Muslim Call to Prayer, which, according to the Koran, makes him a Muslim, and makes the American people infidels and his enemies.
- He said, The sweetest sound I know is the Muslim call to prayer.

- When asked during an interview about his faith, he responded, My Muslim faith.
- He boycotted the National Day of Prayer and then turned around and invited his Muslim brothers into the White House to pray.
- He said: America isn't a Christian Nation and called the Quran the Holy Quran.
- He said he would reduce the U.S. military to a level acceptable to his Muslim brothers.
- He pushed the Iranian nuclear deal, removed sanctions on Iran, loaded pallets of money on planes, and delivered them to Iran in a secret operation.
- At a UN General Assembly meeting, he said: The future must not belong to those who slander the Prophet of Islam.
- He stated that the U.S. "is not" and never would be at war with Islam. This despite their threats and terrorist attacks on the U.S.
- During his time in office, chaplains were prevented from praying in the name of Christ.

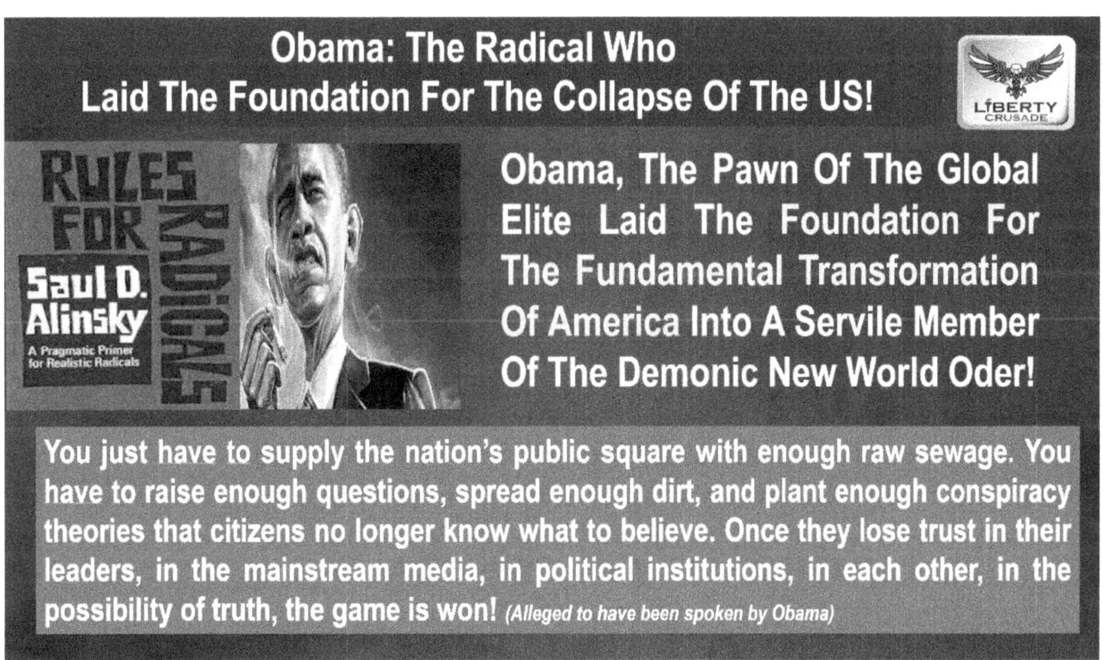

It should be noted that Obama taught from the *Rules for Radicals* while serving as a community organizer in Chicago and implemented the strategy while president of the U.S. He amassed more debt than any of his 43 predecessors!

The following quote is from the foreword to *Rules for Radicals*, the hate-mongering book by Saul Alinsky, which was the primer for Obama's political platform.

Lest we forget an over-the-shoulder acknowledgment of the very first radical...
The first known to man who at least won his own kingdom, Lucifer.

Obama's endorsement of a book dedicated to Satan, teaching strategies to divide the U.S., and bury it under a mountain of debt, demonstrated that he had no business holding public office at any level, much less as the President. Yet he was elected not *once* but *twice*. Or was he?

I believe that soon we will find out that he was not elected, but rather appointed to office through election fraud. If that is proven, our entire political landscape will undergo a radical change. There will be the removal of many from office. Many regulations will be stricken, and laws overturned. I believe there will soon be whistleblowers who will come forward and reveal what they know. When that happens, the army of insurrectionists hiding within our government will be removed from their hiding places, and our Republic will be restored. Remember, God says that all will be revealed, and all is known.

Obama sat under Jeremiah Wright, a preacher who routinely spouted racial hatred and division. He is a man who was mentored by and whose books, *Dreams From My Father* and *The Audacity of Hope*, were reportedly ghostwritten by Bill Ayers, founder of the Weather Underground, which was responsible for bombing the Pentagon in 1972. Arizona Sheriff Joe Arpaio alleged his birth certificate to be a forgery. Drudge Report says that a forensic test proves Obama's birth certificate is a forgery. Why Obama would need to hide his real identity is explored in the documentary *Dreams From My Real Father* by Joel Gilbert. The documentary provides compelling evidence that Obama's birth father is Frank Marshall Davis, a card-carrying communist organizer, and not a goat herder from Kenya.

I ask you, how many red flags do we need before we realize Obama is an enemy of America and Christianity? How is it that a man with this ideology and this history was ever elected President of the United States? The answer lies in the ability of what Trump calls the "Fake News" to control the narrative so that the public is unable to tell fact from fiction, truth from lie, or friend from foe.

Looking back at Obama's presidential campaign and his time in office, it is clear that the *fake news* ran interference for him and censored any stories that raised the slightest question whether he was friend or foe. So, if a man with as many hidden secrets as Obama can be elected, what does it say about the integrity of our election process? It raises the question as to how many of our political figures and presidents were provided the same whitewashing to ensure they were elected to serve the interests of the globalist financial elite and not the interests of American citizens. Our government has been hijacked by those who are intent on destroying the sovereignty of our great nation.

It is difficult for the common good to prevail against the intense concentration of those who have a special interest, especially if the decisions are made behind locked doors.
President Jimmy Carter

Ironically, closing our border and stopping this incursion of illegal immigrants has a simple, straightforward solution. To secure or close the border and secure our sovereignty, all we would have to do is:

- Finish the wall Trump started.
- Withdraw from the UN, which wants open borders and calls migration a human right.
- Place economic sanctions on Mexico to encourage it to cooperate with the U.S. immigration policies.
- Impose severe penalties on all drug dealers, without excluding the death penalty.
- Do not allow children born in the U.S. to illegal immigrants to be granted U.S. citizenship.
- Stop All Entitlements.
- Do not allow admittance into public schools.
- Do not issue driver's licenses or IDs of any kind.
- Impose severe fines and or prison sentences for anyone employing illegal immigrants.
- Impose severe fines and or prison sentences for anyone providing housing to an illegal immigrant.
- Trigger immediate deportation for treatment in an emergency room.
- End chain migration and implement a merit-based immigration system.
- End catch and release.
- Deport all illegal immigrants who commit a crime, any crime, while in the U.S.

- Invoke mandatory prison sentences for anyone deported who returns to the country.
- End sanctuary cities.
- Allow the "grandfather clause" for anyone who has been in the country for ten years or more with no criminal record.

NOTE: Though not a political and social solution, Trump has mitigated the crisis by deploying the military and stopping the influx of new immigrants.

In effect, what these simple measures would do is remove the invitation to come to America as an illegal immigrant. Because even if you get across the border into the U.S., you will have no means of support. Those who want to use illegal immigration to collapse the U.S. will say these policies are inhumane. They are not. Any nation may impose laws and enforce them; anyone who ignores those laws is subject to the prescribed punishment—end of statement.

Implementation of the measures listed above would all but put a stop to illegal immigration. Sounds simple. But wait, there is a major problem. Our traitorous puppet politicians in Washington would never stand for such measures to pass because it is not in the interest of the special interests they represent. So, where does this leave us? As Trump would say, we have no choice but to drain the swamp.

> **I think there are 25,000 individuals who have used offices of power, and they are in our universities, and they are in our Congress, and they believe in One World Government. And if you believe in One World Government, then you are talking about undermining National Sovereignty, and you are talking about setting up something that you could well call a Dictatorship – and those plans are there.**
> Congressman Ron Paul, TX, Austin, TX, August 30, 2003

I saved this until now because I wanted it fresh in your mind as we close out this chapter. I want to reinforce the fact that illegal immigration is a covert war, not some humanitarian migration. These caravans are not organic. They are orchestrated and paid for by various organizations, all of which are serving the interests of the financial elite and their agenda to collapse the U.S. from within.

FUNDING AND COORDINATION FOR THESE CARAVANS COME FROM

Studies reveal that some groups aid in financing unlawful immigration. They are:

- Our bought-and-paid-for Globalist Washington politicians
- The Globalist UN
- Numerous non-governmental organizations (NGOs), the most prominent of which is the globalist Catholic Church

HOW THE ILLEGAL IMMIGRATION INVASION OF AMERICA IS FUNDED AND ORCHESTRATED!

THE ROLE OF THE UN

The UN serves as the travel agent for U.S.-bound caravans. They do so by:

- **Providing Brochures:** Providing illegal immigrants with all the necessary information to facilitate their journey.
- **Offering Funding:** Paying for transportation, travel expenses, food, water, clothing, and all the necessities needed for the journey of illegal immigrants from their nation of origin to the U.S. border.

THE ROLE OF THE U.S. GOVERNMENT

Cross-Border Travel Agreements: This invasion would not be possible without the aid of the U.S. Government, which signed an agreement with six South American Countries to facilitate transit through their countries to the U.S. border. In the simplest possible terms: No cross-border travel agreements/no caravans!

U.S. Funded Entitlements: Upon reaching the U.S. border, the U.S. government provides a range of entitlements, including free cell phones, medical assistance, food, shelter, and travel into the interior. And they are given interest-free loans, which, in reality, the government knows will never be paid back; so, in actuality, they are grants, not loans. And if in the process of illegally entering the U.S. you are separated from your child, the U.S. government will graciously give the parents a $1/2 million remuneration.

THE ROLE OF NGOS

Let's start with the definition of an NGO. They are non-governmental organizations established to allow charitable organizations to assist those in need without governmental red tape, supposedly. In reality, they are a mechanism to facilitate money laundering on a global scale. The Clintons hide behind NGOs, as do George Soros, Bill Gates, the globalist Catholic Church, and a multitude of other globalists who run treasonous operations of various sorts.

You do not have to be a U.S. citizen to establish an NGO. You can be a foreign country, like say China, and set up an NGO to further your agenda. All this under-the-table money laundering is made possible by our bought-and-paid-for corrupt Washington politicians.

THE ROLE OF THE CARTELS

Our lying media and corrupt politicians would have us believe that it is the cartels that make the illegal immigration crisis a reality. Not so. They are simply the mules who get paid to conduct the invading army of immigrants on their journey. And it just so happens that they benefit from the caravans by using them as a cover for their drug and sex trafficking. Which, in my opinion, if the truth be known, is facilitated by the CIA, which is the ultimate agent of the globalists who are intent on ending U.S. sovereignty.

Make no mistake, illegal immigration is a U.S. government-, UN-, and NGO-funded invasion of the U.S. intended to end U.S. sovereignty. Wake up. Stand up.

God inspired this book to empower the public to learn the truth about our slavery so that *the truth can set us free.* All we must do to take our country back is refuse to participate in our slavery. Stand up and refuse to be a part of your slavery. Do what India did to win its freedom from Britain. The people rallied around Mahatma Gandhi and refused to participate in the British economic system; eventually, Britain granted India its independence. Like him or not, Trump is God's David sent to guide us.

Trump promised to make America greater than ever, and right out of the gate, he is taking action to restore U.S. manufacturing, which is the backbone of any economy. He put China on notice that if they built a proposed auto plant in Mexico, he would put a 200% tariff on them, and they would never sell a single car in the United States. Likewise, he notified John Deere that if they built a plant in Mexico, they too would be subject to a tariff, ensuring they could not sell their farm equipment in America.

Remember, trade is the backbone of any economy, and to that end, Trump is giving the world notice that a new sheriff is in town. He is committed to bringing back that symbol of pride that says, "MADE IN AMERICA." Trump may be gruff, but he has a heart for God and the American people. He will keep his promise to:

Make America prosperous again.
Make America proud again.
And make America Godly again.

I say to those who have bought into the media narrative that Trump is a dictator: Nothing could be further from the truth. Within days of being elected, he launched an initiative to unite the nation, restore its Christian foundation, and revitalize its economy. What I refer to is his "America's 250 Birthday Celebration Tour," which is a yearlong traveling tour with stops in all 50 states. It is a celebration of American heritage, including family, faith, patriotism, and technological innovation. These are the very things that made America great in the first place.

The intent behind the Birthday Celebration Tour is to unite the nation and restore American pride. As a nation, we need to be reminded of the greatness of America and inspired by realizing the marvels that promise to MAKE AMERICA GREATER THAN EVER. We are still that shining light on the hill and God's chosen nation.

We harken back to America's Centennial Celebration in 1876, where America showcased the marvels of American technology, including the transcontinental railroad and the Industrial Revolution. In just 34 years, America was the youngest nation in the world and the wealthiest. The steps that Trump is taking will make America energy independent and restore America's status as the world's leading manufacturing powerhouse. As mentioned previously, to date, Donald Trump has secured $18 trillion in commitments to build new factories and infrastructure.

These policies are reminiscent of the ones he implemented during his first term, which resulted in the stock market increasing from 10,000 to 30,000 and led to record-low unemployment across all demographics, ultimately yielding a strong and stable economy. What he did then will be dwarfed compared to what he will do during his second term.

Why is that? Because during the first term, he was an outsider and didn't know who his friends or foes were. So much of what he wanted to do was thwarted by those in our government who served the globalist agenda rather than the people.

This time around, he is familiar with the political landscape, and he will remove those who are opposed to the best interests of the United States. Before you finish this book, you will have a comprehensive plan for restoring America to greatness, and you will come to realize that America is indeed God's covenant nation.

Along with this revelation, you will discover why America will rise from the ashes like the phoenix and usher in peace, prosperity, and unity not only for America but for the entire world. You will realize that no nation in the world can bring this about but America, God's chosen nation. Soon you will know the truth, and it will set the captives free.

We must remember that, as Sun Tzu says, *we are on death ground.* Either we win this last battle, or most of us will die. Those who are allowed to live will live in poverty with virtually no human rights. We are many, and they are few. The Elite cannot control us unless we let them. United we stand, divided we fall. Victory can be ours if we will step out in faith and trust in God.

CLOSING COMMENTS

We have no recourse but to take drastic measures and sweep Washington clean. Our elected government has become the enemy within.

The case for government by elites is irrefutable.
William Fulbright, U.S. Senator

EXCERPT FROM THE DECLARATION OF INDEPENDENCE

We hold these truths to be self-evident, that all men are created equal, that they are endowed by their Creator with certain unalienable rights, that among these are Life, Liberty and the pursuit of Happiness. That to secure these rights, Governments are instituted among Men, deriving their just powers from the consent of the governed. That whenever any Form of Government becomes destructive of these ends, it is the Right of the People to alter or to abolish it, and to institute new Government, laying its foundation on such principles and organizing its powers in such form, as to them shall seem most likely to affect their Safety and Happiness.

Let's rewind to the year 1871 to see how we do that. The phrase, "of the people, by the people, for the people," was illegally stripped from the U.S. Constitution. A corporate charter illegally replaced it with only one mandate: to optimize the profits of the illegal corporation's shareholders.

The Bible states that a thief must return the property he stole. If the Corporation is illegal, which it is, then all the laws passed, and all those elected or appointed under its illegal purview are subject to removal.

TRANSLATION: We go back to our original Constitution, elect new political leaders, and write new laws reflective of the founding principles that made America the greatest nation the world has ever known.

In a subsequent chapter, we will look back at the foundation stones that underpin America's greatness and examine how they have been systematically removed. Restoring America to greatness is simpler than most imagine. The Bible says in Ecclesiastes:

That which has been is what will be . . .
And there is nothing new under the sun.
Ecclesiastes 1:9 (NKJV)

In short, to revive our Republic and America's greatness, we must restore its original foundation. We have the blueprint for rebuilding what has been torn down. Corrupt politicians must be removed, and the laws they have passed must be repealed.

However, there is more to restoring America than simply removing our corrupt politicians and the laws they have passed. We have lost our moral compass, and that must be restored as well. That is where our covenant with God comes in. America must return to God, and we will!

CHAPTER 8

HOW AND WHY CHINA
AND THE U.S. WILL FALL!
God Will Restore the U.S. to Lead the World Into
an Unparalleled Period of Peace and Prosperity

TOPICS COVERED IN THIS CHAPTER:
- HOW AND WHY CHINA WILL FALL
- WHY THE WORLD VIEWS CHINA AS A PARIAH NATION
- WHY CHINA WILL FALL AND BE RELEGATED TO BEING A REGIONAL POWER
- HOW AND WHY THE U.S. WILL FALL AND THEN RISE LIKE THE PHOENIX
- HOW AND WHY THE PRIVILEGE OF BEING THE WORLD'S SOLE RESERVE CURRENCY IS TAKEN FROM THE U.S.
- WHY THE U.S. IS THE ONLY NATION CAPABLE OF BEING THE WORLD'S ECONOMIC SUPERPOWER

BOTH THE U.S. and China have overextended their power, awakening the masses, which will ultimately be their downfall. The removal of China's mask is its greatest weakness, and the world now sees it as the pariah nation that it is. The world finally realizes that it must end China's ability to control the global supply chain. The world has also come to realize that a world controlled by China would be one where there would be virtually no freedom. As for China's future, there are internal problems that will probably relegate it to being a regional power, rather than the world power it aspires to be—details to come.

Regarding the U.S., it has abused the privilege of its position as the world's reserve currency, and that privilege will be removed. In essence, the nations and people of the world are saying that they can no longer allow China or the U.S. to control them. Power, resources, technology, and money must be more evenly distributed among the nations, which means significant changes are on the horizon for both China and the U.S., as well as the world.

The global monetary system is on the verge of collapse, and its failure will profoundly alter the entire global landscape. America is in for a rough time. But when the dust settles, it will rise from the ashes like the Phoenix. It is the only nation in the world capable of restoring order to the world after the forthcoming economic meltdown.

A U.S. free from control by the financial elite will lead the world into a better tomorrow. As Trump says, America will be greater than ever, and the world will be better for it. Don't worry, what is to come must happen to set the captives free. God has planned this all since before the creation of the world. As to exactly how America and the world will be restored, that is the topic of another chapter. We are about to enter God's Harvest of Souls and the purification of his church. The best is yet to come.

The hold the global financial elite has on the nations of the world is about to be broken. It will be painful, but it is in God's hands. He has a new beginning planned, one with peace, prosperity, freedom, the likes of which we cannot even imagine. All's well that ends well!

HOW AND WHY CHINA WILL FALL!

CHINA'S WOES

I remind you that both China and the U.S., and for that matter, every nation in the world, are puppets of the global financial elite. So, when evaluating their actions, we must consider both the nations' motivations and those of their puppet masters as well.

FIRST: CHINA'S FLAWED ECONOMIC MODEL

When the Communist Party of China (CCP) massacred peaceful students protesting in Tiananmen Square, they drove the first nail in their coffin. I say this because it is challenging to govern people who perceive you as an enemy. This blunder led the CCP into a trap of its own making. To pacify the public and quell additional protests, the CCP had to give the people something they wanted, even if it would create problems down the road. That "something" was the promise that, if the people would submit to communism, the government would guarantee them jobs and a better standard of living.

This resulted in an unsustainable economic policy that is now biting the CCP in the butt. Every time there was a slowdown in the economy, instead of laying people off, they would build another ghost city or start a new infrastructure project. The problem is that these projects were not developed based on sound economic policies that consider return on investment. So, as long as the world was investing money in China by the boatload, their Ponzi scheme worked.

Now it has reached the point where the Communist Party of China can no longer keep its promise of jobs and a better standard of living. People have become increasingly disillusioned, and protests are breaking out all over the country. So, the situation has gone full circle. The CCP tried to appease the people by offering them a carrot on a stick. Still, now the people have woken up and realized that, instead of their situation improving, it is getting worse.

NOTABLE EXAMPLES OF INFRASTRUCTURE BLUNDERS

China built an excellent high-speed rail system and ghost cities, motivated by the promise to keep people working, but gave little to no consideration to whether the projects were economically sustainable. The high-speed rail system is a debt trap for the CCP. It loses $44 million per day. Many of the ghost cities are being demolished after sitting vacant for so long.

The Three Gorges Dam may prove to be a real Achilles' heel for China. It reportedly has structural defects that could threaten its collapse. Should that happen, a significant portion of China's arable land would flood, and an estimated 50 million people would be affected. It is worth noting that, of the seventeen Chinese dynasties, five fell because of weather-related events.

There is another, much more important infrastructure project that appears to be in trouble. It is perhaps China's most ambitious undertaking yet and certainly the most strategically important. I am referring to the Belt and Road Initiative (BRI), which represents a modern-day reimagining of the Silk Road, as popularized by Marco Polo. In ancient times, the Silk Road served as a trade route between China and Europe. It is a four-thousand-mile land and water transportation network.

SECOND: FEARS OF REVOLT AGAINST THE CCP TRIGGERED BY

- **Bank Protest**: Prompted by bank closures in Hunan Province.
- **Refusal to Make Mortgage Payments**: Protest triggered by the default of real estate giant, Evergrande, and its associated real estate Ponzi scandal. More on this momentarily under the heading *Real Estate Crisis*.
- **Protests over Lockdowns**: Precipitated by the forcible confinement of 400 million people in their apartments, leading to starvation and, in one instance, death when a fire broke out in a building under lockdown.
- **Oppressive Surveillance State**: Implemented because of the fear that people will revolt against the CCP's oppression. Measures include facial recognition, limited internet access, and the implementation of Social Credit Scores and CBDCs, which punish any action that in any way challenges the CCP's absolute authority.
- **Bridge Protest**: It was an unprecedented call to dissolve the CCP and for Xi Jinping to step down. This is the very fear that led China, following the Tiananmen Square Massacre, to *make the promise to give the people jobs and a better standard of living if they would submit to communism*. The people no longer believe that the CCP and Xi Jinping can keep that promise. China's greatest fear could soon catch up to it. That is the fear of an internal uprising that could topple the government from within. China fears this more than any external threat. That is why China is increasingly reverting to more and more repressive control mechanisms to keep the people in submission. However, this could well prove to be the cause of China's downfall.

THIRD: CHINA IS SEEN AS A GLOBAL PARIAH BASED ON

- **Its Stated Goal of Global Dominance**: For decades, China hid its plans for global dominance, but now they are out in the open and threaten the world.

- **A Belief That China Intentionally Released COVID-19**: COVID-19 was patented, which means it was manmade. The events surrounding the release of COVID-19 led many to believe that it is a bioweapon released by those intent on committing global genocide. The suspected culprits in this atrocity include China and the UN's World Health Organization, and possibly elements in the U.S. government.
- **Chinese Debt Trap**: China has modeled its economy after the centuries-old British Free Trade System, which has been *criticized for its role in systematically driving* competing nations into unmanageable debt. And where money is loaned to poor countries to build vitally essential infrastructure projects that are invariably *debt traps*. Through various means, they are forced to default on the loans, resulting in confiscation of the very assets they borrowed money to build. I will discuss this in more detail later in this chapter.
- **Forced Surrender and Theft of Intellectual Property**: As a condition of doing business in China, companies are required to surrender their intellectual property. Because of the vast market China represented, they reluctantly agreed; however, market conditions are changing, and companies now realize they made a deal with the devil. There is also outright theft of intellectual property that occurs at university research centers and elsewhere.
- **Graft and Influence Peddling**: When the truth finally comes out, we will discover that China has acquired power and influence on a global scale, using it to dominate international markets.
- **Violent Takeover of Hong Kong and Threats to Take Over Taiwan**: Reminders of the fact that China is an aggressor nation that poses a global threat.
- **Deployment of Invasive Corporate Spying Technology**: The world is waking up to China's invasive technologies, as witnessed by the banning of social media company TikTok and telecommunications company Huawei.
- **China's Threat to Attack Taiwan**: This could pose a significant threat to the global semiconductor market, potentially leading to a virtual shutdown of the worldwide supply chain. That's because virtually all our modern technology depends on semiconductors to work. As a result, measures have been taken to restrict China's access to the latest semiconductor technology.

FOURTH: NEIGHBORING NATIONS ALIGNED AGAINST CHINA

The nations depicted in the graphic that follows are all U.S. Allies who stand with the U.S. because they see China as a threat to their sovereignty. However, the most critical nation in the region is not officially a U.S. ally. And, it is not a friend of China. That nation is India. India and China have a long-standing border dispute. And India represents the most significant deterrent in the region to Chinese aggression.

- **India's *Necklace of Diamonds* vs. China's *String of Pearls*:** These terms refer to a string of strategic seaports that both nations have developed in the region of the Indian Ocean to prevent either nation from achieving strategic control over vital trade routes. It is possible that, in this regard, India has outsmarted China. I say this because India's ports, which it has either built or negotiated access to, were secured because all those countries see China as a threat.

By contrast, the ports that China has either built or gained access to through deceptive means are now backfiring on them. As part of its Belt and Road Initiative (BRI), China loaned money to surrounding nations for infrastructure projects, luring them into a debt trap that allowed China to take control of their seaports.

China's tactics are now out in the open, driving countries in the region away from China and toward infrastructure projects and strategic alliances with India, rather than with China. China's deceptive and hostile actions have backfired on them and exposed them for the pariah they are. Not only is naval security in the region impacted by China's underhanded actions, but they also threaten the success of the BRI, a vitally important initiative.

China does nothing without a deceptive ulterior motive, and more and more countries are realizing this. However, this strategy is beginning to backfire on China. And it may well be the second nail in China's coffin.

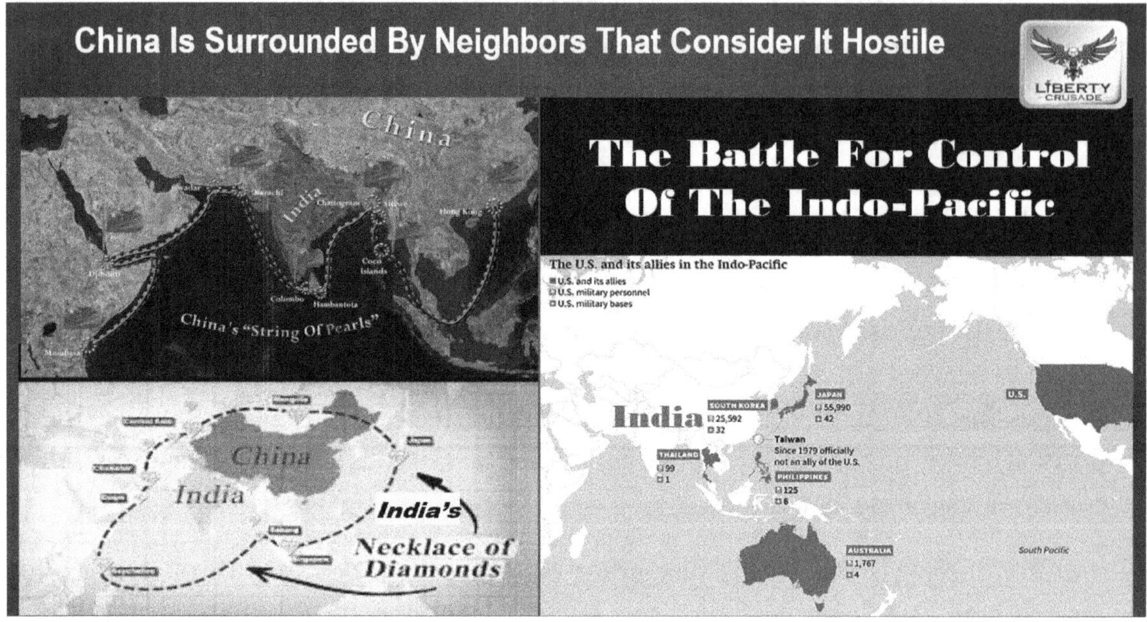

FIFTH: VULNERABILITY OF SUPPLY LINE

- **The Strait of Malacca**: This is a choke point that could threaten China under the right circumstances. (see graphic on the following page)
- **Issues with completion of the Belt and Road Initiative (BRI):** This was caused by China's predatory actions.

A nation's economic security depends on its access to natural resources, which form the basis of all wealth. As we have discussed, natural resources are converted into manufactured goods, which are then sold and converted into money. This money pays for developing the nation and for buying power and influence at every level of society.

China may appear to be sitting in the proverbial catbird seat, but it is a precarious seat. Any major industrial nation depends on energy, and in that regard, China finds itself in a less-than-ideal situation. It imports 75% of its oil. The oil supply could be cut off if, for some reason, the Strait of Malacca and other straits in the Indian Ocean were to be closed to it. Estimates state that in such an event, their economy would come to a screeching halt within 90 days.

Additionally, 53% of China's GDP depends on manufacturing and trade, which in turn depend on access to the same supply lines as the oil. Surrounded by nations that view China as a hostile predator, supply lines are vulnerable.

Additionally, there is the issue of China's long-term goal of global dominance, which hinges on the success of its BRI. Without access to vital natural resources in the Middle East and Africa, China's aspirations for global dominance appear somewhat questionable.

As I mentioned earlier, China is destined to fall and become a regional power. I hope that when that happens, the CCP and the financial elite lose their grip on China, and the people of China are set free. For those of you who don't know, China has one of the largest underground Christian churches in the world.

I have faith that God will liberate the Chinese people, and China will no longer be the aggressive nation it is now. There are still other issues that threaten China's future success, and some of them are potentially very serious.

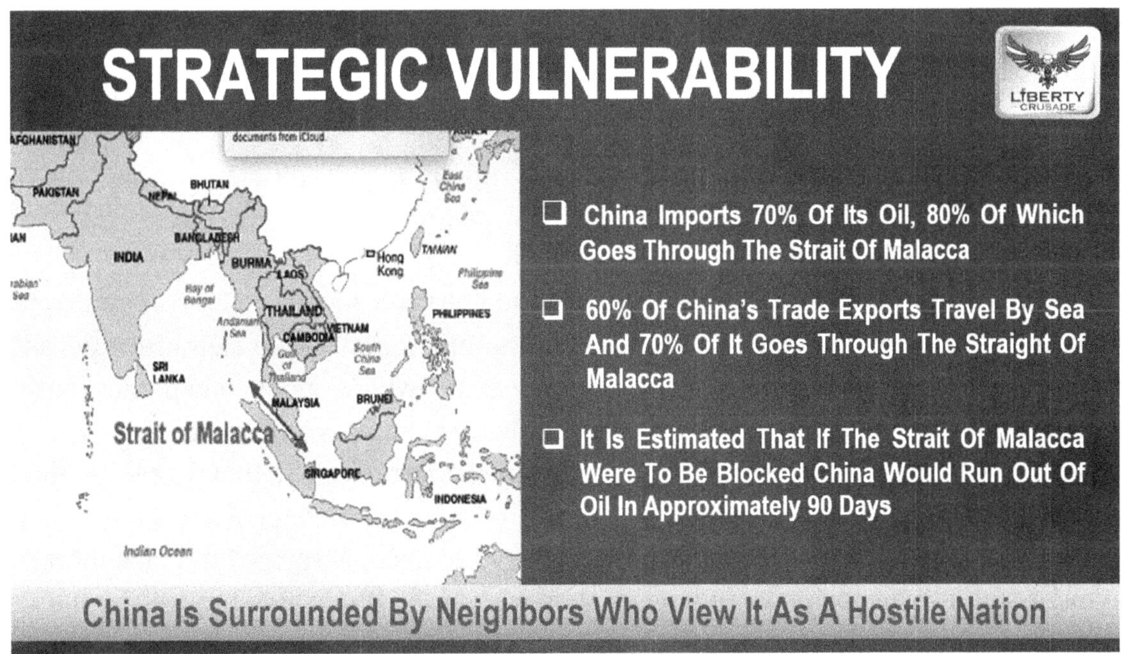

SIXTH: ECOLOGICAL ISSUES

- **Water Crisis:** China has 20% of the world's population and only 6% of the water.
- **Surface Water**: 26% is unusable for human consumption.
- **Groundwater:** 46% is unusable for human consumption.
- **Water Distribution Problem**: Prone to severe flooding in the South and droughts in the North. 80% of the water is in the South, and is needed in the populated North.
- **Dams Causing Severe Flooding:** 94,000 Mao Zedong-era dams are failing.
- **Food Security:** Five out of seventeen of China's dynasties fell because of famine.

China's disregard for water pollution has exacerbated an already serious situation. And their dams have caused more problems than they have solved.

SEVENTH: CATASTROPHIC DEMOGRAPHIC CRISIS

- **Aging Population:** China has one of the world's oldest populations.
- **Social Issues:** By 2030, there will be more people of retirement age than those of working age.
- **Labor Shortages:** By 2050, the population will be half of what it is now, down from 1.4 billion to 650 million.
- **Exodus from China:** With no immigration into China to replace them.

EIGHTH: REAL ESTATE CRISIS

Real estate represents 33% of China's GDP, and the market is in crisis! The real estate giant Evergrande has defaulted, and the Chinese Community Party had to step in to prevent a total collapse! The crisis emanates from a Ponzi scheme, where people buy homes that are yet to be built and are forced to start making mortgage payments immediately!

But corrupt builders leverage buyers' money to start new projects so that people are forced to make mortgage payments on properties that are often not started for years and may never be completed. This caused the real estate protest, where people refused to make mortgage payments until their houses were built or they were at least given assurances by the CCP that they would be built!

NINTH: REDISTRIBUTION OF THE GLOBAL SUPPLY CHAIN

China currently controls 28% of global manufacturing. Approximately 53% of China's GDP is based on manufacturing and trade, and several factors threaten a significant loss of both, with a severe impact on the country's GDP.

- **Manufacturers Pulling Out of China**: For example, Apple is relocating its Foxconn iPhone production plant, which employs 100,000 people, and many other companies are following suit.
- **International Investment Has Dried Up**: Investors recognize that the world is moving away from further globalization and transitioning to decentralized regional manufacturing facilities. It is significantly affecting China's future economic outlook negatively.

- **China Has Caused Severe Disruptions in the Global Supply Chain:** As a result, the world is deglobalizing, and consequently, factories in China are closing in droves. Contributing factors include COVID-19 lockdowns, rolling blackouts due to energy shortages, and labor shortages resulting from an aging population. Disillusioned workers are leaving the cities and returning to their villages, or immigrating to neighboring countries.

The net of this situation is that the world is waking up to the reality that China can no longer be allowed to dominate the global supply chain. It must be distributed to multiple nations around the world, and the economic implications for China are devastating. China is headed into the sunset, never to dominate the world again. Between real estate, manufacturing, and trade, 86% of China's GDP is expected to suffer a significant and potentially devastating decline.

TENTH: VITAL SIGNIFICANCE OF THE BELT AND ROAD INITIATIVE (BRI)

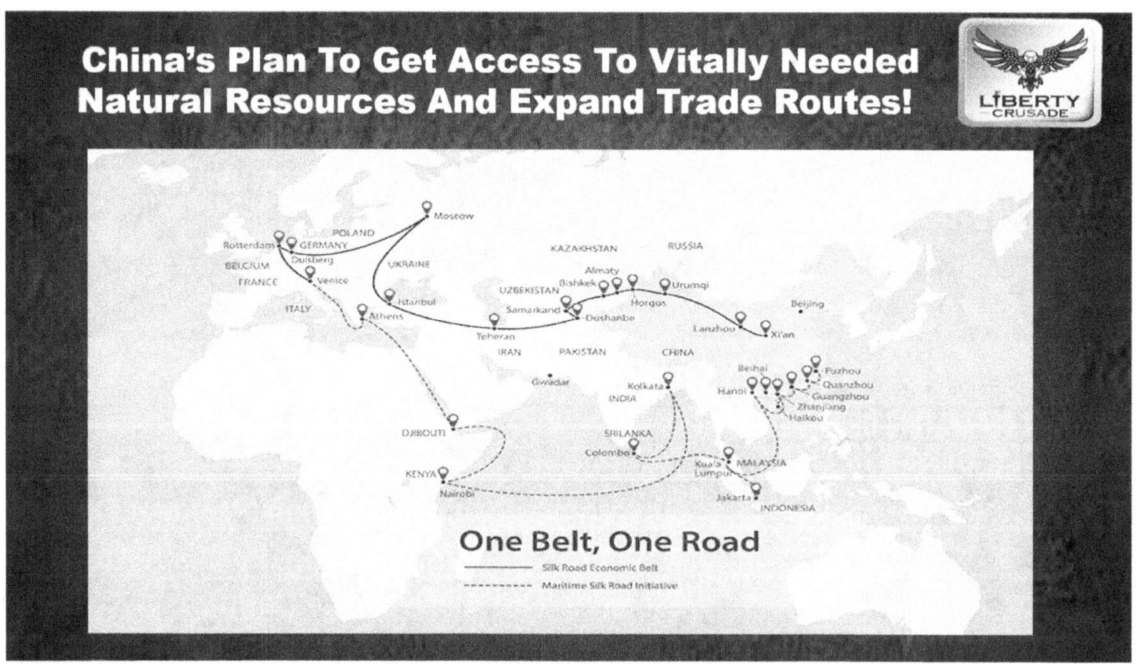

There is nothing new under the sun, and to understand what China is trying to accomplish with its BRI, we need to go back to the Colonial Era. Examine the graphic above, which depicts China's Belt and Road Initiative, and compare it to the next graphic, which illustrates Britain's Colonial Empire at its peak. Let's see what conclusions we draw.

The BRI has no relevance to North or South America; therefore, focus your attention on Europe, Asia, the Middle East, and Africa. China seeks a trade route to these four geographic regions of the world because they contain over 80% of the world's population and a corresponding share of global trade. Add to that the vast natural resources in Africa and the Middle East. It should come as no surprise that the BRI is China's master plan for world dominance, just like it was Britain's during the Colonial period.

If the U.S. and Europe want to maintain their global power, they had better pay attention to this part of the world. China has already made significant inroads into Africa. However, as I have maintained, ultimately the BRI is destined to fail. China will collapse economically and be unable to complete the project. The world is in a race to control the vast resources in Africa. Later, we will discuss just how important Africa is to the world's future.

HOW AND WHY THE U.S. WILL FALL AND THEN RISE LIKE THE PHOENIX

Like China, the U.S. is now considered a rogue nation. What? How can that be? America is the hope of the world. It once was, and soon it will be again. We must first break the financial elite shadow government's hold. Let's take a step back in history to see how we arrived at our current position.

The Year is 1945, World War II has ended, and America is the champion that saved the world from the grip of the Nazis. We are heroes, and there is no nation the world trusts more than the United States of America. In addition, Europe has suffered widespread destruction. But America emerged from the war richer than ever. America was the only nation in the world with the resources needed to rebuild a ravaged world.

So, the countries of the world met at Bretton Woods and conferred on the U.S. the status of the World's reserve currency. A brief explanation for those who might not know the significance of being the world's reserve currency. To conduct international trade, there must be a stable currency against which the values of all other currencies compare. They agreed that the currency was the U.S. dollar. Consequently, all international commodity purchases are made using the internationally agreed-upon stable currency, the gold-backed U.S. dollar.

That arrangement has been in place since 1945, but the U.S. has abused that privilege and, in the process, harmed the economies of the nations of the world. The harm we have done expresses itself in two ways:

1. When the U.S. abandoned the gold standard, no longer tying its currency to gold, under Nixon in 1971, it ceased being a stable currency. Meaning, the financial elite that had hijacked the U.S. economy were free to run the FED printing presses 24/7/365 days a year, devaluing the U.S. dollar. That meant that the dollar was now a fiat currency backed by nothing instead of the stable currency it was intended to be. Effectively, the banker gangsters had breached the terms of the Bretton Woods Agreement. Still, even a fiat dollar was more stable than most other currencies. So the world tolerated what the U.S. had done, at least for the time being.

   Then, in 1974, in what has been dubbed the "Money Laundering Deal," Saudi Arabia and the U.S. signed what is commonly referred to as the Petrodollar Deal. Under the terms of the deal, Saudi Arabia agreed to sell oil exclusively in U.S. dollars in exchange for U.S. military, security, and economic development. The banker gangsters had effectively pulled off a financial coup. To buy oil, which is essential to all technologically advanced economies, nations of the world now must continue using the U.S. dollar. The dollar was no longer backed by gold. It was subject to fluctuations in inflation and deflation, which negatively impacted the economies of those countries.

2. The U.S. used the dollar as a weapon against nations that adopted policies the U.S. felt were against its interests, which meant policies that were in opposition to the interests of the financial elite's central banking system. U.S. leverage was exerted against our adversaries by imposing sanctions on them, which effectively froze their assets and prevented or hindered international trade. Such sanctions have been used against North Korea, Iran, and Russia, and other nations, effectively making America a bully, or, as seen through the eyes of many countries, a rogue nation just like China.

Additionally, even though the U.S. government will adamantly deny it, any country that threatened U.S. interests in any serious way, or should I say the interests of the central bank banker gangsters, was not only sanctioned but was subject to experiencing the wrath of the U.S. military. The point at hand: Iraq was offered the same oil deal as Saudi Arabia, but Saddam turned it down. Today, Saudi Arabia is one of the wealthiest nations in the world, and Saddam's body is rotting in a grave. Iraq is in shambles, and its currency is virtually worthless.

More recently, Muammar Gaddafi, the leader of Libya, was attempting to coordinate an alliance of Middle Eastern and African nations to adopt a gold-backed currency. Along came Hillary, and the Arab Spring, which destroyed all the Middle East. Coincidence? Remember, in politics, there are no coincidences. *If it happened, then you can bet it was planned that way.* History has repeatedly shown us that any person or nation threatening the Central Banking System's control over the global economy will be dealt with summarily. The examples being Lincoln, Kennedy, Saddam, Gaddafi, and who knows how many others.

The shadow government of the global elite controls America, and as long as that exists, our politicians are irrelevant; they are nothing but pawns. America is not a republic, not a democracy, not a free nation, but a uniparty Communist dictatorship. The Federal Reserve controls U.S. domestic policy, and the United Nations and the International Monetary Fund regulate international policy. Soon, the chains of slavery will be broken, and America will lead the world into a better tomorrow, where the world experiences peace and prosperity, the likes of which it has never experienced. However, for that to happen, both China and the U.S. must collapse, triggering a global monetary crisis. That is the only way we can take away the ability of the banker gangsters to print the worthless fiat currency that enslaves the world!

> The modern banking system manufactures money out of nothing.
> The process is perhaps the most astounding piece of sleight of hand that was ever invented. Banking was conceived in iniquity and born in sin. Bankers own the earth.
> Take it away from them, but leave them the power to create money and control credit, and with the flick of a pen, they will create enough money to buy it back again...
> But if you want to continue being the slaves of bankers and pay the cost of your own slavery, let them continue to create money and to control credit.
> Sir Josiah Stamp, Director and President of the Bank of England during the 1920s

China abused the power of being in control of the global supply chain, and the U.S. has abused the power that comes with being the world's reserve currency. So, God has orchestrated events that are removing that power from both countries. Both nations have proven to be unreliable stewards. Under the economic system which God is about to birth, no one nation or, for that matter, group of nations, will be endowed with enough power to control the world. Power will be distributed more evenly and equitably. However, how that will be done is the topic for another chapter. Don't worry, God has a plan, but for now, let's move on.

HOW AND WHY THE PRIVILEGED STATUS OF BEING THE WORLD'S RESERVE CURRENCY IS BEING TAKEN FROM THE U.S.

Let's take another trip back in history and see where this process started. The process may have started as far back as the assassination of Kennedy or even further. For decades, the U.S. has abused its power as the World's reserve currency. As discussed, it ran its printing presses 24/7/365 a year, creating currency inflation and devaluation. It placed sanctions on any country that dared oppose U.S. policies.

On November 22, 1963, President Kennedy joined Abraham Lincoln as a martyr for the cause of liberty and freedom. Lincoln had given the nation an interest-free currency, the *Greenback,* and for that, the financial elite orchestrated his assassination. Eight British spies were hanged. Kennedy represented a quadruple threat because he had:

- Issued Silver Certificates to replace the dollar and put the FED out of business!

- Refused the demands of the Military Industrial Complex to commit more ground troops to the Vietnam War!
- Taken steps to strip the CIA and other intelligence organizations of much of their power.
- Begun to implement an entirely new financial system called the *National Economic Security and Recovery Act* (NESARA). More on NESARA shortly.

Then came the assassination of President John F. Kennedy. By sealing the documents, they hid the truth of what happened on that infamous day from the American people. I believe the documents would have shown that:

- Oswald was a patsy.
- The financial elite, elements in both the CIA and Pentagon, orchestrated Kennedy's assassination.
- Johnson was their puppet, put in the Presidency to reverse the policies Kennedy had put in place. I say this based on the fact that he orchestrated the removal of the silver certificates from circulation. He authorized the false flag event, *The Bay of Token*, discussed in an earlier chapter, to justify committing 100,000 troops to the Vietnam War. A war we later learned, based on the release of *The Pentagon Papers*, was a war for profit intended to drive the U.S. deep into debt. The CIA and other intelligence agencies kept their power.

If I were at the racetrack, I would call this the "Trifecta" because there are no sheer coincidences here. As Roosevelt said, "In politics, there are no coincidences. If it happened, you can bet it was planned that way."

The financial elite are not as smart as they think they are. They leave footprints in the sand that allow us to piece together their actions, not only tracking them but also predicting their future actions. What am I referring to? Sun Tzu says:

To secure ourselves against defeat lies not in our own hands, but the opportunity of defeating the enemy is provided by the enemy himself.

The enemy has repeatedly employed the same tactics, thereby exposing their plans and rendering themselves vulnerable to defeat. The point at hand: the assassinations of Presidents Lincoln and Kennedy, the events of 9/11, which led to the deaths of Saddam and Gaddafi, and the destruction of the Middle East in the ensuing wars. What all these events have in common is that they were all moves on the chessboard to protect the interests of the financial elite shadow government that controls all the nations of the world.

The only possible exception to this statement is Russia, which is the only major nation in the world without a central bank controlled by the Rothschilds. Throughout its history, Russia opposed globalization and the Rothschilds. It seems to me that, at this juncture in history, Russia, our past and future enemy, is our friend. Why? Because both Putin and Trump are for deglobalization and in opposition to the Rothschild central banking system. The adage "My enemy's enemy is my friend" may currently apply to the relationship between the U.S. and Russia.

Russia is currently at war with Ukraine. Putin was maneuvered into starting the war just like Japan was maneuvered into attacking Pearl Harbor, giving the U.S. the excuse it needed to enter World War II. NATO, which the G7 controls, is doing everything it can to bring Russia down, just like they have every country that has ever opposed the Rothschild central banking system. Ask yourself if it is possible that the mainstream news, which Trump calls the *Fake News*, is lying to you about the war in Ukraine. Is it possible that, instead of being the victim, Ukraine is a hub for money laundering, child trafficking, and biolabs? Do your research. You may be surprised at what you find.

I want to raise a point for later discussion. The U.S. is part of the G7, which comprises the seven wealthiest countries in the world. They are: 1) the United States, 2) the UK, which, from our inception, has been our mortal enemy, 3) France, 4) Italy, home of the Vatican, 5) Germany, 6) Canada, and 7) Japan.

Besides the United States, the first five nations were European monarchies. As their monarchies fell, these nations took their vast fortunes and birthed the central banking system that today enslaves the world. They all appear in the Book of Revelation as part of the combination beast that is responsible for the tribulation. The two remaining members of the G7 are Canada, which, under Mark Carney, appears to be controlled by the financial elite, and Japan, which, due to our interconnected trade, may be an ally. The point is that the U.S. is sleeping with the enemy, and we'd better wake up.

The following quote is repeated from a previous chapter. Still, I think it is essential to revisit it in the context of this chain of events. The seventh fleet at Pearl Harbor was the bait for Japan to attack America, so we had an excuse to enter World War II.

> **The question was how should we maneuver them (Japan) into firing the first shot...**
> **it was desirable to make sure the Japanese be the ones to do this**
> **so that there should remain no doubt as to who were the aggressors.**
> Henry Stimson, U.S. Secretary of War prior to World War II, Nov. 25, 1941

Japan didn't just wake up one day and decide to attack the U.S. No. They were baited into attacking. Neither did Putin wake up one morning and decide to attack Ukraine. There were several reasons why Putin attacked Ukraine. Still, the one most Americans will be able to identify with is the parallel between the Cuban Missile Crisis and the threat posed by Ukraine joining NATO and putting missiles on its border, just minutes from Moscow. From a Biblical perspective, Russia will play a critical role in World War III, but this is not that time. The Ukraine war is not a war of expansion, as we are led to believe. Russia will do what it must in order to protect its interests and then go back to sleep until it reemerges when we enter the book of Revelation, which is not now. (Remember the earlier biblical reference to Russia as the "sleeping bear")

Then there is this from FBI Agent Ted Gunderson (in charge of the Los Angeles Bureau), who was thought to have said, "The CIA is behind most of our terrorist attacks."

> **What the CIA has done to this country is unbelievable.**
> **The CIA is behind most, if not all, of our terrorist attacks: We had Pan Am 103.**
> **We had the USS Cole; we had Oklahoma City!**

By the way, the Oklahoma City Bombing and the Patriot Act both resulted in the passage of draconian laws that took away many of our rights!

It is becoming evident that unless we stand united and take back our country, most of us will die, and the survivors will be slaves. Sun Szu refers to our current situation as being on *death ground*, of which he says:

> **Confront them with annihilation, and they will then survive;**
> **plunge them into a deadly situation, and they will then live.**
> **When people fall into danger, they are then able to survive for victory.**

People don't fight back against their government until they feel they have no other choice. We are at that point. All we must do is stand united, and we will regain our freedom.

WE ARE ON DEATH GROUND: EITHER WE STAND UNITED AND DEFEAT OUR ENEMY,
OR MOST OF US WILL DIE, AND THE SURVIVORS WILL BE SLAVES

Once again, we need to take a step back and see where this process started. What I am about to lay out will stretch your mind because, at first glance, it seems to be a dichotomy. However, it is a brilliant military strategy, and we need to understand that it threatens the whole of the Earth.

UNDERSTANDING THE ENEMY'S ENDGAME STRATEGY

PHASE I: BRITISH SUPREMACY

During the Colonial Period, European monarchs, particularly England, in concert with the Catholic Church, embarked on the largest land grab in human history. They acquired approximately 75% of the world's land. Then they implemented laws that effectively denied the masses the right to own land. As previously discussed, we became **renters** at the pleasure of the global financial elite, our land barons.

PHASE II: SEED POWER TO THE U.S.

This would enable them to protect their landholdings by utilizing the U.S. military as their police force and using the dollar to enforce policies favorable to the financial elite.

PHASE III: SEED POWER TO CHINA

To create a hybrid super-capitalist, communist economy with the innovation of capitalism and the control of communism! I repeat a quote provided earlier:

The Rockefeller File is not fiction. It is a compact, powerful, and frightening
presentation of what may be the most important story of our lifetime – the drive of the
Rockefellers and their allies to create a one-world government combining
super-capitalism and communism under the same tent, all under their control...
not one has dared reveal the most vital part of the Rockefeller story:
that the Rockefellers and their allies have, for at least fifty years,

[cont'd next page]

PHASE IV: COLLAPSE THE ECONOMIES OF BOTH CHINA AND THE UNITED STATES

They plan to cause a worldwide financial crash, using the fear and panic it creates to make us accept their totalitarian New World Order, promising economic stability. **That is a lie from the pit of hell.**

Don't panic; their plans will backfire. We are in the Book of Esther, where the enemy's plans backfire and bring them down. Unlike with other financial collapses, we will wake up and refuse to participate in our slavery. We will strip them of their ability to print currency. And that will utterly take away their ability to control the nations and people of the world.

Here is how it will come down:

- Once the economy collapses, whistleblowers will expose their corruption. The masses will stand united and demand the removal of their puppets from all their positions of power. They will be convicted of treason!
- Governments, banks, and corporations will collapse worldwide, and power will return to "We the People."

America will rise from the ashes and lead the world into an unparalleled period of peace and prosperity. How that will happen is the subject of our next chapter.

CLOSING STATEMENTS

I am flabbergasted when considering all that has transpired. There are still people who believe everything is hunky-dory. They say the stock market is booming, and the economy is on the path to recovery. Nothing could be further from the reality of the situation. We are in the midst of the biggest financial collapse the world has ever seen. But contrary to what most people think, that is a good thing, no, it is essential. Like Joseph Stamp said:

Remember, an enemy's greatest strength is also his greatest weakness. The enemy's greatest strength is his control of the monetary system. That is why they must utterly collapse the financial system and destroy the fiat U.S. dollar. Only then can the world function under God's economic system, with commodities at its core. Unlike manipulated fiat currency. China must lose control of the supply chain. No nation or group of nations can be allowed to control world affairs the way the U.S., China, and the global elite have.

HOW THE HOUSE OF CARDS WILL COME TUMBLING DOWN

When COVID-19 afflicted the world, the U.S. became a pariah like China. There was more money printed in a couple of years than had been printed in our entire history. Justified based on the lie that the U.S. and the world had to be protected by shutting down. Small businesses and churches around the world were forced to shut down. But go figure.

Big-box mega-infection-spreading stores were allowed to remain open. Yet a benevolent, no, a corrupt government stepped in and sent *stimulus checks* to the public to keep them afloat. No, but to make them indebted. I should note that the shadow government of virtually every country in the world did likewise. After all, you never want to fail to take advantage of a crisis.

This resulted in placing all nations in a situation where they could only service their debt at interest rates of 0% to 1%. They set the trap. Enter the FED with its interest rate hikes, and the death spiral, which leads to the global financial collapse, was triggered. BRICS, the consortium comprising Brazil, Russia, India, China, and South Africa, was already in place. Still, it was about to enter hyperdrive and potentially undermine the U.S. dollar. For those unfamiliar with BRICS, it represents an effort to trade oil outside the U.S. dollar.

BRICS formed because the nations involved sought to break free from the U.S. and the Petrodollar Agreement, which required them to purchase inflated U.S. dollars to buy oil. Using the fiat dollar was causing their economies to experience inflation. The cost of servicing their debt posed a serious threat to the economies, exacerbated by their ties to the dollar. So, they had no choice but to back their economies with gold and escape the negative effects imposed by being forced to transact oil purchases in U.S. dollars.

This entire process has gone full circle. No longer can the collapse of the U.S. dollar be avoided; it is imminent. The final nail in the coffin of the U.S. dollar occurred on January 9,

2024, when Saudi Arabia, Iran, and the United Arab Emirates joined BRICS. When this happened, it spelled the death of the dollar. We are just waiting for a printed obituary.

Ask yourself this: why in the world would any nation voluntarily choose to transact business in a fiat, inflating, virtually worthless U.S. dollar when they could conduct business based on the gold-backed currencies of the BRICS nations? Obviously, no one in their right mind would make such a decision. So, the U.S. dollar is dead. We are just waiting for the funeral, if we are to have any semblance of a controlled crash. In that case, the nations of the world will need a few months to divest themselves of U.S. Treasuries and completely abandon the dollar.

No crystal ball here, but if I were a betting man, I would say that it will take a few months. So, my prediction for sometime in 2026 is one of extreme volatility. An avalanche of whistle-blowers will follow the collapse of the dollar, which will wake up even the living dead.

That will cause people all over the world to realize that it is true, the global elite do intend on killing most of us and enslaving the survivors. At that point, God will use Trump to lead the U.S. and the world into God's new economic system, ushering in an era of unprecedented peace and prosperity. You may ask how that is possible if the dollar is dead? Don't worry. At the appropriate time, the U.S. will join BRICS. We have plenty of gold. Trump went on a capitulation tour in 2016 and 2017. Watch the documentary, *The Greatest Show On Earth, Part 1,* and you will understand that this is a true statement.

We will find out that, yes, in fact, the 2020 election was stolen, and we have not had an honest election for over 100 years. That realization will be the catalyst that will drain the swamp. Then, like India before us, we will stand united and take back our freedom. A better world is about to be born. For how that happens, read on, and you will find out how and why the kingdoms of man must fall. Also, you'll learn that God planned for the U.S. to lead the world into His economic system.

CHAPTER 9

WHY THE KINGDOMS OF MAN MUST FALL
to Make Way for God's Kingdom

TOPICS COVERED IN THIS CHAPTER:

- THE FIVE KINGDOMS OF MAN MUST FALL
- HOW AMERICA BECAME A DEMOCRACY
  AND WHAT THAT MEANS
- WHAT IT MEANS TO BE A REPUBLIC
- THE SIGNIFICANCE OF THE ACT OF 1871
- THE ENEMY'S CONTROL MECHANISMS

AMERICA IS EXPERIENCING A 1776 MOMENT

WAIT—THAT IS NOT CORRECT. The *world* is experiencing a 1776 moment! As Sun Tzu would say, "We are on death ground, and the only outcome is victory or death!" I choose victory! What do you choose?

> In the time of those kings, the God of heaven will set up a kingdom that will never be destroyed, nor will it be left to another people. It will crush all those kingdoms and bring them to an end, but it will itself endure forever.
>
> Daniel 2:44 (NIV)

So, what kingdoms is God referring to in the passage above? He is referring to the kingdoms of man, all of which, in one fashion or another, are flawed, resulting in division and oppression of different sorts. Let's start our discussion by briefly identifying the principal governmental systems of man.

THE KINGDOMS OF MAN

- MONARCHY

- OLIGARCHY

- AUTHORITARIANISM

- TOTALITARIANISM

- DEMOCRACY

These kingdoms all show, to different extents, abuse of power, resource hoarding, and internal division. That invariably leads to rivalry, division, oppression, war, and economic and social instability, eventually resulting in societal collapse.

Conversely, God's economic system is based on unity, sharing of resources, respect for one another and all of God's creation, peace and harmony, and brotherly love! God's governmental system is as different from man's as night is from day. God is about to take us out from under the oppression of man's flawed governmental systems and into His own, based on unity, brotherly love, and a deep understanding of the true meaning of peace, happiness, prosperity, and unity.

Let's briefly examine each of man's governmental systems and discover the flaws that God was referring to in Daniel 2:44.

MONARCHY

This is a system where power is vested in a hierarchical structure composed of a king and queen, along with their nobles and knights. They derive their absolute power from the family lineage! (a supposed royal bloodline) The general population, referred to as peasants, has absolutely no say in the government, cannot own land, and has no rights whatsoever except those arbitrarily granted by the monarch.

A monarchy is the governmental system our forefathers fled in search of freedom of religion and the pursuit of life, liberty, and happiness. This monarchical system originated in Europe and the Middle East. As the monarchies fell, they took their vast wealth. They established the maniacal Central Banking System that holds the world today in *slavery without chains,* controlled by an oppressive monetary system.

The most powerful of the Monarchies was arguably England, the nation from which our forefathers fled when they came to America. As we have discussed, their system of slavery was based on what they referred to as "British Free Trade," which was in reality a calculated system of slavery and oppression!

The following quotes highlight the British Free Trade's primary means of oppression:

**It is the most gigantic system of slavery the world has yet seen,
and therefore, it is that freedom gradually disappears from every country over which
England is enabled to obtain control.**
Henry C. Carey, an economic advisor to Abraham Lincoln

Note: That system of slavery continues to this day as Chinese Free Trade!

**Free trade with its fiat currency shaves down the workingman's labor first, and then
scales down his pay by rewarding him in a worthless and depreciated State currency.**
William McKinley, October 4, 1892

**Slavery is but the owning of labor and carries with it the care of laborers, while the
European plan (British Free Trade System) is that capital shall control labor by
controlling wages..."**
Hazard Circular, July 1862 [Emphasis added]

Think about the rampant inflation being inflicted on us. There's no question we are in a debt trap that is, in fact, a system of slavery without chains! We'll remain under the control of the European monarchs we sought freedom from unless we abolish the Federal Reserve's unjust and illegal tax system.

OLIGARCHY

An oligarchical governmental system is one in which power is concentrated in a small number of individuals, families, or institutions. Despite any illusion of individual rights, it is *government by the wealthy.* As they say, money buys power, and power corrupts, and absolute power corrupts absolutely!

Russia is commonly thought of as an Oligarchy with Putin at its head over an assortment of wealthy Oligarchs who control the economy and influence the government! Ask yourself if you would like to immigrate to Russia and live under its oppressive government. I'm guessing the answer is no.

AUTHORITARIAN

This is a single-party government with a strong man in leadership who wields near-dictatorial power. A modern-day example of an Authoritarian government is China, with the Chinese Communist Party (CCP) headed by Xi Jinping. China's rise as a global superpower was orchestrated by the financial elite global shadow government, which controls the global central banking system that enslaves the world in a debt trap.

If given the choice, would you like to move to China and live under constant surveillance? There, you would be subject to a social credit score and live in a country that imprisons people based on their religious practices and then harvests their organs for sale to the highest bidder. Again, I'm guessing the answer is no!

TOTALITARIAN

A totalitarian government is analogous to Authoritarianism, with the distinction that it is based on a religious state ideology that dictates daily tasks, beliefs, and freedoms. As an example of what it means to be a zealot, both the Koran and the Iranian government endorse and reward the killing of what they call "infidels" (non-believers).

And under Sharia Law in Iran, women have virtually no rights. These beliefs and customs are the opposite of the governmental system of God, which is based on peace, harmony, and brotherly love. Who would want to live under such an oppressive governmental system? Based on the ongoing social protest in Iran, it is evident that the people of Iran want freedom from the oppression of their totalitarian zealot government!

DEMOCRACY

A democracy is a form of government where the public elects leaders and supposedly has a say in the government, enjoying certain prescribed freedoms. Wealth accumulates over time, leading to a corporatocracy of banks, corporations, and a large, corrupt government. These entities use their vast wealth to buy power and influence in every stratum of society and become a shadow government that is the real ruling power of the nation.

We have been duped into thinking that America was founded as a democracy and that a democracy is a system of government where there is freedom from tyranny. Neither of these statements is true! America was founded as a republic—a government of the people by the people for the people! Knowing the flaws of democracy, our forefathers dubbed democracy a "Mobocracy." This is because they recognized the fundamental flaws in democracies, which inevitably result in division and anarchy.

The founders of America understood that every democracy ever devised eventually suffered from the same fatal error. Ultimately, those least willing or least able to work (the Mob) would realize that they could extort money from the public coffers. From that moment on, those people vote for those who promise the most handouts, and a system of vested interest takes over the government. Then division and anarchy (mob rule) set in and festers until the nation descends into a debt trap that tears the country apart from the inside out, culminating in anarchy!

This is the trajectory that the Shadow Government is taking America, but God has other plans for America! He intends to expose and remove the shadow government that currently controls America and *restore the Republic*. Then, He plans to use a restored America to usher in His governmental system! Stand firm! God's knocking at the door, ready to free the captives and use America. Please don't take my word for this.

The democracy will cease to exist when you take away
from those who are willing to work and give to those who will not.
Cal Thomas

Once those least willing or able to work realize that they can obtain money from the public coffers, democracy is lost. Because they will not vote for what is in the nation's best interest, but rather for who will give them the most handouts. At that point, the debt trap is set, and it is just a matter of time until the democracy degrades into a *Mobocracy*. Rather than being based on constitutional law, Mobocracy is based on the vested interest of special interest groups!

We can either have democracy in this country,
or we can have great wealth concentrated in the hands of a few,
but we can't have both.
Louis Brandeis, Supreme Court Justice

Isn't that precisely what has happened with the government's endless array of unfunded entitlements, most egregious of which are the handouts to the mass of illegal immigrants invading our nation, with who knows what malevolent intent!

Democracies have ever been spectacles of turbulence and contention;
have ever been found incompatible with personal security or the
rights of property; and have, in general, been as short in their lives
as they have been violent in their deaths.
James Madison

Here's how things go when the government levies an illegal IRS, a federal tax, and an unlawful personal property tax, enabling property seizure for unpaid taxes. This also explains government-mandated mortgages and credit cards that unlawfully levy compound interest on outstanding balances each month and year. That is a breach of the *usury laws* put in place to protect us from the implementation of the very corporatocracy that today enslaves us in their debt trap.

CONCLUSION

America and all the nations of the world are puppets of a *global shadow government* that controls humanity by forming a corporatocracy that controls us cradle to grave by combining the power of *big government, big banks, and international corporations.* They control the monetary system and write the laws that impose a legal dictatorship on us!

> I see in the near future a crisis approaching that unnerves me
> and causes me to tremble for the safety of my country. . .
> corporations have been enthroned
> and an era of corruption in high places will follow,
> and the money power of the country will endeavor to prolong its reign
> by working upon the prejudices of the people
> until all wealth is aggregated in a few hands and the Republic is destroyed.
> President Abraham Lincoln, November 21, 1864,
> written in a letter to Col. William F. Elkins

Lincoln's prediction has become today's reality. It should also be noted that Lincoln referred to America not as a democracy, but as a *republic.*

> I pledge allegiance to the United States of America,
> and to the Republic for which it stands, one nation under God,
> Indivisible, with liberty and justice for all.
> As taken from The Pledge of Allegiance

I say again, America has become that which it sought to escape! Once, as Ben Franklin was leaving the Constitutional Convention, he was approached by a woman who inquired, "What form of government have you given us?"

He replied, "A republic, if you can keep it."

That seems a curious response, but there was a reason for it. You see, a republic differs from any of the other five forms of government we have discussed thus far. The framers of our Constitution referred to our republic as a "great experiment" because only this government genuinely allows self-governance by the people!

REPUBLIC

A republic is a government of the people, by the people, for the people, based on constitutional law and the Declaration of Independence. The goal is to grant freedoms and rights previously denied by the English Monarchy. A republic requires a moral, educated public, honestly informed of the issues facing the nation, and a public willing to vote based on what is in the best interest of the nation as opposed to their own vested interest! The following quotes explain how our republic was systematically transformed from a constitutional republic into a democracy, based on the majority rule of a public stripped of the values necessary to sustain a republic.

**If a nation expects to be ignorant and free, in a state of civilization,
it expects what never was and never will be.**
Thomas Jefferson, 1816

That is why today our education system, media, and politicians have become nothing but talking heads, spewing lies and misinformation, feeding us an unending stream of half-truths and out-and-out lies intended to turn the masses into immoral, passive, docile, mindless sheep! I remind you once again:

**America is like a healthy body, and its resistance is its patriotism,
its morality, and its spiritual life. If we can undermine these three areas,
America will collapse from within.**
As quoted by Ben Carson during the 2016 Republican presidential debate

Therefore, Obama said, "America is not a Christian nation." And Henry Kissinger said, "Military men are just dumb, stupid animals to be used as pawns in foreign policy."

It is also why there are no longer any moral absolutes, and the very definition of marriage is in dispute! Please make no mistake. Our core values are under attack to collapse America from within!

THE UNDOING OF THE AMERICAN CONSTITUTIONAL REPUBLIC

Two separate and distinct events in American history ended our Republic—a government *of the people, by the people, for the people*—and morphed it into a Democracy (a socialist communist order).

The first event that contributed to the undoing of the American Constitutional Republic was the **Act of 1871.** On February 21, 1871, Congress passed the Act of 1871. On this date, Congress passed an Act titled "An Act to Provide a Government for the District of Columbia," also known as the Act of 1871. It meant that Congress, without the constitutional authority to do so, created a separate form of government for the District of Columbia. This was an act of treason!

It should be noted that this same corporate governmental status is in force for the District of Columbia, the Vatican, and the City of London. (The Control Centers for The Corporation) You can read more about it by visiting the website: foundationfortruthinlaw.org, and searching for "Acts of the Forty-first Congress," Section 34, Session III, Chapters 61 and 62.

The Act of 1871 superseded the U.S. Constitution and created a new constitution, i.e., a corporate charter!

Remember, I explained that our original Constitution reads: "The Constitution *for* the United States of America." However, the altered version reads: "The Constitution *of* the United States of America" [emphasis added]. Do you notice the difference? As minor a change as this may seem, it meant that our Constitution was altered so that it no longer invoked Constitutional rights and privileges for *We the People.* It was simply a declaratory statement!

CORPORATION

The term "Corporation" refers to a legal entity that is separate and distinct from its owners. Its sole obligation is to the financial interest of its shareholders! That is why we are taxed to the point of submission and why the laws that our puppet politicians pass serve the vested interest of the financial elite and not *We the People.*

Given that the corporation is based on an illegal act, all the laws passed, and people elected or appointed under its charter are also unlawful. Consequently, the laws are subject to being expunged, and the individuals themselves behind this are subject to being removed. We will drain the swamp!

The second event responsible for the downfall of the American constitutional republic was the **Declaration of Bankruptcy in 1933.** As previously discussed, in the depths of the Great Depression, America declared bankruptcy. It became "a democracy—a socialist, communist order!"

With all offices, officials, and departments operating in a "de facto status," an administrative vacuum was created that the illegal corporation filled with an army of *unelected bureaucrats.* It is they—not our elected officials—who write the bills that systematically create the legal dictatorship that today controls the U.S.

As we have discussed, our elected politicians are just figureheads who are selected, groomed, and financed. Those figureheads are put in office to give us the illusion that we have a representative government. However, in reality, U.S. domestic policy is controlled by the Fed, and the UN-controlled IMF controls international policy.

Former FED Chairman Alan Greenspan was once a guest on PBS's *The Lehrer Report*. He was asked, "What is the proper relationship between the Chairman of the Federal Reserve and the President of the United States?" Greenspan's response, provided earlier, is shown once again in the quote below:

> **Well, first of all, the Federal Reserve is an independent agency,**
> **and that means basically that, uh, there is no other agency of government**
> **which can overrule actions that we take. In so long as that is in place ...**
> **What the relationships are, don't frankly matter.**
> Alan Greenspan, Fed Chairman

Congress and the president are just figureheads of a uni-party controlled by the shadow government of the global elite! Going back to our discussion at the beginning of this chapter, that makes America neither a republic nor a democracy. Instead, it becomes a socialist-communist order, meaning an authoritarian single-party government (like, for example, China), where we have only the illusion of having any say in our government.

Today, the sad truth is that America is utterly and entirely controlled by an unelected, dictatorial shadow government that is the enemy of all Americans! Even worse is that literally every government in the world has succumbed to the same fate. There are no longer any sovereign nations, with the possible exception of Russia, that do not have a Rothschild-controlled central bank. But remember, Russia is an oligarchy, which is just another one of the oppressive governments of man!

What this all means is that the world is at a point in time where the prophecies of Daniel 2:44 and Proverbs 29:16 will come to pass. And the corrupt global shadow government that controls the governments of men will fall, to be replaced by God's government. The world will enter an unparalleled era of peace, harmony, and prosperity!

> In the time of those kings, the God of heaven will set up a kingdom that will never be destroyed, nor will it be left to another people. It will crush all those kingdoms and bring them to an end, but it will itself endure forever.
> Daniel 2:44 (NIV)

> When the wicked are in authority, sin flourishes,
> but the godly will live to see their downfall.
> Proverbs 29:16 (NIV)

MORE GOOD NEWS

According to the Bible, all human governments are corrupt. They steal that which was meant for the righteous and hoard it for themselves! The Bible states that what a man steals must be returned, which brings us to the concept of the promised transfer of wealth. Remember, when the Israelites left Egypt, the Pharaoh and his army were defeated, and the Israelites took with them the riches of Egypt. God is not a man that He should lie. In this present time, the corrupt kingdoms of man will fall, and the ill-gotten wealth they have hoarded will be given to the righteous.

> Men do not despise a thief if he steals to satisfy his hunger when he is starving... Yet if he is caught, he must pay sevenfold, though it costs him all the wealth of his house.
> Proverbs 6:30, 31(NIV)

Soon, the oppressive tax system that binds us in a system of slavery without chains will be broken, and the wealth of the wicked will be given to the righteous! That means:

- No more central banks
- No more demonic UN
- No more selected and appointed politicians who pass laws intended to impose a legal dictatorship
- No more progressive income tax
- No more compound interest on credit card and mortgage balances

We will go back to the economic system we had when America was founded, with no illegal Fed, IRS, and no illegal income tax! Back to a time when the government was run on a simple and fair sales tax. We will get out from under the fee simple ownership real estate laws that allow a corrupt government to orchestrate financial crashes and then take our homes when we fall behind on our illegal property taxes. Instead, property tax will be abolished!

It will be hard for you to believe it until you see it, but the wealth of the wicked has been stored up, and it will be given back to *We the People*. And those that God has ordained as stewards will be given so much wealth that when the governments and corporations of the global elite fall, they will take them over and end their ability to control the spheres of influence through their control of the corrupt financial system!

Remember, an enemy's greatest strength is also always his greatest weakness. The Elite's loss of monetary control will cripple their bribery, black ops, and funding of leftist groups that cause hatred, social chaos, and economic instability. In other words, they will lose their power!

The following graphic illustrates how organized minorities (i.e., financially elite-funded organizations) consistently prevail over the unorganized, unfunded majority. However, this will no longer be the case! We will have the money, and we will prevail over them. And the voice of the people will finally be heard!

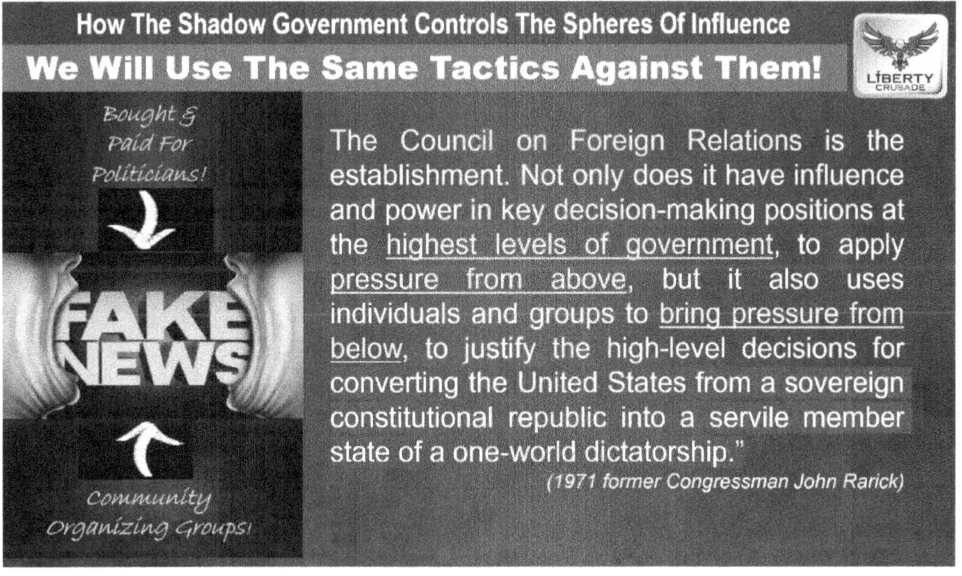

The following list outlines all the ways the financial elites have been able to influence us, as they have had the means to buy power and influence in every sphere of influence. When we regain control of the money, we will re-establish the values that made America great in the first place! We win; they lose!

THE ENEMY'S CONTROL MECHANISMS

- Infiltrate the seven spheres of influence to control every aspect of our lives.
- Drive us into unmanageable debt.
- Attack our Christian and moral values and undermine our patriotism.
- Orchestrate wars for profit that drive us into debt and kill and maim our loved ones for no other reason than greed.
- Destroy the nuclear family because it is the foundation of civilized society.
- Get control of the educational system to dumb us down and foster socialism.
- Divide us because a nation divided cannot stand.
- Infiltrate the media (Press, radio, television, motion pictures) to brainwash us.
- Promote immorality by promoting pornography in books, magazines, motion pictures, and television.
- Promote Homosexuality, same-sex marriage, and promiscuity as normal and acceptable.
- Undermine our Christian values and use social justice rhetoric to promote the philosophy that there is no absolute right and wrong, and those who believe so are intolerant, etc.

Imagine what the world will be like when we take away the money and power from the financial elite and when America returns to its founding roots based on God, country, and family. A better tomorrow awaits us—that's God's promise. And God always keeps His promises!

> So do not be afraid of them, for there is nothing concealed
> that will not be disclosed or hidden that will not be made known.
> Matthew 10:26 (NIV)

The collapse of the global monetary system is inevitable, and it will lead to the downfall of the kingdoms of man. The collapse will usher in God's governmental system and an unparalleled period of peace, prosperity, unity, and God's Harvest of Souls. Celebrate—a new day is dawning!

Once the economy collapses, whistleblowers will expose corruption, and the masses will stand united and demand their freedom. Governments, banks, and corporations will collapse worldwide. America will rise from the ashes, and God will use America to restore financial stability and create a new, more equitable governmental system! We will explore how that occurs in the next chapter.

CHAPTER 10

WHY AMERICA IS THE PROTOTYPE
for God's Governmental System

TOPICS COVERED IN THIS CHAPTER:

- AMERICA IS UNDER ABRAHAM'S COVENANT
- WHY THE WORLD IS ON THE BRINK OF A GLOBAL FINANCIAL COLLAPSE
- WHAT GOD'S GOVERNMENTAL SYSTEM LOOKS LIKE
- WHAT IS NESARA, AND WHAT IS ITS ROLE IN RESTORING THE GLOBAL ECONOMY?

AMERICA IS UNDER ABRAHAM'S COVENANT

And I will make of thee a great nation, and I will bless thee
and make thy name great; and thou shalt be a blessing:
Genesis 12:2 (KJV)

The angel of the LORD called to Abraham from heaven a second time and said,
"I swear by myself, declares the LORD, that because you have done this
and have not withheld your son, your only son, I will surely bless you
and make your descendants as numerous as the stars in the sky
and as the sand on the seashore. Your descendants will take possession of the cities of
their enemies, and through your offspring
all nations on earth will be blessed, because you have obeyed me."
Genesis 22:15-18 (NIV)

THIS SCRIPTURE DOESN'T tell us whether America is under God's Abrahamic covenant. Still, it provides us with an important indicator to look for, which is that to qualify, America would have to be a great nation (which it is), and it would have to be blessed and be a blessing (which it has been).

It is not only Israel that qualifies to be under the covenant of Abraham. The Bible says:

And other sheep I have which are not of this fold; them also I must bring, and they will
hear My voice; and there will be one flock and one shepherd.
John 10:16 (NKJV) [Emphasis Added]

- God intends that all men be saved.
- Salvation is not by bloodline but by obedience to God's commandments!
- Now is the time of the fulfillment of Abraham's covenant and God's Harvest of Souls.
- America is under Abraham's Covenant. America, more than any other nation, has been blessed and has been a blessing.

- It is the melting pot where the lost sheep came to learn to put aside their differences and to learn to live together in peace and harmony.
- America was dedicated to God on three very significant occasions.

Let's examine critical time points in history where God establishes His covenant with America:

THE YEAR: 1607

A Virginia Trading Company landed in America at what is called "First Landing." The first thing they did was cut the mast from their ship, erect a cross, and dedicate America to God.

> We do hereby dedicate this land, and ourselves, to reach the people within these
> shores with the Gospel of Jesus Christ, and to raise up Godly generations after us,
> and with these generations take the Kingdom of God to all the earth.
> May this Covenant of Dedication remain to all generations,
> as long as the earth remains, and may this Land...be Evangelist to the World.
> May all who see this Cross remember what we have done here,
> and may those who come here to inhabit join us in this Covenant,
> and this most noble work that the Holy Scriptures may be fulfilled.
> Rev. Robert Hunt's prayer over America, April 29, 1607; Cape Henry, Virginia

America's global evangelism will play a crucial role in the imminent Great Awakening.

THE YEAR: 1620

This was the year when the Pilgrims fled England in pursuit of religious freedom. Before even departing the Mayflower, they wrote and signed the Mayflower Compact.

> Having undertaken, for the Glory of God and Advancement of the Christian faith,
> and Honour of our King and Country, a Voyage to plant the first Colony
> in the northern parts of Virginia, Do by these Presents solemnly and mutually,
> in the Presence of God and one of another,
> covenant and combine ourselves together into a civil Body politick...
> Written by the pilgrims on the Mayflower,
> just off the shore of what is now Cape Cod, Massachusetts

THE YEAR: 1789

On the 1st day as a nation, President George Washington made his inaugural speech at Freedom Hall, NY, and then proceeded to St. Paul's Chapel, where he consecrated America to God.

THE SYMBOL OF AMERICA'S COVENANT WITH GOD

Contrary to what you have been told, the symbol of God's covenant with America is not the Statue of Liberty. There is a little-known, yet much older and more symbolically important statue representing the foundation upon which America was built. It is the Plymouth Monument pictured on the graphic below.

Our forefathers migrated to America to escape the tyranny of the European Monarchs and the Catholic Church, which denied them political and religious freedom. They sought to establish a government based on the Ten Commandments of God, on the principle that all men are created equal and have certain inalienable rights granted by a loving and merciful God.

NO MATTER HOW THINGS LOOK, GOD ALWAYS WINS!

The following are several tipping points in Biblical and modern-day history where it looked like all was lost until God intervened on behalf of His remnant and the impossible happened.

478 BC: KING XERXES OF PERSIA SIGNS A PROCLAMATION CONDEMNING THE JEWS TO DEATH

Long story short: Mordecai, the uncle of (Jewish) Queen Esther, had made an enemy of Haman, who tricked King Xerxes into issuing an edict condemning the Jews to death. Queen Esther risked her life by approaching the king without being summoned and orchestrated events that exposed an assassination plot against the king by Haman.

In the end, Haman was hanged on the gallows that he had built for Mordecai. And the Jews were not killed. The Israelites are under Abraham's covenant. Therefore, no plot by any man ever had a chance of ending a bloodline that God ordained.

THE RED SEA

With their backs to the Red Sea and an army threatening annihilation, God intervened and kept his covenant! In an instant of time, Pharaoh and his army were annihilated. And Egypt, the most powerful nation in the world at that time, was stripped of its power and to this day has never recovered. Touch not my anointed! God is faithful to keep his covenant.

THE BATTLE OF JERICHO

Jericho was a mighty walled city. It is believed that the wall of Jericho was so thick that six chariots could ride abreast on it at one time. Without siege equipment to break down the wall, it seemed impossible that the Israelites could breach the wall. But they obeyed God and marched around the city blowing their Shofars and praising God, and the impossible happened. The walls came tumbling down! God kept his promise that they would take the cities of their enemies.

Not everyone reading this is Christian, and even many Christians believe that these accounts of miracles from the Bible are just folklore. So let's jump forward to more modern times, to accounts of similar miracles straight out of our history books. For those who doubt their own history, in some instances, there are people still alive who lived through these events and attest to their accuracy. Just as always, God keeps his covenant.

1588: THE SPANISH INVASION OF ENGLAND

Prince Philip of Spain, at the direction of the Pope, led an Armada of warships intent on conquering England and imposing the horrors of the Catholic Inquisition on England. The provocation for this attack was that King Henry VIII had broken away from the Catholic Church and established the Church of England. This was considered an act of heresy that the Catholic Church could not allow. King Henry and the people of England had to be made an example of, so they were to be crushed.

At the time, Spain was the naval superpower of the world, and England was no match for it. It looked hopeless. The English had few actual warships, so in an act of desperation, they fitted small merchant ships with cannons and took on the mighty Spanish fleet in what looked like a hopeless battle.

But God's favor was not with the Spanish and the Catholic Church that had orchestrated the death of Christ and the usurping of his throne! He made a way for the impossible to happen. The English had a single advantage against the mighty Spanish Armada. Their smaller ships were more maneuverable. So, the admiral of the Spanish fleet ordered that their anchors be cut.

Not long after that happened, God whipped up a hurricane. The English dropped anchor and weathered the storm, but the Spanish ships were tossed to and fro and smashed against the rocks! When the storm was over, the Spanish Armada was decimated. On that day, the power structure of the world shifted, and England went on to be the naval superpower of the world, the empire upon which the sun never sets!

> He makes nations great and destroys them.
> He expands nations and disperses them.
> Job 12:33 (NIV)

God is faithful to His Covenant, and He is a Waymaker. God interceded on the side of England, not because they were righteous, but because they had a future role to play in the founding of America. Additionally, He was not going to allow the coalition of Spain and the Catholic Church that was responsible for the death of his Son to prevail. Spain's fate was sealed before the battle even began.

Moreover, God knew that in the future His Remnant would suffer religious persecution in England and leave to find religious freedom in His Covenant Nation, America! Queen

Elizabeth 1st of England commissioned a medallion commemorating what she called "The Miracle of the Raging Sea."

1940: WORLD WAR II AND THE EVACUATION OF DUNKIRK

America had not yet entered the war. Allied troops were in an impossible position. Their backs were to the English Channel, and Hitler's troops were bombarding them. English Prime Minister Churchill later said they were within three days of surrender. But instead, another miracle happened. Hitler thought it seemed too easy, and it must be a trap, so he called a meeting with his generals. The second the meeting convened, a fog fell over France, grounding the German Air Force.

At the same time, the English Channel, which was usually very rough at that time of year, became as smooth as glass. Churchill called on the British people to muster every available boat and launch a rescue of the ill-fated troops. By the time the fog lifted, 338,000 troops had been rescued from the shore of Dunkirk. They lived to fight another day and went on to defeat Hitler and keep the world from falling to Nazi occupation. God had orchestrated yet another miracle.

This one was proclaimed the Miracle of the Calm Sea! God is faithful, and no enemy can prevail against him! No matter how hopeless the situation may look, God always makes a way. He is the Waymaker!

WORLD WAR II AND THE GERMAN ENIGMA ENCRYPTION MACHINE

This machine was an ingenious device used by Hitler to encrypt military intelligence transmissions. Here is how it worked: a typist would type an outgoing message, and the machine would scramble each character they typed so that instead of the character they typed appearing on the message, any one of 150 million possible character choices would print. When the message was received, the machine would decipher the scrambled text into a legible message.

Hitler had air and naval superiority. His planes were superior to those of the Allies! He had a two-pronged strategy to force England's surrender. He conducted brutally effective bombing raids on British cities and military installations. He had developed a naval strategy that deployed packs of submarines, called "wolf packs," which were wreaking havoc with Allied convoys delivering supplies to England. It appeared that he was on the verge of winning the war by cutting England's supply lines and forcing its surrender.

But never underestimate God. Should England fall, the war would be over! Against odds of 150 million million million against them, the British cracked the German Code and managed to keep it a secret for the duration of the war. Had it not been for this miracle and the Miracle of Dunkirk, Hitler would have most certainly won WWII and imposed his brutal dictatorship on all of Europe and possibly the entire world!

No matter what things look like, God always comes through. What I didn't mention is that Churchill called Britain to national prayer, and God answered. No matter what it looks like in the natural, only a fool would wager against God Almighty, the creator of heaven and earth!

So, we have just covered six different instances where, from the human perspective, it seemed like evil would prevail. And in each instance, God orchestrated an event beyond the capabilities of man (a miracle) and saved the day! He will do the same thing in our present-day struggle with the demonic forces of the global financial elite. God has never lost a battle, and He never will.

THE YEAR: 2025

The world is on the brink of a global financial collapse. And the global elite believe that it will usher in their New World Order! Despite all the miracles God has performed on behalf of His Covenant nations, Israel and America, many people believe that the grip of the global elite's shadow government is so complete that it can't be defeated!

Many mistakenly believe that we are in the Book of Revelation, and therefore, it is time for the rise of the Anti-Christ and his Beast System. This would be a time when no one can buy or sell except those who pledge allegiance to him.

Both are wrong! King Belshazzar of Persia displeased God when he took the gold and silver vessels from the temple of the house of God and drank from them in what was probably a drunken orgy. Suddenly, a hand appeared, and the following inscription was written on the wall of the palace:

> **MENE, MENE, TEKEL, PARSIN**
>
> "Here is what these words mean:
>
> **MENE:** God has numbered the days of your reign and brought it to an end.
>
> **TEKEL:** You have been weighed on the scales and found wanting.
>
> **PERES:** Your kingdom is divided and given to the Medes and Persians."
>
> Daniel 5:26-28 (NIV) [Emphasis Added]

God raises up nations and rulers, and He removes them. This is not the time in the Book of Revelation where the anti-Christ implements his Beast System. This time is the time of the fulfillment of Abraham's Covenant and the Harvest of Souls foretold in Genesis 22:15-18 (NIV), which this chapter opened with. That means that just like for King Belshazzar, for those with eyes to see, the handwriting is on the wall for the global shadow government and all those who have aided and abetted them in their effort to usher in a demonic one-world government.

The next section describes what will happen with the collapse of the global monetary system and the fall of a one-world government.

COLLAPSE OF THE GLOBAL MONETARY SYSTEM

The global elite is about to lose control of the central banking system that has allowed them to print money out of thin air. When this happens, their greatest strength (their control of the printing of fiat currency) will become their greatest weakness.

IMPLEMENT A NEW COMMODITY-BASED FINANCIAL SYSTEM

The current fiat system allows the value of money to be intentionally inflated and deflated. It also allows wages to be controlled and financial boom and bust cycles to be intentionally inflicted on the public. None of this manipulation will be possible under a commodity-based system, which, by the way, is the basis of God's economic system.

FALL OF THE FINANCIAL ELITE'S SHADOW GOVERNMENT

Once they no longer have an inexhaustible supply of money, their house of cards will collapse!

THE FALL OF CHINA AND THE MOVEMENT FROM GLOBALIZATION TO DEGLOBALIZATION

This situation will be triggered by China losing control of the global supply chain, resulting in a movement from globalization to deglobalization. When this happens, it will trigger the collapse of China. Like Egypt before them, they will never again regain their superpower status. They will be relegated to being a regional power.

COLLAPSE OF THE U.S. ECONOMY AND GLOBAL FINANCIAL SYSTEM

When, on June 9th, 2024, Saudi Arabia terminated the U.S. Petro Dollar agreement, the final nail was put in the coffin for the U.S. economy. The collapse of China and the U.S. will cause the collapse of the entire global monetary system! This collapse will be so devastating that numerous nations will face financial and governmental ruin.

GOD'S TRANSFER OF WEALTH TO THE RIGHTEOUS

Because of the magnitude of this collapse, there will be no bailouts! There will be an onslaught of governments that will collapse (declare bankruptcy), as well as banks, and blue-chip corporations! Some banks and corporations will disappear, and others will be taken over when God transfers the wealth of the wicked to the righteous!

A NEW ECONOMIC SYSTEM WILL EMERGE

The current Fiat system will collapse and be replaced by the National Economic Security and Recovery Act (NESARA). This act will take America back to its founding economic system—details and explanation to follow later in this chapter.

GOD'S HARVEST OF SOULS IS AT HAND

This economic collapse must finally happen to strip the global financial elite of their power and usher in God's Harvest of Souls!

AMERICA IS THE PROTOTYPE FOR GOD'S GOVERNMENTAL SYSTEM!

America will rise like a phoenix from the ashes and restore order out of chaos! God always gives us a foreshadowing of what is to come. In this instance, that foreshadowing comes in the form of a little-known economic system called "The American Economic System," which was responsible for America's meteoric rise as a global superpower.

GLOBAL ELITE WILL LOSE CONTROL OF THE SEVEN SPHERES OF INFLUENCE

If the financial elite lose control of money, they can't buy power and influence. Nor will they be able to fund their black ops programs or organizations like Black Lives Matter, or fund caravans of illegal immigrants, or any number of other nefarious organizations. They will lose the ability to control the seven spheres of influence, and the power will shift to *We the People.*

WHISTLEBLOWERS WILL COME OUT

Loss of control of the money will unleash an avalanche of whistleblowers. The public will finally find out just how evil the financial elite are and that they intend to kill billions and enslave those they allow to live.

THE ACT OF 1871 USURPED OUR CONSTITUTION AND CREATED THE CORPORATION

This Act was illegal, unconstitutional, and passed by a treasonous Congress! Given this, an unconstitutional government resides in Washington! This knowledge allows us to deem our current 2,700-plus-page constitution invalid and reinstate our original one. It also allows us to remove those elected and/or appointed under this *illegal corporation* and to expunge the illegal laws they have passed to impose their legal dictatorship.

REINSTATE OUR REPUBLIC

To do so involves more than simply reinstating our Constitution and draining the swamp of those who were illegally elected or appointed! That alone does not reinstate our Republic. A republic is a government *of* the people, *by* the people, and *for* the people. We need a well-informed electorate that votes in the national interest. To accomplish that, we must reclaim our original Constitution and regain control over all areas of influence, which are:

- Family
- Religion

- Education
- Media
- Entertainment
- Politics
- Military
- Economy

It also means that we must take away powers that the federal government has usurped from local and state governments and give them back to those that are entitled to them. This means we have before us a complete overhaul of our political, economic, and social systems. Given the degree to which the public has been brainwashed, we must reeducate the public and reinstate the Christian and family values and patriotism that made America great initially. The economic system and laws can be revamped relatively quickly, but restoring America's founding principles and unity will take years, perhaps decades.

If this is not done, America will never be anything but a shadow of its former self. It will not fulfill its destiny, which is to be that shining light on the hill that is an inspiration to the world. Fear not, we will realize our destiny, but it requires a complete revamping of our social structure, which will take time.

THE ELITE WILL FIGHT BACK

There is no telling what they will do to try to hold on to power—I put nothing past them! They may release another virus, try to start another war, or use the army of illegal immigrants they let into the country to execute a series of terrorist attacks. But trust in God. There will be some significant events, but in the end, they will fail.

Nothing is going to stop the fall of the governmental systems of man, the birth of God's government, and the Harvest of Souls. It was ordained before the foundation of time. Refer to the miracles which were discussed in the opening of this chapter! God has never lost a war, and He never will. They lose; we win!

THE TRUTH WILL SET US FREE

Once the whistle-blowers come out, the public will stand united and refuse to participate in their own slavery, and an unparalleled period of peace and prosperity will be unleashed.

SIGNS, WONDERS, AND MIRACLES WILL BE RELEASED

When this happens, the entire world will be forced to acknowledge that God is a God of miracles. And that God, not any man, was responsible for this, the greatest miracles the world has ever seen. Against all odds, the world as a whole will gain its freedom!

God's governmental system is not like the current state of America's corrupt government! It refers to a time in America's past when it birthed what was known as "The American Economic System." The following quotes express why the American economic system is the basis of God's governmental system! God knows the end before the beginning. He has made a way for His children to finally live in peace and harmony!

In 1876, the U.S. hosted its Centennial Celebration, attended by nine million people from around the world who came to witness how America, the world's youngest nation, had become the world's wealthiest nation, supplanting Britain that had a 300-year head start! America had found a way to break free from the British free trade slavery system. In the words of Henry C. Carey, economic advisor to Abraham Lincoln:

> It [the British System] is the most gigantic system of slavery
> the world has yet seen, and therefore it is that freedom gradually
> disappears from every country over which England is enabled to obtain control.
> Henry C. Carey, economic advisor to Abraham Lincoln [Emphasis added]

What was it about the British Free Trade System that made it "the most gigantic system of slavery the world has yet seen?"

> Free trade shaves down the workingman's labor first, and then scales down his pay by
> rewarding him in a worthless and depreciated state currency.
> William McKinley, Oct. 4, 1892

Think about what is happening to the dollar. It is rapidly depreciating due to inflation, yet salaries are remaining static, so our standard of living is evaporating, which is exactly what the financial elite want! They want us desperate and fearful enough that we will surrender what freedom we have left in exchange for their promise to fix the very crisis they caused. Stand firm! God is our refuge, not a corrupt government.

> ...Slavery is but the owning of labor and carries with it the care of laborers,

[cont'd next page]

> while the European plan... [British Free Trade System]
> is that capital shall control labor by controlling wages...
> *Hazzard Circular,* July 1862

Free Trade controls wages, stifles ingenuity, and hoards resources. It creates conditions that foster lack, exploiting this lack to pit people against one another and create division and economic disparity between nations, which it then leverages to fuel endless wars for profit and control. Free Trade creates circumstances where the majority of people are caught in a debt trap. And no matter how hard they work, they never seem to get ahead.

This occurs because the system ensures that wages are always suppressed relative to the inflation or deflation of the currency! In the instance of the United States, intentionally losing trade deals was inflicted on us in an effort to weaken the U.S. economy. This also happens because the U.S. is the only nation in the world that poses a threat to the financial elite's plans to impose their New World Order Dictatorship!

HOW THE AMERICAN SYSTEM OF ECONOMICS ELEVATED WHILE EQUALIZING THE CONDITION OF MAN THROUGHOUT THE WORLD

Rather than controlling wages, stifling ingenuity, and hoarding resources as the British Free Trade Slavery System did, the American System encouraged innovation, which it shared with the world. As the innovators of the technology, America benefited, as did those who adopted it. The condition of mankind was "equalized and elevated!" To break free from the British Free Trade System, America needed to:

GAIN ACCESS TO ITS NATURAL RESOURCES

So, they built the transcontinental railroad, which connected the U.S. from the East Coast to the West Coast. Then they shared that technology with countries around the world.

DEVELOP DOMESTIC MANUFACTURING

So, it would not be dependent on British-made goods. To achieve this, a tariff of up to 50% was imposed on British imports. This forced American innovation to flourish, leading to the birth of the Industrial Revolution in America, marked by the assembly line and numerous revolutionary inventions. As a result, America, the world's youngest nation, became the wealthiest. Like the transcontinental railroad, all the inventions from the Industrial Revolution were shared with the world.

ENTER INTO FAIR AND EQUITABLE TRADE AGREEMENTS

So, America had a market to sell its finished products. It could use the proceeds to build additional infrastructure projects, such as more factories and Railroad spur lines, to gain even more access to its natural resources.

WHAT BECAME OF THE AMERICAN SYSTEM OF ECONOMICS?

While much of this has been discussed elsewhere, its significance necessitates repetition. The American System of Economics so threatened Britain that it orchestrated WWI to crush it! Plans were to connect all the nations of the world by rail, except for Australia, which, of course, is an island. Plans were in process to cross the Bering Strait and connect Europe, Asia, and North America. President McKinley was spearheading efforts to connect North and South America. Lastly, there were plans to build a bridge at Gibraltar connecting Europe and Africa. Had this network of interconnecting railroads been completed, it would have forever ended Britain's control of trade by sea, thereby ending its stranglehold on trade and the global economy.

Germany posed a double threat to Britain, as it was not only constructing railways but also adopting American technology to establish modern factories that could produce goods more quickly and at lower costs than Britain. So, Germany in particular had to be crushed!

Britain was desperate, and its situation called for desperate measures. They would orchestrate events that would cause WWI. They knew the war would be fought on the mainland, so as an island nation, while the rest of Europe would be demolished, they would be relatively unscathed!

Additionally, the economies of all European nations would be severely impacted. Yet given that most of their economy was based on their colonies, their economy would be relatively unaffected. To ensure victory, Germany, its primary economic rival in Europe, had to be crushed. To ensure victory, it was imperative that America enter the war on the side of Britain against Germany.

The war started in 1914, and it just so happened that in 1913, the traitor Woodrow Wilson was elected president (no coincidence). He had run on the pledge that under his presidency, there would be no central bank implemented in the United States. He lied! His campaign had been financed in large part by J.P. Morgan on behalf of the (British) Rothschilds. So, by the time WWI started, Wilson had signed the Federal Reserve Act!

Wilson sold out the American people to the British central bank and its global shadow government. Prior to the war, the United States and Germany were trading partners, with no significant friction between them. So, what changed?

The global elite always hedge their bets, so with the traitor Wilson in office, a plan was hatched to create a false flag event that would bring the U.S. into the war on the side of Britain against their former ally, Germany. The passenger ship, RMS *Lusitania*, would be sacrificed as an excuse to enter the war. It was loaded with munitions, making it a legitimate target.

German spies in New York knew the ship was carrying munitions. They went so far as to take out ads in New York papers, warning America that if the ship entered the war zone, it would be sunk. America denied the allegations, and the ship sailed with 1959 passengers and crew who were to be sacrificed as an excuse to enter the war. Years later, the wreckage of the RMS *Lusitania* was found, and just as charged, it was carrying munitions. Go figure!

WHAT ENTICED AMERICA TO COMMIT SUCH AN ATROCITY?

First, we had a traitor as our president, and we had a British central bank, which meant that the global elite shadow government was controlling America. They cared about nothing but power and money.

- They stood to maintain control of global trade by sea, which meant that they continued to control the global financial system!
- There was a powerful financial incentive for the puppet politicians in Washington. America would emerge from the war as the undisputed superpower of the world. We would loan money to the allies to fight the war. The U.S. Military Industrial Complex would make a fortune, as would the financial elite. After the war, Europe would be ravaged, and U.S./Globalist banks would loan European countries the money to rebuild, and U.S./Globalist contractors would do the building!
- The war would present the perfect opportunity to push the League of Nations under the guise of promoting world peace. But it was a covert effort to establish a global governance organization to further the endgame agenda of establishing a one-world government!

- The greedy U.S. politicians made a deal to sleep with the enemy! Regardless of how much power and money the U.S. stood to make by agreeing to enter the war, we stood to lose much more. Had the network of transcontinental railroads not been destroyed, the British Free Trade System would have been crushed, and the American Economic System would have gone on to "equalize and elevate the condition of all the nations of the world." It would have ushered in an unparalleled period of peace and prosperity with America at the helm.

AMERICA IS UNDER ABRAHAM'S COVENANT

America will fall because it must fall to break the control of the financial elite. But America will rise like a phoenix and be greater than ever. The American economic system was a foreshadowing of the governmental system that will underpin God's economic system! An America that is free of the control of the global shadow government (with Donald Trump at the helm) will lead the world back from the soon-to-come financial collapse that must befall the world.

WHAT WILL GOD'S GOVERNMENTAL SYSTEM LOOK LIKE?

THE MONETARY SYSTEM WILL BE BASED ON A COMMODITY-BASED CURRENCY

There will be no CBDC (Central Bank Digital Currency). Our monetary system will be tied to blockchain technology! Unlike under a fiat system, the currency will not be subject to manipulation through inflation and deflation. This new system guarantees economic stability, wage protection against inflation and deflation, and prevents orchestrated economic crashes.

THE WORLD WILL MOVE FROM GLOBALIZATION TO DEGLOBALIZATION

This change means that the supply chain will be decentralized, making it more difficult to create supply shortages intentionally, as has been done in the past. This, in turn, will result in stable prices.

RESOURCE-RICH UNDERDEVELOPED NATIONS WILL BE PROVIDED INTEREST-FREE LOANS

The primary purpose of the money will be to develop infrastructure and technology, so they are no longer dependent on first-world nations to mine and process their raw materials. To ensure that the funds are used for the designated purpose, they will be given to an intermediary who will serve as the general contractor for the projects. The companies building the projects will be required to establish an apprenticeship program and enroll a specified number of workers in it, ensuring a transfer of expertise.

ALL NATIONS WILL SHARE RESOURCES AND TECHNOLOGY

This will help equalize the standard of living between nations. It will also streamline the supply chain, which will appreciably cut the cost of finished goods!

ALL NATIONS WILL DEVELOP SHARED RESEARCH AND DEVELOPMENT CENTERS

Participating organizations will share costs and technology. This will prevent the hoarding of technology, which has been the case in the past. Additionally, changes to patent laws will prevent the elite from suppressing technology, particularly technology that will end our dependency on the grid and the elite's stranglehold on access to cheap, clean energy solutions! Reversal of the Chevron Case will take away power from the corporations and their unelected bureaucrats and put the power back in the hands of Congress and the courts, where it belongs!

INCUBATOR PROGRAMS WILL BE ESTABLISHED IN UNDERDEVELOPED NATIONS

The purpose of these programs is to develop educational initiatives that train nationals to become self-sufficient by providing essential services, including basic education, vocational training, and medical care.

INTERNATIONAL PROGRAMS WILL BE ESTABLISHED TO STUDY AND IMPLEMENT PROJECTS WITH GLOBAL IMPLICATIONS

Listed below are examples of such projects:

- Implementing a global network of fish hatcheries to repopulate our oceans.
- Addressing ecological problems like cleaning our oceans and rivers.
- Implementing biodiversity programs to reinstate heirloom seeds so we are not so dependent on GMOs (genetically modified seeds), controlled by a few corporations. It is insane to allow our food supply to be controlled by giant corporations!

The world is facing a catastrophic clean water shortage that could lead to a famine of biblical proportions. Clean water, not our carbon footprint, is the most pressing crisis facing mankind! I will keep this brief, as an entire chapter is devoted to this subject.

Suffice it to say that Trump said we would get free energy, so for now, let's take him at his word and assume that is true. A free energy technology currently exists that will allow us to have an abundance of clean water anywhere in the world. It is a highly sustainable system that captures water evaporating from the oceans, causes it to reach the condensation point, and releases the water on demand from the atmosphere.

Our lakes, rivers, and aquifers will be replenished because we will no longer have to drain them to irrigate millions of acres of farmland. We will tap into God's ever-replenishing hydrological cycle, where water flows from the oceans and returns to its source. In the process, we will clean our oceans, lakes, and rivers. God is a Waymaker!

There are assuredly other projects with global implications, but this gives you an understanding of the type of projects that need to be addressed.

WHAT IS NESARA?
AND WHAT IS ITS ROLE IN RESTORING THE GLOBAL ECONOMY?

NESARA: NATIONAL ECONOMIC SECURITY AND RECOVERY ACT

Here's the caveat: I try to base my analysis on historical events that can be substantiated. However, in this case, NESARA has not yet been implemented (at least its implementation has not been formally disclosed). Nonetheless, what I am about to tell you is essential, even if I am unable to validate it fully.

The general components of NESARA are available, but as to how it is implemented remains to be seen. Some believe it is already running in tandem with our current banking system. I believe it, but I'm not certain enough to confirm it.

Having said that, I will explain my understanding of NESARA's components. The prevailing story that underpins NESARA's inception goes back to the assassination of President Kennedy. It is also related to the efforts of farmers to get out from under financial policies that threatened their financial livelihood.

Kennedy had issued a silver-backed currency and was in the process of terminating the Fed. This required the implementation of a new economic system, NESARA. Fast forward to 2016, and what was referred to as the "Capitulation Tour." Trump says he has all his enemies' hidden secrets! God says that nothing is hidden.

So, here is what is postulated to have happened. Trump went on a world tour where he reportedly presented the leaders of the nations he visited with evidence of their treasonous activities, and one by one, they capitulated and agreed to submit to NESARA and its global counterpart, GESARA.

Additionally, many nations of the world sought to escape China's control through global trade. Likewise, they sought to escape U.S. control over their economies, leveraging the U.S. dollar as the world's reserve currency. They were therefore in favor of both NESARA and BRICS with its gold-backed currency.

PROVISIONS OF NESARA AS CURRENTLY AVAILABLE TO THE PUBLIC

NOTE: Following each provision, I will give my understanding of its implications. But please understand that I am not an insider, so take what I say with a grain of salt. That being said, I believe events have already occurred that strongly indicate these are accurate deductions.

FED AND IRS TO BE DISSOLVED

There are indications that the FED is bankrupt and has already been put under the Treasury. This would mean that debt obligations under the FED would be forgiven due to bankruptcy. The implication is that mortgages, at least those that predate the bankruptcy, would be forgiven.

GOLD/COMMODITY BACKED CURRENCY

With Saudi Arabia announcing it will no longer sell oil in U.S. dollars, the death of the dollar is inevitable. The financial elite will no longer be able to use the dollar to inflict nations with inflation, deflation, and orchestrated financial crashes. The current fiat dollar will be replaced with a gold-backed commodity-based system, i.e., BRICS. Unlike fiat currencies, commodity-backed currencies are based on commodities with intrinsic value, making them resistant to manipulation. Trump has pledged that, under his presidency, there will be no Central Bank Digital Currency (CBDC). This stops central banks from manipulating the currency.

It should be noted that the Elite's version of the financial reset requires the implementation of Central Bank Digital Currency (CBDC), which would effectively usher in the Beast System. It allows the currency to be programmed so that the public can only buy those items sanctioned by the Elite. For example, they could program the currency to prevent you from purchasing meat, sugar, bullets, guns, or any other items they wanted to control. This would effectively mean that all the governments of the world would be irrelevant! The result would be a global totalitarian one-world government.

ILLEGAL DEBT FORGIVENESS

Although I cannot confirm this, it makes sense. The Federal Reserve System, the IRS, and the compound interest charged on mortgages and credit cards were illegally imposed on the public. Therefore, I believe they are subject to being forgiven. Additionally, when America was founded, there was no property tax. It is also illegal, and I think it will be abolished.

SALES TAX REPLACES INCOME TAX

With the FED being dissolved, there would be no more illegal federal income tax. Trump says we will be able to complete our taxes on a postcard. When America was founded, there was no federal income tax, and the nation was funded based on a sales tax, just like what is supposed to be the case under NESARA!

TAXES ON NEW NON-ESSENTIAL ITEMS ONLY

Driven solely by profit maximization for shareholders, an unlawful corporation exploited the public for every possible dollar. But a government that represents *We the People,* as under NESARA, would not need to bleed the public. This is credible.

REINSTATES OUR CONSTITUTION

The reinstatement of our constitution excites me because I believe that laws have been passed to establish a legal dictatorship. And they must be stricken. Laws passed under an illegally instituted, i.e., the Corporation, are subject to being dissolved. Additionally, all those elected or appointed under such an illegal system are subject to removal. We must drain the swamp of all the global elite puppets!

RELEASE OF 6,000 PATENTS

My research confirms that many patents have been shelved. I cannot confirm the exact number, but I do not doubt that it could be as many as 6,000. We need laws that, in the future, prevent such abuse of power. Additionally, the Chevron Supreme Court Case (discussed previously) provides the means to access technology that has been denied to us by a corrupt corporatocracy.

INCREASED BENEFITS TO SENIORS

On July 4, 2025, the Big Beautiful Bill was put into place by the 119th United States Congress. Rather than jeopardizing Medicaid as the Left was pushing, the bill makes sweeping changes to Medicaid work requirements, getting rid of fraud and abuse. Also, it removes those, including illegal immigrants, who shouldn't be on Medicaid.

The bill underpins Trump's Make America Great Again Agenda. It renews Trump's first-term tax cuts and extends them, thereby stimulating the economy. The bill removes obstructionist environmental regulations and implements tax cuts that attract investment in his Build America, Buy American Agenda. It also weans us off the folly of the $93 trillion Green New Deal.

The Big Beautiful Bill restores oil and gas independence while transitioning to revolutionary new, cheap, clean energy technology, which is forthcoming as a result of the Chevron Supreme Court Decision. The transition to clean energy opens the door to revolutionary energy technology that has been denied based on claims of national security, when in actuality the technology was withheld to protect the trillions of dollars of oil and gas revenues controlled by major corporations.

REQUIRES STANDDOWN OF ALL MILITARY AGGRESSION

My understanding is that a gold-backed Rainbow Currency will be issued, and it will be exchanged on a one-to-one basis with the dollar. If true, it means we do not need to be worried about bank failures. They must happen to collapse the fiat system and usher in NESARA. There are laws in place that say that those found guilty of racketeering or treason are subject to having their funds confiscated. In this instance, this means that rumors of mass confiscations of gold and other assets are credible.

What I think the future will hold is an economy where the national debt is forgiven. We can look forward to an economy where the wealth of the wicked has been confiscated and will be used to free us from the debt trap that we have been under, virtually from the inception of the United States. Additionally, because of their illegal activities, the financial elite will be prohibited from participating in the currency swap.

Lastly, there is a provision that says that for nations to participate, they must stand down from their wars. Maybe, just maybe, that explains why there were no wars under Trump's Presidency. Regardless, this means that with everything you have read, the division and economic disparity that cause wars may end, leading to an unprecedented period of peace and prosperity.

The kingdoms of man, with their corruption, division, poverty, and wars, are coming to an end (at least till we enter the Book of Revelation, which I hope is a long time away). It is time for God's Harvest of Souls and for the Great Spiritual Awakening!

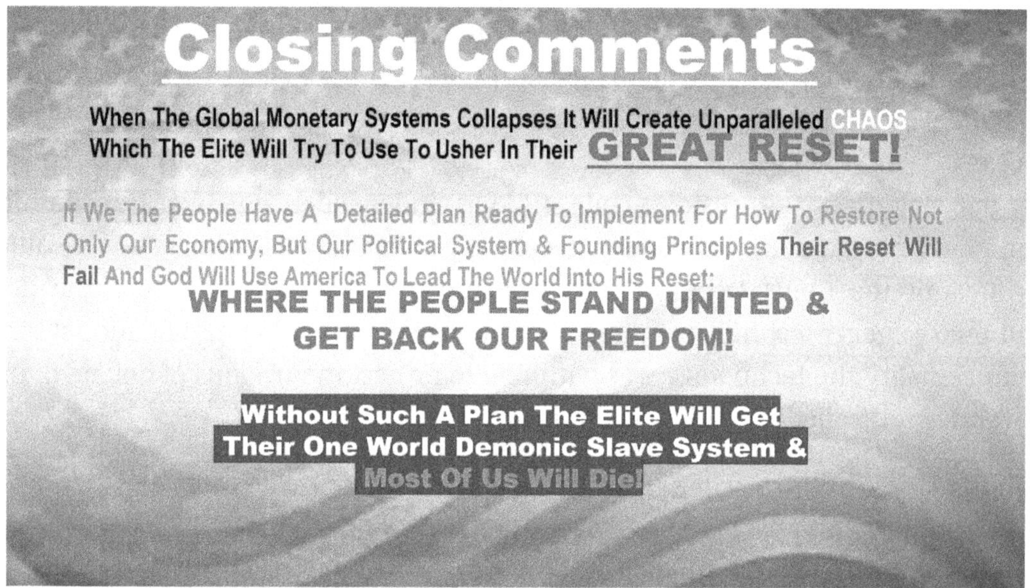

As the graphic above details, the Elite are trying to usher in unparalleled chaos. And they want to implement a one-world demonic slave system. My prayer is that God will not let that happen. But we need to be informed! And we need to stand united, demand our freedom, and repent to God. It is then that He will come to our aid.

CHAPTER 11

GLOBAL INSIGHTS
Analysis of the Global Power Structure Post-Collapse

POST-COLLAPSE AMERICA will rise from the ashes and restore economic stability not only for the U.S. but for the world. However, post-collapse, the U.S. will not emerge as an all-powerful nation that controls the world's nations through control of the global financial system. As we will discuss in another chapter, power and resources will be more equitably distributed, so that no single country or group will be able to dominate the world, as has been the case for hundreds of years.

When the world rises from chaos and the dust settles, this will be a far better, far kinder, far more prosperous, and more peaceful world. But before that can happen, the foundation of our political and economic systems must be leveled and rebuilt on a new foundation! Both America and China must fall so that the new system can emerge! In reaching my conclusions, I will:

- Consider what God's Word says about where we are in the Bible,
- Analyze what it takes structurally to be a global superpower, and lastly
- Project into the future to predict the structure of the world post-financial collapse.

This book is unique because it provides the 60,000-foot view that most authors and strategists are unable to see! It can do this because it combines insights from history, the Bible, and current events to see trends that are impossible to see without these three perspectives.

WHERE WE ARE IN THE BIBLE

Many people believe that the Bible offers no insights into strategic analysis. But they are mistaken. The Bible is a history book, a military strategy book, a book that prophesies future events with extraordinary accuracy, and a book that provides a covenant with the Creator of all things. Throughout the Bible, God repeatedly demonstrates that He knows the end from the beginning. When combined with human history, compelling trends can be seen and outcomes projected!

Many people reach a point where they are so discouraged and disillusioned that they yearn for a way out. So, they are all too happy to believe that things are so bad that any day they will be raptured and spared what is coming! That is defeatist, wishful thinking. So, let's revisit biblical history and set the record straight, starting with God's covenant with Abraham.

Abraham was tested and proven righteous! He was told to sacrifice his son, Isaac. But just as the knife was about to be thrust in, God spared Isak and showed Abraham a lamb caught in the thicket that he was to sacrifice instead of his son. Because of his obedience, God judged him righteous and told him that his descendants would be as the sands of the seashore and the stars of the sky. At that time in history, it is estimated that the global population was somewhere around one-half billion, and today it is approaching eight billion. Looks like God fulfilled his promise!

God also told Abraham that he would make of him a great nation. So, did God keep that promise as well? It would seem so. Historical records indicate that the lost tribes migrated up the Euphrates River, eventually settling in England. Even though England is evil to the core, God knew the plans he had made for them to be a family of great nations by having them colonize the world! Finding no religious freedom in England, the Pilgrims made the journey to the New World. They founded America, which God used to evangelize the world!

Going back in history, we find ourselves in Egypt with Moses at the Red Sea, where God delivered the Israelites from the hand of Pharaoh! Just as today, circumstances looked hopeless, but at the last minute, God intervened. Today, things look hopeless, but that's not the case. The coming financial collapse will strip the financial elite of their wealth and power. Just like the Israelites were delivered from captivity then, America and the world are about to be delivered today!

Then there is Queen Esther, who stood in the gap for her people! Haman plotted to have the Jews massacred, and Ester's cousin Mordecai hanged. But at the last minute, events were reversed, and it was Haman who ended up being hanged! In America, we had a plot where the 2020 election was stolen, and Biden, the usurper, conspired with the financial elite to destroy America and kill most of us!

However, just as in the story of Esther, a reversal has taken place; Biden and Harris have been removed from power. And the people of America and the world will be delivered. The truth is coming out, and soon the enemy will be removed from power. Trump is ordained by God to set the captives free. An avalanche of truth is about to expose the enemy's lies and, with it, their power!

So, where does this leave us today? Do you think God orchestrated all these events only to let the Harvest of Souls go to the devil and his minions, the financial elite? Remember the devil is a liar and a thief, and God is not a man that he should lie!

No, God has a plan. Everything that has occurred has happened for a reason, and the outcome was predetermined from the beginning of time. Christ is coming back for a spotless church. As the financial collapse hits us full force, men's hearts will faint with fear!

Then God will release the Holy Spirit, just like He did in the upper room when the disciples were anguishing over the crucifixion of Christ. That tragedy was not the end; it was the beginning! These men, previously paralyzed by fear, now boldly shared their message, knowingly facing potential repercussions. The latter-day rain is about to fall, and the church is about to be purified. End. Of. Story!

It is not a time of defeat, but a time of the Harvest of Souls. We're living in the greatest time ever. The future that awaits us is more marvelous than we can imagine.

God is not a liar.

THE REQUIREMENTS TO BE AN ECONOMIC SUPERPOWER

- An abundance of natural resources (the basis of God's wealth)
- The ability to process those natural resources into finished goods
- The ability to trade the finished goods efficiently by transporting them where they need to go, which requires an adequate infrastructure

THE END OF THIS PROCESS IS THE CONVERSION OF THE FINISHED GOODS INTO MONEY (MAN'S BASIS OF WEALTH)

This last step is where things have historically gone awry because the money is used to:

- Buy power and influence at every stratum of society.
- Inflict the people of the world with boom-and-bust cycles that keep the masses in a constant state of indentured servitude.
- Inflict on us all manner of control mechanisms to make us so dependent that we are unable to break the invisible chains that enslave us.

The graphic on the next page allows you to see the big picture at a glance.

How The Elite Control Mankind!

LIBERTY CRUSADE

The Basis Of All Wealth Is
- Control Of Natural Resources
- Control Of Manufacturing
- Control Of Trade
- Converts Into Money

Create A Boom Bust Cycle
- Increase Money Supply
- Lower Interest Rates
- Push Investment Opportunity
- Increase Interest Rates
- Dry Up Credit & Instant Crash

Control The 8 Spheres of Influence
- Family
- Religion
- Education
- Media
- Entertainment
- Politics
- Military Industrial Complex
- Economy

Events That Enslave Us
- Wars For Profit
- Fiat Currency (Fed)
- Open Borders
- Drug Epidemic
- Division
- Rigged Elections
- Control Of Energy
- Control Of Healthcare
- Control Of Food & Water
- Control Of Jobs & Housing

In subsequent chapters, we will discuss in detail how this cycle of corruption and abuse of power will be broken, and money will be used to benefit mankind.

POWER DISTRIBUTION POST-COLLAPSE

In the past, wealth has not trickled down to the masses. On the contrary, it has been used to enslave them. What follows is a brief overview of the political and economic structure required to allow the implementation of a fair and equitable economic and political system.

No country currently satisfies all of these requirements. A lot of changes must be made. There are too many to cover here, so that topic will be addressed later. For now, suffice it to say that once the U.S. gets out from under the control of the global financial elite's shadow government, we will make those changes to a greater degree than any other nation! America will then lead the world in an era where all nations join to share resources and technology, and solve the problems facing individual nations and the world.

We will build a world based on cooperation and mutual assistance as opposed to the plunder, pillage, and slavery imposed on the world by the global financial elite. God intends America to be the shining light on the hill once again! America will lead the world into a better tomorrow, and before you finish this book, you will know exactly how we will do that!

STRUCTURAL REQUIREMENTS FOR GLOBAL LEADERSHIP

Global Leadership capabilities require the following:

- **A LARGE ENOUGH GDP TO AFFECT WORLD EVENTS**–God will use America to revitalize the global economy, not to dominate, but to lead and assist!

- **LEADERSHIP ROLE IN DEVELOPING SOLUTIONS TO SOLVE PROBLEMS FACING HUMANITY**–Clean water and air, food security, energy independence, and robust health and education systems are especially critical for us.

- **INNOVATION**–This will be necessary to accommodate a transition from cheap throwaway products to products designed for longevity and reusability!

- **TECHNICAL KNOW-HOW**–This knowledge is critical for engineering and manufacturing technology that other countries may not be able to produce.

- **MANUFACTURING CAPABILITY**–This will enable rapid gearing up of manufacturing to fill the vacuum created by China's economic collapse.

- **ADEQUATE INFRASTRUCTURE BACKBONE**–This will ensure that we are a significant component of the global supply chain.

- **FAVORABLE DEMOGRAPHICS**–Economic and social stability is significantly dependent on population size and age distribution. Overpopulation reduces per capita income. Too large a *retired* population can create an economic drain on society.

GOVERNMENTAL and SOCIAL REQUIREMENTS

Global leadership requires not only structural elements but also governmental and social elements, as well, including:

- **HONEST LEADERSHIP WITH HONEST ELECTIONS AND THE RULE OF LAW** -Economic and social stability are impossible without honest leadership, which means the absence of special interests, nepotism, and the fostering of division.

- **NATIONAL UNITY AND COMMON LANGUAGE**–This will make our communication more efficient and stable.

- **NATIONAL SECURITY CAPABILITY**–Only a nation with internal and external security can assume a global leadership role!

- **ADEQUATE EDUCATION**–In a technological era, an educated population is essential for both economic and social stability.

RESOURCES

To lead globally, sustainable resources are essential.

- **NATURAL RESOURCES**–Raw materials and manufacturing capability are must-haves.

- **FOOD, WATER, ENERGY, AND HEALTH**–These necessities of life are essential to economic and social stability! In the post-economic collapse society, nations will cooperate to ensure that all nations have access to these basics. Collaborative research and development projects are needed to address our common threats. The top priorities are clean water and energy independence.

- **FAVORABLE GEOGRAPHY**–Climatic conditions significantly affect economic development. Technology can mitigate this to some extent, but not completely.

Once the Shadow Government is removed from the U.S., our deficiencies can be quickly solved. In many other countries, their problems run much deeper and are much more difficult and complex to solve. However, with international cooperation, these issues can also be resolved over time. For today and the foreseeable future, the U.S. is best positioned to fill the vacuum created by the collapse of China and the global monetary system.

Based on the requirements for leadership and analysis of the statistics presented in this chapter, we will develop an economic model that predicts the most likely power structure of the world following a collapse. An economic scorecard will be developed for specific nations and regions. Solutions to specific problems will be discussed.

The subsequent chapter details a new economic model that supersedes both capitalism and communism, establishing God's economic order. By the time we are finished, you will have a global perspective on what is to come and how humanity will put dominance and greed behind us, ushering in an unparalleled era of peace and prosperity.

In the final chapter, we will face the reality of eventually entering the Book of Revelation and the "Beast System" being restored. To delay that day as long as possible, we will examine the mechanisms by which the financial elite will regroup and reclaim power.

But remember, God is in control. The story ends with the millennial reign of God's peace on earth, where it will be said: *"On Earth, as it is in Heaven!"*

AN ANALYSIS OF THE GLOBAL POWER STRUCTURE AS OF 2024

TOP TEN COUNTRIES BY SHARE OF GLOBAL MANUFACTURING

1. China 28.4%
2. United States 16.6%
3. Japan 7.2%
4. Germany 6.8%
5. South Korea 3.3%
6. India 3.0%
7. Italy 2.3%
8. France 1.9%
9. United Kingdom 1.8%
10. Mexico 1.5%

Output measures on a value-added basis in current U.S. dollars. Source: United Nations Statistics Division

China has been labeled as a pariah nation. As a result, control of the global supply chain is being stripped away from them. Investment in China has virtually dried up. Companies are relocating to other countries worldwide.

The most notable example is the Foxconn iPhone manufacturing facility, which employs approximately 100,000 people. It is not only leaving China but also distributing manufacturing across five countries (deglobalization). As the global supply chain is stripped away from China, a large part of it will go to neighboring nations, such as Vietnam, Laos,

Cambodia, and Thailand. This action is based on the labor force and the level of technology of these nations.

The two countries that will benefit the most in the region are India and Vietnam. The U.S. will get many of the more technical items. As all the vital statistics required for global leadership are presented in this chapter, you will see that America is the only nation in the world capable of restoring economic stability post-collapse.

Concurrent with the fall of China will be the collapse of the U.S. dollar. These two events will mark the fall of man's economic systems and the birth of God's economic system. God is no longer going to allow any nation or group of nations to dominate the world. The era of globalization is over, giving way to regionalization or deglobalization. But don't worry, God has plans for the U.S., and I guarantee you will like them.

THE WORLD'S TEN MOST RESOURCE-RICH NATIONS

1. Russia .... $75.0 Trillion
2. U.S. .... $45.0 Trillion
3. Saudi Arabia .... $34.4 Trillion
4. Canada .... $33.2 Trillion
5. Iran .... $27.3 Trillion
6. China .... $23.0 Trillion
7. Brazil .... $21.8 Trillion
8. Australia .... $19.9 Trillion
9. Iraq .... $15.9 Trillion
10. Venezuela .... $14.3 Trillion

Africa is currently the poorest continent in the world. However, when we transition to God's gold-backed, commodity-based economic system, it will perhaps become the wealthiest. Africa has been denied access to its vast wealth, but that is about to change. Africa will finally be allowed to prosper. As to how that occurs, that is a subject for another time.

It's essential to note that, although these nations are among the most resource-rich in the world, this does not necessarily mean they will have the highest GDP or per capita income, nor does it guarantee that they will be a global leader. As we review all the statistics, please note that only the U.S. is at or near the top of the list for all the crucial economic leadership indicators.

The following chart might be somewhat confusing because at first glance, you get the impression that the U.S. is heavily dependent on oil imports. But that is only because the Biden administration wanted it that way. Biden shut down the Keystone Pipeline and banned drilling on much of our federal lands. Most significantly, before leaving office, Trump had opened Pergo Bay, Alaska, for drilling. But as soon as Biden came into office, he shut it down. Pergo Bay is estimated to be the largest oil field in the world.

So, it is not that the U.S. does not have oil. It is that we are being denied access by the Globalist Shadow Government that wants a weak and oil-dependent United States. Remember when Trump was in office, we were oil independent and even exporting oil. So, in truth, the U.S. is perhaps the world's most oil-rich nation, which bodes well for the U.S. when the world goes on a commodity-based economy, and we get access to our oil reserves.

IMPORTS OF OIL BY COUNTRY IN METRIC TONS

Country	Metric Tons
China:	549,925,112
United States:	362,523,000
India:	276,000,000
South Korea:	114,000,000
Japan:	113,000,000
Germany:	97,302,814
Spain:	64,743,580
Netherlands:	57,167,594
France:	55,305,516
Italy:	54,223,689

Trump is once again the 47th President of the United States. Will he be the 48th? Refer to the introduction to see what I am referring to! He has come back promising to make America greater than ever. It is not complicated. All he must do is what he did in his first term, which is to:

- Give us access to our natural resources, particularly gas and oil.
- Remove job-killing regulations.
- Remove regulations that negatively affect our ability to build infrastructure (especially factories).

- Enforce fair trade agreements.
- Place tariffs on nations that attempt to disadvantage U.S.-made products in the global marketplace.
- Enforce policies that support made in America.

As soon as Trump was inaugurated, he began the process of draining the swamp and reducing the size of the bloated federal government. The *swamp* is defined as the corporatocracy, comprised of the banker gangsters, their corporate accomplices, and the bought and paid for politicians that write the laws that force the public to pay illegal taxes and inflict us with all manner of laws that enslave us.

Trump has already announced a yearlong celebration of American heritage. We will learn our true heritage, and with the swamp rats removed, America will once again become the land of the free and the home of the brave. This was demonstrated on June 14, 2025, in the tremendous birthday celebration for the U.S. Army. Commonly known as "Flag Day," this date also coincided with the 250th anniversary of the Army's birthday and was celebrated in grand style at our nation's capital.

Celebrations like this will help unify our nation. We will once again be the United States of America, and the undisputed leader of the world. America will understand what it means to be a republic. We will harken back to what made America great in the first place: our family and Christian values, our Constitution, innovation, work ethic, and rugged individualism. God ordains America to be the nation that restores the world to God and, in the process, ushers in God's kingdom on earth where men finally learn to live together in peace, harmony, and prosperity greater than we can currently envision.

Getting back to China: It imports 75% of its oil and faces a threat to its oil supply because of its dependency on access through the 1 ½ mile-wide Strait of Malaysia. If access through the Strait were to be cut off, it would cripple China because it depends on it for shipping both oil and manufactured goods. China has a substantial supply of oil, but it is nowhere near enough to support its industrial base without relying on massive imports.

Regarding the other nations listed in the chart above, the amount of oil imported is tied to population and the level of manufacturing. However, the U.S. still possesses greater reserves than any of them. For example, Japan imports virtually 100% of its oil. So, you see once again that the U.S. is in a very enviable position!

I believe that in the future, oil and gas, though vitally essential resources, will be less of a determinant of global power than today. I do not necessarily say this because of green technology. In my opinion, wind and solar are not optimal energy solutions, and neither are batteries necessarily the answer either. My research leads me to conclude that we have revolutionary technologies that have been suppressed, that will provide virtually free, off-the-grid energy. Read some examples below.

HYDROGEN ON DEMAND

Hydrogen on demand was touched on in a previous chapter, but it warrants repeating here. This is a much better solution for electric cars than Lithium batteries. Toyota just announced the production of a car that runs on hydrogen, on demand. In my opinion, this will be a death blow for the evolving lithium-dependent electric vehicle (EV) market.

ZERO POINT ENERGY

This type of energy utilizes powerful electromagnets to create electric generators capable of powering an automobile or a home without dependency on the grid. These magnets have a lifespan of approximately 300 years. The generator, powered by magnets, can run continuously or be disengaged, similar to the ignition in an automobile, and then be restarted with a battery.

GARBAGE RECYCLING

There are currently operational facilities that take waste (anything but silica) and convert it into crude oil, carbon char, and methane. Methane is used as the primary power source for the facility, making it highly energy-efficient. The process is called "thermal depolymerization" and was invented by visionary leader and waste-to-energy pioneer Brian Appel, who said:

> **We can conservatively convert all the agricultural waste in the U.S.**
> **which is six billion tons, into over four billion barrels of light oil a year.**
> **That is the same number we import.**
> Brian S. Appel, Founder, Changing World Technologies

These and other patents and technologies have been shelved or suppressed because they end our dependency on the global financial elite. There is every reason to believe that Tesla harnessed the energy of the Earth's magnetic field and developed technology to electrify the stratosphere, making it possible to have free energy anywhere on Earth. The technology is referred to as "standing wave" electricity.

It is reported that when Tesla demonstrated this technology to his financial backer, J.P. Morgan, he said, "This technology would make me a G## da## antenna salesman!" Shortly afterward, Tesla's funding was stopped, he was blackballed, and his research facility was torn down! We must get access to the shelved patents that could potentially solve most of the ecological crisis facing the world. But as the quote below exposes, that is the last thing the global elite want.

> **In fact, giving society cheap, abundant energy at this point would be the moral equivalent of giving an idiot child a machine gun.**
> Paul Ehrlich, Stanford University

TECHNOLOGY DRIVES INNOVATION AND GDP IN THE MOST TECHNOLOGICALLY ADVANCED COUNTRIES

1. South Korea:............................ 6.52
2. U.S.:... 5.10
3. Denmark:................................. 5.02
4. Switzerland: 4.72
5. Taiwan:.................................... 4.63
6. Singapore:................................ 3.97
7. Japan: 3.94
8. Netherlands:............................ 3.94
9. Finland:................................... 3.90
10. Israel: 3.86

This ranking is based on four metrics: internet users, LIE users as a percentage of a country's population, digital competitiveness score, and the portion of GDP a country allocates to research and technological development as of 2022. (Source: Global Financing Ranking Royals).

You will note that the U.S. holds the number two slot in technological advancement. However, there is a mitigating factor that gives the U.S. a distinctive advantage going forward: its leadership position in artificial intelligence. And that can provide the U.S. with a substantial advantage in research and development.

At this point, I noticed that nations with the largest manufacturing bases and the most abundant natural resources are not necessarily the most technologically advanced. That distinction is bestowed on many small countries that have discovered, through technology, they can carve out market niches that provide economic stability and prosperity for their people. One such example is Taiwan, a leader in semiconductor technology used in virtually every electronic device on the planet.

Think about what the world would look like if technological advancements were shared instead of being suppressed and hoarded. The key to peace on earth lies in the shared use of resources and technology, which enables greater equality worldwide.

> Is there any man here or any woman, let me say any child here
> who does not know that the seed of war in the modern world
> is industrial and commercial rivalry?
> President Woodrow Wilson

A BETTER WORLD AWAITS IF WE EMBRACE IT!

With a declining population, innovation is key to economic development! The following graphic considers human capital and institutions. Technology and creative output, market and business sophistication, among others. (Source: World Intellectual Property Organization).

THE WORLD'S MOST INNOVATIVE COUNTRIES

Switzerland:	65.5
Sweden:	63.1
U.S.:	61.3
United Kingdom:	59.8
South Korea:	59.3
Netherlands:	58.6
Finland:	58.4
Singapore:	57.8

This information originates from the Global Innovation Index 2021, a survey of innovation trends in 132 economies. 100 = most innovative. The saying below comes to mind when I look at this graphic.

Necessity is the mother of invention.
Danish Economist Ester Boserup

Isn't it time we woke up, opened our eyes, and realized that we are controlled from cradle to grave and the necessities of life are intentionally held in short supply? We have reached a point where mutual cooperation and development are necessary to solve the problems facing humanity and the planet that sustains us.

The whole is greater than the sum of its parts.
Aristotle

COOPERATION IS THE KEY TO A BETTER WORLD!

There is one statistic that does not seem (at least on the surface) to favor the United States. That is education! The U.S. is ranked 30th out of 195 countries worldwide. That is alarming, but not as significant as you might think, and not an insurmountable problem. Two questions come to mind when I look at the U.S.'s Education ranking:

1. *How is it possible that a nation (the U.S.) whose education system is ranked 30th in the world for education can be ranked 3rd in the world for innovation? This seems like an oxymoron. But upon further reflection, there is a rational explanation! NOTE: Donald Trump says we rank 40th. I have a hunch his data is superior to mine.*

The first factor in unraveling this enigma is to understand that the U.S. is not as dependent on its own education system as poorer countries. The best, the brightest, and the richest can attend school anywhere in the world, or they can attend a private school, or have a personal tutor!

The second factor is that the U.S. creates a brain drain in other countries by extending work visas to their best and brightest. This works to the benefit of the U.S. and to the detriment of poorer nations!

The third factor is that in this era of Artificial Intelligence (AI), a technological society like the U.S. is much less reliant on human brain power than poorer, less technologically developed countries, because much of our research and development can be driven by artificial intelligence. Given this, the U.S. has a significant advantage over less technologically developed nations!

2.   *How is it possible that America, which once had one of the best education systems in the world, has now slipped to 30th in the world? (Or as Trump says, "40th")*

The answer is that it was done intentionally. There is no nation in the world other than the U.S. that can prevent the global financial elite from implementing their New World Order Dictatorship!

So, the financial elite have sabotaged and undermined the quality of our public schools as a control mechanism and to dumb down the general population. After all, they select the best and brightest from all over the world, and they have the technology to conduct their own research and development. So, they are not dependent on a well-educated general population!

As a matter of fact, the last thing they want is a well-educated general population because they might wake up and lead a coup that would remove them from power. How brilliant a strategy! What a maniacal plot! The power must be taken away from these monsters, and it will be!

By the time you've finished this book, you'll understand how it's accomplished. In the meantime, I have some quotes for you that will hopefully convince you that what I say is true. The goal is to turn us into docile, dumbed-down sheeple who are incapable of revolting against them!

Education is dangerous. Every educated person is a future enemy.
Hermann Göring, Hitler's designated successor

If I could control Hollywood, I could control the world.
Attributed to Joseph Stalin, Russian leader and mass murderer

To achieve world government, it is necessary to remove from the minds of men their individualism, loyalty to family traditions, national patriotism, and religious dogmas.
Brock Chisholm, Director, UN World Health Organization

The bewildered herd is a problem. We've got to prevent their rage and trampling. We've got to distract them. They should be watching the Super Bowl or sitcoms or violent movies or something ... and you've got to keep them pretty scared because unless they're scared properly and frightened of all kinds of devils that are going to destroy them from outside or inside or somewhere, they may start to think, which is very dangerous because they're not competent to think, and therefore it's important to distract and to marginalize them.
Professor Noam Chomsky, *Keeping the Rabble in Line*

To give you an idea of just how deep this indoctrination goes, consider this: at one point, the California Appellate Court ruled parents do not have a Constitutional right under California law to homeschool, a decision that was later overturned. Their justification was, "A primary purpose of the education system is to train schoolchildren in good citizenship, patriotism, and loyalty to the State and the Nation as a means of protecting public welfare."

TRANSLATION: School is an indoctrination center.

The following table highlights that GDP isn't necessarily linked to economic stability or higher per capita income. Because the size of the population dilutes the GDP. Demographics matter. This is one of the destabilizing factors regarding China and is a limiting factor for India and Africa.

TOP TEN ECONOMIES 2022			
Data per IMF	$GDP	$ Per capita	Growth Rate
U.S.	$25.340T	76.027	3.7%
China	19.912	14.096	4.4%
Japan	4.912	39.243	2.4%
Germany	4.256	51.15	2.1%
India	3.535	2.516	8.2%
Britain	3.376	49.741	3.7%
France	2.937	44.747	2.9%
Canada	2.221	67.506	3.9%
Italy	2.058	34.777	2.3%
Brazil	1.833	8.57	0.8%

In summary, if one examines all the metrics for global leadership, the U.S. emerges as the nation best positioned to lead the world out of the chaos that will result from the impending global financial collapse. America is the world's best hope for fostering a more equitable society where all nations have the opportunity to share in the world's wealth.

KEY INDICATORS TO GLOBAL LEADERSHIP

Core Indicators of Power	$GDP	$ Per capita	Natural Resources	% Global Manufacturing
U.S.	$25.340T	76.027	$45T	16.9%
China	19.912T	14.096	23T	28.4%
Russia			75T	
India	3.53T	2.516	N/A	3.0%

CHINA

As discussed, I project that China will fall and be demoted to a regional power. Manufacturing is leaving. Investment is drying up. They are highly dependent on oil imports. They have food and water security issues. Importantly, the people are primed for an internal coup! The sentiment of the world has turned against China, and they are considered a pariah nation, not to be trusted!

RUSSIA

Russia is an isolated nation. To put it plainly, the world does not want to place its future in the hands of any communist nation. Their economy is heavily skewed toward natural resources. It does not rank in the top 10 in GDP, per capita, or percentage of global manufacturing, which are requirements for a global leadership role. To be a global leader, a nation must have a diversified economy that can address global issues. That is not Russia! In this technological age, Russia lacks the necessary technology and skill set to lead the world.

INDIA

This is where China was 40 years ago! It is an emerging economy with a lot of potential. It will greatly benefit from China's fall, but it suffers from many of the same issues that China does. Its population holds down GDP, making it difficult to bring prosperity to the entire nation. It suffers from a lack of unity that makes effective governance truly difficult! This is because it has 23 official languages, and there are deep-seated cultural and religious differences between its many provinces!

THE UNITED STATES

Like I have said many times, America is God's covenant nation! It was chosen before the foundation of time to gather God's lost sheep. Many things have been done in the name of America that put a blemish on its reputation. But at the same time, it has been the leading light of freedom to the world.

When the global elite's shadow government falls (as it soon will), the heart of America will brighten the world. If you examine the key indicators of financial prosperity and leadership, the inescapable conclusion is that the U.S. is the only nation in the world capable of filling the power vacuum created by the collapse of the global monetary system, the fall of China, and the collapse of the financial elite. America is #1 in GDP and per capita income, #2 in natural resources, manufacturing, trade, and technology, and #3 in innovation!

To become a superpower, a nation must hold a leadership position in all three of the following areas: natural resources, manufacturing, and trade. No nation other than the U.S. holds this distinction! China is the only nation that even comes close to the U.S., and, as we have discussed, for a myriad of reasons, it is destined to collapse and be relegated to being a regional power.

OVERARCHING GLOBAL PERSPECTIVE

GOD'S RESET VS. THE GLOBAL ELITE'S RESET

The plans of the financial elite are falling apart, and God has written on the wall (just as He did in Persia), forecasting their downfall. The global elite's defeat began when the miracle of miracles, Hillary (the witch), was defeated by Trump, the bull in the china shop (God's Cyrus). Trump promised to "Make America Great Again," to which Obama (the son of perdition) responded, *"What are you going to do, wave a magic wand?"*

Go figure that in a matter of months, the U.S. economy experienced a miraculous recovery! To anyone who knows the least thing about history, what Trump did was entirely understandable and replicable. With Trump, the world will experience the greatest economic turnaround in human history, which will ripple through all nations worldwide. To review his actions, Donald Trump:

- Gave America access to its vast storehouse of natural resources. The U.S. has perhaps more oil and natural gas than any nation in the world. However, we have been intentionally denied access to them.
- Got rid of regulations intended to hamper the building of U.S. infrastructure and the building of factories. Our infrastructure (once the best in the world) has been intentionally allowed to atrophy. But we still have a serviceable backbone, and once the financial elite are removed from power, our infrastructure will be rebuilt. And, in the process, it will supply massive amounts of construction jobs, just like what happened in China.
- Placed tariffs on China and negotiated fair trade deals, not intentionally losing trade deals, and instantly, the tables were turned on China. And China began to bleed economically while the U.S. started a stellar recovery. This is simple stuff, but it is absolutely what determines which countries will rise to the position of being a global superpower.

Soon—very soon—the eyes of the people will be opened, and the global financial elite will fall! If that occurs, the United States is the only nation capable of guiding the world toward a brighter future, and God will ensure it happens. Once the swamp has been drained (which is happening even now), the handcuffs will be taken off America, and the world will be set free.

God does nothing less. He gives us a foreshadowing of what He has planned. What I am about to tell you will shock you! God's plan to set the captives free already exists, and it is embedded in U.S. history! In the next chapter, I will outline that plan for you. It is not my plan. It is God's plan, and it is infallible! The best is indeed yet to come!

IMPLICATIONS FOR RUSSIA AND THE U.S.

The two nations in the world that the global financial elite most want to see fall are the U.S. and Russia. On the following page, we will explore why for each nation.

RUSSIA

Earlier, I touched on the war in Ukraine, but I need to punctuate something here that the people of the world need to open their eyes to! The Rothschild Central Banker Gangsters control the world! They control virtually all the world's governments. Presidents who oppose them are killed (e.g., Abraham Lincoln and John F. Kennedy, who tried to end the FED).

Countries that try to oppose them are invaded, and their leaders are killed. For example, Iraq, which refused its oil deal, and Libya, which tried to put together a coalition of African nations to go on a gold-backed currency! So, both Saddam and Gaddafi are dead, and their countries are in ruins. Now it is Russia's turn. But this time, their plans will backfire. Russia will not suffer defeat. Russia is being used by God!

The War in Ukraine is not what the talking heads on TV tell us it is. I covered this previously, so I'll keep it short. Russia is the only major country in the world without a Rothschild-controlled central bank. Putin may be many things, but he is no fool, and he is not a globalist. For this reason, Russia is a target. But wait! Russia is the bad guy here, right? No, not true! But Putin invaded peaceful Ukraine. Things are not as they look!

Remember how, in the chapter on false flags and wars for profit, the Elite always do one of two things to justify the war they want! Either they create a false flag event and blame it on the nation they wish to attack, i.e., 9/11 and Iraq, or they provoke the other nation into attacking them. For example, consider how Roosevelt goaded Japan into attacking the U.S. to pull us into WWII, or their attempts to instigate a war with the Cuban Missile Crisis!

Putin was placed in a position where he had to attack Ukraine. Just like with the Cuban Missile Crisis, they were trying to put missiles on Russia's border. Go back and read what I wrote about the history of Ukraine. They are not the poor innocents they are portrayed to be. They are the heart of the global elite's money laundering syndicate.

Here is what my Bible tells me! Just like God used Nebuchadnezzar, he is now using Putin. God is using Russian President Putin to clean the viper's nest! Then Russia will go back to sleep until its reappearance as part of the Combination Beast in the Book of Revelation!

THE UNITED STATES

In a nutshell, the U.S. is God's Anointed nation. As you just read, it is the only nation in the world capable of filling the vacuum created when China falls (and it will)! They are afraid of the U.S. and the power it is capable of projecting. The following quote has been stated previously, but I think it warrants repeating in this context. As the quote shows, the Elite's fear of the young U.S. necessitates the U.S. terrifying them today.

> If that mischievous financial policy, which had its origin in the North American Republic, should become indurated down to a fixture, then that Government will furnish its own money without cost. It will pay off debts and be without a debt. It will have all the money necessary to carry on its commerce. It will become prosperous beyond precedent in the history of the world.
> The brains, and the wealth of all countries will go to North America.
> That government must be destroyed,
> or it will destroy every monarchy on the globe.
> Abraham Lincoln, issuing the debt-free Greenback Currency,
> Senate document 23, page 91. 1865

All the nations that the Israelites went up against feared them because they knew God was with them. If you knew what God has shown me, you would not bet against the United States. Let's go back in history to glimpse God's hand intervening to ensure America's destiny was fulfilled. This has been mentioned before; therefore, I will be brief.

1588: MIRACLE OF THE RAGING SEA

Spain sent an Armada of ships to crush England, and they surely would have, had it not been for the Spanish Admiral instructing the fleet to cut their anchors to increase maneuverability. Then, all of a sudden, God whipped up a hurricane, and most of their fleet was sunk. England replaced Spain as the superpower of the day.

1940: MIRACLE OF THE CALM SEA

Allied forces were backed up against the sea at Dunkirk, France, and were on the verge of surrender! But a fog rolled in, and the German Air Force was grounded, and the English Channel became as smooth as glass. A flotilla of small pleasure boats rescued over 300,000 Allied troops who lived to fight another day and went on to win the war!

WWII: THE BREAKING OF THE GERMAN CODE

Allied troops were near defeat. They had one hope! Break the German Code. The Germans had a cipher machine that was so sophisticated that the odds of breaking their code were

150 million, million, million. But against all odds, the British broke the code without which they would have undoubtedly lost the war! God is a Waymaker!

2024 -2028: THE MIRACLE OF THE FALL OF THE GLOBAL FINANCIAL ELITE

The global financial system is on the verge of collapse. Both China and the U.S. will collapse. But the U.S. will rise from the ashes to lead the world into God's kingdom and an era of peace and prosperity.

Do you think that this time God is going to abandon His nation, the United States? Or, for that matter, the rest of His beloved children? No way.

God always knows the end before the beginning, and He is the Waymaker. He has made a way for this generation, and in the next chapter, you will find out what that plan is.

CHAPTER 12

THE TRUTH ABOUT CLIMATE CHANGE:
We Are Intentionally Poisoning the Earth

TOPICS COVERED IN THIS CHAPTER:

- THE TRUTH BEHIND THE ELITE'S CLIMATE CHANGE NARRATIVE
- WHY WIND, SOLAR, AND LITHIUM-POWERED ELECTRIC VEHICLES ARE NON-SOLUTIONS
- THE TRUTH ABOUT THE UN'S AGENDA 21
- WHY ARE ALL 17 OF THE UN'S SUSTAINABLE DEVELOPMENT GOALS LIES?
- WHY GETTING ACCESS TO SUPPRESSED ENERGY TECHNOLOGY IS THE KEY TO SUSTAINABLE DEVELOPMENT, PEACE, AND PROSPERITY

ARE WE KILLING MOTHER EARTH?
THE TRUTH BEHIND THE LIES!

THE ELITE WOULD have us believe that there are too many people consuming too many natural resources, and human activity is killing the planet. There is some truth to that, but as usual, they skew the facts to create a false narrative. The truth is that humanity is systematically poisoning Mother Earth.

And the Elite are doing it to create a worldwide crisis of their own making. One that, at the last minute, they intend to step in and offer solutions that will solve the very problems they intentionally caused. You are about to get your eyes opened as to the truth behind the "Green New Deal."

Let's break down the various ecological crises we are facing and see if we can't unravel the truth behind one of the biggest lies ever fostered on humanity.

THE TRUTH BEHIND THE ELITE'S CLIMATE CHANGE NARRATIVE!

THE PROBLEM

Our carbon footprint is supposedly the principal cause behind what we call "climate change" and "global warming"—lies we will expose later in this chapter.

THEIR SOLUTION

To achieve zero carbon emissions by 2050, they expect to do so by adopting the clean energy solutions listed below.

THE REAL SOLUTION

To avoid redundancy and confusion, the real solutions will be presented in the following chapters as a comprehensive, practical, and cost-effective solution that exposes the flaws of the Elite's Green New Deal Agenda.

WIND TURBINES ARE A COMPLETE JOKE AND ARE:

- **Expensive to manufacture and maintain:** The Green New Deal is estimated to cost up to a staggering $93 trillion, which is about $600,000 per U.S. household. This solution is utterly impractical from multiple perspectives!

- **Inefficient**: And up to 60% of the energy they produce is lost during transmission through landlines on our outdated, obsolete electrical grid.
- **Harmful and kills birds/marine life**
- **Prone to icing**: In inclement weather, when energy is most needed. Realistically, this limits their use to limited climatic zones!

SOLAR FARMS ARE SIMILAR TO WIND TURBINES IN THAT THEY ARE:

- **Inefficient:** As with wind turbines, solar panels lose up to 60% of the energy they produce during transmission through our outdated, obsolete electrical grid.
- **Wasteful of critical supplies of silver,** which is needed for the electronic devices that run a technological society.
- **Highly susceptible to storm damage:** As a result, massive numbers of solar panels end up in our landfills. They contain toxic materials, such as lead and cadmium, which pose a biohazard.
- **Limited in their life expectancy** (typically 25-30 years). Between transmission loss, weather damage, limited life expectancy, and the biohazard they represent, they are neither an environmentally friendly nor cost-effective energy solution. And don't forget they are connected to our obsolete grid system, which enriches our slave masters!
- **Impractical**: In many climatic zones and under a variety of weather conditions.

LITHIUM-POWERED ELECTRIC VEHICLES:

- **Depend on the grid.** Which, I will remind you, is an integral part of the problem they are professing to solve.
- **Have a limited range.** Meaning these vehicles are impractical for most people, except as a second car that is driven only locally. During a recent heat wave in California, which prompted the use of electric cars, people were advised that they could not use their electric vehicles because it would overload the grid, potentially triggering power outages. Go figure.
- **Are highly toxic when disposed of in landfills.** They contain Cobalt, Magnesium, Chromium, Thallium, Nickel, Copper, and Lead, as well as organic chemicals such as

electrolytes containing LiCLO4, LiBF4, and LiPF6. If these substances enter the water supply, they could potentially pose a risk to human health and ecosystems.

These three technologies represent the baseline solution that the Elite claim will solve all the world's power and environmental problems, saving the planet from a catastrophic ecological crisis. That is a lie from the pits of hell! Not only will they not do what they are touted to do, but they are actually a step backward. They are not only still connected to our carbon-belching, inefficient electric grid, but they also introduce new ecological biohazards and are so expensive as to utterly collapse the financial system.

This renders us at the mercy of the banker gangsters and their bought and paid for corrupt swamp creature politicians! That is the lie behind the Green New Deal! This so-called "deal" is a ploy to create chaos, forcing our surrender and acceptance of the New World Order, a supposed solution to the problems they caused. The trap is set and baited, but we will not take the bait because the truth will set us free!

They are lying to us about creating a "Zero Carbon Footprint by 2050" narrative. Solar, Wind, and lithium-powered electric cars are all connected to our obsolete carbon-dependent electric grid. Talk about a shell game. As I have said before, their intent is not and never was to eliminate our carbon footprint. Their goal is to divert our attention away from their non-solutions, keeping our focus off the correct solutions, which lie in releasing suppressed free energy technology. More on this later.

We are about to have our eyes opened so that the truth can set us free. The graphic on the next page offers a glimpse into the future that awaits us if we don't stand against this evil agenda.

Let us dig a little deeper into this monumental lie. **Agenda 2050** promises to solve 17 problems that they say will save the planet. The sad truth is that their magic bullet—comprising wind, solar, and lithium-powered electric cars—will not solve even one of the 17 issues they claim to address. They are nothing but a distraction.

Before you finish this chapter, we will unravel this tangled web of deception. However, first, I want to take you down another rabbit hole and discuss the Elite's hidden agenda. The intent is to poison us and pollute the planet, and as the Georgia Guidestones said, to reduce the global population to 500 million people. Then those of us that are allowed to survive will be nothing but "chattel" personal property—livestock. It's time to wake up!

Let's take a closer look at precisely what they have planned for us cockroaches. **Agenda 21** specifies what the Elite intends to do with us pesky sheeple.

THE UNITED NATION'S PLAN FOR SUSTAINABLE DEVELOPMENT
(AGENDA 21)

AGENDA FOR THE 21ST CENTURY

Agenda 21 calls for many things that will place limitations and restrictions on the world. They are:

- An end to national sovereignty
- Abandonment of the Constitution
- Presumption of guilt till proven innocent. i.e., no unalienable rights.
- An educational system focused on the environment as the central organizing principle of society
- Restructuring the family unit with education focused on allegiance to the state.
- Limitations on mobility, with up to 75% of land being off limits
- State control of access to higher education and career opportunities

- Limitations on private ownership of property with state-owned residences along rail corridors

The graphic below provides further information about the solutions that Agenda 2050 aims to implement to address the 17 problems the Elites believe are harming our planet.

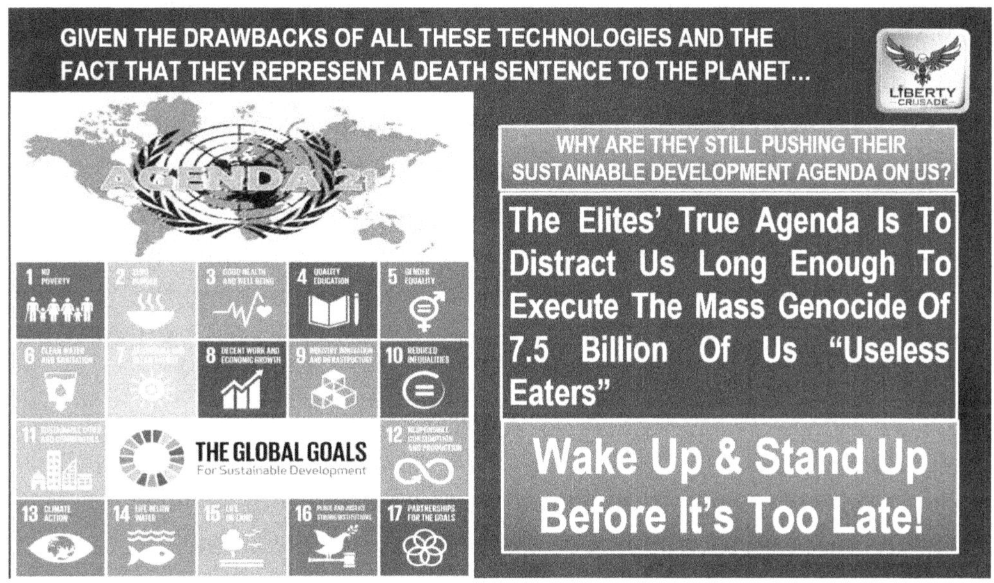

AGENDA 2050 AND THE ELITES' NON-SOLUTIONS
THE TRUE AGENDA IS TO POISON US AND THE PLANET AND USHER IN THEIR NEW WORLD ORDER THROUGH ORDER OUT OF CHAOS!

Their intention was never to restore ecological balance or cure any chronic disease. Instead, the intent is to poison us and the planet that sustains us. The poisons to which we are exposed are creating the underlying cause of many of our illnesses. We're then given toxic medications that mask symptoms, often creating worse problems than the original illness.

It may not be immediately apparent, but their poison pharmaceuticals make their way into our water supply, along with hormones and other additives they put in our food. Obama's science advisor, John Holdren, springs to mind; he promotes a global authority to pave the way for a one-world government. In his book, *Ecoscience: Population, Resources,*

Environment, Holdren wrote that we are facing a global overpopulation catastrophe that must be resolved at all costs. Holdren advocates:

- A "Planetary Regime" to control the global economy and dictate by force the number of children allowed to be born, which is what Communist China has done.
- The surrender of national sovereignty to an armed international police force. Can anyone say, "The United Nations?"
- Mass sterilization of humans, as long as it doesn't harm livestock. They need livestock, but with the advent of AI and Robotics, they can see the day when they no longer need us. And on that day, the mass of humanity becomes expendable!
- That single mothers should have their babies taken away by the government, or they could be forced to have abortions. While I write, the government is issuing threats to remove children from parents who don't agree to surgeries changing their children's sexual characteristics or hormone blockers, actions that caused Elon Musk's son's sterility.

The Elite are the enemy of humanity, and as I have said repeatedly, their true agenda is to kill a vast percentage of the population in the name of *"Resource Sustainability."* Then, when they have gotten rid of us, they plan to release shelved energy and medical technology and birth their utopian one-world dictatorship! Wake up before it is too late!

THE ELITE'S SELF-INDICTMENT

Rather than trying to prosecute or indict someone for crimes against humanity, it is often easier to let their own words convict them. In light of that, here are quotes that are a scathing critique of the Elite. They open their mouths and stick their foot in them.

Or if they don't, there are patriots who do it for them. But one way or another, the Truth always comes out. In Luke 8:17, God says,

> For there is nothing hidden that will not be disclosed, . . .
> Luke 8:17a (NIV)

You're about to have your world rocked!

INDICATIONS OF THE ELITE'S TRUE AGENDA!
THE ELITE ADMIT THEY ARE LYING TO US ABOUT THE CAUSE OF CLIMATE CHANGE

**'Protecting the environment' is a RUSE. The goal is the political and economic
subjugation of most men by the few, under the guise of preserving nature.**
J.H. Robbins [Emphasis Added]

**We've got to ride this global warming issue.
Even if the theory of global warming is wrong...**
Timothy Wirth, former U.S. Senator, D-CO

**A global climate treaty must be implemented
even if there is no scientific evidence to back the greenhouse effect.**
Richard Benedict, State Dept. Employee
While working on an assignment from the Conservation Foundation

THE ELITE ADMIT THEY REALLY WANT TO COMMIT MASS GENOCIDE:

**Isn't the only hope for the planet that the industrialized civilizations collapse? Isn't it
our responsibility to bring that about?**
Maurice Strong, executive director of the UN Environmental Program
Opening Speech, Rio Earth Summit 1992

*Global Sustainability requires the deliberate quest of poverty...
reduced resource consumption...and set levels of mortality control.*
Professor Maurice King, Director of the UN Rio Accord

**A total world population of 250-300 million people,
A 95 percent decline from present levels would be ideal.**
Ted Turner

**The United Nations' goal is to reduce population selectively by encouraging abortion,
forced sterilization, and control of human reproduction, and regards two-thirds of the
human population as excess baggage, with 350,000 people to be eliminated per day.**
Jacques Cousteau (UNESCO Courier, November 1991)

Depopulation should be the highest priority of foreign policy
towards the third world,. . .
Henry Kissinger, Secretary of State Under Richard Nixon

A part of eugenic politics would finally land us in an extensive use of the lethal
chamber. A great many people would have to be put out of existence simply because it
wastes other people's time to look after them.
George Bernard Shaw, Lecture to the Eugenics Education Society
(Reported in The Daily Express, March 4, 1910)

THE ELITE ADMIT THEY WANT WORLD DOMINATION AT ANY COST:

We are not going to achieve a New World Order
without paying for it in blood as well as in words and money.
Arthur Schlesinger Jr., *The CFR Journal of Foreign Affairs*, August 1975)

We are on the verge of a global transformation. All we need is the right major crisis and
the nations will accept the New World Order.
David Rockefeller, Sept. 23, 1994

The supranational sovereignty of an intellectual elite and world bankers
is surely preferable to the national determination practiced in past centuries.
David Rockefeller, Council on Foreign Relations

To achieve world government, it is necessary to remove from the minds of men their
individualism, loyalty to family traditions, national patriotism, and religious dogmas.
Brock Adams, Director, UN Health Organization

No one will enter the New World Order unless he or she will make a pledge to worship
Lucifer. No one will enter the New Age unless he will take a Luciferian Initiation.
David Spangler, Director of Planetary Initiative, United Nations

The New World Order cannot happen without U.S. participation, as we are the most
significant single component. Yes, there will be a New World Order, and it will force
(cont'd next page)

the United States to change its perceptions.
Henry Kissinger: World Affairs Council Press Conference,
Regent Beverly Wilshire Hotel, April 19, 1994

THE ELITE ADMIT BIG BROTHER IS HERE TO CONTROL AND ENSLAVE US:

The technetronic era involves the gradual appearance of a more controlled society.
Such a society would be dominated by an elite, unrestrained by traditional values.
Soon, it will be possible to assert almost continuous surveillance over every citizen
and maintain up-to-date, complete files containing even the most personal
information about the citizen. These files will be subject to instantaneous
retrieval by the authorities.

Zbigniew Brzezinski
Between Two Ages: America's Role in the Technetronic Era, 1970

NOTE: Add Central Bank Digital Currency, and their slavery system is complete. Wake up, stand up, before it is too late!

EXECUTIVE ORDER 11921

This order states:

When a state of emergency is declared by the President,
Congress cannot review the action for six months.

There are three branches of government. To have all the power in the hands of the executive branch undermines the entire concept of the balance of power and seriously erodes our civil liberties, not to mention opening the door to a dictatorship.

NOTE: This is precisely how Hitler rose to power through "The Enabling Act," and that same authority is conveyed to the president in the "Patriot Act," which creates a legal dictatorship.

TRANSLATION: *They want to end the sovereignty of all nations, especially the U.S.,*
which is the only nation in the world capable of stopping their maniacal plan to establish
their New World Order Dictatorship.

WHISTLEBLOWERS SAY THE ELITE WANT TO IMPLEMENT THE BEAST SYSTEM:

The New World Order under the UN will reduce everything to one common
denominator. The system will be made up of a single currency,
single centrally financed government, single tax system, single language, single
political system, single world court of justice, single state religion...
Anonymous

Each person will have a registered number, without which he will not be allowed to buy
or sell; and there will be one universal world church. Anyone who refuses to take part in
this universal system
will have no right to exist.
From *Assessment of the New World* by Dr. Kurt E. Koch

I risk sounding like a conspiracy theorist, but it is no longer a theory.
What I am about to say is fact. The secret organizations of the world power elite are no
longer secret. They have planned and are now leading us into a One World Communist
Government. The combining of national governments started with the European
Union. That union started with trade agreements, then a common currency, the Euro,
and now a European Parliament that is feverishly passing laws . . . A constitution was
drafted, but was rejected by a few of those nations; but never mind, they implemented
it anyway. Now it is North America's turn. Building on the 'North American
Free Trade Agreement', the NAFTA section of the Commerce Department
is busy drafting laws and regulations for a North American Union—
a union of Canada, America, and Mexico. The President [Former President Bush] has
attended secret meetings and signed at least two agreements under the 'Security and
Prosperity Partnership Program.' Information leaked out about the meetings,
and now it is all in the open. No treaty has been signed,
so Congress has not become involved; however, money from our treasury
is now being spent for this effort. We will have a new currency, the Amero and a new
Constitution modeled on the Soviet Union's Constitution.
Stan Jones, U.S. Senate Candidate for the Libertarian Party in a CSPN Debate 2006
[Emphasis Added]

NOTE: The Amero Union has, as yet, not been birthed, but not for lack of trying. See graphics
on the next page.

NORTH AMERICAN UNION
International Rights Supersede Those Of US Citizens

Bureaucrats Write Regulations
Merging The US, Mexico & Canada

Transportation
Law Enforcement
Agriculture
Banking
Manufacturing
Construction
Education
Immigration
Military

Both Bush Sr. & Biden Plotted to End U.S. Sovereignty by Merging the U.S. With Canada & Mexico!

The Plan Is To Create A 10 Nation
Servile Trading Block Beast System!

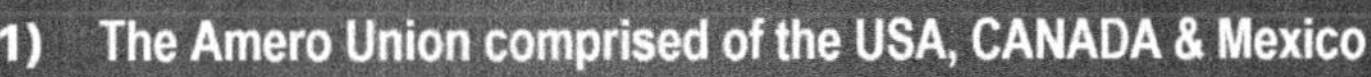

1) The Amero Union comprised of the USA, CANADA & Mexico
2) The E.U. – countries of the European Union, Western Europe as a whole
3) Japan
4) Australia, New Zealand, South Africa
5) Eastern Europe, Pakistan, Afghanistan, Russia and the former countries of the Soviet Union
6) Central and South America, Cuba and Caribbean Islands
7) The Middle East and North Africa
8) The rest of Africa, except South Africa
9) South and Southeast Asia, including India
10) China and Mongolia

Let's break down the UN's Agenda 2050 (17 Sustainable Development Goals) one by one and analyze them to see if they are realistic or just a pack of lies intended to distract us. Remember, it is not what our leaders *say* that is important. It is what they *do* that matters. Over at least the last 50 years, under Nixon, Carter, Clinton, the Bushes, Obama, and Biden, we have been censored, lied to, and driven into economic repression. So, why should we believe anything they say? We should not!

What I am going to lay out are real solutions based on my years of research and my walk with God. I believe God has anointed Trump for this pivotal time in world history. So, I will be referring to Trump and what he is doing to drain the swamp, and how it will chart the course to accomplish most, if not all, of the 17 goals the UN is taunting in their Agenda 2050 lie-fest. What the UN and our corrupt politicians are proposing is nothing but a bunch of lies and hyperbole.

As I've reiterated, this is the time of God's Harvest of Souls, and He is the Waymaker. The future God has in store for mankind is the exact opposite of the one envisioned by our elite slave masters! The following two quotes from a few pages back tell us the truth about the Elite's hidden agenda. It is to enslave us, impoverish us, and kill most of us. Don't forget what the Georgia Guidestones said: They called for a global population of 500 million.

By now, I am sure you have noted that I tend to use quotes more than once. That is a form of reinforcement, and it applies in different contexts as a means to reinforce what is being said at the time.

> **Global Sustainability requires the deliberate quest of poverty...**
> **reduced resource consumption...and set levels of mortality control.**
> Professor Maurice King, Director of the UN Rio Accord

Think about it! This quote contradicts everything the Elite claim they will do to save the planet and improve life for all of us. Wait! Better for whom? Us? Or for themselves? Remember, their idea of Utopia doesn't include us because we are consuming too many of their natural resources, so we must be exterminated the way you would exterminate an infestation of cockroaches!

NOT ONE OF THESE GOALS IS ACHIEVABLE UNDER THE UN'S GREEN NEW DEAL AGENDA 2050
WITH THEIR BOGUS WIND, SOLAR AND LITHIUM BATTERY TECHNOLOGY!

NOTE: There are solutions to all these crises, but the UN's Agenda 2050 addresses none of them. To avoid confusion, the solutions will be presented separately after we have covered all the UN's non-solutions

UNITED NATIONS GOALS

1)   **NO POVERTY:** There is a real disconnect here! I hate to be redundant, but the following quotes shout the truth for all to hear. They convict our slave masters out of their own mouths.

> **The one aim of these financiers is world control by the creation of
> inextinguishable debts.**
> Henry Ford, Industrialist

> **It [the depression] was a carefully contrived occurrence . . ..
> The International bankers sought to bring about a condition of despair here
> so that they might emerge as the rulers of us all.**
> Congressman Louis Thomas McFadden, [Emphasis Added]

Comment: The 1929 Great Depression, 08 Collapse, and soon-to-come Financial Reset were all orchestrated as part of the plan to create the *"Inexhaustible Debt"* that enslaves us in invisible chains!

> **Whoever controls the volume of money in our country is absolute master
> of all industry and commerce... when you realize that the entire system is very easily
> controlled, one way or another, by a few powerful men at the top, you will not have to
> be told how periods of inflation and depression originate.**
> President James A. Garfield stated two weeks before he was assassinated.

> *TRANSLATION: Financial collapses are intentionally orchestrated to take your homes
> and investments and to impoverish you to make you dependent on the Elite's system of
> slavery without chains!*

These are not benign statements! They are malevolent statements declaring war on us. You cannot have inextinguishable debts *and* collapse industrial civilization while achieving prosperity. They are mutually exclusive concepts.

Then consider the track records of the last several administrations. When Carter was elected president in 1977, the National debt was a scant $660 billion, and now it is over $38 trillion. The principal causes for this astronomical increase in national debt are attributed largely to the intentionally losing NAFTA trade deal signed under Clinton, the Iraq war (for profit), which Bush said would be a *generational war*, and the trillions in stimulus checks printed during the Plan-demic.

We practiced what I call 'losing trade,' deliberately losing trade, over the last 50 years...
Congressman Duncan Hunter (R-CA)
During debates about U.S. trade policy in 2006

There is no instance of a nation benefiting from prolonged warfare.
Sun Tzu in *The Art of War*

It [war] depletes assets and affects morale, and at some point,
the cost of victory is too great.
King Pyrrhus of Epirus [Emphasis added]

There are two ways to conquer and enslave a nation.
One is by the sword. The other is by debt.
President John Adams

Remember, the Elite want a financial reset, and that requires that the current system implode. I say again they are liars, and they are capable of committing mass murder or any other atrocity necessary to achieve their New World Order Dictatorship.

2)   **ZERO HUNGER:** Another lie! Remember when I said that our carbon footprint (though it is a factor in what the Elite call "climate change") is not the real threat. So, what is? The real threat the world is facing is a biblical-level famine caused by a global shortage of clean water for irrigation and drinking. Our lakes, rivers, and aquifers are drying up at an alarming rate. This is not because there is less rainfall. It is because since the turn of the century, the population has increased from approximately two billion to approximately eight billion. As a result, we are simply drawing more water from these sources (for irrigation and manufacturing) than can be replenished by rainfall. Additionally, countries like China and India face a serious water pollution problem, rendering much of their water supply unusable for both agricultural and human consumption. Don't worry, there are solutions, and we will discuss them soon.

3)   **GOOD HEALTH AND WELL-BEING:** I guess that when our slave masters patented and released COVID-19, they thought they were doing us a favor. *Not So!* Likewise, I suppose that when they forced us to take unproven vaccines, of which manufacturers were indemnified

against lawsuits, they were protecting us from ourselves. *Not So!* And when we protested because of all the deaths and health issues caused by the vaccines, they had our well-being in mind when they told us to shut up and take the shot or lose our jobs. *Not So!* These people are the enemy of humanity.

4)   **QUALITY EDUCATION:** I suppose that putting tampons in boys' restrooms was a good thing. *Maybe Not!* And I guess teaching our children to despise our flag and that socialism is a good thing was to strengthen our nation and bring us closer together. *Maybe Not!* Maybe it was to divide us! And I guess it was for *our* well-being when they created one education system for the Elite, a second for the middle class, and a third for an "undereducated entitlement class." *Maybe Not!* But it did an excellent job of creating division and economic disparity. That was the plan all along.

Education is dangerous. Every educated person is a future enemy.
Hermann Göring, Hitler's designated successor

If a nation expects to be ignorant and free, in a state of civilization,
it expects what never was and never will be.
President Thomas Jefferson, 1816

Comment: That is why we have propaganda centers disguised as schools.

Every kingdom divided against itself is brought to desolation,
and every city or house divided against itself will not stand.
Matthew 12:25b (NKJV)

Those who manipulate this unseen mechanism of society constitute an invisible
government which is the true ruling power of our country...In almost every act of our
lives, whether in the sphere of politics or business, in our social conduct or our ethical
thinking, we are dominated by the relatively small number of persons...
who understand the mental processes and social patterns of the masses.
It is they who pull the wires which control the public mind.
Edward Bernays, Father of Modern Advertising

The Central Intelligence Agency owns everyone of any significance in the major media.
William Colby, Former CIA Director

5)   **GENDER EQUALITY:** I suppose society is better off when schools teach children to question their gender. *Not!* Every society that has ever taken that path has degraded into immorality and ultimately fallen from within. Could there be a hidden agenda to such policies? *Yes!* Consider the following:

To achieve world government, it is necessary to remove from the minds of men their individualism, loyalty to family traditions, national patriotism, and religious dogmas.
Brock Adams, Director, UN Health Organization

Comment: They want a unisex, one-world dictatorship. The philosopher Confucius tells us precisely the opposite.

To put the world in order, we must first put the nation in order.
To put the nation in order, we must first put the family in order.
To put the family in order, we must first cultivate our personal life.
And to cultivate our personal life, we must first set our hearts right.
Confucius

I am sure there is no malevolent intent when the government threatens to take children from parents who refuse to comply with its LGBTQ Gestapo legislation. *No, not much!* Nor is there any when Obama's science czar threatens to either force unmarried women to have abortions or have their children taken by the state. *They are so kindhearted!*

6)   **CLEAN WATER AND SANITATION:** According to the UN, our carbon footprint is killing the planet, and extreme measures are required. Say the $93 trillion Green New Deal—Agenda 21—Agenda 2030, etc. But if this is true, how is it that all the solutions offered by the UN are still dependent on our carbon-belching, inefficient, outdated electric grid? And how is it that millions of solar panels and lithium batteries are buried in landfills where the heavy metals and other biohazardous materials they contain can leach into our water supply and destroy ecosystems?

Could it be that the last thing they want to do is provide us with actual solutions? Could they be protecting their multi-trillion-dollar revenue stream based on oil, gas, and coal, as well as the electric grid? They have no incentive to sunset these technologies. But they have a very real incentive to reduce the population to 500 million because we are consuming too many of their valuable resources.

NOTE: We are facing opposition from powerful men who make decisions in dark rooms that control our lives. They represent the interests of a cabal of European bankers and bought and paid for swamp creatures in Washington. They have no allegiance to the Constitution of *We the People.* Their only allegiance is to maximize the profits of an illegal, unconstitutional banking cartel in Europe. They are the enemy of all humanity and must be removed for us to have freedom!

> **The illegal we do immediately. The unconstitutional takes a little longer.**
> Henry Kissinger, Secretary of State and CFR Member

> **Since I entered politics, I have chiefly had men's views confided to me privately. Some of the biggest men in the United States, in the field of commerce and manufacture, are afraid of something. They know there is a power somewhere so organized, so subtle, so watchful, so interlocked, so complete, so pervasive, that they better not speak above their breath when they speak in condemnation of it.**
> President Woodrow Wilson

As I have said, the genuine crisis that must be addressed is not our carbon footprint, but access to clean, usable water for irrigation to avoid a biblical-level famine. Our lakes, rivers, and aquifers are being sucked dry from the demand placed on them to irrigate millions of acres of farmland to grow the food to feed eight billion people. This crisis can be solved by gaining access to free energy technology, which would enable the implementation of super-sustainable water from the atmosphere technology, as explained later in this chapter. (See heading titled: **Ecological Issues—Implications of free/cheap, clean, renewable energy**).

But that technology alone does not solve the problem. We must also implement water conservation technology. We start by turning from wasteful above-ground irrigation to underground drip irrigation like that used to re-green the deserts in Israel. However, if we are to re-green, for example, the Sahara Desert in Africa, which is characterized by its porous sand, technology must be deployed to prevent water from leaching through the sand. There is such technology. It is called an "*Evaporative Control System*." Essentially, it involves placing catch basins beneath the sand, connected by a network of pipes that fill the basins and regulate the water level. With these technologies, vast areas that are currently non-arable can become re-greened, and the world's food and water crisis can be solved. All we need is a government that actually wants to solve the problem!

7) **AFFORDABLE AND CLEAN ENERGY:** We just discussed why wind, solar, and lithium are not clean energy solutions. Neither are they cost-effective. See graphic below.

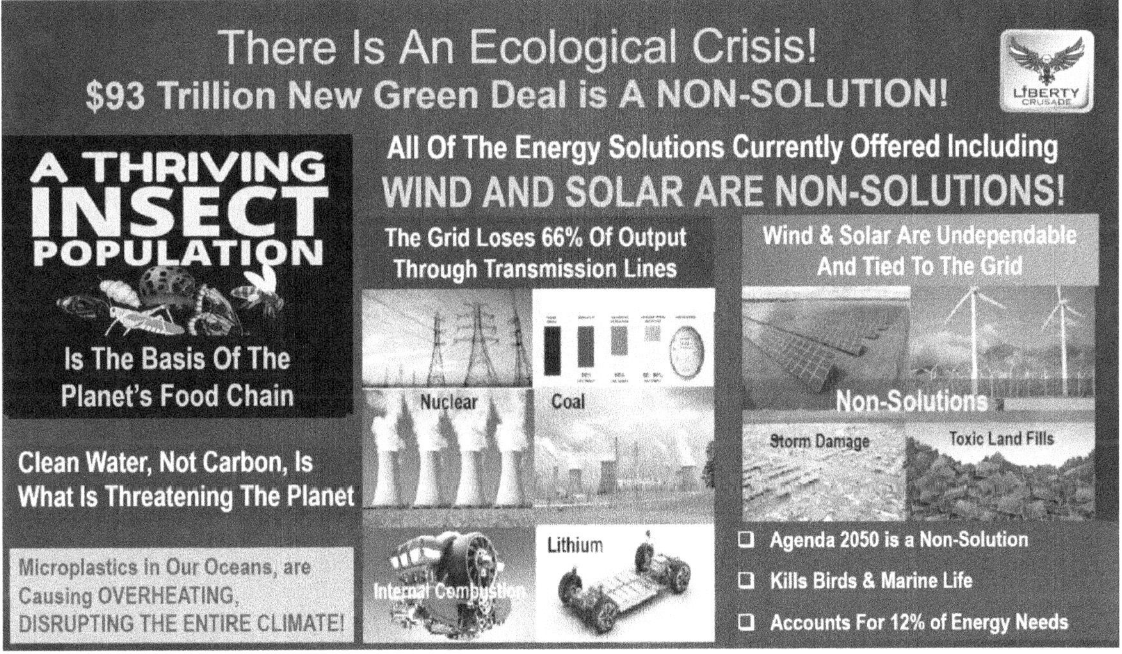

NOTE: Why is that? Because, from the perspective of our elite slave masters, it would break the chains of our economic slavery. A little history lesson is in order. At the turn of the 20th century, Nikola Tesla discovered a free energy technology that would enable the atmosphere to be electrified, making free, non-polluting electricity available worldwide. His financier, J.P. Morgan, replied that "that would make him nothing but a goddamn antenna salesman," upon which he pulled Tesla's funding, suppressed his research, and saw to it that no one would fund the project or any other like it. The truth is that it is not in the interest of the Elite to provide us with clean, cheap energy because it would render them obsolete as antenna salesmen, and they would no longer be able to control us and our access to the necessities of life.

We would break free, which is the last thing they want. We should heed the warning of President Ronald Reagan:

> **Approximately 80% of our air pollution stems from hydrocarbons**
> **released by vegetation, so let's not go overboard in setting and enforcing tough**
> **emission standards from manmade sources.**
> President Ronald Reagan

Before you finish this chapter, you will find out that there are cheap, clean, renewable solutions that can solve the problems the UN only pretends to want to solve. Hang in just a little longer. The truth will set us free!

8)   DECENT WORK AND ECONOMIC GROWTH: Once again, the UN is lying to us. It is not in their best interest to provide us with decent work and economic growth. I remind you of their true agenda, which is to collapse *"the industrialized civilization."*

> **Isn't the only hope for the planet that the industrialized civilization collapses?**
> **Isn't it our responsibility to bring that about?**
> Maurice Strong, executive director of the UN Environmental Program
> Opening Speech, Rio Earth Summit 1992

Just open your eyes! Retail stores are busy installing and ordering checkout kiosks, which take away jobs. More and more sophisticated robots are being invented to take away still more jobs. AI is on the fast track to do just about everything a human can do faster and better. Dystopia is on the horizon.

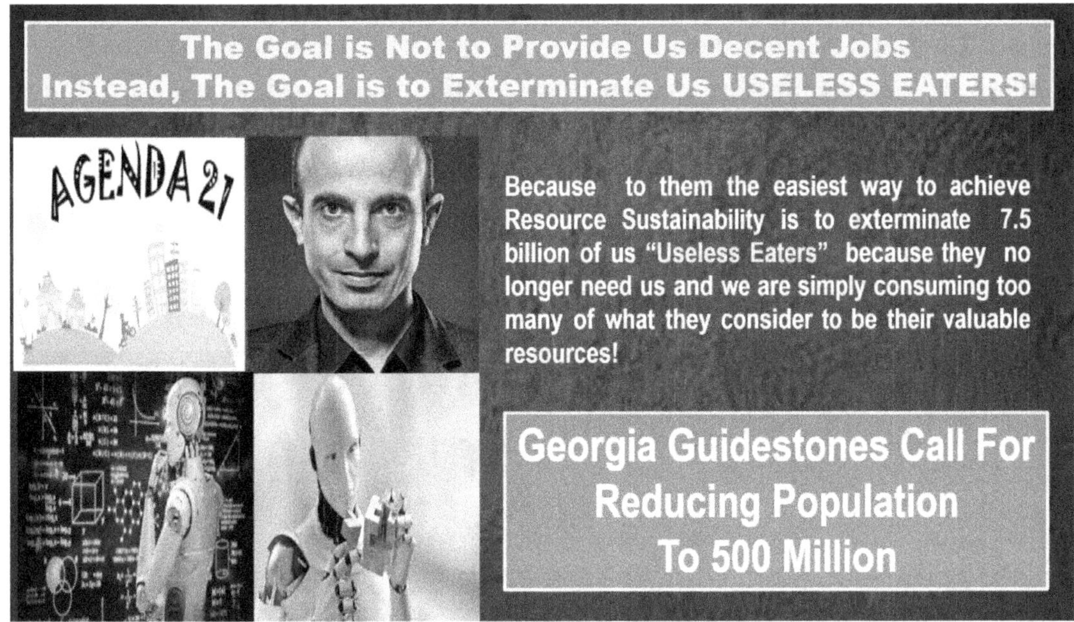

9) INDUSTRY, INNOVATION, AND INFRASTRUCTURE: So, while the Elite blocked Tesla's Free Energy technology, they were all too happy to allow Henry Ford to birth the automobile industry in 1903, making way for John D. Rockefeller to build an oil empire that to this day fuels our cars. Go figure, technology is doubling in capacity every two years, and yet we have not been able to devise a better mode of transportation than the internal combustion engine, which is likely the largest source of carbon pollution on the planet.

Since the invention of the automobile, we have put a man on the moon, developed supercomputers, robotics, nanites (aka nanobots), 3D Printers, artificial intelligence, and a plethora of other inventions. Yet we still drive cars based on technology that was invented 122 years ago. Finally, along comes the electric vehicle, and we become less dependent on gasoline. But things aren't always as they seem. Because, you see, those electric cars get their power from the carbon-belching grid. The one constant is that the Elite still have control of their multi-trillion-dollar energy cartel!

Several alternative energy technologies have been suppressed by the corporate mafia and their partners in crime, our swamp-dwelling Washington politicians, who pass laws that allow such technology to be kept from ever seeing the light of day. But that is changing! As Trump says, we will have free energy, and before you finish this chapter, all will be revealed.

10) REDUCED INEQUALITIES: Let me ask you a question: When have you ever seen an election where the Swamp Monsters failed to play the race card, the class card, the socio-economic card, the gender card, the political party card, the Union VS Worker card, and virtually every card they could come up with to divide us and pit us against one another? When has there ever been a time when we were not pitted against some other nation or group of nations or class of people? Never. That is when! Remember the Bible says, "A nation divided cannot stand." Division is a control mechanism of our slave masters.

The whole aim of practical politics is to keep the populace alarmed
(and hence clamorous to be led to safety) by [menacing it with]
an endless series of hobgoblins, most of them imaginary.
H. L. Mencken [Emphasis added]

SUSTAINABLE CITIES AND COMMUNITIES: To understand why this is another lie, we need to understand how our current tax structure works. We are under an illegal Federal Reserve (which illegally taxes your labor). 100% of the money you pay in federal income tax goes to European bankers to pay the national debt that is created by printing the fiat dollar. Then, to collect the illegal tax, our Washington swamp creatures join forces with the European banking mafia and pass laws that force you to pay an unlawful tax.

At that point, you are locked into a debt trap where every dollar printed creates additional debt. So, under that system, the debt keeps climbing until we reach the point where we are today (which is where the national and personal debt stands)—at the point where it is about to collapse the fiat Ponzi Debt Trap.

Their **progressive tax structure** works like this: Initially, when the national debt is low, they collect enough money from federal income tax to service the debt. Then, eventually, the debt increases to the point that not enough money is collected from federal income tax to service the national debt, so a bunch of new taxes are created, i.e., inheritance tax, petroleum tax, capital gains tax, etc. Eventually, these new taxes are insufficient to service the national debt, so they raise the tax rate and keep raising it until the system implodes on itself. Then they say that the banks are too big to fail, so we, the people, must bail them out. And at the end of the cycle, they start all over with a new Ponzi scheme.

Here is how the last reset worked. When the Banks failed in 1933, the Washington swamp creatures passed legislation stating that we had to turn in our gold at the going rate of $35 an ounce or face a $10,000 fine and/or ten years in prison. Once they got our gold, they raised the price of gold to $65 an ounce. Gold is a store of value against inflation. At the time of this writing, a one-ounce gold coin buys exactly what it bought in 1933. Meanwhile, the dollar has devalued from $1 to four cents, headed to zero.

This time, they have something even more diabolical planned. They intend to go to digital currency (which, in and of itself, is not bad). But they want to tie it to a Central Bank Digital Currency (CBDC), which is effectively the beast system that determines who can buy and sell and what you can buy and sell, i.e., meat substitutes only, no meat, no guns, no bullets, etc.

So, the bottom line to this story is that the reason I know they have no intention to give us sustainable cities and communities is that the money is not earmarked for that purpose. It is intended for European bankers. They not only tax us into poverty, but they also indenture future generations as well. They do that by spending money they don't have, by dragging us into protracted wars for profit, funding all manner of entitlements, and then, finally, when they get around to building infrastructure projects, they are out of money, so those projects are funded by driving us even further into debt because they are funded with borrowed money, not tax revenues.

This was all based on abandoning our Constitution and putting the U.S. under a corporate charter. Under a corporation, the only obligation our Washington Swamp Creatures have is to optimize the profits of the shareholders of the Illegal U.S. Corporation, none of whom are U.S. citizens or, for that matter, U.S. Banks. They are all foreign European banks. The graphic above should help you understand just how this travesty operates.

The bottom line is that we have a shadow government in place in Washington. It is they who run the U.S. on behalf of a European banking cartel headed by Britain, the Vatican, and overseen by the UN, the World Bank, and the IMF. The following quotes explain that because of this, our Washington Swamp Rats are just puppets of an international banking cartel. It is they who run our nation on behalf of the shareholders, none of whom are any of us.

Someone once warned in the 1960s that:

> ... both houses of Congress are irrelevant. America's domestic policy is now being run by ... The Chairman of the FED and the Federal Reserve. America's foreign policy is now being run by the IMF (International Monetary Fund).

11) RESPONSIBLE CONSUMPTION AND PRODUCTION: Yet another lie. During the Carter administration, the decision was made by the puppet masters to shift control of global manufacturing to China and to begin the process of financially collapsing the United States.

The Cliff Notes version of the story is that trade was opened with China. Then, the NAFTA trade deal was passed to create intentionally lost trade deals. Major U.S. corporations were acquired in hostile takeovers and then sold off in pieces to make holes in the U.S. markets.

Effectively, this reinstated the British free trade slavery system, rebranded as Chinese free trade. Chinese workers were employed in sweatshops to make cheap Chinese products that undercut U.S. labor costs. This resulted in capturing a huge portion of U.S. manufacturing, with products designed to wear out quickly, necessitating frequent replacement. A massive amount of natural resources was squandered because manufactured products were designed to wear out. In contrast, we had the ability to build products that last. The following disclosure cost Larry McDonald his life.

> **The Rockefeller File is not fiction. It is a compact, powerful, and frightening presentation of what may be the most important story of our lifetime.**
> The Rockefeller File by Gary Allen, American Journalist

> **The drive of the Rockefellers and their allies is to create a one-world government combining super-capitalism and communism all under the same tent, all under their control....**
> Congressman Larry P. McDonald, GA

> **Not one has dared reveal the most vital part of the Rockefeller story: that the Rockefellers and their allies have, for at least fifty years, been carefully following a plan to use their economic power to gain political control of first, America, and then the rest of the world.**
> Congressman Larry P. McDonald, GA, in his Introduction to The Rockefeller Files

> **Do I mean conspiracy? Yes, I do. I am convinced there is such a plot, international in scope, generations old in planning, and incredibly evil in intent.**
> Congressman Larry P. McDonald, GA

So, the intent was to collapse the U.S. financially, getting it out of the way as the only nation in the world with the power to block the formation of the Elite's demonic one-world dictatorship!

12) **CLIMATE ACTION:** We have already discussed why wind, solar, and lithium batteries are a non-solution—just a distraction and another lie. So, we will move on to the next topic.

13) **LIFE BELOW WATER:** This implies the intent to clean our oceans and replenish endangered marine species, **But No!** Given the plight of our oceans, one would think they would stop polluting them, **But No!** One would think they would prevent plastic waste from contaminating our lakes, rivers, and oceans, **But No!** On this topic, remember plastic is a forever product, meaning it does not biodegrade. As a result, it poses a significant threat to marine life. Over time, the plastic breaks down into small microparticles. The colored particles are mistaken by marine life as food and ingested, which kills them. Do some research. This is a very serious problem that is not receiving the attention it deserves.

The even bigger problem is that those nanoparticles of plastic (of which it is said there are trillions) act as a heat sink, causing our oceans to heat up. In simple terms, water flows from the two poles to the equator, acting to regulate the planet's temperature. This in turn controls the planet's weather patterns. If the ocean water heats up too much, the convection current from the poles to the equator and back to the poles stops, and the planet is plunged into an ice age. What more serious problem could there possibly be, but they ignore it!

Could it be that they plan on killing billions of us and then employing suppressed technology that can clean our water and air? Such technology exists. More on this later.

14) **LIFE ON LAND:** Again, if they were serious about solving this crisis, they would not ram inefficient, energy solutions connected to our carbon-belching grid on us. They would not suppress thousands of patents because they threaten their revenue stream (particularly affecting their multi-trillion-dollar energy revenues).

Trump said we would have free energy, and we will. The reversal of the Chevron Supreme Court case will provide us with the means to access these technologies. More on this later. Lastly, they poison our food and spray us with chemtrails. Yes, they are real, and they contain heavy metals. Do some research.

15) PEACE, JUSTICE, AND STRONG INSTITUTIONS: We have discussed how wars for profit are perpetrated on us by our Swamp Creatures in Washington and their partners in the Military Industrial Complex. We have also discussed how those wars were justified based on false flag events. We have discussed how those wars were intentionally dragged out to drive us deep into debt. Consider the following:

> **The question was how we should maneuver them [Japan] into firing
> the first shot ... it was desirable to make sure the Japanese be the ones to do this
> so that there should remain no doubt as to who were the aggressors.**
> Henry Stimson, U.S. Secretary of War before WWII, Nov. 25, 1941,
> [Emphasis added]

> **It [war] depletes assets and affects morale, and at some point,
> the cost of victory is too great.**
> King Pyrrhic of Epirus [Emphasis added]

Does this sound like a government that wants peace, justice, and strong institutions?

16) PARTNERSHIP FOR THE GOALS: There is no partnership for goals because the public wants peace and prosperity, and our Swamp Creatures want CHAOS, leading to our surrender and genocide of most of us.

> **I am concerned for the security of our great nation;
> not so much because of any threat from without,
> but because of the insidious forces working from within.**
> General Douglas MacArthur

> **In this present crisis, government is not the solution to our problem;
> government is the problem.**
> President Ronald Reagan

Today, this statement is true across a wide range of events. The quote on the following page, taken from *Confessions of an Economic Hit Man* by John Perkins, says it all:

> Economic hit men (EHMs) are highly paid professionals
> who cheat countries around the globe out of trillions of dollars.
> They funnel money from the World Bank, the U.S. Agency for International
> Development, and other foreign "aid" organizations (UN Organizations)
> into the coffers of huge corporations and the pockets of a few wealthy families who
> control the planet's natural resources. Their tools include fraudulent financial reports,
> rigged elections, payoffs, extortion, sex, and murder. They play a game as old as
> empire, but one that has taken on new and terrifying dimensions during this time of
> globalization. I should know I am an EHM.
>
> John Perkins

I close our discussion of the lies behind the UN's Agenda 2050 goals to achieve zero carbon emissions with the following graphic.

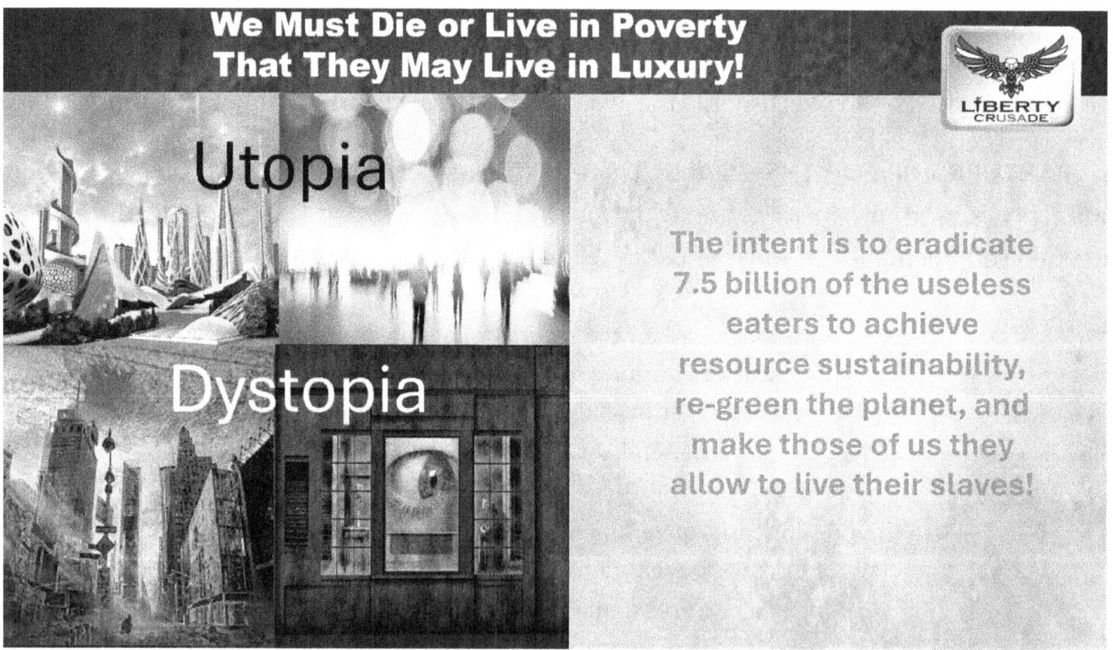

Need I say More? Convicted out of their own mouths and by truth seekers who spoke out before our media became little more than a propaganda weapon!

TIME FOR THE TRUTH AND REAL SOLUTIONS!

It is much easier to fix a problem than it is to enslave a nation or birth a one-world dictatorship. I think you will be surprised at how easy it is to actually do the things the UN claims it intends to do. Simply speaking, you look at what they have been doing and do the opposite. We do not need to rehash all 17 of the Agenda 2050 goals because they all fall into four general categories:

- Sovereignty—Restoration of Our Republic
- Ecological Issues—Implications of Free/Cheap, Clean, Renewable Energy
- Financial Stability—Not Intentionally Imposed Poverty
- Social Issues—Economic and Social Parity

Let's examine each of these categories in more depth.

SOVEREIGNTY—RESTORATION OF OUR REPUBLIC

As we have established, the solution is not wind, solar, or lithium batteries because they are costly, inefficient, and connected to the carbon-belching grid; their disposal also poses a biohazard. In 1951, the Swamp Rats (representing the Corporation) codified their technology suppression policies with the passage of the "Invention Secrecy Act," resulting in the suppression of a reported 5,915 patents. That suppression is about to end. Donald Trump is committed to getting access to these patents and the technology we need to innovate America and the world out of the financial collapse that must happen. As this collapse occurs, entire countries and their governments will collapse, along with massive numbers of blue-chip corporations and banks.

This financial collapse is essential for breaking free from our slave masters. As we have discussed, this collapse is underway. It is evidenced by the shift away from globalization to deglobalization, which is triggering the collapse of China, as well as the movement away from the dollar as the world's reserve currency to a commodity-based economy, led by the BRICS (Brazil, Russia, India, China, and South Africa). As with China, the U.S. economy must transition to a commodity-based economy that is not subject to manipulation, unlike a fiat system.

As to how all this will come about: When the financial collapse occurs, we will need a new economic system. That system is called NESARA, the *National Emergency Security And*

Restoration Act (to be discussed in the next chapter). It provides the framework for our new economic system as well as provisions for the release of the suppressed patents.

An indication that this is happening can be seen in the recent Chevron Supreme Court decision. It paves the way for the revitalization of America's manufacturing might. Simply speaking, it takes control of technology and related regulations away from the Banks and Corporations and their army of unelected bureaucrats (that represent the interests of the financial elite) and gives it back to our elected politicians, where it was intended under our Republic.

NOTE: I said "*republic.*" That is because, as this financial collapse occurs, the Act of 1871, which gave birth to the Corporation, will be repealed. At that point, America will once again be a REPUBLIC. When this happens, the FED and IRS will also be terminated (supposedly already has happened), and the printing of Commodity Backed Currency will be under the Treasury, as intended. These events will restore the SOVEREIGNTY of the U.S. and the REPUBLIC. Then we will be free to solve the problems that were imposed on us by our slave masters.

Trump says he will get rid of massive numbers of regulations (10 regulations to be removed for every new regulation). This will make way for restoring our infrastructure. Trump also said he will enable permits to be issued quickly to allow new factories to be built. Then, between NESARA and the Chevron Decision, we will be positioned to launch a new era where the motto is once again "Built In America and Buy American." To this end, Trump is threatening to put up to 200% tariffs on a proposed Chinese auto plant and a John Deere plant planned to be built in Mexico.

With that said, there is still one major problem that must be resolved, which is that the Washington Swamp needs to be drained. There is another Supreme Court case, the Brunson case, that might take care of that for us. As of January 2026, this case is in the early stages of the legal process and names three Supreme Court Justices as plaintiffs before the court. It alleges that those three justices breached their oath of office when they previously refused to hear the Brunson case, arguing that a national emergency would be declared if it were found that there was election fraud in the 2020 election.

These justices have had to recuse themselves, opening the way for the election fraud case to finally be heard. This could then lead to breach of oath charges against some 300-plus Senators and Congressmen, who could be subject to being removed from their elected positions. Instantly, the swamp would be drained. There is a second way the swamp could be drained. If whistleblowers were to come out with proof that the 2020 election was stolen, there would be a special election called, resulting in the draining of the swamp.

In any regard, the people are waking up. It is just a matter of time till the coming global financial collapse strips the financial elite of their money, and with that, they will lose control of the spheres of influence (banks, corporations, the Uni-Party, Military Industrial Complex, media, religion, education, and family) that they use to enslave us.

So, what do any of these have to do with ecological issues? Everything! The UN's promise to reduce our carbon footprint to zero by 2050 is bogus based on the technology that we have established. Not only that, but it represents a step backward. Getting access to truly revolutionary, free, clean, and renewable energy is a game-changer for humanity.

ECOLOGICAL ISSUES—IMPLICATIONS OF FREE/CHEAP, CLEAN, RENEWABLE ENERGY

The primary claim of Agenda 2050 is that it will create a carbon-free environment by 2050, which we have proven to be impossible based on current wind, solar, and lithium battery technologies. So, is there a solution, and if so, what is it?

There is absolutely a solution. Actually, there are multiple solutions just waiting to see the light of day. They come in the form of currently suppressed technology. As these technologies have not been released to the public yet, I will provide a brief overview of a few of the suppressed technologies that will change the world for the better. They provide real ecological solutions, unlike the bogus solutions that underpin the UN's Green New Deal Agenda 2050.

Hydrogen on demand: Toyota has just announced it is going into production with a car engine that fractures hydrogen on demand. Say goodbye to lithium EV vehicles. Dead on arrival.

Technology to clean the planet: Some technologies can clean up radioactive material and convert carbon pollution into clean, breathable oxygen. God has made a way for us to clean our land, air, and water. We just need to get access to suppressed technology. See graphics on the next page.

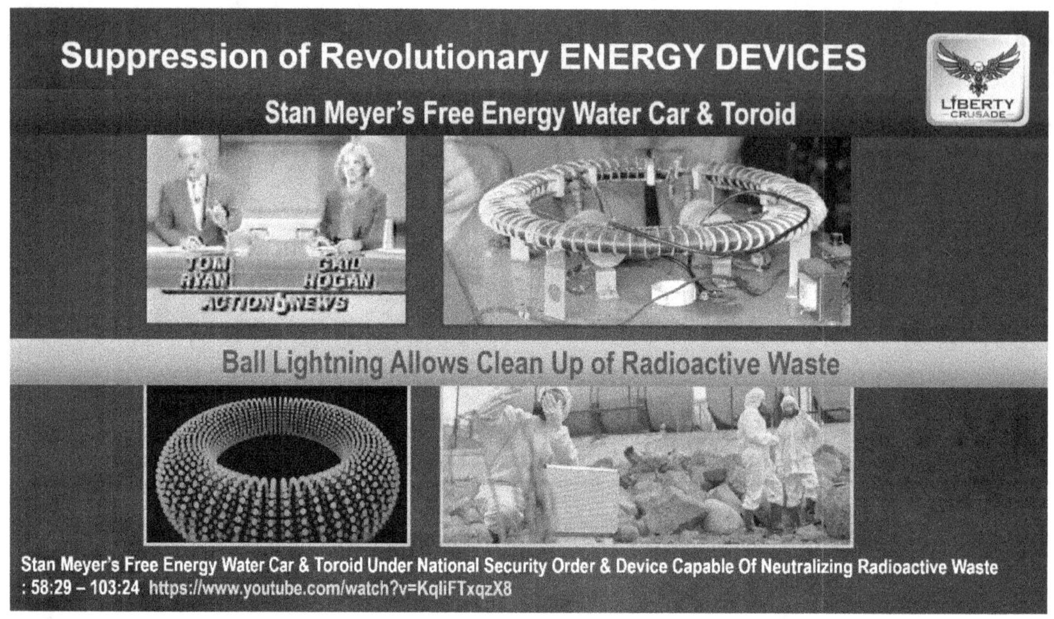

Energy from the vacuum and the Earth itself: Almost 100 years ago, Nikola Tesla demonstrated that electricity could be pulled from the vacuum of space and from the Earth itself. When he presented his revolutionary technology to his financial backer, J. P. Morgan, he responded that such technology would make him nothing but a damn antenna salesman, whereupon Morgan pulled Tesla's funding and blackballed him.

Sustainable water supply from the atmosphere: The Elite tell us that the most pressing problem facing the planet is our carbon footprint. *That is another lie!* Don't get me wrong, carbon pollution is an issue, but it is dwarfed by the looming crisis we face from a catastrophic clean water shortage that threatens to usher in a biblical-level famine. The reason they push the carbon issue is twofold. People can see the smog in big cities, so it is believable.

However, the real reason they promote reducing our carbon footprint is that they are advocating for the imposition of a "carbon tax," which would tax every item you buy and even the air you breathe. It is the perfect way to enslave us utterly and control the necessities of life by making them too expensive for most.

Our lakes, rivers, and aquifers are drying up, not because there is less rainfall but because weather patterns are changing. Think *HAARP:* **H**igh-frequency **A**ctive **A**uroral **R**esearch **P**rogram, the government's weather control technology used to create chaos and push us toward their New World Order (described in Chapter 2).

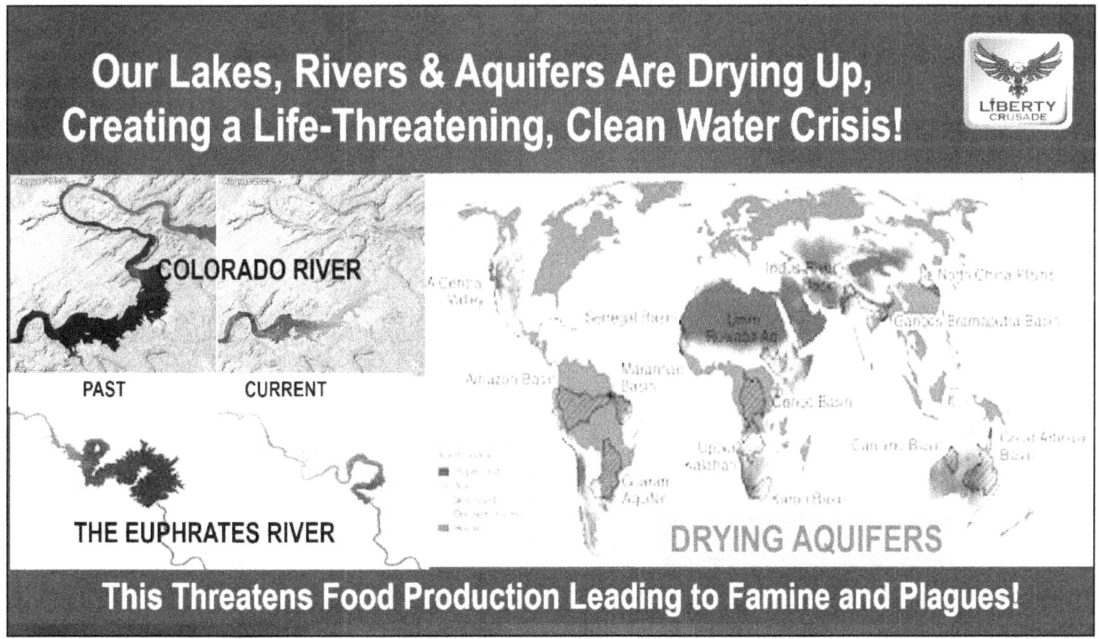

There is no reason there needs to be any hunger anywhere in the world! So, what is this technology that can provide us with water from the atmosphere and help us solve what I believe is the real crisis facing planet Earth? Water is the basis of all life, so access to clean, usable water outweighs any consideration of our carbon footprint as the basis of the Green New Deal. The liars are about to be exposed!

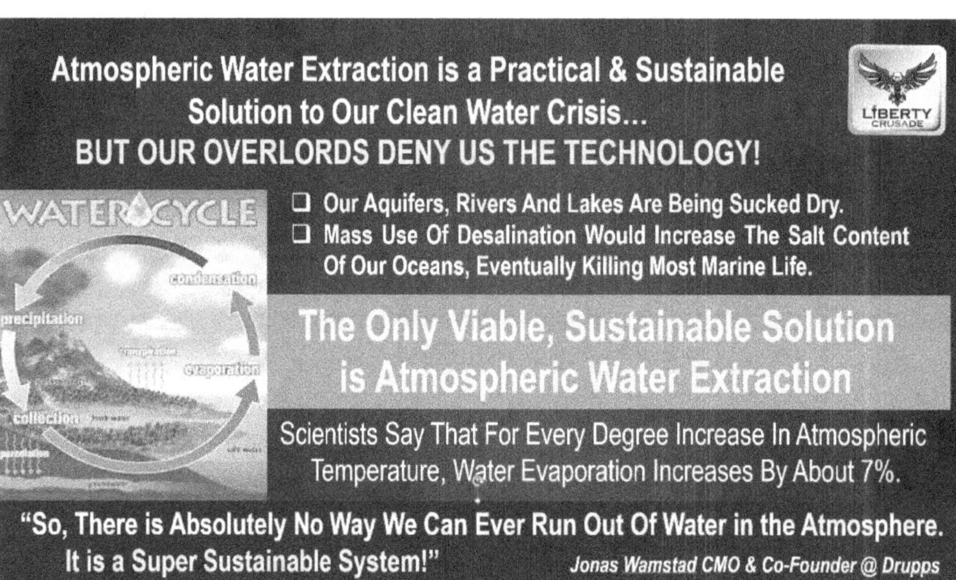

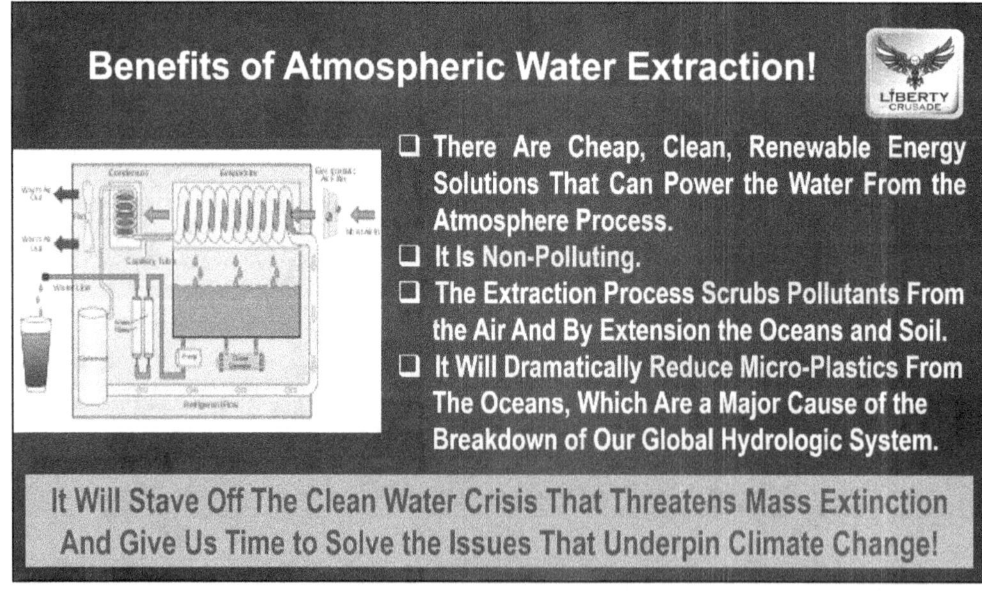

FINANCIAL STABILITY, NOT INTENTIONALLY IMPOSED POVERTY

Think about this: The UN and its global elite slave masters talk out of both sides of their mouths. On the one hand, they claim to have developed 17 Goals for Sustainable Development, which will achieve zero carbon emissions by 2050 and, in the process, end poverty and hunger, provide better health, and usher in an era of peace and prosperity. Sounds great! And it would be if it were true. But their words and actions expose their real intentions, which are to:

- Create order out of chaos.
- Economically and politically subjugate us by ending industrial civilization. This event would bring untold hardship, poverty, hunger, famine, and disease to the masses of humanity.
- Forcibly reduce the population to 500 million in the name of *resource sustainability* (per the Georgia Guidestones). So, we must *die* that they may have their New World Order Utopia!
- Withhold revolutionary energy and transportation technology that could do what they falsely claim to be able to achieve through their (grid-dependent) wind, solar, and lithium batteries (per the 1951 Invention Secrecy Act).

THE FOLLOWING QUOTES BEAR REPEATING

"Protecting the environment" is a RUSE. The goal is the political and economic subjugation of most men by the few, under the guise of preserving nature.
J.H. Robbins [Emphasis Added]

Global Sustainability requires the deliberate quest of poverty... reduced resource consumption...and set levels of mortality control.
Professor Maurice King, Director of the UN Rio Accord

**The one aim of these financiers is world control
by the creation of inextinguishable debts.**
Industrialist Henry Ford

SOCIAL ISSUES—ECONOMIC AND SOCIAL PARITY

As we have discussed throughout this book, the intent of the Elite has always been to rule over us *peasants*, us *chattel* (livestock, personal property). A synopsis of their game plan will provide a quick review. Their bad intent:

- Causes wars to drive nations into unsustainable debt.
- Inflicts them with a central bank debt trap.
- Controls the bulk of the world's natural resources.
- Produces finished products in sweatshops and undercuts competing nations as another means of driving them into unmanageable debt.
- Takes the money from trade and creates a shadow government by buying power and influence at every stratum of society.
- Inflicts on us a system of slavery without chains. This system is the culprit behind the deceptive Green New Deal and its seventeen sustainable development goals.

CLOSING COMMENTS

Solving the problems enumerated in the UN's *Global Goals for Sustainable Development* is impossible with wind, solar, and lithium-powered vehicles. These technologies actually represent a step backward because wind and solar are only practical in limited climatic zones under ideal conditions. Solar panels and lithium batteries end up going into landfills, where they pose a biohazard. We are told these technologies will allow us to reach zero carbon emissions by 2050. This is an absurd lie because they are all connected to our outdated carbon-belching grid.

The entire Green New Deal is a ruse. It is impossible without the release of free energy technology that is being withheld from us to protect the Elite's multi-trillion-dollar energy revenue stream. This chapter has enumerated all seventeen of the UN's Sustainable Goals and pointed out that every one of them is based on nothing but lies and misdirection.

As discussed, all the UN's Sustainable Development Goals can be solved. But for that to happen, the UN and all its global governance organizations must be terminated because they are keeping us from the very solutions they claim to solve. Their true agenda is to reach resource sustainability by killing billions of us. Then, and only then, will they release the suppressed free energy technology that can solve this very real ecological crisis threatening planet Earth.

CHAPTER 13

EQUALITARIANISM:
God's Plan to Usher in an Era of Peace and Prosperity

TOPICS COVERED IN THIS CHAPTER:

- THE EVENTS THAT MADE AMERICA, THE YOUNGEST NATION, THE MOST PROSPEROUS
- WHY CHINA AND THE US MUST FALL & THE US WILL RISE LIKE THE PHOENIX
- THE FOUNDATION STONES THAT UNDERPIN AMERICA'S GREATNESS
- A NEW ECONOMIC SYSTEM: EQUALITARIANISM
- NESARA—NATIONAL ECONOMIC SECURITY RESTORATION ACT
- RESTORING THE REPUBLIC—OUR MOST URGENT CHANGES

WE ARE GOING to rewind the clock again! Do you remember my mentioning that God always hints at future events? Let's explore the past, starting with the colonial period, to see God's plan unfold. Only then can we have our eyes opened to the truth, so that the truth can set us free!

Those who know our true history know beyond a shadow of a doubt that England is our mortal enemy. They know that England is the home of the Rothschilds' global banking cartel, and they know that it is they who have time and time again thrust the world into bloody wars for profit! It is they and the descendants of the other European monarchs who are the puppet masters that, to this day, rule the world from the shadows.

To walk into the future God has in store for us, we must know how wars are caused and how to break that cycle. Recall this quote, also mentioned in Chapter 1:

If my sons did not want war, there would be none.
Gutle Schnapper Rothschild, wife of Mayer Amschel Rothschild

If you need a reminder of how virtually every war the U.S. has been involved in was started based on some false flag event, then go back to Chapter 6. I am about to tell you the story of the confluence of events that, over the span of a few years, shocked the world and petrified the British.

1828: TARIFF ACT

This tax imposed up to 50% tax on British goods to protect U.S. manufacturing. The South dubbed the act the "Tariff of Abomination." This, along with other moves by the industrial North to protect domestic manufacturing, started the U.S. on the road to the Civil War.

1861: THE CIVIL WAR BEGINS

The underlying issue was that the industrial North was becoming increasingly less and less dependent on the British Free Trade Slavery System. At the same time, the agricultural South was still very dependent on cheap British goods. Fearing that America was emerging as a formidable industrial power, Britain, Spain, and France agitated circumstances to trigger the war. By changing the name from British Free Trade to Chinese Free Trade, the system of economic slavery can still be recognized to drive nations into economic submission, which is a significant factor in why China must fail for the world to be free.

1862: GREENBACK IS ISSUED

To the dismay of the British, Abraham Lincoln issued the (debt-free) *Greenback*. Remember, nations and presidents that interfere with Britain's control of money suffer dire consequences.

1863: THE U.S. TRANSCONTINENTAL RAILROAD

The track began being laid in 1863, and by 1869, it was completed. With this event, Lincoln was not only threatening Britain's control of the money supply but also threatening its control of natural resources.

APRIL 15, 1865: ABRAHAM LINCOLN WAS ASSASSINATED

As a result, eight British spies were hanged. Go figure, just two months after Lincoln's death, the war ended (on May 13, 1865), and before the year was over, the *Greenback* was taken out of circulation. Will coincidences never cease? But with the war over and the transcontinental railroad completed, even Britain couldn't stop God's plan for America!

1876: THE U.S. HOSTS THE UNITED STATES CENTENNIAL CELEBRATION

The Marvels of American Technology were exhibited. America's high tariffs and technological innovations have made America—the world's youngest nation—also the world's most *prosperous*.

This is the story of God's plan: America's past greatness, and the coming era of global peace. The economic system that catapulted America to become the world's economic superpower is known as the *"American Economic System."* Very few Americans have ever heard of it. But regardless, it was the foreshadowing of the economic system that would usher in God's ordained era of peace and prosperity. We will discuss this shortly, but first, we must return to the present and examine the events unfolding.

For the world to be free, man's governmental systems must fall. A statement like this evokes a vision of the fall of capitalism and communism. But we must think bigger. Virtually every nation in the world has lost its sovereignty and is a puppet of the global elite shadow government. So, it is they who must fall, and when they fall, which they will, they will lose control of the global financial system. At that point, their greatest strength will become their greatest weakness. By that, I mean they will no longer be able to print their fiat currency and use it to wield their power over us.

At that moment, an army of whistle-blowers will emerge, and their control over the nations of the world will collapse like a house of cards. This will usher in God's economic system modeled after the American economic system from way back in the late 1800s.

I am certain that the thought of this happening frightens the average person to death. But if we are to be free, the old system must be destroyed.

It is imperative that when the coming financial collapse occurs (which will be soon), the global financial elite are not bailed out. The current fiat system must be allowed to crash and burn. As the quote above states, the power to issue money must be completely stripped away from the global financial elite. Easier said than done, you say. I didn't say it was easy, but it is imperative, and God has made a way.

The global elite think they are so smart. But they forget they are attempting to play chess with God, who knows every move they are going to make before they make it. When the financial elite used China to release COVID-19, they drove the final nail in both their coffin and China's. We discussed this before, so I will keep this brief. Here is what is about to happen:

CHINA'S FALL

This is not a maybe! The world has woken up to the fact that China is a pariah. The world was also awakened to the fact that China can no longer be relied on to control the global supply chain. They are the reinstatement of the British Free Trade Slavery System, and that system must be ended. They are fading into the sunset. Their dream of replacing the U.S. as the undisputed global superpower will never be realized. Manufacturers are fleeing their sinking ship—end of story.

AMERICA'S FALL

When the shadow government, which controls the U.S., used the release of COVID-19 to expand the money supply (to an unsustainable point), they signed their death warrant as surely as that of the U.S. economy. Then, when they used the FED to increase interest rates to trigger a banking collapse intentionally, they put a nail in their coffin.

Then they put the final nail in their coffin when they decided to use the power of the U.S.'s status as the "world's reserve currency" as a weapon to sanction other nations to control them. At that point, Brazil, Russia, India, China, and South Africa (BRICS) banded together to collapse the dollar by buying oil in currencies other than U.S. dollars. When Saudi Arabia joined in, the handwriting was on the wall for the dollar.

Where does this leave us? Exactly where God wants us. If you are going to build a new house on the site of an existing home, you first have to tear the old house down and lay a new foundation. That is precisely what is happening.

The global supply chain must be stripped of China, and the world must move from globalization to deglobalization. It is also essential that the U.S. dollar be allowed to collapse. These two events will trigger a collapse of the global monetary system. This will signal the end of the Rothschild global financial elite's ability to control the world through control of the printing of fiat currency. That, in turn, will trigger a new commodity-based economic system and strip the financial elite of the ability to create worthless currency with the flick of a pen. They will no longer be able to suppress wages, inflate and deflate the currency, or trigger financial crashes at will.

THE ENTIRE BEAST SYSTEM MUST BE ALLOWED TO FALL SO THAT WE CAN REINSTATE OUR FOUNDING PRINCIPLES!

- The UN and all its global governance organizations must fall!
- Governments around the world must fall!
- The FED and the Central Banking Network must fall!
- The stock market must fall!
- Many international corporations must fall!
- Our 2,700-plus-page Constitution has been usurped, and we must reinstate our original Constitution!
- All the corrupt laws inflicted on us by the financial elite's illegal shadow government must be voided, and new laws passed based on our original Constitution!
- Most of our politicians are puppets of the financial elite and must be removed!
- As Trump says, the swamp must be drained!
- We must go back to the founding principles that made America great!

Below are the twelve foundation stones that underpin America's greatness. Regardless of what the financial elite may say, America is exceptional, and it shines the light of Liberty for the entire world. Should America ever fall, the entire world would be poorer for it, both economically and culturally. As America goes, so goes the rest of the world!

THE 12 FOUNDATION STONES THAT UNDERPIN AMERICA'S GREATNESS!

1) **GOVERNMENT.** A republic serves the people, but all other forms of government are self-serving, resulting in an elite ruling class with a perverted shadow government that operates behind the scenes. Our republic (a government of the people, by the people, for the people) must be restored. And equally important, our Christian and family values, as well as our patriotism, must also be restored. Without its founding values, America is not the nation God intended it to be!

2) **BORDERS.** This term describes a territory over which a nation is sovereign. Erase the borders, and there is no nation to be sovereign over! All we have to do to end illegal immigration is build the wall and make it so that absolutely no entitlements or rights are given to illegal immigrants! Once they get the memo that, in fact, the border is closed, they will stop coming. War and money are the ultimate control mechanisms! We can end wars by "equalizing and elevating the condition of all mankind!"

3) **MILITARY.** Our armed forces provide safety and security, but if perverted, the military becomes a means of domination and oppression. We must wake up to the fact that every war we have been in was started based on a false flag event. War is intended to drive us into unmanageable debt. And our sons and daughters were killed and maimed not to protect our nation but to enrich the financial elite!

4) **LEGAL SYSTEM.** The system provides order and defines the people's rights, but if perverted, it oppresses them. Today, our puppet shadow government passes laws intended to serve special interest groups and to create a legal dictatorship. They must be stricken, and those who pass and enforce them must be removed.

5) **PATRIOTISM.** The source of national allegiance and strength is found in patriotism; undermine it, and the nation falls from within. We must regain control of all spheres of influence. In this instance, it starts with the education system, media, and entertainment industry, which have perverted America's founding principles. For America to be great, its founding principles must be reinstated.

6) **PROPERTY RIGHTS.** A republic protects property rights, but other forms of government allow the government to *'take rights'*, leading to Socialism. Illegal *"property tax"* and 'take' rights must be abolished. Because of the take rights, no American actually owns property (land or a house) because they are, in reality, renters, and their landlord is the corrupt shadow government.

7) **MONETARY SYSTEM.** This system utilizes a medium of exchange, but if perverted, it becomes a means to enrich the ruling class at the expense of the public. The Fiat monetary system must be allowed to crash and burn, to be replaced with God's economic system based on commodities, so the economic system cannot be manipulated.

8) **NATURAL RESOURCES.** The basis of all wealth and the necessities of life are found in our natural resources. If perverted, it becomes the ultimate control mechanism. As Trump says, we must get access to our oil and other natural resources because they are the basis of all wealth.

9) **TRADE AND COMMERCE.** This is the conversion of natural resources into useful goods and is a basis of wealth; however, if intentionally restricted, it becomes a means by which a nation can be bankrupted. Trump imposed tariffs on China. They must remain in place. He got us out of the intentionally losing the NAFTA trade deal and negotiated fair trade deals. He also removed many regulations that prevented us from building factories and other infrastructure, so all we need to do is continue and expand his policies. Lastly, because of deglobalization, it will be more difficult to cause supply chain issues and product shortages intentionally.

10) **EDUCATIONAL SYSTEM.** Education is essential to a republic because it forms the basis for voters' informed decision-making and the basis for the innovations that drive economic growth. If perverted, it becomes a weapon to sow social discourse and division! Our entire education system must be revamped.

11) **RELIGION AND FAMILY VALUES.** These values form the basis of the moral system that determines a civilized society. But if perverted, society collapses from within. As much as I hate to say it, our churches are filled with dogma, and thanks to the 501 (c)'s, our pastors are silent. The 501 (c) laws need to be abolished. The Rothschild-controlled

seminaries need to be revamped, as does our education system, and that also includes our Rothschild-controlled medical schools. The lies must be exposed.

12) MEDIA: The media informs the public, or, if perverted, becomes propaganda used to manipulate and brainwash. We must regain control of the media and restore freedom of speech.

Our Founding Fathers referred to America as "The Great Experiment." Why was that? It was because America represented a unique form of government. It was not a monarchy. It was not a democracy. It was not socialism or communism. It was a republic, which is the only form of government ever designed to "limit the power of government and allow the people to govern themselves in a manner they felt best served their needs." The American Republic was founded on three coequal branches of government: the Executive, Legislative, and Judicial, which were intended to give control of the government, not to an all-powerful federal government, but to the states and the people who were to be responsible for keeping their freedom intact.

As the story goes, Ben Franklin left the Constitutional Convention when he was met by a woman who inquired, "Sir, what form of government have you given us?"

He responded, "A republic, Madam, if you can keep it."

That may seem a strange response, but it gets to the heart of what a republic is. A republic is unlike any other form of government because it truly gives the people the power of self-government, but with that privilege comes responsibility.

Let's take a look at precisely what a republic is and what makes it unique. A republic is a government "of the people, by the people, and for the people." It requires an educated, well-informed public. That is why education is one of the founding principles of America, and that is why President John Adams said,

Liberty cannot be preserved without a general knowledge among the people.
President John Adams

Knowing this truth is why the financial elite have hijacked the education system and the media in America. Under a republic, the people must be willing to abide by the Constitution (the rule of law). Leaders must pass laws in the people's best interest, not in the interest of special interest groups or the financial and political elites. By contrast, a democracy is based on majority rule, and our Founders referred to it as "Mobocracy." James Madison famously said of democracies:

> **Democracies have ever been spectacles of turbulence and contention;**
> **have ever been found incompatible with personal security or the**
> **rights of property; and have, in general, been as short in their lives**
> **as they have been violent in their deaths.**
> James Madison

Why would that be? Democracies invariably degrade into chaos when those least willing or least able to work realize they can vote themselves handouts. For this reason, democracies invariably morph into socialism and communism, which is precisely what is happening in America today. You may have heard it said:

> **The democracy will cease to exist when you take away from those**
> **who are willing to work and give to those who would not.**
> Anonymous

America was founded as a republic. Two events morphed it into a socialist, communist order! The first event was the Act of 1871, which took away our constitution and placed America under a **corporate charter** that served the interest of its shareholders (European Bankers) instead of *We the People.*

The second event occurred in 1933, when the U.S. government declared bankruptcy. The receivers of the bankruptcy (the financial elite banker gangsters) declared that under the National Emergency Act of 1933, all U.S. offices and officials existed in name only. The U.S. had a new form of government, a Socialist Communist Order. At that moment, an army of non-elected bureaucrats was embedded in the government, forming the Shadow Government that is the actual ruling power of the country!

> **If we are ever to be free, the Republic must be restored. And for that to happen, we**
> **must take back the printing of our currency. Their shadow government must be rooted**
> **out, and our Constitution and Foundation Stones must be reinstated! This lays the**
> [cont'd next page]

necessary foundation to allow us to delve into exactly what "The American Economic System" is and how it differs from the British Free Trade System, and every other economic system in the world!
Henry C. Carey, economic adviser to Abraham Lincoln, when comparing the British Free Trade System to the American Economic System.

So, what was it about the American Economic System that allowed America, the youngest nation in the world, to (in the span of just a few years) surpass Britain (that had a 300-year head start) and become the most economically prosperous nation in the world?

It is a simple and replicable formula that we have discussed before. But we need to take another look at it in the context of why China must fall and how and why, as Trump said, he will "Make America greater than ever."

WHY CHINA MUST FALL

China must fall because it is just a replay of the old British Free Trade System that kept the world in a state of slavery without chains for hundreds of years. Our Founding Fathers were fleeing Europe to escape the oppression of feudalism, alternatively referred to as the British Free Trade Slavery System. The entirety of the American governmental system was structured to free them from that oppression and hopefully to protect future generations from once again falling victim to it.

THE AMERICAN SYSTEM OF ECONOMICS!

The year is 1876, and the United States is hosting the U.S. Centennial Celebration, exhibiting the marvels of American technology. America's high tariffs and technological innovations had made the United States the world's youngest and most prosperous nation. Trump understands the power of tariffs to protect U.S. domestic markets, create fair trade agreements, and stoke the U.S. economic engine. He reversed our decades-old policies of intentionally losing trade policies imposed on us by every U.S. President from Carter to Obama. Back to the Centennial Celebration.

1876

The Civil War is over, and Henry C. Carey has organized the United States Centennial Celebration. The world is invited to witness the technological marvels of human ingenuity and see how America, the youngest nation in the world, has become the most prosperous. Nine million visitors attend, including official foreign delegations of scientists, engineers, industrialists, and economists. They saw the potential for uplifting the human condition, such as had never been seen before.

It was all attributable to the American system of Economics, which prized human creativity as the key to material wealth, as opposed to control of natural resources and labor. It imposed high tariffs as a form of protectionism necessary to allow economic development to flourish in opposition to the British Free Trade System.

Change the name from British Free Trade to Chinese Free Trade, and you can see that we have gone full circle. The financial elite are once again up to their old tricks, and America is their primary target. Perhaps now you can see why President Trump has imposed tariffs on Chinese goods.

Seeing America's success, the world realized that it could emulate the American System, escape the British free trade system's oppression, and transform its national economies. With that realization, American technology was exported worldwide, and the world held the promise of a better tomorrow.

- **IN RUSSIA:** The Russian Transportation Minister imposed a system of high tariffs and worked with American engineers to construct a Trans-Siberian rail system modeled after the American Transcontinental Railroad system. By 1890, there were plans for a Bering Strait bridge to connect by rail to America.

- **IN FRANCE:** Tariffs were also imposed, and plans were made to develop the Nile River area. Perhaps most important was a plan to connect to the Russian Trans-Siberian project.

- **IN GERMANY:** German Chancellor Otto von Bismarck wholeheartedly embraced the American System and transformed Germany into Europe's leading industrial power. He also began plans to connect to the Russian Trans-Siberian Railway system and develop a rail line from Berlin to Baghdad.

The world was changing. Instead of fighting over natural resources, nations were cooperating to develop rail systems that connected the nations of the earth. The world saw the promise of the American System to "elevate while equalizing the condition of man throughout the world." The future held the promise of an era of prosperity and peace as nations joined together in cooperation and mutual benefit. Once completed, the rail system's network promised a cost-effective and efficient way to transport goods worldwide, significantly reducing the world's dependency on maritime shipping.

While the rest of the world rejoiced at the prospects for the future, the powers behind the British Empire laid plans to make certain that no such future would ever be realized. The world's dependency on naval power had to be maintained, and nations couldn't be allowed to develop their technological potential. Should such plans ever be realized, it would mean the demise of the British Empire's stranglehold on world resources, labor, and commerce, and with it the end of their ability to pillage the wealth of other nations. There was only one hope for the British. It was risky, but they were desperate. They would orchestrate WWI.

THE TRUE CAUSE OF WORLD WAR I

World War I was intended to safeguard England's maritime dominance from the threat posed by a transcontinental rail system connecting the nations of the world. On June 14, 1914, the heir to the Austro-Hungarian throne, Archduke Ferdinand, was assassinated. As history records, World War I began. But few people realize that the groundwork for the war had been in the making for over twenty years, ever since plans were announced in 1890 to build the Trans-Siberian Railway.

The American economic system held the hope of a better world for all. But that hope threatened England, often referred to in the 18th through 20th centuries as "the empire on which the sun never sets". They are the founders of "Globalism."

The American System was based on the belief that the *single most important resource is human creativity, which it saw as the basis of material wealth.* Thus, the American System did not struggle to control resources, unlike the British System. Instead, it sought to encourage creativity as the basis of technological advancements, which can enrich the nation that invents the technology while simultaneously raising the standard of living for the country that adopts it. Thus, unlike the British System, which oppresses people, the American System is seen as using technology to elevate the standard of living for all.

The key to allowing a nation to withstand the cheap goods of the British Free Trade System was to impose high tariffs as a form of domestic protection that protects wages while allowing for the development of manufacturing capability and long-term infrastructure projects, all of which led to economic stability and a higher standard of living. That is the exact opposite of what our last several administrations have done. Along comes President Trump, the "Disruptor," the billionaire business executive, and common sense reemerged.

Trump's policies reinvented the American economic system, and the U.S. economy once again flourished. With Trump's return, the swamp will be drained. He will lead the U.S. and the world into an unparalleled era of peace and prosperity. As we have discussed, the U.S. is the only nation in the world capable of leading the world into God's era of peace, prosperity, and spiritual enlightenment. America is God's covenant nation!

THE FAILED POLICIES OF THE PAST

Read the following quote and ask yourself if this isn't exactly what has happened to the American worker since the implementation of Chinese free trade under President Carter. It began when the financial elite took control of the printing of our currency in 1913.

We are opposed to British political economy...Free Trade shaves down the workingman's labor first, and then scales down his pay by rewarding him in a worthless and depreciated State currency.

Henry C. Carey, economic adviser to Abraham Lincoln

The proof that this quote accurately reflects our current situation can be seen in our rampant inflation caused by the fact that today, the fiat dollar is reportedly worth only four cents. So, it is the reduced buying power of the deflated dollar that is driving the rampant inflation, leading to the imminent collapse of the dollar. I think most of us are painfully aware of the truth of this quote and how we have indeed become slaves without chains. It is time to break the chains of our bondage!

Would you like some proof that tariffs work, that President Trump's policies worked and will work again for a second term? If so, then read on. On September 5, 1901, President McKinley delivered a speech at the Pan-American Conference in Buffalo to 50,000 North and South Americans, espousing the virtues of the American economic system. The following quote is from that speech.

Thirty years of protection have brought us to the 1st rank in agriculture, mining, and manufacturing development. We lead all nations in these three great departments of industry. We have outstripped even the United Kingdom, which has a century's

[cont'd next page]

head start on us....For thirty-one years, the protective tariff policy of the Republicans has, by any test, measured by any standard, vindicated itself.
President William McKinley

So, now you know how the American economic system made America great in the first place.

It is a foreshadowing of the economic system that God has ordained to usher the world into the era of peace and prosperity He intends for mankind!

This foundation, however, must be expanded upon to solve the problems that today divide nations and the issues that threaten the planet that sustains us. Because the essence of the American economic system was "to equalize while elevating the condition of all mankind," Therefore, I am using "Equalitarianism" as the name for the modern American economic system!

A NEW ECONOMIC SYSTEM: EQUALITARIANISM!

BASED ON EQUALIZING WHILE ELEVATING ALL MANKIND

Equalitarianism is the key to ushering in an era of peace and prosperity, and is accomplished by the following.

- **A monetary system based on natural resources (commodities):** This ensures that no nation or group can inflict the world with fiat currency. So, our slave masters are prevented from inflating and deflating our currency, causing financial booms and busts cycles, and suppressing wages relative to the cost of goods and services. So, the supply chain cannot easily be controlled to create shortages and drive up prices.
- **A decentralized supply chain:** So, no nation or group can control the supply chain and intentionally create supply shortages.
- **Promoting resource sustainability:** By engineering products based on product longevity and reusability rather than the wasteful Chinese model of planned obsolescence.
- **International research facilities:** To promote shared technology and natural resources and solve the ecological issues threatening the planet, i.e., overpopulation, resource sustainability, pollution, clean water, energy, and food security.

- **Access to suppressed technology:** That may well hold the answers to the most critical issues facing humanity, i.e., clean water, energy, medical patents, etc.
- **Regional manufacturing centers:** To minimize disruptions in the supply chain and to ensure that developing nations can develop their economies.
- **Building projects:** To develop infrastructure in developing countries so they can access their natural resources and process them. Interest-free loans would fund such a project. To improve efficiency and minimize graft, funding for such projects would go through an intermediary who would serve as a general contractor. Lastly, participating nations would be enrolled in apprenticeship programs, thereby facilitating a transfer of knowledge.

Way back in 1968, when I had my near-death experience, God told me that when my hair was salt and pepper (which it is now), capitalism and communism would fall to be replaced by His economic system. He told me that His new system would require a new, more sophisticated ledger system than what was in place at the time. I didn't know what that meant until recently. It is called NESARA, the National Economic Security and Restoration Act.

When combined with Equalitarianism, NESARA completes the foundation for God's economic system. NESARA has been in the works for some time, but it finally looks poised to be implemented. Below, I summarize what NESARA is.

NESARA: NATIONAL ECONOMIC SECURITY AND RESTORATION ACT

NOTE: I have no connection to the inner circle responsible for implementing NESARA, so although I believe everything presented here to be factual, I cannot verify it.

- **Reinstates our Constitution:** And our founding legal system.
- **Establishes a gold/commodity-backed currency:** Thus, eliminating worthless fiat currency and the ability to inflict us with boom-and-bust cycles, inflation, and deflation.
- **Dissolves the FED and IRS:** 100% of the money we pay to the FED goes to pay the interest for printing our worthless fiat currency. It is my understanding that the FED has declared bankruptcy, and the printing of our currency is now under the control of the U.S. Treasury Department, as our founders intended. I am not a lawyer, but my understanding is that by virtue of the bankruptcy of the Fed, all mortgages that were in place under the FED at the time of the bankruptcy will be forgiven.

- **FED dissolved and income tax repealed:** To be replaced by a sales tax on new nonessential items. This reinstates the tax structure that was in place when America was founded.
- **Compound interest on credit cards and mortgages is banned:** Because they violate usury laws that were in place when America was founded. They must be revoked, and a new system implemented. No details as to exactly what that looks like.
- **Personal property tax and take rights are banned:** Because our original real estate laws were based on "Spanish Land Grants" that guaranteed ownership for perpetuity. It was replaced by illegal "Fee Simple Real Estate Laws" that inflicted us with an illegal property tax and *took* rights. The implementation of these laws meant that the government became the owner of all real estate, as failure to pay property taxes resulted in the confiscation of the property. This is a fundamental component of the Communist Manifesto!
- **Monetary system based on a quantum computer:** Based on blockchain technology, which provides security and privacy. Additionally, a quantum computer eliminates election tampering. That is because the quantum computer would instantly detect voting irregularities. We need to clean up our database!
- **Shelved patents to be released:** There are reportedly approximately 6,000 revolutionary shelved patents that could help solve many of the issues facing humanity and the planet that sustains us.

NOTE: The Chevron Supreme Court decision, recently rendered, opens the door to accessing these previously suppressed patents and the technological benefits they offer. Release of this technology will enable America to reinstate the American economic system, which was responsible for announcing (at its centennial celebration in 1876) that America, the youngest nation in the world, was the wealthiest. Trump said he would give us free energy, and the Chevron decision is how he plans to fulfill that promise.

Think about this: Energy is a major cost component of all finished goods, so free energy will drastically reduce the cost of all manufactured goods (both industrial machinery and consumer goods). Get ready for everything you buy to be less expensive. The chains of financial slavery are being broken. When you couple these cost reductions with the elimination of all taxes, except a sales tax on nonessential items, and financial freedom is truly on the horizon!

- **Increased benefits to Seniors:** As a result, they will no longer live hand to mouth.
- **Currency swap:** U.S. dollars are to be exchanged on a one-to-one basis with a new commodity-backed "Rainbow Currency." This protects the American people from financial loss due to the soon-to-come financial collapse that must happen to strip power from the financial elite, who enslave mankind with their illegal banking and tax system. We win. They lose. God is the Waymaker!
- **Requires standdown of military aggression:** Would end our endless wars for profit. NESARA prevents wars in two ways. First, by implementing an economic system that equalizes and elevates the condition of all nations, the primary cause of war is eliminated. Second, to participate in the one-to-one currency swap, nations must agree to stop all military aggression.

NOTE: Although I cannot confirm this, it is my understanding that there is a provision specifying that for a person, i.e., an illegal immigrant, to receive any benefits arising from the implementation of NESARA- GESARA, they must be in the country with legal status. If this is true, this would go a long way toward solving our open border crisis!

God keeps His promises. He promised that the wealth of the Wicked would be stored up for the righteous, and NESARA will accomplish that! In keeping with the principles of the American economic system, what Trump did to create the economic recovery in his first term was to:

- Give us back access to our natural resources (particularly energy)
- Remove bogus regulations that block infrastructure development, i.e., the building of factories, etc.
- Change taxes so corporations could return billions of dollars to the U.S. to be used to build factories
- Place tariffs on China
- Negotiate fair (not intentionally losing) trade agreements

Add to this equation "EQUALITARIANISM and NESARA," and there will be nothing to stop the U.S. from rising from the ashes like the phoenix and leading the world into God's era of peace and prosperity. Just think about all that Trump accomplished in the face of opposition from the swamp. And imagine what he can do now that he's back to drain the swamp and remove our traitors from power.

SUMMARY

To end the financial elite's grip on the world, we need to strip the global supply chain from China and let the dollar collapse so the entire global monetary system will implode (*not to be bailed out*)! This is essential to being able to restore the U.S. Republic. As I have said, we need to reinstate our constitution and *nullify the thousands of illegal laws* that have been passed to enslave us and allow the imposition of a legal dictatorship. This will take some time, so I want to close this chapter with a short list of the most urgent foundational changes that must be made.

RESTORING THE REPUBLIC'S MOST URGENT CHANGES!

NOTE: Some of the items listed below were discussed during our previous discussion on NESARA. Also, as previously stated, our constitution has been usurped, and our laws are largely unconstitutional, so we need a complete reset. I only mention these items because they are some of the most pressing changes that must be made if we are to restore our Republic.

- **Implement election reform:** Taxpayer-funded elections with no Super PACs and with a constitutional amendment to set term limits to prevent amassing of power.
- **Return power to state and local governments:** The Federal government has usurped powers from state and local governments that the Constitution never intended. Those powers must be removed. This requires that our bloated federal government be drastically reduced in size and scope.
- **Repeal usury laws:** Change laws to set interest rate limits and to make it illegal to charge interest on unpaid balances.

NOTE: In early 2026, Trump announced a 10% cap on credit card interest rates! At one time, all but six states had usury laws in place to protect consumers. The banker gangsters got around those laws by incorporating in those six states and inflicting the entire country with their corrupt credit system based on illegal compound interest.

- **Implement mortgage reform:** Change mortgage laws so that interest is no longer front-loaded, and so it is no longer necessary when refinancing or buying a new home to have a completely new loan. Instead, the existing loan can simply be modified. Hence, there is no need to start over at month one on the amortization table. Given that the average American moves or refinances seven or more times in their life, that means that under current laws, many people are never able to pay off their mortgages and be debt-free! This is a system of slavery that must be abolished!
- **Do away with property taxes:** Abolished with no *take* rights!
- **Close our borders and build the wall:** Very simply, no entitlements at all, and if you step foot on U.S. soil illegally, you are deported! **The only exception:** TRUE POLITICAL ASYLUM, and then, only if applied for in the first country you pass through when leaving your country of origin, which nullifies most requests.
- **Block censorship:** Legislation to make news agencies liable for their lies, propaganda, and censorship. A republic is impossible without an informed public, which means we must regain control of the narrative, meaning control of the pulpit (Separation of church and state, as our founders intended, not as the 501 (c) (3)s have corrupted it). We must also have control of the media, the education system, Hollywood, and the courts (as our adjudicators under the blind justice system we were intended to have). In other words, the Swamp must be drained just like Trump has said all along.
- **Redo our education system:** Must be completely revamped because a republic is impossible without an informed, well-educated public!
- **Update campaign contribution laws:** Must be changed so special interest groups cannot control the outcome of our elections.

The truth will come out, proving that the 2020 election was, in fact, stolen. But the truth is, we have not had an honest election since the election of McKinley in 1897. Here is what happened:

McKinley was pro-big business, and his opponent, William Jennings Bryan, sought to break up the monopolies that had emerged and were undermining our constitutional rights through their influence over special interest groups and the buying of power and influence. Three of the most powerful men in America (JP Morgan, Rockefeller, and

Carnegie) combined their money, power, and influence and got McKinley elected. That represented a repeatable moment in U.S. politics that the financial elite exploited. At that moment, they understood that power was for sale at every stratum of the government, corporate, and private sectors. Even the presidency was for sale. Since 1897, they have groomed, financed, and placed in power men willing to represent their interests over those of *We the People.*

Here is how they worked to steal political power. They backed both Republican and Democratic candidates, so no matter which party won, their interests were served. Our government has been hijacked and, as we have discussed, we have a shadow government that is the true ruling power of the nation and virtually every nation in the world.

These men, who were put in power by the financial elite, were turncoat traitors. They broke their oath of office to protect the nation from all enemies, both foreign and domestic. As a result, they are subject to removal from office, and all the laws they passed are subject to being expunged. We must lay a new foundation! Speaking of illegal and unconstitutional laws, these two quotes reflect on this issue.

When I speak of turncoat traitors, I do not limit my comments to past presidents! Our illustrious congressional representatives and Senators must not go unnoticed, for most of them are puppets of the financial elite as well. Most of our politician power brokers long ago sold out to the global financial elite, so they must be removed from their offices.

Given that the CFR wants to end U.S. sovereignty and given that all the people whose names are listed on the graphic below are CFR members, they have openly admitted to being traitors to the oath of office they swore. As the Bible says, a man cannot serve two masters. Therefore, these people and most of our current politicians must be removed from office, and our government must be swept clean, or as Trump would say, *"The swamp must be drained."*

The truth will come out about our stolen elections. And, consequently, that will lead to the removal of huge numbers of legislators, judges, and non-elected bureaucrats!

THE SHADOW GOVERNMENT!

MOST OF OUR POLITICIANS ARE GUILTY OF TREASON!

COUNCIL on FOREIGN RELATIONS

The Council on Foreign Relations (CFR) and Trilateral Commission (TC) are committed to ending US sovereignty and birthing the One-World Government

Brzezinski	Presidential Advisor & Founding Member	CFR	TC
Colin Powell	Chairman Joint Chiefs of Staff	CFR	
George H. Bush	U.S. President	CFR	
William Clinton	U.S. President	CFR	TC
Jimmy Carter	U.S. President	CFR	
Walter Mondale	U.S. VP	CFR	
John McCain	Senator [Arizonian] Presidential Candidate	CFR	
Albert Gore. Jr.	U.S. VP	CFR	
Hillary Clinton	Secretary of State Obama Admin		TC
Condoleezza Rice	Secretary State Bush Admin.	CFR	
John Kerry	Senator & Chairman Foreign Relations	CFR	
James Woolsey	Director CIA	CFR	
Robert Gates	Sect of Defense & Former Dir. CIA	CFR	
Henry Cisneros	Sect. Housing & Urban Development	CFR	
Dick Cheney	Vice President		

Virtually Every Politician in Washington Belongs to These Traitorous Organizations!

"The case for government by elites is irrefutable." – William Fulbright U.S. Senator

GOD IS WITH AMERICA!

GOD WILL KEEP HIS COVENANT WITH AMERICA!

That in blessing I will bless thee, and in multiplying I will multiply thy seed as the stars
of the heaven, and as the sand which is upon the seashore;
and thy seed shall possess the gates of his enemies.
Abraham's Covenant, Genesis 22:17 (NKJV)

Trump knows just how simple it will be to restore the republic once we have drained the swamp. All he has to do is what he did before:

- Give us back access to our natural resources.
- Rebuild our factories and infrastructure.
- Give us fair trade agreements, not intentionally losing trade deals.
- Finish the wall and finally close our border.
- Impose tariffs as a way to force products to be: *"Made In America."*

America will come roaring back and lead the world into an unparalleled period of peace and prosperity. We Win! God Wins! The global financial elite lose, and all their puppets along with them. This is the time of God's Harvest of Souls. God is the Waymaker, and He has already made a way!

CHAPTER 14

THE ENEMY WILL TRY TO REGAIN POWER:
Anticipating What He Will Try To Do Next

TOPICS COVERED IN THIS CHAPTER:

- A REVIEW OF WHAT HAS BEEN DONE TO US SINCE 2019
- A REVIEW OF THE ENEMY'S ENDGAME AGENDA
- HOW HE CONTROLS US
- REQUIRED SOCIAL CHANGES
- HOW THE ELITE ARE LIKELY TO REGROUP AND TRY TO TAKE BACK POWER

AS WE DELVE into how we restore our republic and how we maintain it, you may be surprised that I don't delve into all the laws that need to be changed to regain control of our banking system, corporations, and political system, otherwise known as "The Corporatocracy." That is because it is not necessary. Entire governments will collapse, huge numbers of blue-chip corporations will collapse, and politicians in governments around the world will be removed en masse. As to how that will be done, you will learn that in the remainder of this chapter and in the final chapter.

In a nutshell, the illegal corporation will collapse. It will lose control of all the spheres of influence, and a deluge of whistleblowers will come out to open our eyes as to how we have been enslaved. Most of the division that has been inflicted on us by our slave masters will fade away as the truth is exposed and people realize that the Elite really do want to end all sovereign nations. They then want to install a UN-controlled 10-nation trading coalition, i.e., the "*Beast System*" talked about both in UN documents and the Book of Revelation.

In the next chapter, there is a draft of the 2nd Declaration of Independence that Trump intends to release during his second term. It removes the illegal corporate constitution and reinstates our republic, the governmental system that made America the greatest nation the world has ever known. We will get back our original constitution, and there will need to be some amendments, the most important of which is to implement *term limits* to prevent career politicians from amassing power.

In the simplest possible terms, the swamp will be drained, and all those in positions of power who serve the illegal corporation will be removed. Special elections will have to be held, and our corporations, banks, and the stock market will be restructured. We will not need 2,000-page bills to accomplish this. As Trump said, we will be able to file our taxes on a postcard, and our laws will be short and to the point because they will not be instruments to enslave us.

Well, folks, now you know the truth, and "The Truth will set you free." As this book has laid out, the global financial elite controls us cradle to grave! They control virtually every aspect of our lives.

Now that we know the truth, our job is to keep our eyes open and question everything our leaders tell us. America was established as a *republic,* which is the only form of government that is "A government of the people, by the people, for the people." It is the only form of government that protects property rights and is based on a set of founding principles that unite the people around *God, Country, Family, Law, and Education.* As previously covered, we lost our constitution in 1871 when it was changed to read:

THE CONSTITUTION *OF* THE UNITED STATES OF America
instead of
THE CONSTITUTION *FOR* THE UNITED STATES OF AMERICA

As simple as this change may seem, it took away our rights and gave them to the banker gangsters and created a Corporate Charter whose only obligation is to maximize the profits of their European shareholders, no matter the harm their actions do to *We the People.*

This loss of freedom was compounded when, in 1933, in the depths of the Great Depression, America once again declared bankruptcy. This time, we lost our republic when the receivers of the bankruptcy declared all government offices and officials to exist in name only and declared that America was a *"Democracy, a Socialist Communist Order!"*

We are about to get our republic back, and when we do, it will be our responsibility to guard it for our children and their children. To that end, we must be informed. We must be willing to stand for those things that are in the best interest of society rather than self-serving interests. We must stand for *"Patriotism, Family, and Christian Values!"* The world is about to see the utter collapse of the global elite's beast system. When that happens, we need to turn to God in thanksgiving and acknowledge that He is our all-powerful, all-knowing, omnipresent, all-loving Father who has, in His mercy, made a way for us. No matter what role Donald Trump or any other man plays in our political and economic restoration, they are just workers in God's kingdom.

What is about to happen is of such magnitude that it can only be described as supernatural. We must remain vigilant, and we must be willing to stand up against evil when we see it. Hopefully, we have learned that our enemy is cunning, secretive, and evil beyond anything most of us can imagine. We must recognize that our enemy is the servant of the evil one, who is the father of lies and deception. But most of all, we must recognize that our enemy is persistent!

This is a war to the finish—a war of good against evil. The time will soon come when we think we have won the war, but not so! It is the time of the Harvest of Souls, but it is not yet time for God's millennial reign on earth. The enemy will walk away from this battle bruised and with his money (which is the source of his power) stripped from him, but he will regroup and come at us again. So, it is good to reflect on all the ways the enemy has controlled us and enslaved us. And then we need to look forward and ask ourselves how our enemy is likely to come at us next time. I guarantee you there will be a next time. But if we cleave to God and are vigilant and watchful, we can keep him at bay for a considerable period!

Most people are beyond frustrated. They are at the point of giving up. However, since Trump won a second term in office, they're hopeful again!

If we are honest with ourselves about what has been done to us since the release of COVID-19, we will realize that the enemy's endgame agenda is to kill 7+ billion humans and that surrender is not an option! The graphic below explains THE MASTER PLAN.

I tell you that if we stand united and refuse to submit, we will win. In truth, we are winning! The enemy panicked when Trump was elected in 2016, and it caused them to overplay their hand, and that will be their downfall. For decades, they have pushed their agenda on us, but when we pushed back, they backed off and bided their time, allowing us to go back to sleep.

But this time, we are not going to go back to sleep, because finally, the masses of society understand what is at stake: our freedom and our very lives! It is hard to believe what we have gone through in just a little over four years. But God allowed the loss (the theft) of the 2016 election to create circumstances that would blatantly expose the financial elite and what they have done to enslave us. With Trump's election, people are optimistic, but the Elite are not about to surrender power without a fight to the bitter end.

I am haunted by something Obama said when it became apparent that Kamala had no chance of winning the election. He said, "Don't worry, we have time." What I am about to say is not prophecy. It is just conjecture on my part. I reflected on history and remembered how it was that FDR was allowed to serve a third term. The nation was in the throes of the Great Depression and World War II, and it was deemed too dangerous to bring in a new administration, so a national emergency was declared, and FDR served a third term.

In our present situation, what God wants more than anything is for his people to repent and return to him so He can gather His Harvest of Souls. Given this, I pondered what it might take to create a situation of sufficient severity to bring this about. I concluded that things had to be allowed to get so bad that when we finally get our freedom, we would realize that only God could have set us free. He wants us to sear into our memories all the atrocities our evil slave masters have committed so we will fully repent and turn to Him. Then He will intercede and heal not only America but the nations of the world!

I remembered how FDR was allowed a third term. We were in the throes of the Great Depression and the beginning of World War II, so it was deemed *too dangerous* to install a new administration; therefore, FDR was allowed to serve a third term. These emergent situations call for unprecedented actions.

This scenario is also like how Hitler became the dictator of Germany. He orchestrated the burning of the German Parliament and blamed it on a Communist. The result was the passage of the "Enabling Act of 1933," giving Hitler dictatorial power for six months. It was posed as a law to relieve the distress of the German people. But of course, Hitler never relinquished power. It just so happens that the Patriot Act contains an almost identical clause. Will coincidences never cease to happen?

Or perhaps this isn't a coincidence but a contingency plan that was hatched way back in 2001. The Elite are patient and game everything out to the nth degree. I don't know exactly what will happen, but I am certain the Elite won't give up power without a fight to the bitter end. America is God's covenant nation that He has chosen to use to set the nations free. I am certain we will win, but not without a fight to the death.

It is important that we reflect on the things the Elite have done to us to enslave us, so we will see through their game plan when they attempt to get their power back. There is nothing new under the sun, so I am confident that they will try many of these same tactics in the future!

Their strategy starts with Wars to bankrupt nations
and force acceptance of a central bank debt trap.

This has been the centerpiece of their slavery system. But we are wise to that strategy, so next time I predict they will attempt their return to power through technology, not war. More on that later.

EVENTS THE ELITE INFLICTED ON US
DURING THE FOUR YEARS OF THE BIDEN ADMINISTRATION

STOLEN ELECTION

The 2020 election was stolen! Whistleblowers are coming out who will prove this. As soon as Biden took office, he reversed all the policies Trump had put in place that had resulted in a historic economic recovery, and the economy plummeted. This was no accident!

FORCED VACCINATIONS

People were forced to take an unproven vaccine, and the pharmacy companies were indemnified against any harm. Blood clots, heart attacks, miscarriages, fertility issues, and an assortment of autoimmune illnesses have been attributed to these forced vaccinations. This was a test to see if we would (under the right circumstances) surrender our freedom without a fight.

ASSAULT ON THE MIDDLE CLASS

Small businesses were shut down (and droves of them went out of business!). Yet big-box, infection-spreading stores were allowed to remain open and made record profits. Churches were shut down and not even allowed to hold services in parking lots. And still, like sheep, we complied.

MANDATORY SHUTDOWNS

Our corrupt Washington politicians used the mandatory shutdowns as an excuse to print more money than had been printed in the last hundred years. This happened in nations around the world and was calculated to create a global debt crisis. This malicious attack was inflicted on us by a consortium of puppet politicians, banker gangsters, greedy corporate CEOs, lying media outlets, and big tech Gestapo propagandists who are all puppets of the financial elite. *They* are the swamp and must be removed!

COLLAPSE OF THE GLOBAL FINANCIAL SYSTEM

Our corrupt politicians knew full well that this reckless money printing would lead to runaway inflation, bank failures, and inevitably, a collapse of the global financial system!

ATTACK ON THE DOLLAR

As if "on cue," the BRICS alliance was released to cause a de-dollarization to bring an end to the dollar as the world's reserve currency.

DISRUPTION OF THE GLOBAL SUPPLY CHAIN

This was intended to strip control of trade from China and create deglobalization.

DE-DOLLARIZATION AND DEGLOBALIZATION

The goal was to crash the global money system, starting the Elite's Great Reset, which would bring in the Best System, governing all buy/sell transactions. Ultimately, the intent is to implement a programmable central bank digital currency to be used for monitoring compliance through a social credit score that penalizes individuals for infractions of dictatorial regulations. It also regulates what can be bought or sold, as well as the quantity allowed, i.e., meat substitutes only, no bullets or guns, limits on electricity, gasoline, and other necessities of life, etc.

NOTE: God does not intend for this system to be implemented. He intends for capitalism and communism to fall, to be replaced by his governmental system based on gold and other commodities.

God intends for His economic system to replace the flawed systems of man. God's gold-backed commodity-based economic system will operate on a quantum computer with decentralized blockchain technology (which, unlike our current fiat currency, cannot be manipulated). The value of various commodities, including precious metals, agricultural products, land, houses, and virtually anything tangible, will be able to be fractionalized using XRP Crypto Tokens to facilitate all types of commerce. See graphics below.

ORCHESTRATED SHORTAGES

The intent is to make us so dependent on our slave masters for the necessities of life that we will simply surrender. Shortages were intentionally orchestrated: cargo ships sat in harbors and were not unloaded, food plants were burned down, railroads experienced derailments, and fertilizer was in short supply, as were oil and natural gas. Make no mistake; these are acts of war.

THE UNITED NATIONS

The United Nations drafted a resolution saying, "Migration is a human right!"

> *TRANSLATION: We have no right to a border,*
> *which means we have no right to sovereignty!*

The UN printed and distributed pamphlets instructing people on how to join a caravan, and provided them with food, clothing, and transportation to the U.S. border. The UN is an enemy of mankind, and the U.S. must withdraw from it.

OPEN BORDERS

Trump's border wall was stopped, and our borders were open to a horde of invading military-age men who represent a genuine threat of terrorist attacks from within our borders. This is an act of war masquerading as human rights.

Most of these invaders have no means of income. Many have health issues, don't speak English, and are poorly educated. They represent a new welfare class that creates a financial drain on the economy at a time when veterans, senior citizens, and natural disaster victims needed financial aid that was denied to them and instead given to these invaders. Again, I say this is an act of treason, and those responsible have no right to hold political office. The U.S. government, the Globalist UN, and an assortment of nongovernmental organizations (NGOs), including the Globalist Catholic Church, have joined forces to fund and coordinate this invasion—this assault on our sovereignty!

Always remember:

> *A nation with no border*
> *has no nation to be sovereign over!*

Hopefully, you now understand just how organized and how evil our enemy is. It is as the traitor President Wilson said:

> Since I entered politics, I have chiefly had men's views confided to me privately. Some of the biggest men in the United States, in the field of commerce and manufacture, are afraid of something. They know there is a power somewhere so organized, so subtle, so watchful, so interlocked, so complete, so pervasive, that they better not speak above their breath when they speak in condemnation of it.
> President Woodrow Wilson, 1913

THE ENEMY'S ENDGAME

If we understand what the enemy's endgame really is, how truly heinous it is, then we will understand that there can be no surrender. In simple terms, the enemy views most of humanity as Useful Idiots—Useless Eaters—Excess Baggage. The global elite see natural resources as the basis of all wealth, and there are too many of us consuming too many of what they consider their valuable resources. So, according to the Georgia Guidestones, the global population must be reduced to 500 million. COVID-19 was just a test run for the mass extermination of most of us. They don't see us as having any value. To them, we are every bit as much of a virus, a plague on the earth, as COVID-19, and we pests or cockroaches must be exterminated by any means necessary.

The following quote serves as a reminder of exactly what the financial elite's End Game really is! There are no ifs, ands, or buts about it—they want most of us dead and the survivors as their slaves.

> **The most powerful cliques in these (CFR) groups have one objective in common:
> they want to bring about the surrender of the sovereignty and the national
> independence of the U.S. They want to end national boundaries
> and racial and ethnic loyalties... What they strive for would inevitably lead to
> dictatorship and loss of freedoms by the people. The CFR was founded
> for the purpose of . . . and submergence of U.S. sovereignty, and national
> independence into an all-powerful one world government.**
> *Harper's Magazine*, July 1958

Is there any evidence that this quote really reflects the financial elite's endgame agenda? You bet! The UN's "Ten Nation Beast System" outlined next lays out their vision for their Brave New World. It is a world where not only U.S. sovereignty is surrendered, but the sovereignty of all nations is surrendered and replaced by "10 Servile Trading Blocs."

The Beast System ties to an end-times prophecy, mentioned in the Book of Revelation, where no one is allowed to buy or sell unless they submit to the forces of evil. The concept derives from interpretations of Revelation 13 and 17, which describe a beast with ten horns, often linked to a coalition of nations or powers.

This system returns to *feudalism*, where we are to surrender our sovereignty and swear our fealty (loyalty) to the king and his noblemen. Under feudalism, fealty is the oath of loyalty of a peasant, and a peasant is defined as chattel, which means personal property. So, we are seen as personal property to be treated and disposed of as our owner sees fit.

*TRANSLATION: We are in a state of war. Not a conventional war,
but a covert war that was inflicted on us from the shadows.*

THE UN WANTS TO CONTROL ALL THE WORLD'S NATURAL RESOURCES!

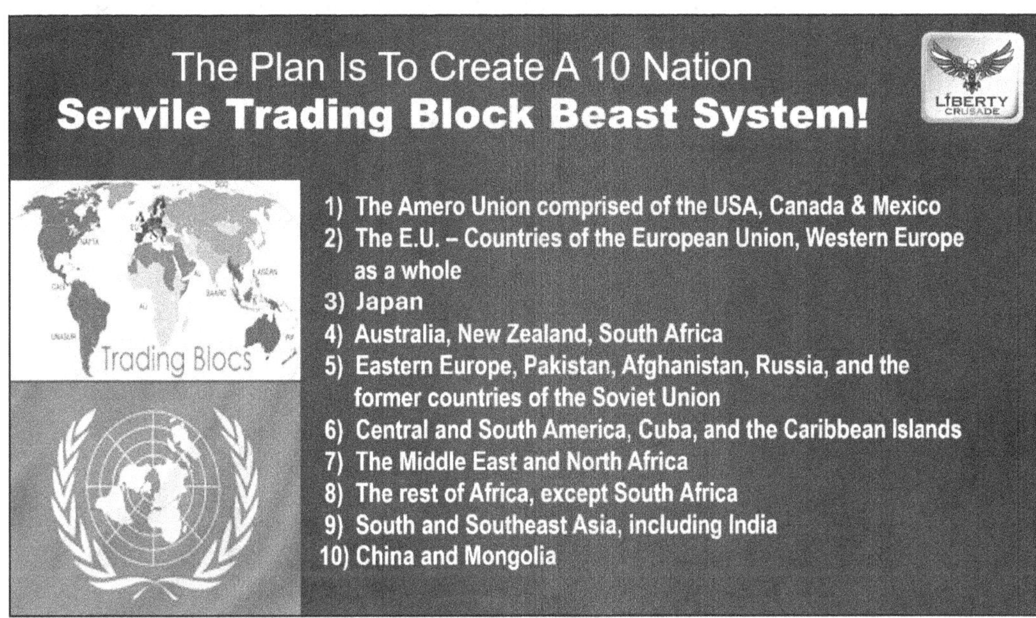

Most of us are blind to what is being done to collapse the U.S. and take away our freedom. It is no coincidence that China has experienced such a remarkable rise to power. As we discussed, starting with the traitorous President Carter, the global financial elite have done everything they could to orchestrate the rise of China and the decline of America. That is because to establish their one-world dictatorship, they needed a hybrid capitalist/communist economy, combining the innovation and productivity of capitalism with the control of communism.

Most of us have been asleep to what was happening because they have not waged a conventional war but a covert, subversive war fought from the shadows!

The financial elite took the virtually inexhaustible amount of money they had at their disposal because they could, with the flick of a pen, print money backed by nothing. With that money, they found bright young men and women and groomed them, financed them, and placed them in positions of power and influence to rule us from the shadows. As we discussed, the global financial elite controls all spheres of influence, including family, religion, education, media, entertainment, politics, the Military, and the economy.

Except for Reagan, Kennedy, and Trump, they have selected and placed every U.S. president in office for the last 100 years. As previously discussed, Congress is irrelevant because the private FED and the IMF run the government from the shadows!

Almost everyone in Washington who is anyone belongs to the traitorous CFR, which is dedicated to ending national borders and establishing One World Government. I'm restating the following quotes to highlight their intent to kill us.

> **The United Nations' goal is to reduce population selectively by encouraging abortion, forced sterilization, and control of human reproduction, and regards two-thirds of the human population as excess baggage, with 350,000 people to be eliminated per day.**
> Jacques Cousteau, *UNESCO Courier*, November 1991

The U.S. is the one nation in the world capable of obstructing the plans of the global financial elite from enslaving the world. It is the only nation in the world capable of filling the vacuum created by the fall of China, the U.S., and the global monetary system. America is God's Anointed nation. We will rise from the ashes to be the city on the hill that guides the world back to God!

The New World Order cannot happen without U.S. participation, as we are the most significant single component. Yes, there will be a New World Order, and it will force the United States to change its perceptions.
Henry Kissinger, World Affairs Council Press Conference,
Regent Beverly Wilshire Hotel, April 19, 1994

So goes America, so goes the world. But don't worry, things are about to get rough, but we will come through it!

The time will come when we will enter the Book of Revelation and the Tribulation, but now is not that time. Now is the time of God's Harvest of Souls. Do not be afraid of the Russian-Ukrainian war and what is happening in the Middle East. The Elite will not get WWIII. Now is not that time. God is using Russia to take down Ukraine because it is the money laundering capital of the world, and there are things there that must be destroyed.

Now is the time when the arrogance of the financial elite brings down their evil empire. As soon as its job is done, the Bear (Russia) will go back to sleep till the tribulation. It will join The Lion (England), The Leopard (Germany), The 10 Horned Beast (The 10-nation trading coalition), and the Catholic Church (in whose name all abominations have been committed), and they will usher in the tribulation.

That day will come as surely as the sun will rise tomorrow. We cannot stop it, but we can slow it down so that as many souls as possible can be saved. So, with that said, let's turn our attention to exploring how, with their control over money taken away from them, the financial elite will regroup and finally usher in the Tribulation!

You may remember that when we discussed the potential superpowers of the world, we did not discuss the European Union. That is because now is not their time. But the EU, led by England, Russia, Germany, the Catholic Church, and the 10-Horned Beast, will be the predominant players during the tribulation. But even then, they are defeated after their seven-year reign of terror has run its course.

That takes us into Daniel's interpretation of Nebuchadnezzar's dream! I will jump to the end of the interpretation where the feet of miry clay mixed with iron are struck with a stone, not hewn with human hands. The generally accepted interpretation is that the feet of miry clay mixed with iron is the "Holy Roman Empire," which is the union of the Roman Empire (the modern-day EU) and the Catholic Church (the lady who rides the beast), in whose name all abominations have been committed.

The stone not hewn with human hands is the return of Christ, marking the fall of the union of the Holy Roman Empire. This unholy union is also referred to as "Mystery Babylon the Great." In current times, it is generally recognized as referring to the global financial elite, which at the time of the tribulation will be represented by the EU and its one-world government.

So, as we examine the global financial elite's efforts to regain their power, we can expect the EU to play a prominent role.

SWITCHING SUBJECTS

With their control over the issuance of money gone, what tactics should we expect the global financial elite to use to regain power? They will not be able to buy power and influence so easily in every stratum of society, but they won't have to. They will use technology to launch their comeback. Supercomputers, AI, robotics, etc., will be the key to the resurgence of their empire of evil.

So, we'd better closely monitor these technologies and do everything possible to prevent them from disrupting the fabric of society to the point where they create an opportunity for our enemies to regain power and implement their global beast system.

BACK TO THE FOUNDING PRINCIPLES THAT MADE AMERICA GREAT!

A republic requires an educated, informed, and moral population,
willing to vote for those things that are truly in the best interest
of the Nation as a whole, as opposed to vested self-interest!
Without these attributes, a republic cannot be sustained!

Despite what our slave masters tell us, America was founded as a republic, not a democracy. Recall that our founding fathers called democracy, *"Mobocracy."* That is because it is based on majority rule. As soon as those least able (or least willing) to work discover they can get handouts (entitlements) from the public coffers, the political system is irreparably damaged.

From that point, those people vote for the party or person who promises them the most handouts. The nation slips into a debt trap, degrades into socialism and communism, and freedom is lost!

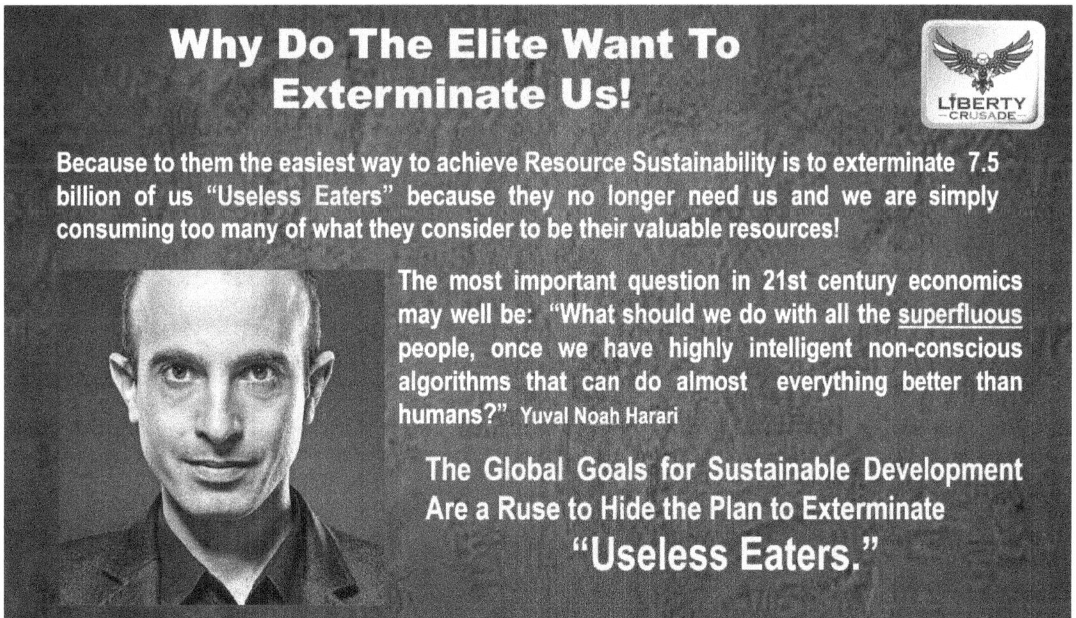

> **Democracies have ever been spectacles of turbulence and contention; have ever been found incompatible with personal security or the rights of property; and have, in general, been as short in their lives as they have been violent in their deaths.**
> James Madison

REQUIRED SOCIETAL CHANGES

The best defense is a strong offense. By that, I mean that if we can anticipate "how" the Elite are likely to come at us, we can build natural defense mechanisms into the very structure of society. But where do we start? We go back to our foundation as a nation and reinstate those things that made America great in the first place.

I can think of no better people to lay out these principles than the men who founded this great nation, so I will let them speak for posterity in their own words. After all, without their insights, courage, honor, patriotism, and reverence for God, this great nation would not exist. Conversely, we need to understand the perversion of those who have connived to enslave us, so we should also hear what they have said, connived, schemed, and plotted to commit all manner of atrocities.

I open this discourse with a quote that is attributed to President John F. Kennedy and is believed to have been made just seven days before he was assassinated:

> **There's a plot in this country to enslave every man, woman, and child.**
> **Before I leave this high and noble office, I intend to expose this plot.**
> President John F. Kennedy, according to Ian Douglas, as stated in his book,
> *Alien Hostiles: Solar Warden* Book Two

Kennedy knew that to expose the plot of the global financial elite was dangerous. He knew he was bucking the political elite, the Federal Reserve, the military-industrial complex, our 3-Letter Agencies, and factions in all three branches of government. Still, he had the courage of his convictions and faced his responsibility, even welcomed it. (see his famous Inaugural quote from 1961 in Chapter 6).

Likewise, our founding fathers knew when they signed the Declaration of Independence that they were pledging their lives and their fortunes to chart a course to freedom for their fellow Americans. When we say the Pledge of Allegiance, I would remind you to reflect on what it took to found this country and what it will take to keep it. If we stand united and honor our pledge, the enemies of this great nation will be defeated. We are many. They are few! We have the protection of God and His divine intervention; they don't.

> **I pledge allegiance to the flag of the United States of America and to the Republic for which it stands: one nation under God, indivisible, with liberty and justice for all.**
> Founding Fathers of the USA

When saying the Pledge of Allegiance, you are entering into an oath to uphold the principles upon which this nation was founded, and you are entering into a covenant with God as well. Remember:

> **We the People are the rightful masters of both Congress and the courts, not to overthrow the Constitution, but to overthrow the men who pervert the Constitution.**
> President Abraham Lincoln, 1859

We are patriots, not insurrectionists, as our corrupt leaders contend. We need to remember that our Declaration of Independence, as shown on the following page, says that:

> **We hold these truths to be self-evident, that all men are created equal, that they are endowed by their Creator with certain unalienable rights, that among these are life, liberty, and the pursuit of happiness. That to secure these rights, governments are instituted among men, deriving their just powers from the consent of the governed. That whenever any form of government becomes destructive to these ends, it is the right of the people to alter or to abolish it, and to institute a new government, laying its foundation on such principles and organizing its powers in such form, as to them shall seem most likely to effect their safety and happiness.**
> Declaration of Independence

United we stand; divided we fall. But with God on our side, we will be victorious. The following quotes reflect the struggle that is being fought to this day by American Patriots!

> **Where the people fear their government, you have tyranny.**
> **Where the government fears the people, you have liberty.**
> John Basil Barnhill

> **All the rights secured to the citizens under the Constitution are worth nothing,**
> **and a mere bubble, except guaranteed to them**
> **by an independent and virtuous Judiciary.**
> President Andrew Jackson

Stop for a second and reflect on the lawfare that has been used against President Trump. You will realize that we no longer have an independent and virtuous judiciary, and for that matter, neither do we have those attributes reflected by our elected officials as a whole. As Trump says, "the swamp must be drained."

This entire book is about exposing the truth so that the truth can set us free. It is about our American Heritage and what this nation stands for. The truth must be told if we are to be free and if America is to survive as a free nation.

The truth of what Kennedy died for is that a cartel of global banker gangsters had hijacked our government, and now all three branches of government have been compromised. The following quote is the sad truth, but we will soon get our republic back.

> **The Trilateral Commission doesn't run the world;**
> **The Council on Foreign Relations does that!**
> Winston Lord, Assistant Secretary of State, the U.S. State Department,
> according to Paul T. Hellyer in *The Money Mafia: A World in Crisis*

WITH THIS SAID, LET'S TAKE A LOOK AT
THE PRINCIPLES THAT MADE AMERICA GREAT!

FAMILY VALUES, NATIONAL PATRIOTISM, AND SPIRITUALITY

There has been an assault on all three of these core values because our slave masters understand that if they can undermine these values, America will become so divided that it slips into immorality and self-destruct from within. The LGBTQ nonsense must be ended, and family values restored. Patriotism must be restored. Pornography must be banned from the internet because it is highly disruptive to the continuity of society.

NOTE: One of the first things Trump did after winning the 2024 election was to announce a year-long celebration commemorating the 250th anniversary of America. The celebration commenced on Memorial Day 2025 and runs through July 4th, 2026. We are honoring the things that made America great. The event highlights our patriotism and unique cultural values, as well as reunites the people as one nation under God. It also showcases U.S. technology and shows how an America free from the swamp rats will usher in an unparalleled period of unity, peace, and prosperity. America will once again be the innovative inspiration of the world and the city on the hill it was ordained to be.

WHAT WE MUST DO

Adults and children alike must be taught to be responsible members of society. That is the only way we can get our republic back and keep it. As stated a minute ago, this means we must have a well-educated, informed, and moral public that is willing to vote for those things that are in the best interest of society at large, rather than for vested self-interest. To that end, we must regain control of all spheres of influence: Family, Religion, Education, Media, Entertainment, Politics, Military, and Economy.

Our entitlement society must shift to one where people learn to be more self-sufficient and community-oriented. Our bloated, power-hungry federal government must be significantly reduced in size, and power must be returned to the states, where it was intended. To accomplish this, the public, not the corporatocracy, must control all the spheres of influence.

The family is the nucleus of civilization.
Will Durant

EDUCATION

One of the first things our forefathers did was to found Harvard University so the public could read. They brought their Bibles from Europe and used them as the basis of our constitution and our legal system. This covenant with God is the foundation of what made America the greatest nation the world has ever known—the shining city on the hill.

RESTRUCTURING THE EDUCATION SYSTEM

Currently, there are intentionally three distinct education systems: One for the Elite that teaches wealth generation and leadership, one for the middle class that teaches basic skills the Elite need to run their day-to-day operations, and one for the lower class that intentionally creates an undereducated, underprivileged class that is intended to be a perpetual welfare class. The intent is to keep the masses in economic slavery while creating class and race division as a control mechanism. Our entire education system will have to be revamped to teach vocational and life skills that are actually meaningful. But I will leave the details of that transition to the experts.

OUR TRUE HISTORY MUST BE TAUGHT IN OUR SCHOOLS

It teaches how our republic has been stolen. Without that knowledge, we cannot understand how we lost our freedoms, how we regain them, and how we maintain them once we have regained them. If a person doesn't have a compass to chart their course, the one certain thing is that they will never reach their destination. That is why our enemy goes to such extremes to dumb us down and brainwash us.

THE MILITARY-INDUSTRIAL COMPLEX

Under NESARA, all nations must end military aggression. Instead of hoarding technology, it will be shared, and all nations will experience financial prosperity; the cause of war will no longer exist. That is why control of the global supply chain was seeded to China. But it is about to be seeded back to America, as Trump puts tariffs on foreign nations to force "Made In America Policies" to spur domestic manufacturing, just as Ulysses S. Grant was responsible for America at its centennial celebration in 1876, announcing that America, the youngest nation in the world, was the wealthiest.

History is about to repeat itself as America spearheads a global technological revolution that equalizes the economic conditions of all nations worldwide and ends the economic disparity that is the principal cause of war. America is under God's covenant, and though the world will experience an economic collapse, America will rise like the Phoenix and restore order out of chaos. The best is yet to come!

Ironically, the man who inflicted us with the unconstitutional Federal Reserve, IRS, and unconstitutional property tax had this to say:

> Our great industrial nation is now controlled by its system of credit. We are no longer a government by free opinion, no longer a government by conviction and the vote of the majority, but a government by the opinion and duress of a small group of dominant men...*A great industrial nation is controlled by its system of credit.*
> Our system of credit is privately centered. The growth of the nation, therefore, and all our activities are in the hands of a few men...Who necessarily, by very reason of their own limitations, chill and check and destroy genuine economic freedom.

[cont'd next page]

**We have become one of the worst ruled, one of the most completely controlled
and dominated governments in the civilized world.**
President Woodrow Wilson, The New Freedom, 1913

NOTE: Written in regret of his having inflicted the American people with the evil Federal Reserve Banking System, the propagators of the very tyranny our forefathers fled Europe to escape.

General and President Eisenhower warned us about the abuse of military power. Under NESARA, that abuse of power will come to an end, and all nations will coexist in an era of peace and harmony, as God's Harvest of Souls brings peace, prosperity, and enlightenment.

As previously discussed, all our wars are the result of false flag attacks—intentionally prolonged to drive us into unmanageable debt! Remember what was spoken of the sheeple:

**The people can always be brought to the bidding of the leaders. That is easy.
All you have to do is tell them they are being attacked...It works every time.**
Hermann Göring

THE ECONOMY

As previously discussed, the fiat dollar is a debt trap. Every dollar printed carries with it an unconstitutional tax obligation in the form of a Treasury Bond that charges interest on every dollar printed and is the basis of both our national and personal debt. This tax is paid to a private, unconstitutional European banking cartel (The Federal Reserve Bank). To ensure that this illegal, unconstitutional tax is paid, our bought and paid politicians have joined forces with this foreign banking cartel and created the IRS, which serves to collect their extortion money forcibly. It can only be described as a criminal extortion ring!

What makes this even more egregious is the fact that both the dollar and the Treasury Bond are backed by absolutely no collateral from the banking cartel. They are issued with the stroke of a pen. If you or I were to do such a thing, we would be arrested and charged with counterfeiting. But that doesn't happen because the banker gangsters and our bought and paid for politicians are partners in this criminal enterprise.

Wait, there is something that gives the dollar value! It is something that was illegally stolen from you and me. That something is an unconstitutional tax on our labor, called the Federal Income Tax, collected by the IRS, with payments tracked by your Social Security number. The only conclusion that can be reached from this analysis is that we are all slaves without chains controlled from cradle to grave by a criminal banking and political partnership. There is one last piece to this crime. As previously discussed in 1871, our Constitution was abandoned and replaced by a corporate constitution that has no obligation to the American people. Its only obligation is to return the highest possible profit to the shareholders of the European banking cartel. We are slaves without chains.

To regain our freedom, the federal income tax, the IRS, and property tax must be abolished, and we must return to the tax structure upon which the nation was founded: a simple sales tax on nonessential items only. Additionally, the stock market is another criminal organization. It must be based on earnings, growth, and dividends, devoid of the speculation that comes with quarterly forecasts. Consider the following:

History records that the money changers have used every form of abuse, intrigue, deceit, and violent means possible to maintain their control over governments by controlling money and its issuance.
James Madison, 4th President of the United States, 1809-1817

**Permit me to issue and control the money of a nation,
and I care not who makes its laws.**
Mayer Rothschild, Founder of the Rothschild banking dynasty

TRANSLATION: Entitlements are a DEPT TRAP.

God plans that their criminal enterprise will be disbanded. When that happens, the banker gangsters and their political partners will be removed from power. We will get back our constitution and control of our political system, our economic system, our legal system, and our constitution. However, as to how that happens, you will have to wait until you read the last chapter of this God-ordained book!

RELIGION

Our founding fathers came to America in pursuit of religious freedom. That is why they embedded the concept of separation of church and state into our Constitution. The intent was to allow political rhetoric from the pulpit so that the public could be informed of political issues without interference from the government. However, with the advent of 501 (c) (3) organizations, a gag has been placed on churches, which precludes them from commenting on political issues. 501(c)(3)s must be abolished and freedom of speech restored.

Additionally, the truth must come out about our religious seminaries and our entire education system. The Rothschilds have hijacked the seminaries, and we must sort out the lies they have inflicted on an unsuspecting public.

**We have staked the whole future of our new nation [American civilization],
not upon the power of government, far from it. We have staked the future of all our
political institutions upon the capacity of mankind for self-government;
upon the capacity of each and all of us to govern ourselves, to control ourselves,
to sustain ourselves according to the Ten Commandments of God.**
James Madison, Father of the U.S. Constitution, [Emphasis added]

**Our constitution was made only for a moral and religious people.
It is wholly inadequate to government of any other.**
John Adams, second President of the United States

**Resistance to tyranny becomes the Christian and social duty of each individual. ...
Continue steadfast and, with a proper sense of your dependence on God,
nobly defend those rights which heaven gave, and no man ought to take from us.**
John Hancock, the first signer of the Declaration of Independence

**Here is my Creed. I believe in one God, the Creator of the Universe.
That He governs it by His Providence. That He ought to be worshipped.**
Benjamin Franklin, Signer of the Declaration of Independence
and the United States Constitution

THE MEDIA

Most of the news outlets, social media platforms, the entertainment industry, and print publications have become propaganda outlets of the Elite and their globalist puppets. They represent the interests of the corporation rather than our original Constitution and the interests of *We the People.* Government and corporate censorship are nothing short of treason, so to get our freedom back and keep it, these institutions must be purged and freedom of speech restored. All political and corporate leaders who have perpetrated this betrayal on *We the People* must be removed from their positions of power. How that will be done will be covered shortly.

**The liberties of the people will never be secure
when the transactions of their rulers can be counseled from them.**
Patrick Henry

**The freedom of speech may be taken, and dumb and silent we may be led,
like sheep to the slaughter.**
President George Washington, in his address to the officers of the Army, 1783

**Don't interfere with anything in the Constitution.
That must be maintained, for it is the only safeguard of our liberties.**
President Abraham Lincoln

Media manipulation in the U.S. today is more efficient than it was in Nazi Germany, because here we have the pretense that we are getting all the information we want. That misconception prevents people from even looking for the truth.
Mark Crispin Miller, professor at New York University

The Central Intelligence Agency owns everyone of any significance in the major media.
William Colby, Former CIA Director

The size of the lie is a definite factor in causing it to be believed, for the vast masses of a nation are in the depths of their hearts more easily deceived than they are consciously and intentionally bad. The primitive simplicity of their minds renders them a more easy prey to a big lie than a small one, for they themselves often tell little lies, but would be ashamed to tell big lies.
Adolf Hitler: Mein Kampf, 1925

NATIONAL SOVEREIGNTY REQUIRES CLOSED BORDERS

There are limits to the number of people a nation can assimilate. Immigration was completely stopped from 1924 to 1965. This was done because we could not afford to take in all the poor people and because there were so many people coming that they couldn't be assimilated, and that threatened national sovereignty and unity. What was true then is true now. The Open Borders policies of the Left are, in truth, a form of covert warfare. It is a military invasion masquerading as a humanitarian obligation. I say again, a nation without a border has no nation to be sovereign over!

The UN, Council on Foreign Relations, Trilateral Commission, World Economic Forum, etc., as well as other organizations, including the CIA, FBI, NASA, and other National Security Agencies, have been co-opted and must be done away with as part of draining the swamp so we can get back our freedom. Please reflect on the following quotes. They tell the truth as seen by people in a position to know!

OPEN BORDERS ARE A MILITARY INVASION

Let me draw your attention again to a quote from Dr. Carroll Quigley on the next page, which was previously noted in this book.

> **The Council on Foreign Relations is the American branch of a society,**
> **which originated in England,... (and) ... believes national boundaries**
> **should be obliterated and one-world rule established.**
> Dr. Carroll Quigley, CFR member,
> College Mentor of President Clinton, Author of Tragedy and Hope
>
> *TRANSLATION: The CFR is our enemy.*

THE CORPORATOCRACY EXPLAINED

> **The Trilateral Commission is intended to be the vehicle for multinational consolidation**
> **of the commercial and banking interests by seizing control of the political government**
> **of the United States...They rule the future.**
> Sources attribute this quote to Felix Frankfurter, Supreme Court Justice

WE MUST CLOSE OUR BORDERS

We must focus on the unique values that made America great! The borders can be closed, and the illegal immigrants can and will be removed. It is easier than most people think. Trump will finish the wall, and that will stem the influx of illegal immigrants. As to how we get the illegal immigrants out of our country and keep others from coming, all we have to do is remove the invitation that the Biden administration, the UN, and a host of NGOs have extended.

Additionally, if things go as I expect, we will see violence in the streets before this is over. If that happens, there will need to be some type of martial law, which would likely allow illegal immigrants in sanctuary cities to be gathered up and deported. We must get our country back!

No handouts, no healthcare, no drivers' licenses, no access to public schools, no jobs. That is all it would take, and that can be done with the stroke of a pen. Additionally, if it is true that, to participate in the wealth transfer under NESARA - GESARA, one must return to their nation of origin. In that case, they will voluntarily leave the U.S.

STOP DRUG AND HUMAN TRAFFICKING ACROSS OUR SOUTHERN BORDER

Mexico is literally under siege by the cartels, and in the U.S., drug addiction is literally at epidemic levels, and it must be stopped. It is tearing the fabric of society apart. There is a solution, but it is rather extreme; nonetheless, it is vitally important. Thump leveraged tariffs to get military assistance from Mexico at the border and to house illegal immigrants in Mexico while awaiting asylum hearings.

The solution to this crisis, this national security crisis, this invasion is for the U.S. and Mexican governments to join in a joint military engagement and do a surgical strike on the cartels and put them out of business. They possess paramilitary capabilities, but they would be no match for a full-fledged military assault. This is vital. We need to defend our borders instead of spending taxpayer money on foreign wars that have questionable motives.

I would rather not see this happen. But if Mexico will not join us, Trump is within his legal rights to take out the cartel (terrorist cartels) alone. But one way or another, they must be taken out.

ADDRESS THE HOMELESS—OPIUM AND FENTANYL EPIDEMIC

What I am about to say will sound harsh. Still, this crisis must be addressed for the sake of society and for the sake of people with an addiction and the mentally ill who live on the streets. Following the Opium Wars in China, the Emperor of China ordered the people with an addiction to be rounded up and executed. I certainly do not condone such an action. But here is what I do see as essential. We must round up the homeless and take them to FEMA camps, where we do everything possible to help them. People with an addiction must be put through rehab. Then those who are able will be assisted to reintegrate into society. This means that halfway houses must be provided and work programs must be offered.

For the mentally ill who were abandoned when we closed mental illness facilities across the nation, they must be provided long-term care. The penalty for drug pushing must be harsh. Long maximum sentences for first-time offenders, mandatory life sentences for second-time offenders, and, in extreme cases, the death penalty.

POLITICS AND THE FED

I saved this until last because none of the problems we face can be solved as long as we have a uni-party comprised of corrupt bought and paid for career politicians. But don't worry. As we have discussed, China and the U.S. must fall, and that will trigger a global financial collapse, the likes of which the world has never seen. The national debt of literally every country in the world has reached the point where it is unsustainable. As a result, we will soon see nations around the world declare bankruptcy, dissolve the national debt, and start over with a new gold-backed economy. Their governments will be dissolved, and their corrupt politicians will either retire or be removed! Likewise, a host of globalist corporations and banks will go under. This represents the fall of the corporatocracy, which rules the world. This is good news because before God's economic system can be installed, man's economic systems (capitalism and communism) must fall!

THE SHADOW GOVERNMENT IS REAL

The real rulers in Washington are invisible
and exercise power from behind the scenes.
Supreme Court Justice Felix Frankfurter, 1952

UNDERSTANDING WHO OUR SLAVE MASTERS ARE

The real truth of the matter is, as you and I know, that a financial element in the larger
centers has owned the Government ever since the days of Andrew Jackson.
A letter written by FDR to Colonel House, November 21st, 1933

TRANSLATION: This is the swamp that can and will be removed.

EXPOSING THE HIDDEN AGENDA OF THE ELITE'S CENTRAL BANKING SYSTEM

...Nothing less than to create a world system of financial control in private hands able
to dominate the political system of each country and economy of the world as a
whole...controlled in a feudalist fashion by central banks of the world acting in concert
by secret agreements arrived at in private meetings and conferences.
Carol Quigley, Author of *Tragedy and Hope*
Member of the Trilateral Commission and mentor to Bill Clinton

TRANSLATION: We are, in fact, controlled by a shadow government

PRINTING SOVEREIGN CURRENCY ISSUED BY THE TREASURY WILL BREAK THE CHAINS OF SLAVERY

Creating and issuing money is a supreme prerogative of government and its greatest
creative opportunity. Adopting these principles will save the taxpayer immense sums

[cont'd next page]

**of interest, and money will cease to be the master
and become the servant of humanity.**
President Abraham Lincoln

TRANSLATION: The FED is our slave master.

CONGRESS IS IRRELEVANT

Someone warned in the 1960s that both houses of Congress were irrelevant because the International Monetary Fund was running the Federal Reserve Chairman.

TRANSLATION: The Fed, acting on behalf of the financial elite, tells the President and Congress what to do, and they do it. They are puppets of the banker gangsters.

PRESIDENT THOMAS JEFFERSON SAID THE CENTRAL BANK WOULD TAKE OUR PROPERTY

**The Central bank is an institution of the most deadly hostility existing against the
principles and form of our Constitution...if the American people allow private banks
to control the issuance of the currency, first by inflation and then by devaluation of the
banks and corporations that will grow up around them will deprive the people of all
their property until their children will wake up homeless
on the continent their fathers conquered.**
President Thomas Jefferson

*TRANSLATION: The Banker Gangsters create financial hardship and steal our homes
based on unconstitutional property tax laws. Need I say this is criminal?*

THE PLAN TO DESTROY U.S. INDEPENDENCE

**I believe that if the people of this nation fully understood what Congress
has done to them over the last forty-nine years, they would move on Washington;
they would not wait for an election...It adds up to a preconceived plan to destroy the
economic and social independence of the United States!**
Senator George W. Malone of Nevada, speaking before Congress in 1957

*TRANSLATION: We have the right to restore our Constitution
if it ceases to serve We The People.*

NOTE: I cannot say for certain, but supposedly, the new quantum financial system has been running in tandem with the old fiat system. Once the dust settles, there will be a one-for-one exchange of the old fiat currency for the new gold-backed, commodity-based currency. This represents the birth of God's economic system that will usher in peace and prosperity.

Now that you know who our enemy is and what his endgame is, we can turn our attention to how we go about *Restoring the Republic*.

CHAPTER 15

HOW WE RESTORE OUR REPUBLIC:
Ushering in God's Governmental System!

TOPICS COVERED IN THIS CHAPTER:

- THE SECOND DECLARATION OF INDEPENDENCE
- THE TWELVE FOUNDATION STONES THAT MADE AMERICA GREAT
- THE ENEMY'S PLAYBOOK
- WHY THE KINGDOMS OF MAN MUST FALL
- HOW WE TAKE BACK OUR FREEDOM

IN THE MIDST of chaos, there is opportunity! We are about to experience a period of chaos as the Elite make their final push to enslave us. But when the dust settles, and we are on the other side of the chaos, we will finally have our freedom. If you don't already know who, what, where, when, how, and why as it relates to our slavery, you will before you finish this chapter. It will bring everything you have learned into focus and provide a simple plan for how we restore our freedom and our republic!

The enemy thinks they are going to cause a catastrophic financial collapse and cause the public to be so overcome with fear that we "sheeple" will bend our knees and surrender to their demonic one-world dictatorship! Nothing could be further from the truth. Their plans are going to backfire! Here is what is going to happen instead! This collapse, which they have orchestrated, will be so large that countries all over the world will collapse, as well as major banks and a host of global corporations!

When that happens, and it must, there will be an explosion of truth the likes of which has never been seen. The people's eyes will be opened, and "The Truth Will Set The Captives Free!" The people will understand that we have been intentionally divided and pitted against one another! They will understand that all our wars have been orchestrated by the financial elite as control mechanisms! They will understand that they are living in an economic system of "Slavery Without Chains!"

As to the reason for what they intend to do, it is simple! If money is their god (*which it is*), then it begs the question: *What is Money?* It is not that worthless piece of paper we call the "dollar!" It is the natural resources that are mined, manufactured into finished products, and sold that are the basis of the global monetary system!

Knowing this and knowing that the earth is a finite sphere with a finite quantity of natural resources, the Elite have decided that with the advent of AI, robotics, nanotechnology, etc., we are expendable! The UN's goal is to exterminate 90% of the world's population. They envision that those of us they allow to live will be their slaves!

United Nation's publications "Agenda 21" and "Agenda 30" reveal the "New World Order" agenda, calling for the end of nationalism, patriotism, private property, individual rights, the two-parent family, automobiles, air travel, and the right to defend ourselves from a tyrannical government. In keeping with their goal of "Sustainable development," they plan to reduce the population by over 90%, ridding

(cont'd next page)

America and the world of dissidents. The remaining "useful servants" are to live in coastal communities, wherein they will be stacked and packed into micro-apartments.
Excerpt from Second Declaration of Independence

If you believe this, as I do, then you realize that we are on *"death ground!"* In that event, we have no choice other than to draw a line in the sand and demand our freedom!

We are many! They are few! If we stand UNITED and refuse to continue to participate in our slavery, they will lose! That is exactly how India got its freedom from England, and it is how we will get our freedom as well.

JUST SAY NO TO YOUR ENEMIES' SLAVERY!

India got its independence from England by rallying around Gandhi and boycotting the British Free Trade System of Slavery Without Chains. They boycotted the British economic system, and eventually Britain caved and gave India its freedom without a single shot being fired. America can do what India did. We are many! They are few! If we refuse to participate in our own slavery, the enemy will lose his power, and we will get our freedom. Below is an excerpt from a 2nd Declaration of Independence released by President Donald Trump on July 4, 2020. It lays out exactly how we get back our freedom!

A 2nd Declaration of Independence,
By the 50 United States of America Signed
by President Donald Trump on July 4,
2020. To the New Republic of the United States
Transcribed by Mark Baughman 2/9/2020 from Parchment Paper from
Original.

Trusting our cause is just and having prayed for the fortitude of brave spiritual wickedness in high places. WE CITIZENS OF AMERICA make this announcement to the SHAREHOLDERS OF US CORP. including THE CITY OF LONDON, THE BRITISH CROUWN, AND THE VATICAN, and their OPERATIVES in the medica government and society. A 2nd DECLARATION OF INDEPENDENCE, By the 50 United States of America

https://operationdisclosure.blogspot.com/2021/02/the-2nd-declaration-of-independence.html

The complete document is included at the end of this chapter. No half measures are adequate to restore our inalienable rights of life, liberty, and the pursuit of happiness. The document proclaims our independence from the U.S. Corp, the District of Columbia, the Vatican, and the City of London! The rights, spelled out in the original Declaration of Independence, say:

> *We hold these truths to be self-evident, that all men are created equal,*
> *that they are endowed by their Creator with certain unalienable rights,*
> *that among these are life, liberty, and the pursuit of happiness.*
> *That to secure these rights, governments are instituted among men,*
> *deriving their just powers from the consent of the governed.*
> *That whenever any form of government becomes destructive to these ends,*
> *it is the right of the people to alter or to abolish it,*
> *and to institute a new government, laying its foundation on such principles*
> *and organizing its powers in such form,*
> *as to them shall seem most likely to affect their safety and happiness.*

I remind you that America was not founded as a Democracy, but as a *"constitutional republic—a Government of the people, by the people, for the people."* The 2nd Declaration of Independence explains the rights that have been taken from us and must be restored so that we may be the free, prosperous nation that God intended. America was intended to be blessed and to be a blessing! Let me remind you why our ancestors gave us a republic, not a democracy, when they escaped the British Monarchy's tyranny.

> *Democracy is just another name for Socialism, Communism, and Mob Rule,*
> *where those least willing to work vote for the political party and candidates*
> *who promise the most money from the public coffers. The result is crippling*
> *taxation, public discord, division, and a government based on "special interest"*
> *rather than on what best serves We the People.*
> *The 2nd Declaration of Independence charts our way*
> *back to our founding principles!*

Believe this! God has not abandoned us! He is a Waymaker. Like him or not, Donald Trump is God's David, and he has outsmarted our enemy. In his first term, Trump did the impossible! Obama scoffed at him and asked him if he was going to wave a magic wand and restore the economy, and he said, "Yes!"

Faced with an army of swamp dwellers, he took the stock market from 10,000 to 30,000. All he had to do was give us access to our natural resources, open the way for new factories to be built, negotiate fair trade agreements, and impose tariffs on China. If he could do that in the face of unprecedented opposition, imagine what he will do when the swamp dwellers have been removed from power. He promised to "*Make America Greater Than Ever,*" and he will.

In previous chapters, I laid out the case for why America is under Abraham's Covenant and why it is the only nation in the world capable of restoring the world from the chaos that is about to befall it from the coming financial collapse! Now is the time God has ordained to set the captives free. There is a single requirement for what we must do! We must stand up and say no to our captivity and surrender to God, and He will do the rest. Provisions have been made.

Now is the time of the transfer of wealth from the wicked to the righteous. Read on, and you will understand this is no idle wish but a fact!

TIME TO JOIN GOD'S REMNANT ARMY!

Let's quickly review so we're all clear before we talk about how to restore our republic. It is time to take what we have learned and turn it into an action plan. We have everything we need to defeat the enemy. We are many! They are few! As previously stated, an army of whistleblowers is about to be released! When that happens, we need to stand up and refuse to continue to participate in our own slavery. Before you finish this chapter, you will know what to do to take back our republic!

REVIEW TIME

WHO IS THE ENEMY?

We have called him by many names: The financial elite, the global elite, the one-world government, the Illuminati, the Corporation, the UN with its global governance organizations, the Uni-Party, etc.! But really, who is he?

The enemy is anyone in a position of power or influence who is willing to support the globalists' agenda in exchange for money, power, or influence, or because they are being blackmailed because of some indiscretion they have committed. Most of them are in some way connected to a sphere of influence that the Elite has used to execute their plans for world dominance!

They are a cast of traitors who have been short-sighted enough to side with the forces of evil and bet against God and his remnant! Bad choice. God is our Waymaker, and He is about to remove our enemies from their seats of power. They lose; we win!

WHAT IS THE ENEMY'S SOURCE OF POWER, AND WHAT IS HIS GREATEST WEAKNESS?

The enemy's greatest strength is always his greatest weakness! In this case, it is the ability to print worthless fiat currency and charge the nations of the world interest on that money because it is actually a loan! I am speaking of the privately owned Rothschild Central Banking System, including the Fed. They use their unlimited supply of money to buy the power and influence that controls all the spheres of influence that control us from cradle to grave!

WHAT IS OUR ENEMY'S AGENDA?

This book is the inspired word of God! The time is now! It is time to stand up and join God's Remnant Army. What follows in this chapter will expose the enemy's playbook, and with that knowledge, you will be empowered to stand, and when you do, we will win, and we will get our freedom back!

As hard as it may be to believe, the wealth of the wicked has been stored up for the righteous. As stated, this chapter contains a 2nd Declaration of Independence, which Trump signed on July 4th,2020. When the people learn the truth, nothing will stop us from getting back our Constitution and our freedom.

It delineates who the illegal corporation is and gives us the legal means to confiscate the wealth they have stored up and to remove from office those they put in power, as well as to nullify the illegal laws they passed to enslave us! As the Bible says, what is stolen must be returned. As I have said repeatedly, we win, they lose! Please stand up and let's take back our freedom!

WHAT IS THE ENEMY'S FATAL ERROR?

Once he finds a strategy that works, he makes the mistake of using it over and over! This behavior creates a pattern that we can use to anticipate what he is likely to do in specific situations. Poker players call this a "Tell." It allows us, with high accuracy, to anticipate what our enemy is planning before he does it. We must have these countermeasures in place to defeat him!

We have the enemy's playbook, and that makes him extremely vulnerable to defeat in any situation. Earlier, we discussed how breaking the German code in WWII turned the tide of the war from almost certain defeat to victory. This is no different!

HOW DO WE USE WHAT WE HAVE LEARNED TO DEFEAT OUR ENEMY?

That is what the rest of this chapter is about. It is what this entire book has been preparing you to do. We have the enemy's playbook, and it holds the key to defeating him! Before you finish this chapter, you will believe that we do, in fact, have the power to defeat our mortal enemy (the globalist financial elite). Everything is about to change. The collapse of both China and the U.S. is now inevitable and imminent.

As we have discussed, China will be relegated to being a regional power! Also, as discussed, the U.S. will rise from the ashes and lead the world into God's governmental system! America will be greater than ever, and the world will experience an unparalleled period of peace and prosperity, during which God will usher in His Harvest of Souls.

RESTORING THE U.S. TO GREATNESS AND LEADING THE WORLD INTO AN UNPARALLELED PERIOD OF PEACE AND PROSPERITY

All Trump had to do to restore the economy in 2016 was give us access to our natural resources, open the way for new factories to be built, negotiate fair trade agreements, and impose tariffs on China. Once the economy has been restored, we must begin the process of *Restoring Our Republic!* It starts with the 2nd Declaration of Independence that Trump signed in 2020! As discussed previously, it calls for the restoration of our "inalienable rights of life, liberty, and pursuit of happiness!"

It also calls for the termination of the Illegal U.S. Corporation. It spells out that we have the legal right to confiscate the wealth they have stored up and to remove from office those they put in power, as well as to nullify the illegal laws they passed to enslave us! In the Bible, this is described as the transfer of riches from the wicked to the righteous.

Then begins the hard work! We must restore the Christian and family values and Patriotism that underpinned our REPUBLIC! A new generation of Americans must learn the values that underpin America's greatness and exactly what is required to be a republic once again and to be able to keep it from being usurped by those who would be the masters of us all. Armed with the truth, we will educate the people, so we are once again empowered to become "A government of the people, by the people, for the people!"

This will require that we restore "The Foundation Stones" that made America great in the first place. The following two graphics outline what I call "The 12 Foundation Stones that Provide the Structure for a Free Society." One by one, they have been either weakened or removed completely. In the simplest possible terms, all we must do to make America great once again is to restore the foundation stones that made it great in the first place!

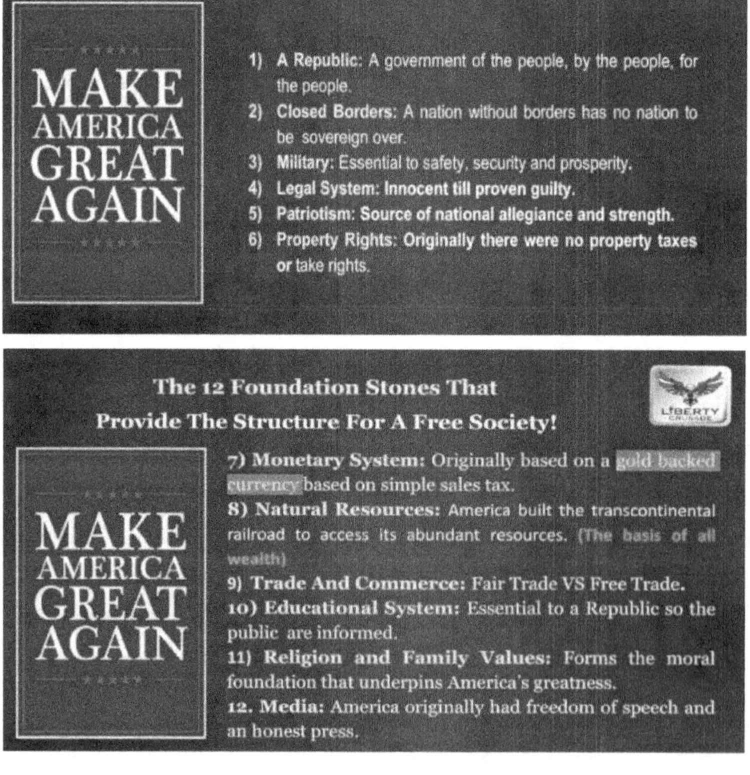

WE HAVE THE ENEMY'S PLAYBOOK
AND IT HOLDS THE KEY TO HIS DEFEAT!

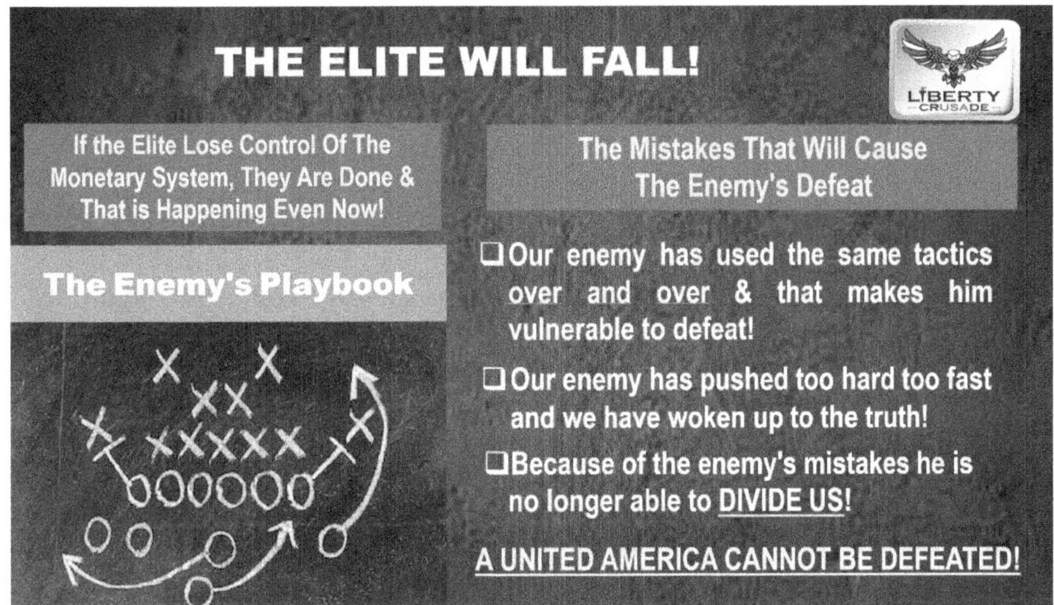

What follows is an account of all the things the agents of the U.S. Corporation have done to enslave us. I call it "*The Enemy's Playbook*." Once you have read the playbook and know what has been done to enslave us, we will use that knowledge to develop a simple counteroffensive that will show you how we take back our freedom. This knowledge will empower you to join the resistance movement that will take back our freedom!

THE ENEMY'S PLAYBOOK IS WAR AS A MEANS OF CONTROL
USE FALSE FLAG EVENTS AS AN EXCUSE FOR WARS FOR PROFIT AND CONTROL

- War is used to drive nations into DEBT and force them to accept a central bank, which is 90% of communizing a nation!
- Wars are intentionally dragged out as a business decision to enrich the financial elite and to drive nations into their debt trap!

- Terrorist attacks like the Oklahoma City Bombing and 9/11 are used to pass draconian laws that take away our freedom by passing laws that create a legal dictatorship.

For example, "The Patriot Act" authorized the federal government to declare a national emergency and seize control of local, state, federal, and tribal governments as well as all means of production, distribution, and financial assets!

FORMS OF MONETARY CONTROL - EFFECTS OF ILLEGAL TAXATION

America is under a corporate charter with only one mandate: to optimize the profits of the corporations' shareholders! To this end, the public is in servitude to an illegal tax system that must be stricken so that we may have freedom!

ILLEGAL TAXES
- Progressive federal income tax
- Mortgages with front-loaded compound interest payments and the requirement to get a new mortgage every time you refinance or buy a new home
- Credit cards with usury rates and compound interest
- Personal property taxes are paid year after year on the same items, etc.

EFFECTS OF FED'S FIAT CURRENCY SYSTEM
- Create inflation and deflation on demand.
- Suppress wages so they never keep pace with inflation.
- People can never get ahead.

ORCHESTRATED BOOM AND BUST CYCLES

HOW THEY ORCHESTRATE BOOM AND BUST CYCLES
- Increase the money supply.
- Lower interest rates.
- Push investment opportunities.
- Increase interest rates.
- Dry up credit and instant crash.
- Layoffs result from a slowdown in the economy.

- People are forced to sell their stocks, which the Elite buy for pennies on the dollar.
- A debt trap is triggered when people are forced to resort to high-interest credit cards as a stopgap measure.
- If a person gets behind on their mortgage, the banker gangsters take their home.

EFFECTS OF AMERICA'S ABUSE OF BEING "THE WORLD'S RESERVE CURRENCY"

The FED runs the printing press 24/7/365 intentionally, causing domestic inflation and devaluation, causing prices to rise relative to wages! Under the terms of the *"Petro Dollar Agreement with Saudi Arabia,"* international oil purchases are made with devalued U.S. dollars, causing inflation in other countries. Because of the financial hardship this caused, BRICS was formed to end this system of monetary extortion.

NATURAL RESOURCES AS A CONTROL MECHANISM
NATURAL RESOURCES ARE FUNDAMENTAL TO WEALTH, INFLUENCE, AND POWER

They are converted into finished goods and sold, creating money that is used to purchase power and influence. To be a global superpower, a nation must lead in all three of these commerce engines.

- Control of Natural Resources
- Control of Manufacturing
- Control of Trade

Profits from the sale of raw material and finished goods are used to run nations and covertly create a Shadow Government by corrupting:

- Politics: All Three Branches of Government
- Economic System: The Corporatocracy—Banks, Corporations, and Government
- Military Industrial Complex
- Media and Entertainment Industry
- Education System
- Family and Moral Values
- Religion: By creating division and the insertion of religious dogma

EFFORTS TO COLLAPSE THE US FROM WITHIN

The goal is to create a network of community organizing groups to apply pressure from the bottom up, which supports pressure from the top down to undermine America and other nations around the world! (i.e., BLM, SEIU, Green Movement, etc.)

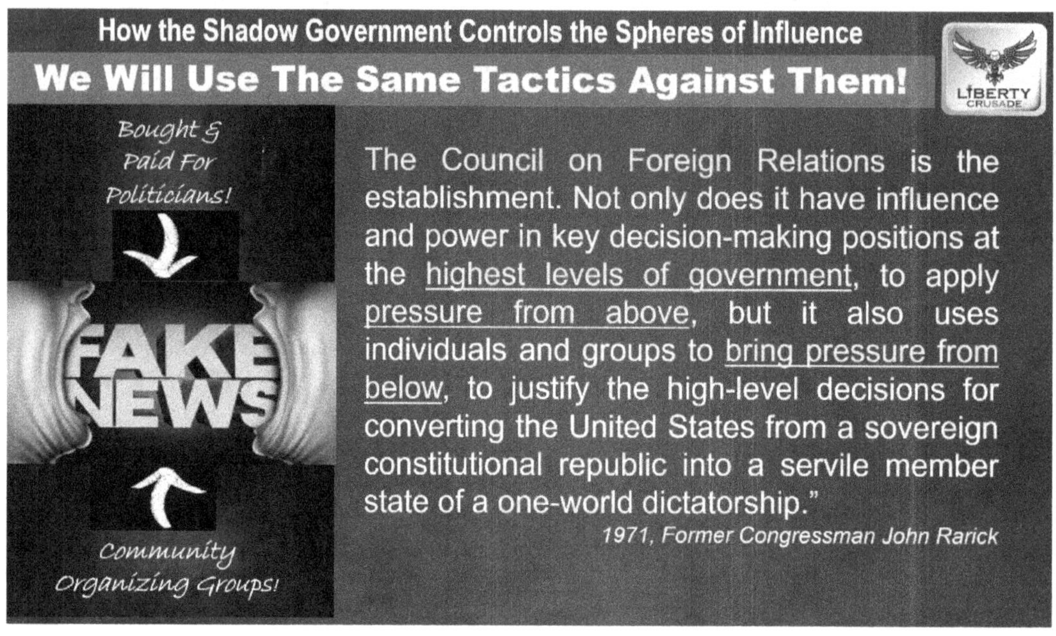

EMBED THESE SUBVERSIVES IN OUR LEGITIMATE GOVERNMENT TO DESTROY IT

- Create the Council on Foreign Relations and the Trilateral Commission, dedicated to ending national borders and sovereignty.
- Place political leaders in these organizations to form a shadow government to rule the nation.

EFFORTS TO END SOVEREGNITY OF ALL NATIONS AND CREATE A ONE-WORLD DICTATORSHIP

- Create the UN to establish global governance organizations with which to enslave humanity, i.e., WB, IMF, UASID, NATO, WHO, WTO, etc.
- Create organizations dedicated to ending all sovereign nations and establishing the 10-nation trading bloc beast system (see graphic above).
- Use the aftermath of WWII to create the 1st servile trading bloc - the European Union (see graphic above)
- Create the Amero-Union to merge the U.S., Canada, and Mexico, and then create eight additional servile trading blocs.
- Inflict us with a fiat currency that is the basis of most of our debt.
- Drive us into wars for profit to keep us in a state of perpetual poverty and dependence.
- Use open borders to create chaos, DEBT, and ultimately end U.S. sovereignty because a nation with no border has no nation to be sovereign over.
- The Oklahoma City Bombing and 9/11 were used to pass Draconian laws that laid the foundation for a legal dictatorship.
- Create a one-world government combining super-capitalism and communism.
- Inflict the U.S. with intentionally losing trade deals to drive it into deep debt.
- President Carter, acting as a puppet, purposefully gave China control over manufacturing and trade.
- Under the puppet President Clinton, NAFTA was signed, a trade agreement designed to bankrupt the U.S.

FORMS OF MIND CONTROL AND BRAINWASHING

All the spheres of influence have been taken over, i.e., the education system, news outlets including social media, the entertainment industry, churches, corporations, banks, politicians, courts, the Pentagon, and other security agencies, the military industrial complex! Jointly, they control access to all forms of information, leaving us in a position where we live in a vacuum devoid of truth. We are literally controlled from cradle to grave. The general population is left in a position where they cannot discern fact from fiction, truth from lie, friend from foe! In other words, we are immersed in a sea of propaganda and are victims of mind control.

> **If we understand the mechanism and motives of the group mind, it is now possible to control and regiment the masses according to our will without them knowing it.**
> Edward Bernays, Father of modern advertising–propaganda

> **Those who manipulate the unseen mechanism of society constitute an invisible government which is the true ruling power of our country...In almost every act of our lives whether in the sphere of politics or business in our social conduct or our ethical thinking, we are dominated by the relatively small number of persons who understand the mental processes and social patterns of the masses. It is they who pull the wires that control the public mind.**
> Edward Bernays

> **To achieve world government, it is necessary to remove from the minds of men their individualism, loyalty to family traditions, national patriotism, and religious dogmas.**
> Brock Adams, director, UN Health Organization

> **The organized minority will beat the disorganized majority every time.**
> Vladimir Lenin, founder of the Soviet Union

NOTE: What better example of this could there possibly be than the decision of the Supreme Court to make gay marriage the law of the land?

> **The CIA owns everyone of significance in the media.**
> Colby William, former CIA director

> **Misinformation in the US today is more efficient than in Nazi Germany because we think that we are getting all the information we want. That misconception prevents people from even looking for the truth.**
> Mark Crispin Miller

> **The bewildered herd are a problem. We've got to prevent their rage and trampling. We've got to distract them. They should be watching the Super Bowl or sitcoms or violent movies or something...and you've got to keep them pretty scared because unless they're scared properly and frightened of all kinds of devils that are going to destroy them from outside or inside or somewhere, they may start to think,**
> [cont'd next page]

which is very dangerous because they're not competent to think,
and therefore it's important to distract and to marginalize them.
Professor Noam Chomsky, Author, *Keeping The Rabble In Line*

A revolt of the plebs would become as unthinkable as an organized insurrection of
sheep against the practice of eating mutton.
Bertrand Russell

EFFORTS TO COMMIT MASS GENOCIDE
AND ALTER OUR DNA

Next are some quotes that demonstrate that it is absolutely a fact that the global elite are committed to killing 7.5 billion of us and enslaving those few who are allowed to live, in what can only be described as labor camps! The following should convince you of the truth of what I just said. As we have discussed, virtually every war we have engaged in was based on a false flag event used to justify a war that killed millions. We know COVID-19 was a man-made virus inflicted on us to cull the herd of humanity.

Based on what the AMA, WHO, and big Pharma did to us during COVID-19, the people are finally waking up to the truth: our food, water, air, and land are being poisoned! We are also at a point where we believe that the Elite do, in fact, intend to genetically alter us to turn us into some form of docile sheeple!

A part of eugenic politics would finally land us in an extensive use of the lethal
chamber. A great many people would have to be put out of existence simply
because it wastes other people's time to look after them.
Lecture to the Eugenics Education Society, Reported in *The Daily Express*,
March 4, 1910

The most important question in 21st-century economics may well be: What should we
do with all the superfluous people once we have highly intelligent non-conscious
algorithms that can do almost everything better than humans?
Yuval Noah Harari

In the event I am reincarnated, I would like to return as a deadly virus,
in order to contribute something to solve overpopulation.
Prince Philip

> …the Fourth Industrial Revolution doesn't change what you are doing. It changes you.
> If you take genetic editing just as an example. It's you who are changed,
> and of course this has a big impact on your identity.
> Klaus Schwab
>
> A total world population of 250-300 million people,
> a 95 percent decline from present levels, would be ideal.
> Ted Turner

Klaus Schwab, head of the World Economic Forum, envisions a world where artificial intelligence (AI) has effectively obsoleted humanity. It is a world where AI and robots have taken over most jobs, and the Elite no longer need us! So, they are free to exterminate the population and birth their New World Order Dictatorship.

EFFORTS TO CREATE A ONE–WORLD CHURCH

Use the Catholic Church, which usurped Christ's throne, to establish a watered-down one-world demonic church.

SEPTEMBER 14-15, 2022, THE 7TH CONGRESS OF WORLD AND CONVENTIONAL RELIGIONS

Members of this congress agreed that in the name of "peace and security," Christianity, Islam, Judaism, and Buddhism are all brothers and sisters under the same God. This denies that Christ is the Son of God and that only through Him is salvation. This is political religion, ushering in the one-world government and the one-world church referred to in the Book of Revelation. Here is what the Bible has to say about peace and security:

> While people are saying, "*peace and safety*," destruction will come on them suddenly,
> as labor pains on a pregnant woman, and they will not escape.
> 1Thessalonians 6:3 (NIV) [Emphasis added]

> Whosoever shall confess that Jesus is the Son of God,
> God dwelleth in him, and he in God. 1 John 4:15 (KJV)

This contradicts the agreement made at the 7th Congress. Draw your own conclusions!

EFFORTS TO CONTROL RESOURCE-RICH UNDERDEVELOPED NATIONS

This is how the Globalists have controlled natural resources for centuries. They make sure resource-rich, underdeveloped nations are denied the infrastructure, money, and technology to develop their own resources, therefore assuring that 1st world countries would be able to keep them under their thumb.

Today they are using this centuries-old strategy to pillage Africa by denying it infrastructure, technology, and education. If we are to have peace in the world, these types of activities must be stopped. For example, Africa (the most resource-rich continent in the world) has been divided into 54 intentionally dysfunctional nations to keep it poor so its resources can be exploited.

HOW WE TAKE BACK OUR FREEDOM!

STEP 1: REGAIN CONTROL OF THE ENGINE OF THE ECONOMY BY REGAINING CONTROL OF:

- Natural Resources
- Manufacturing
- Trade

Also, we should replace our fiat currency (that is subject to inflation, devaluation, and enables the orchestration of boom-and-bust cycles) with a commodity-based financial system that is not subject to manipulation and accumulation of insurmountable debt that invariably leads to societal collapse! This falls under NESARA.

Trump is committed to making America energy independent by giving us access to oil and clean coal. We have suppressed technology that allows us to scrub carbon from the air and convert it into oxygen. The missing component is access to suppressed energy inventions. The 47th President says we will have free energy. All our ecological problems can be solved with access to suppressed technology. Wind, solar, and lithium batteries are a joke!

STEP 2: RESTORE THE TAX STRUCTURE OUR CONSTITUTION SPECIFIED

- Terminate the illegal IRS and federal income tax
- End the illegal property tax
- End compound interest on mortgages and credit cards
- The U.S. initially ran the government based on a simple sales tax, and how we return to that tax structure is laid out under the provisions of NESARA, to be enumerated shortly

STEP 3: CONFISCATE/REPATRIATE THE WEALTH OF ALL PERSONS AND INSTITUTIONS THAT AMASSED VAST FORTUNES UNDER PROVISIONS OF THE ILLEGAL U.S. CORPORATION

Use the funds to take control of all spheres of influence that have been used to control the masses. The Bible says that what is stolen must be returned, and our Constitution makes provision for that to happen! Power and finances must be taken from all these organizations and institutions! These are the enemies of humanity, and they must be stripped of all their power!

The global financial system is about to collapse. When that happens, the wealth of our slave masters will be confiscated. They will lose their power and influence, and whistleblowers will come out by the droves. Our eyes will be opened, and *We the People* will stand united, and freedom will reign. When this happens, political figures put in power illegally will be removed, and the laws and regulations they passed to establish a legal dictatorship (The Corporation) will be subject to removal.

At the same time, governments, banks, and corporations will collapse by the droves, their money and power taken to be used by those God has chosen as stewards. We will have righteous leaders, and the republic will be restored. A prosperous, righteous U.S. will rise from the ashes and lead the world into a brighter future where humanity learns to live together in peace and harmony.

Expect us to regain control of the following:

- **Economy–the corporatocracy:** i.e., Central banks, international corporations, and big government
- **Politics–all three branches of government:** This includes both elected and non-elected persons

- **Media:** i.e., news outlets, social media outlets, the internet, etc.
- **Education:** Public schools, colleges, universities, and publishing companies that can be used to undermine the republic
- **Entertainment industry:** i.e., Hollywood and the music industry
- **National heritage—the foundation that made America great:** 501c churches (muzzles removed) and any organizations that undermine our Christian heritage, family values, and our patriotism! Obstructionist organizations: i.e., Planned Parenthood. ACLU, Anti-Defamation League, fallacious fact checkers, etc.
- **Military industrial complex:** The collaboration of arms companies, bankers, politicians, and national security agencies that inflict us with false flag events and wars for profit, i.e., the Pentagon, NSA, CIA, etc.

STEP 4: REMOVE ALL THOSE THAT WERE PLACED IN OFFICE UNDER THE ILLEGAL U.S. CORP AND DISSOLVE OR RESTRUCTURE THOSE INSTITUTIONS AND ORGANIZATIONS THAT HAVE BEEN HIJACKED OR IMPLEMENTED TO END NATIONAL SOVEREIGNTY

- Remove from office all politicians, judges, and bureaucrats elected or appointed illegally under U.S. CORP and dissolve all unconstitutional laws, provisions, and regulations implemented by them.
- Restructure all national security agencies that have been infiltrated and used against *"We the People,"* i.e., FBI, CIA, DOJ, NASA, etc.
- Dissolve the UN and all of its global governance organizations, i.e., NATO, WB. IMF, WTO, WHO, etc., because they should end national sovereignty, and their UN Agenda 21, Agenda 2030, and Agenda 2050 specify plans to commit global genocide, making them enemies of humanity.
- Dissolve or reorganize all organizations instituted to end U.S. sovereignty, i.e., the Council on Foreign Relations, Trilateral Commission, World Economic Forum, etc., and remove from office any person belonging to these or similar subversive organizations.

STEP 5: REINSTATE THE REPUBLIC AND THE AMERICAN ECONOMIC SYSTEM

Ours was the only system ever devised that, instead of hoarding resources and oppressing people, shared resources and technology. It was the only economic system of which it was said: *"Equalized while elevating the condition of all mankind."*

The American economic system is the economic system God ordained from before the foundation of time to replace the kingdoms of man and to usher in His kingdom on earth and an unparalleled period of peace, prosperity, and spiritual enlightenment!

America is under Abraham's Covenant with God. America is the nation God chose to be blessed and to be a blessing. Many horrible things have been done in the name of America, but the shadow government of the financial elite did them. Once out from under their control, God will use a morally restored America to be an inspiration to the world and to establish an economic system based on God's foreshadowing, the American economic system.

You will note I have mentioned no laws that need to be changed. That is because destroying the shadow government of the global financial elite does not rest with changing individual laws. **The enemy must be destroyed at the root.** We do that by executing the five-step plan laid out above.

Once that is done, it is an easy matter to change individual laws. An enemy's greatest strength is always his greatest weakness as well. In the instance of the global financial elite, that is, his control of the global monetary system. Take away his ability to print fiat currency, and he no longer has the money, power, or influence; he is rendered impotent! The five-step process outlined above does exactly that. Once that is accomplished, all that remains is to grasp a simple truth. Everything has an opposite, a yin and a yang! Whatever the enemy has done to control us, we do the polar opposite, and it will have the opposite effect.

For example, the enemy has controlled us by implementing globalism because it allows them to control the supply chain to create shortages that control prices and disrupt manufacturing, allowing them to bring production to a halt at any time they want. For example, during COVID-19, they created a shortage of semiconductor chips, which affected virtually all electronics and the products that depended on them. It took a year to get a cell phone, a car, and a plethora of other products!

So, in this context, the opposite of globalism, with its ability to control us, is deglobalization, which insulates us from such disruptions. The graphic on the following page enumerates several opposites that either allow the Elite to control us or allow us to take back control from them. So, taking back control is a simple matter of knowing how we are being controlled and doing the opposite.

The same is true of laws: find a law that oppresses us and implement a law that does the opposite, and we have taken control from the enemy. It is that easy!

There are two more components to the process of *Restoring our Republic*! First, we take away the enemy's control of the fiat currency system and replace it with a commodity-based system! This enables the implementation of a new economic system. The first step in that process is to implement the National Economic Security and Restoration Act (NESARA), which began when Kennedy tried to shut down the FED by issuing a silver-backed currency.

The provisions of NESARA are required to move us to a new economic system based on commodity-based assets that prevents the enemy from using his control of money to control us. It also provides for God's transfer of the wealth of the wicked to the righteous, which allows us to take control of all the spheres of influence the enemy has used to control us. See the graphic below for the provisions of NESARA!

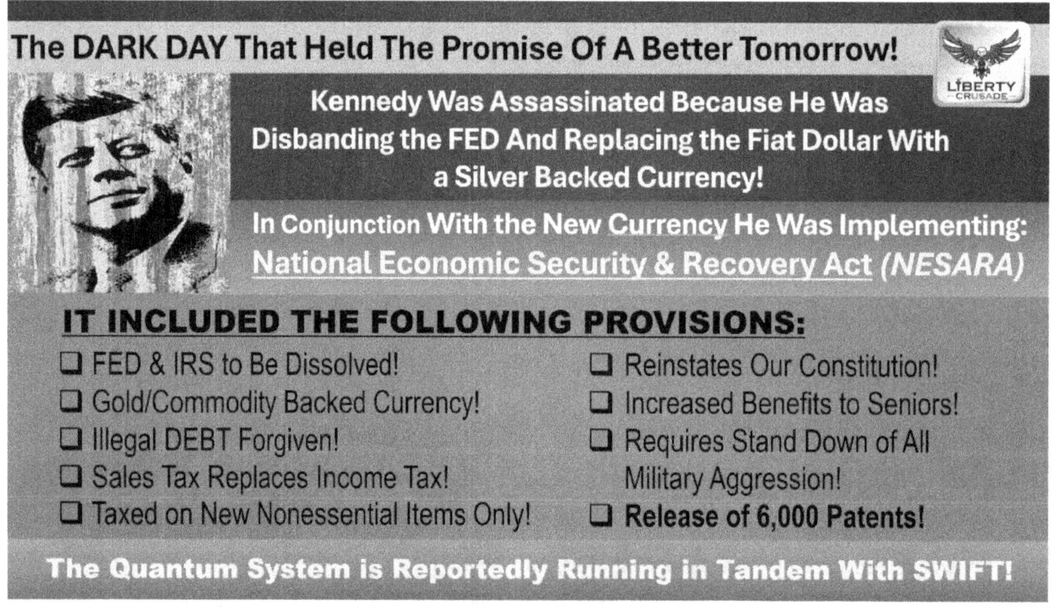

This positions us to reimplement the American economic system that, in 34 years, catapulted America, the youngest nation in the world, into being the richest. It is a tried and proven system that God gave as a foreshadowing of His economic system intended to usher in an unprecedented period of peace, prosperity, and spiritual enlightenment. The American economic system stands in stark contrast to man's flawed governmental system, based on hoarding of natural resources, controlling access to technology, and manipulation of the monetary system. It shares natural resources and technology and is based on a commodity-based economic system that cannot be manipulated as a control mechanism!

As you would expect, it afforded people unprecedented financial freedom. It was said of the American economic system that it was, "The only system ever devised that had the tendency of elevating while equalizing the condition of all mankind!"

It prospered America as the innovator of the technology that birthed the Industrial Revolution, while simultaneously prospering the nations that implemented those innovations. In the simplest of terms, the system that will underpin God's governmental system will see:

- A commodity-based economic system.
- Nations who will share resources and technology.
- Underdeveloped nations who will be assisted in developing their infrastructure, developing technology, and implementing education and medical systems.
- Natural resources stockpiled on every continent.
- Nations participating in joint ventures to develop technologies that affect the world and all its inhabitants.
- NESARA providing a provision for shelved patents to be released to benefit mankind.

In a nutshell, humankind will cease to be divided. It will come to see all men as their brothers, and the division and economic disparity that causes war will be a thing of the past. God will use America to lead the world in a wondrous time where men learn to live together in peace and harmony. The best is yet to come. God is a Waymaker, and He has made a way, and He intends to use America greatly!

In concluding this chapter, I feature a direct copy of the *Second Declaration of Independence*, which is the final piece that is needed for *Restoring the Republic*!

A 2nd Declaration of Independence, by the 50 United States of America,

Signed by President Donald Trump on July 4, 2020.

To the New Republic of the United States

Transcribed by Mark Baughman 2/9/2020 from Parchment Paper from Original.

Trusting our cause is just, and having prayed for the fortitude of brave spiritual wickedness in high places. WE CITIZENS OF AMERICA make this announcement to the SHAREHOLDERS OF US CORP, including THE CITY OF LONDON, THE BRITISH CROWN, AND THE VATICAN, and their OPERATIVES in the media, government and society.

A 2nd DECLARATION OF INDEPENDENCE, By the 50 United States of America

With the utmost respect and admiration for the founders of America and the framers of the original DECLARATION OF INDEPENDENCE, the American people humbly emulate their thoughtful measured response to certain perpetual and ascending tyranny and despotism. We too believe it is moral obligation of those privileged with knowledge and opportunity to work on behalf of THE PEOPLE, that THE PEOPLE are served best when their benefactors choose unity over division, nationalism over globalism, sovereignty over submission, and liberty over oppression, that all human beings are equal in their innate value, that America was founded under God, and that our God-given rights may not be revoked, suspended, negated or abridged without due process. What distinguishes the 2nd DECLARATION OF Independence from its progenitor is the object from which we seek independence.

Regrettably, to our great misfortune, shame, and dismay, and despite the recurrent warnings, and accorded safeguards, a cabal of foreign investors and privateers have managed to gain possession of our land, our wealth, our labor, our well-being, our future, and even our children.

Although history has become muddied with varied interpretations of cardinal events, including the surreptitious adoption of a second "corporate" constitution, and uncertain ratification of several amendments destructive to THE PEOPLE, it matters only that one or more alien groups lay claim to America and its assets. Rather than speculate on motives and weigh unprofitably to biased accounts, unverifiable information, and plenteous theories and opinions, we engage a perfect solution, wherein we exact independence from all claimants, past and present, proclaimed, identified, or veiled. As such, the usurpers named in this declaration are representative, and not specific, or exhaustive, regardless of supposed, ancestry, preceded, instrument or process.

Although simply enumerating transgressions and usurpations would suffice to justify insularity, recounting significant events reveals important facts that are missing from history. These forgotten facts, add insight, perspective, and clarity, illuminating our best way forward.

1.   The inevitable Civil War destroyed America's economy, ripped families apart, and cast a questionable shadow on the future of a once promising nation. America was in trouble financially and needed a massive infusion of capital to get back on its feet.

2.   A cabal of nation-building venture capitals, from Europe, agreed to finance America's recovery, but demanded an active role in government to ensure their investment. In 1871, mired in debt, Congress worked out a partnership. In exchange for boundless financial support, the foreign investors handle America's administrative needs.

3.   Although initially it seemed to be an innocuous concession, the consequences of allowing the nation-building venture capitalists to conduct America's business beyond the protections of the U.S. Constitution proved catastrophic. The investors quickly embedded OPERATIONS throughout the foreign-owned corporate government, and Washington D.C. began serving the interests of America's financiers over THE PEOPLE. In 1871, America effectively lost its independence, and the nation-building venture capitalists became our new masters.

4.   By the early 1900s, the foreign investors who bankrolled America controlled the major newspapers and news services, enabling them to shape what is reported and how it is to be framed. They had to cover their tracks before being exposed and repudiated by THE PEOPLE.

5.   The nation-building venture capitalists worked to soften America's imperturbable elevated system of government. The founders had formed a Constitutional Republic instead of a Democracy specifically to prevent citizens in the majority from oppressing those in the minority. By doing what is best for their District (or State), rather than enforce the majority will, representatives serve all citizens equally, eliminating the noise, division, and violence intrinsic to Democracies. Being in control of the narrative, the foreign investors ingeniously promoted the fallacy that America is a Democracy, trusting that the deception would lead to unrest and chaos that would make the world vulnerable to America, creating additional opportunities for infiltration and manipulation.

6.   In 1913, the foreign investors established the Anti-Defamation League to slander anyone who exposed them and their infiltration into American politics.

7.   In 1913, by the way of the 16th Amendment, the foreign investors were granted the authority to tax the American people directly, something expressly prohibited by the

original Constitution. That THE PEOPLE would willingly subject themselves to forced confiscation of their property (their labor) is illogical, putting the legitimacy of ratification in question.

8. In 1913, by way of the 17th Amendment, the foreign investors breached an important safeguard that protected our Constitution Republic from infiltration of enemy forces. Previously, Senators were "Statesmen" appointed by the respective State Legislatures, as a check on the House of Representatives, raiding the public treasury, Henceforth. Senators would run as glorified House Representatives, reduced to promising "free" public money and services for votes. The authenticity of ratification is unlikely because the State Legislatures would not willingly surrender their authority to bridle the appetite of THE PEOPLE's House, nor would they accede to transfer more power to the Federal Government, opening yet another door for the international bankers to buy the influence they need to further their grip on America.

9. In 1913, the foreign investors gained control of our currency by pushing through Congress the Federal Reserve Act, establishing a foreign-owned central banking system despite the dire warnings of presidents Thomas Jefferson, Andrew Jackson, Abraham Lincoln, Andrew Johnson, James Garfield, and William McKinley. The Federal Reserve Act passed with the help of compromised legislators between 1:30 AM to 4:30 AM on December 22nd, when most members were away on the Christmas holiday.

10. In 1920, Congress, by the way of the independent Treasury Act, turned over the U.S. Treasury Department, and its assets (our gold and silver), to the Federal Reserve, the central banking system owned by the foreign investors, established 1913.

11. In 1921, the Council on Foreign Relations was formed under cover advancing America's interests in the world. In fact, the CFR is sponsored by THE CITY OF LONDON, and serves to advance the interests of the foreign-owned Federal Reserve, by direction the president, Congress, and the narrative through OPERATIVES in their news and information networks.

12. In 1925, the owners of the Federal Reserve formed the UNITED STATES corporation. Just 5 out of the 100 shares issued were identified, with the balance of the shareholders of US CORP remaining anonymous, yet the money trail leads to THE CITY OF LONDON, THE BRITISH CROWN, and THE VATICAN. The tax dollars we send to the Internal Revenue Service go to the International Monetary Fund and the World Bank, which are under their control.

13. The official formation of US CORP set the stage for the transformation of America from a Constitutional Republic of THE PEOPLE to a corporation owned by foreign interests and their families. Over the next few years, the individual States were registered as corporations as well, making them franchises of US CORP. Representatives and Senators neither represent nor work for the American People. Rather, they are managers of US CORP. and, as such, they are obligated first to serve its best interests. The president is just the President of America. He is the CEO of US CORP.

14. The abbreviated term "United States" was purposely used to represent both America and US CORP. to blur the distinction between them. Similarly, the original U.S. Constitution was quietly supplanted by an impostor "corporate (all-capital letters) constitution" that bears a similar name and appearance, again, to confuse and deceive the American people. Specifically, the "Constitution for the United States of America" was replaced by "THE CONSTITUTION OF THE UNITED STATES," with the latter's corporate statutes becoming the supreme law of America.

15. In 1933, the U.S. federal government declared bankruptcy, and President Roosevelt, its acting CEO, signed over to US CORP. America and its assets, including THE PEOPLE, and our labor. The bankruptcy of 1933, which was arguably unnecessary, ceremonial in nature, and contrived and orchestrated without the consent of THE PEOPLE, completed the heist and transfer of America and its assets to the same foreign interests that own US CORP.

16. In the bankruptcy of 1933, US CORP forced the American people to surrender their gold in trade for debt notes called "dollars." Fiat currency that has no real value, and that is continually depreciated through inflation to where it is worth just 4 cents today.

17. The bankruptcy of 1933 put US CORP in a state of emergency, allowing it to implement Admiralty Law, made evident by the gold fringe around the American Flag. When in a US CORP courtroom, you are considered at sea and not a citizen of America.

18. In 1936, US CORP began issuing Social Security Numbers to turn otherwise sovereign Americans into trustees of corporate fictions, making our labor taxable, which would otherwise be unconstitutional. According to US CORP. you are not a love man or woman, but rather a representation of a corporation in your name.

19. In 1945, the anonymous owners US CORP founded the United Nations, under the guise of spreading peace, civility, and humanitarian assistance throughout the world, yet the true purpose is to condition citizens to recognize an international authority, a first step in

establishing their promised "New World Order," in which the U.S. Constitution is retired to make room for a universal totalitarian government.

20. United Nations' publications "Agenda 21" and "Agenda 30" reveal the "New World Order" agenda, calling for the end of nationalism, patriotism, private property, individual rights, the two-parent family, automobiles, air travel, and the right to defend ourselves from a tyrannical government. In keeping with their goal of "sustainable development," they plan to reduce the population by over 90%, ridding America and the world of dissidents and "useless eaters." The remaining "useful servants" are to live in coastal communities, wherein they will be stacked-and-packed in micro-apartments.

21. The only thing standing in the way of their "New World Order" is a strong, prosperous, and secure America. To achieve their goal of world domination. America must lose its sovereignty and leadership position, which is why the owners of US CORP quietly work to undermine our culture, systems, beliefs, standards, aspirations, and morals for over 100 years, employing unrestrained methods and tactics.

22. With millions of dollars at their disposal every year from taxing our labor, the owners of US CORP. fund leftist non-profit groups, including the COUNCIL ON FOREIGN RELATIONS, that work to subvert our nation and silence anyone in opposition. They ingratiate the officials and administrators who run the largest charities and organizations, including the A.M.A., the APA, the CDC, the FCC, the SEC, and the FDA, and they embed OPERATIVES in the State Department, the Department of Justice, and the intelligence agencies, official and covert, including the NSA, FBI, and CIA.

23. In trade for generous grants and endowments, the anonymous owners of US CORP shape the curriculum and political sentiment of the public schools, colleges, and universities, ensuring the next generations, our children, harbor disdain for their country, their history, their culture, their families, and even their ethnicity.

24. The anonymous owners of US CORP keep THE PEOPLE in the dark about the true history of America, the greatest heist and cover-up in history, by controlling public education, the major publishers, the news services, the airwaves, and the social and information networks.

25. The foreign owners of US CORP prop up "puppets" throughout society and government, allowing them to make millions of dollars in trade for perpetrating their agenda of secrecy and subjugation of America. These traitors include prominent politicians, news readers, pundits, authors, movie stars, and the heads of the social, news,

and information networks, major sports teams, music, and entertainment industries, and corporate conglomerates responsible for over 90% of the products designed, manufactured, advertised, purchased, financed, and consumed.

26. By the way of funding campaigns and fixing elections, the owners of US CORP obligate the most influential politicians to further their agenda of breaking America socially and financially. They promote disdain for country, dependency on government, indulgence, lawlessness, and immorality, to spoil and dishearten citizens, predisposing them to trade their sovereignty for the false promises of an international unelected government, sponsored by the world elite.

27. By the way of the Democrat Party, and OPERATIVES posing as television hosts, entertainers, journalists, pundits and policy experts, the owners of US CORP brainwash and condition THE PEOPLE to accept invalid arguments and pseudoscience, that call for globalism, socialism, and a godless society, in which technology is our moral compass.

28. The OPERATIVES of the foreign-owned US CORP are deeply rooted throughout the news and information networks, academia, government, and society. Colloquially referred to as "the Deep State," "the Shadow Government," and "the Swamp," the OPERATIVES perform with a hive mind because they are guilty of treason, a crime punishable by death. They are desperate to hide their complicity, and thus they systematically target, demonize, and even "s*****e" all who threaten to expose their treachery and malfeasance.

29. The OPERATIVES of US CORP favor unbridled immigration because it is the most expedient way to destroy the country from within. Flooding America with illegal immigrants, without allowing them time to assimilate, ensures arrogance, separation, and anti-Americanism, and anger, animosity, and conflict with THE PEOPLE. By design, we can also expect a steady dilution of the principles, ethics, and systems that made America successful. Moreover, the majority of illegal immigrants are against the ethics and systems that made America successful. Moreover, the majority of illegal immigrants are likely to vote for Democrats, who legislate according to the will of the foreign owners of US CORP.

30. Because the free, open, largely unchained internet reveals the hidden heist of America, and the criminal network that operates in the shadows, the owners of US CORP, the predators of crimes against America and Humanity, are tightly concerned about exposure. To ensure THE PEOPLE do not wake up, organize, and enact justice, they censor the information we see, ply us with psychoactive drugs, make us complacent with money

from government, distract us with sempiternal video games, and promote us with meaningless sporting events after another.

31. In conjunction with skewed statistics, deceptive polls, false facts, and the omission of decisive information, the owners of US CORP promote anti-Americanism and their "New World Order" agenda. Fake news keeps THE PEOPLE disoriented, misinformed, and divided over ethnicity, gender, sexual orientation, religion, and economic class. Meanwhile, their debt system enslaves us; their grip ever tightens through surveillance, and fluorination, vaccinations, and other technologies are deployed to weaken any substantive opposition.

32. The owners of US CORP are working incessantly to disarm the millions of law-abiding Patriots who stand in the way of their totalitarianism, oppressive "New World Order." By the way of orchestrated mass shootings, the owners of US CORP will continue to terrorize THE PEOPLE until we assent to "comprehensive background checks." The word "comprehensive" is nebulous and undefined, allowing for a battery of psychological and medical testing, ever-expanding, until individuals are largely deemed emotionally unstable and a danger to society. True to the predictions of every futuristic book and movie, patriotic Americans will be disarmed by the way of political profiling, under the guise of screening for mental health.

33. Through their vast indoctrination machine, the foreign owners of US CORP have convinced THE PEOPLE that America is a Democracy, and that Democracy is the highest form of government. This is problematic because Democracy is by definition, "mob rule." Democracies invariably fail because "the majority mob" always demands more and more public monies and services, procured through excessive taxation and other Socialist-like policies, resulting in economic ruin, runaway debt, fiscal collapse, and ultimately, social implosion, opening the door for the promised, predicted, dreadful, and ever-looming "New World Order." Because sovereignty is not sustainable without exploring the ills of Democracy, and reestablishing our elevated Constitutional Republic, we are compelled to make the following proclamations:

a)   The word Democracy does not appear anywhere in America's founding documents because the framers knew that Democracy, in any form or disguise, is fatally flawed, leading invariably to oppression, unrest, societal failure, violence, and death.

b)   All modern forms of government are elected democratically. They are differentiated only by who makes their decisions, after the elections are over.

c)   In a Democracy, citizens in the majority make the rules, leaving those in the minority oppressed. Consequently, a Democracy is always noisy, divisive, insufficient, unsteady, combustible, fiscally irresponsible, and short-lived.

d)   America was established as a Constitutional Republic; those elected must NOT do the bidding of the citizen majority. Rather, they must do what is best for their District (or State), despite the majority will. In this way, all citizens are represented equally, and no one is suppressed, making a Constitutional Republic quiet, steady, efficient, and preferred.

e)   Although the word "democracy" feels good, it is founded on mob rule, making it akin to socialism, communism, and every other tyrannical form of government.

f)   Finally, Article QV. Section 4 of the U.S. Constitution resolves any doubt: "The United States shall guarantee to every State in this Union a Republican Form of Government".

Having exposed the greatest heist and cover-up in history, we are able to summarize. America and its assets were quietly hijacked, and the cover-up has resulted in unthinkable crimes against THE PEOPLE and humanity. Allowing the hostile takeover to stand will lead eventually to compete and irreversible subjugation and the eradication of truth, justice, and all that is good.

This 2nd DECLARATION OF INDEPENDENCE distinguishes the United States of America from the subversive UNITED STATES CORPORATION. It asserts that the **US CORP was formed illegally**, that it is foreign-owned, and that its shareholders have been quietly at war with America for over 150 years. Treasonous OPERATIVES, embedded within government and the "fake news" networks, purposely divide the citizenry, and facilitate conflict among the nations, to hide that US CORP was formed illegally, that is foreign-owned, and that its shareholders have been quietly at war with America for over 150 years. Treasonous OPERATIVES, embedded within government and the "fake news" networks, purposely divide the citizenry and facilitate conflict among the natives to hide that US CORP is and always has been the only real enemy of America. This 2nd DECLARATION OF INDEPENDENCE also repudiates, with conviction, US CORP's satanically inspired plan for world governance. In addition to being, of, by, and for THE ELITE, and not THE PEOPLE, their falsely advertised pseudo-Utopian unelected totalitarian "New World Order" would supplant America's sovereignty, and extinguish forever any semblance of liberty and prosperity.

Because natural inclinations predispose human beings to be shortsighted, malleable, and easily bamboozled, one might presume the American people should bear responsibility for being swindled out of their homeland, inherited from their forefathers who procured and secured it at great expense and much sacrifice, and for slowly but steadily trading their largely unappreciated blessings of liberty, opportunity, and prosperity for "trinkets" in the form of unearned comforts, frivolous indulgences, and gluttonous pleasures.

However, the transfer of ownership form the American people was not conducted openly and with candor, but clandestinely, through calculated design, and nefarious means, without body consent, and unconstitutionally. It is for the latter reason that American people claim their right to rectification. That the greatest heist in history was effected outside the constraints of the U.S. Constitution, and that those who were elected to represent America's best interests transgressed their fiduciary responsibility, and exceeded their authority, warrants this proclamation, that the American people are rightful owners of our land, our labor, our well-being, or future, and our children, for our benefit, and the benefit of our posterity.

As with any negotiated peace after years of atrocities committed by parties at war, we seek neither vengeance nor demand justice for past transgressions. The simply adjure the return of what rightly belongs to THE PEOPLE, and avow firmly, emphatically, publicly, and officially, that America shall forever remain a sovereign nation, free, selfdirected, and not affiliated or dependent upon any version, or variation, of the present, planned, or innovated "New World Order".

We entreat a bloodless solution, wherein you cease all destruction activities, including false flag events, dissolve US CORP and other illicit legal structures and custodial instruments, return our land, and assets, including our gold and silver, redirect the tax collected on our labor back to America, and have your "Deep State" and "Shadow Government" OPERATIVES retire, withdrawing your influence in a orderly fashion, so society continues to thrive, in trade for you keeping your wealth, your position, and your heads.

In response to questions regarding legitimacy, efficacy, and process; throwing off the shackles of national thralldom is elementary and unambiguous, as evidenced by the separation of the 13 Colonies from Britain in 1776, and the Mexican people from Spain in

1825. A formal declaration, hailed by authorized representations, procures independence that is immediate, whole, consummate, infrangible, and unencumbered by obligation, condition, or imposition.

As we enter grievous territory, we reflect on the precarious road our forefathers forged when they judiciously severed the political and familial ties that bound them. Or hearts also are filled with melancholy and trepidation, yet we too are resolute in our posture and positions from being confronted with no better option. Despite the manifest peril, the consequences of acquiescence are graver still, compelling us to claim solemnly our independence once again. So, in support of this Declaration, with its firm reliance on the protection of divine providence, we mutually pledge to each other our Lives, our Fortunes, and our sacred Honor.

(The 56 signatories of THE TASK FORCE are to be affixed at the time of presentation to Congress, the President, the 50 State Legislatures, and the Governors of the respective States.)

More about this document can be found at:
https://operationdisclosure.blogspot.com/2021/02/the-2nd-declaration-of-independence.html

CHAPTER 16

A CALL TO ACTION:

You Can Make a Difference

TOPICS COVERED IN THIS CHAPTER:

- DEATH OF THE AMERICAN DREAM CRIPPLING DEBT
- ONE WORLD GOVERNMENT WARS FOR PROFIT
- ELECTION TAMPERING
- BORDER CRISIS
- POLITICAL CORRUPTION
- DOMESTIC TERRORISM
- ECOLOGICAL CRISIS
- HEALTHCARE CRISIS
- MIND CONTROL
- GLOBAL GENOCIDE

PUTTING IT ALL TOGETHER

NOW THAT YOU KNOW the truth about what has been done to enslave humanity, the questions are: What can you do? What will you do? That is the topic of this chapter.

HOW DO WE FREE SOCIETY AND RESTORE PERSONAL FREEDOMS?

Restoring the Republic and getting back our freedom is not nearly as difficult as we have been led to believe. If we get back control of the monetary system, everything will begin to fall in place. Why do I say that? Because it is a simple truth. He who controls money controls the world.

As discussed, our global slave masters have created so much debt that we are facing a global financial collapse and monetary reset. Not to worry: Trump and an army of "White Hats" are executing a plan to strip power from these globalists. De-globalizing Trade is doing this, so no one nation (China) or group of nations can control trade. Trade is the genesis of the money that is used to buy power and influence at every stratum of society. Simultaneously, efforts are underway to de-dollarize global trade by removing the U.S. dollar as the world's sole reserve currency.

The dollar is to be replaced by a basket of currencies so no one nation (The U.S.) or any group of nations can control the monetary system. The plan is to create a new monetary system backed by Gold and other commodities that, unlike fiat central bank currency, cannot be manipulated. Though the U.S. will not emerge from this reset as the world's sole reserve currency, it will emerge as the dominant reserve currency. This financial restructuring eliminates:

- Inflation
- Deflation
- Wage Suppression
- Orchestrated Boom-Bust Cycles
- Orchestrated Stock Market and Real Estate Crashes
- Orchestrated Credit Crises

GETTING RID OF THE FED WILL RESTORE SOVEREIGNTY

Implementing a commodity-based financial system will signal the demise of the Fed's fiat central banking system. Our currency will be put back under the Treasury, where it belongs. It will be backed by gold and other commodities that cannot be manipulated. This lays the framework for the restoration of our republic and prevents the Globalists from being able to buy power in all the spheres of influence. The graphic below depicts what I have repeatedly called "the corporatocracy," which is the merger of banks and corporations. It depicts how these bankers' gangsters literally got control of all the nations of the world.

Abraham Lincoln had this to say about this unholy union.

> I see in the near future a crisis approaching that unnerves me and causes me to tremble for the safety of my country. Corporations have been enthroned and an era of corruption in high places will follow, and the money power of the country will endeavor to prolong its reign by working upon the prejudices of the people until all wealth is aggregated in a few hands and the Republic is destroyed.
>
> President Abraham Lincoln, November 21, 1864 (letter to Col. William F. Elkins)

Lincoln's fears were realized when this unholy union got control of our political system to write laws that serve their interest as opposed to serving the interest of *We the People.* At that point, they made up what is known as the "global shadow government." They could create false flag events to create wars intended to drive the nations of the world into wars for profit, intended to bankrupt them. With control of the banks, corporations, and politicians, it was easy to get control of the remaining spheres of influence: education, media, entertainment, and religion, which are used to brainwash the masses.

In a nutshell, here is how they have brainwashed the masses of humanity without most of us even realizing it. By controlling all these communication channels, they create a narrative and repeat it over and over. In the absence of any narrative to the contrary, even the deepest, darkest lie becomes an irrefutable truth.

> The size of the lie is a definite factor in causing it to be believed, for the vast masses of a nation are in the depths of their hearts more easily deceived than they are consciously and intentionally bad. The primitive simplicity of their minds renders them a more easy prey to a big lie than a small one, for they themselves often tell little lies, but would be ashamed to tell big lies.
>
> –Adolf Hitler: Mein Kampf, 1925

The previous graphic gives a pictorial representation of the spheres of influence, which make up the power structure of a global shadow government. As formidable as it is, it can be rendered powerless by taking away its control of the monetary system, which is currently being dismantled by transitioning from the current fiat system to the commodity system discussed in the opening paragraph of this chapter. It is not as difficult as they would have us believe.

Like I already mentioned, the shadow government of the financial elite is not invincible. As Sun Tzu says, you take down a powerful adversary by taking advantage of their mistakes. So, what mistakes have our enemies made that make up their Achilles' heel? Simply put, they have used the same strategies for decades, which has allowed us to figure out their playbook.

This knowledge will lead to their demise. David is about to take down Goliath. The following two graphics provide further insight into the tactics and methods our enemies use for subjugating us.

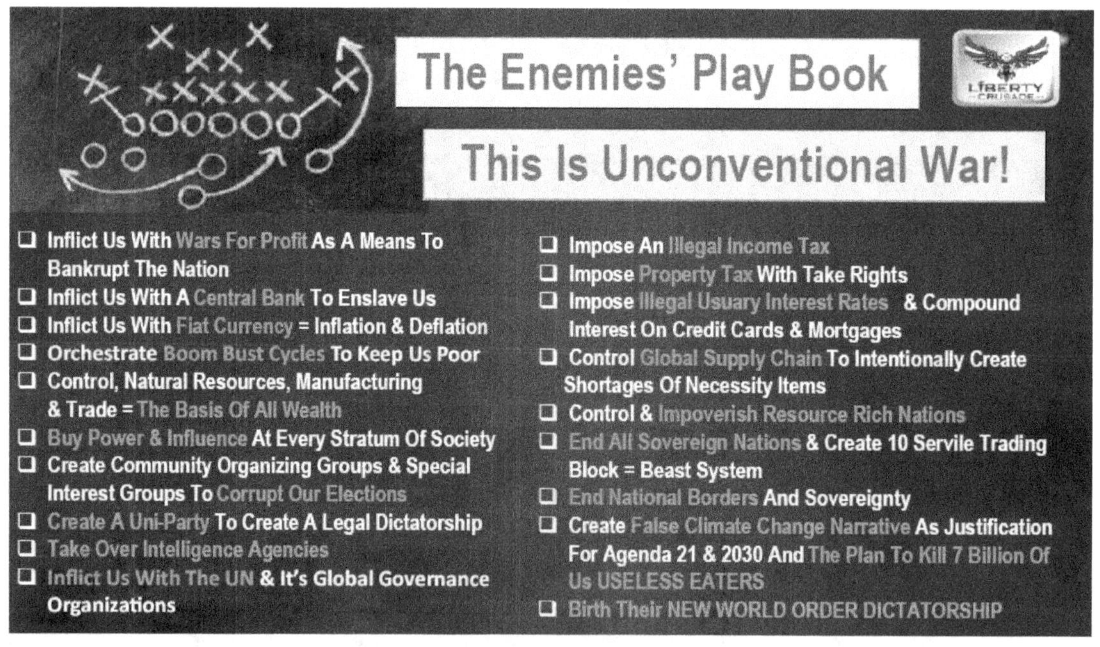

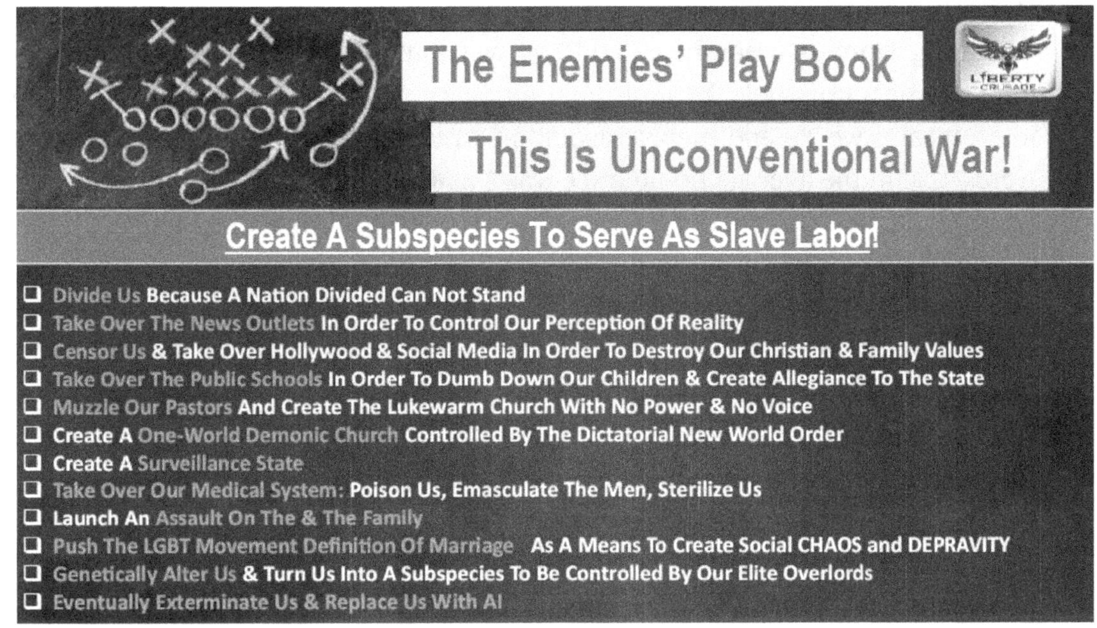

Now that we have a high-level understanding of how our enemy controls us, let's take a thorough analysis and explore the subtleties of what I call "unconventional warfare."

THE WORLD IS IN CRISIS

-What has been done to you?

-What can you do about it?

-What will you do?

-How will you vote?

A RECAP OF THE WAYS THE GLOBALISTS CONTROL US!

Within these pages, I've illustrated the global elite's transparent, yet disguised, plans to manipulate us. Here's an overview of the many control mechanisms they use, ultimately resulting in a crisis.

DEATH OF THE AMERICAN DREAM

- **Declining Home Ownership:** COVID-19 was intended to create a situation where home ownership would become unattainable except for the wealthiest. In 2019, interest rates we 3% and the average home price was $200K. By 2025, interest rates were 7%, and the average home price was $400K. Magically, the American dream of home ownership was out of reach for most, especially 1st time home buyers. Finally, tens of thousands of starter homes were built as rental-only properties.
- **Political Corruption:** Ask yourself this question: Short of bribery, insider trading, and other illegal activities, how is it possible that so many politicians come to Washington broke and in no time, they are multimillionaires?
- **Unequal Justice:** Political privilege and protection of political operatives show that the judicial system has been politicized and corrupted.
- **Crippling Progressive Tax Structure:** This is a plank of communism. The strategy calls for massive unfunded entitlements and wars to drive prices and taxes higher and higher till the masses are hopelessly in debt and dependent on a corrupt government.
- **Debt Trap:** By design, every fiat dollar printed carries a debt obligation (In the form of a Treasury Note) to the Central Bank, enriching them while driving the masses into crippling, unmanageable debt. The FED must be dismantled, and Trump is committed to doing just that.
- **Orchestrated Boom-Bust Cycles:** These are intentionally caused by lowering interest rates to attract investors. Investors are then driven to what looks like a great investment (Usually in stocks or real estate). Prices are driven up, and at the appointed time, the bubble is popped, followed by credit being dried up. Magically, the trap is set. The criminals get rich, and the public loses its hard-earned money!
- **Wage Suppression:** As productively increase due to automation, wages are supposed to go up, but that doesn't happen because the intent is to keep the masses perpetually struggling to survive.
- **Inflation:** Occurs because every dollar printed carries a debt obligation, which drives up the national debt. Additionally, our slave masters keep the printing presses operating 24/7/365, which adds to inflation.
- **Declining Job Security:** Automation may seem like a good thing, but not when greedy, corrupt corporations see their workers as useless eaters who are expendable.

- **Clean Water Crisis:** Simply put, our lakes, rivers, and aquifers are using water faster than it can be replenished. Little is done by way of conservation efforts. At the same time, sustainable water from the atmosphere technology is suppressed. Never mind! There may not be enough water for a population of eight billion, but there is plenty for a population of 500 million.
- **Exorbitant Energy Costs:** Ultra-low-cost, virtually non-polluting energy technology is available, but it is being kept from us to protect the profit margins of the energy cartel. Be encouraged. Thanks to Trump and the overturning of the Chevron Supreme Court Decision, nearly 6,000 suppressed patents will be released, and they will spur the greatest technological revolution the world has ever seen. Trump is positioning the U.S. to lead this Technological revolution.
- **Rising Food Prices:** It is simple. Take farmland out of production, withhold water, and build corporate farm factories, and you get higher food prices.
- **Cost of Healthcare:** The U.S. has the highest healthcare prices in the world because we underwrite the cost of many countries just the same way we carry most of the cost of being the world's police force, and struggling under the burden of unfair trade agreements. But thanks to Trump, all that is changing. It is America First in action.
- **Crumbling Infrastructure:** While China and many other nations build gleaming cities and incredible infrastructure projects, American cities are allowed to crumble.
- **Blighted Cities:** Thanks to Trump's America First Agenda, as new factories are being built ($18 billion committed to rebuild America), homes and communities will grow up around them, creating an American comeback.
- **Assault on the Nuclear Family:** Since Obama and his same sex marriage agenda, there has been a war on the family, but thanks to Trump, the LGBTQ movement is in retreat.
- **Neighborhood Safety:** You allow millions of illegal immigrants into the country, breeding homelessness, gangs, and drugs, and it should be no surprise that crime is up. It is all by design. But Trump is deploying military, and the tide is turning.
- **Rising Crime Rates:** Arrest criminals and then release them without bail, and how could you not expect crime to go up?
- **Defund the Police Movement:** This is nothing but domestic terrorism. What can you expect when you turn the cities over to the criminals?

- **Attacks on Patriotism:** Our left-leaning public school system and colleges teach socialism, and illegals burn our flag, and we are expected to stand by and do nothing. Patriotism is under attack by those who want to collapse America from within.
- **9/11 and the Patriot Act:** As previously discussed, the Patriot Act was modeled after the Enabling Act, which was responsible for the rise of Hitler. The Patriot Act created a U.S. surveillance state and laid the foundation for a legal dictatorship.
- **Broken Education System:** By design, Americans spend more per student on education than any nation in the world. Yet we rank 40th. Our schools have been dumbed down because our slave masters see an educated person as a threat.
- **Declining International Education Rankings:** You ask how America's schools can be so bad and yet America is an economic superpower. It is simple. The plan is to dumb down our students and then bring in lower-paid workers from foreign countries.
- **American History Not Taught in Schools:** Of course not. The intent is to paint America as a monster while extolling the virtues of socialism.
- **Religious Freedom – Prayer in Schools:** Christian exceptionalism is a threat, so prayer must be kept out of the school. At the same time, the Vatican is pushing to create a demonic one-world church to go with their one-world government.
- **Parental Rights:** The intent is that the schools are indoctrination centers, and the powers to be don't want the parents getting in the way.
- **Forced LGBTQ Story Times:** The intent is to destroy the nuclear family because it is the foundation of society.
- **Same Sex Bathrooms:** Push the LGBTQ movement as a means of division and civil decay.
- **Boys Participating in Girls' Sports:** Another effort to divide us.

CRIPPLING PERSONAL DEBT

- **Illegal Federal Income Tax:** In 1913, the income tax was one percent on incomes above $3,000, with a top tax rate of six percent on those earning more than $500,000 per year. Now the progressive income tax rate has ballooned from a low of 10% to 37%. Can you say "debt slavery"?

- **Usury Credit Card Debt:** We originally had Usury laws to cap interest rates, but the credit card companies (loan sharks) got around the laws. Currently, they charge (revolving rates on the unpaid balances) as high as 36%.
- **Price Gouging:** The global corporatocracy, in conjunction with a global logistics supply chain, regularly controls availability, which in turn allows them to control prices. A decentralized supply chain would markedly lower prices.
- **Illegal Property Tax:** Our founding fathers came to America to own land and homes, which was not permitted under European Feudalism. Originally, there was no such thing as take rights, so when real estate was paid off, it granted ownership for perpetuity. Sadly, today under Fee Simple Real Estate Law, the government has *take rights*, meaning no person in America actually owns a home. They are relegated to being renters, and their landlord is the federal government and the banker gangsters.
- **Inflation/Deflation:** With a worthless fiat dollar, inflation and deflation can be controlled the way you would work a math formula.
- **Mortgage Refinancing:** The average American moves seven times in their life, and given that each time they move or refinance, their amortization table starts over at month one, most Americans retire still having a mortgage over their head. This is by design, and it is nothing short of criminal.
- **Wage Suppression:** As automation drives up productivity, wages are supposed to go up as well, but no. The debt slavery system requires that wages never keep up with rising prices; otherwise, it wouldn't be a debt trap.
- **Retirees' Debt Crisis:** The debt trap means that we never get out of debt. The plan is that you retire still having a mortgage. Add in rising property taxes, and you retire with higher housing costs in retirement than when you bought the home, so much for the dream of home ownership.

ONE-WORLD GOVERNMENT

The globalists want to end all sovereign governments and implement a one-world dictatorship. They see the U.S. as being the only country that could stop them, so the U.S. is enemy number one.

HEALTHCARE CRISIS

- **Poison in our Food and Water:** We have known or at least suspected it for decades, but now RFK is confirming it. Our slave masters want us sink and be hooked on their poison drugs. They want us docile and passive, and spending our hard-earned money on drugs designed to hide symptoms without curing the underlying cause of our illness.
- **Drug Costs:** Some drugs have markups of as much as 4,000%. By design, America has the highest drug costs in the world. However, Trump struck a deal with Pfizer to significantly reduce drug expenses.
- **Suppression of Natural Cures:** Going all the way back to the Rockefellers, they systematically drove all homeopathic practitioners out of business so they had a monopoly. Add in the AMA and insurance companies, and their grip on healthcare is near total. At least it was. Post Covid people are waking up and seeking alternative healthcare solutions based on light therapy, frequency, herbals, etc.

ELECTION TAMPERING

- **Counting Illegal Immigrants on the Census:** This allows Illegal immigrants to be packed into Democrat states, giving them more federal funding and more House seats. By denying this simple question to be asked on the census (*Are you a U.S. citizen?*), election fraud was carried out unbeknownst to most.
- U.S. citizens. Elections can be stolen in many ways, and the most effective ways occur long before election day.
- **Lobbyist:** Former politicians who use their political connections to secure under-the-table deals that benefit their benefactors to the detriment of We the People.
- **Voter Id:** We have to have a driver's license, a hunting license, a business license, a building permit, etc. It begs the question: Why not a voter ID? I will tell you. Not having a voter ID makes voter fraud much easier.
- **Paper Ballots:** These aren't used because they significantly hinder voter fraud.
- **Drop Boxes:** These facilitate voter fraud. Are you getting the drift?
- **Mail-In Ballots:** The story just keeps repeating itself. It makes cheating easier.
- **Same Day Election Results:** Prevents ballots from being recounted multiple times and doesn't allow enough time to cheat big enough to steal an election.

- **Gerrymandering:** Redrawing congressional districts in such a way as to pack them with voters of the preferred party.
- **Term Limits/Carrier Politicians:** Having term limits allows the amassing of power and wealth in a way that couldn't happen if there were no term limits. We need a constitutional amendment to impose term limits. Without them, the Swamp will never be completely drained.

CRISIS AT THE BORDER

- **Chain Immigration:** Constitutes a non-kinetic attack on America, which allows a literal army of immigrants into the country without regard for whether they speak English or can support themselves. The only requirement is sponsorship by a relative currently in the country. So, one immigrant gets into the U.S. (illegally) and then their entire family gets carte blanche and potentially becomes a financial burden, and or takes a job from a U.S. citizen because they will work for less.
- **Merit-Based Immigration:** This is the system used by virtually every other country. The person has to show that they can support themselves and have a skill that is sought after.
- **Catch and Release:** This absurd policy of the Democrats releases millions of Illegal immigrants into the U.S. pending a hearing to occur months or years later. As you might guess, many, if not most, of these illegal immigrants disappear into the interior and never show up for their hearing. This policy clearly shows government complicity.
- **Role of NGOs, the UN, and the Federal Government in Illegal Immigration:** The illegal caravans were not organic. They were orchestrated and funded by the UN, an assortment of NGOs, and multiple governments, including elements within the U.S. government. Their actions constitute an act of covert war and, in some cases, may constitute treason.
- **Birth Tourism and Birthright Citizenship:** Travel agencies advertise for pregnant women in foreign countries to book a vacation to America, where they conveniently have their baby. This process makes the baby a U.S. citizen. As the baby's guardian, the mother is allowed to stay in the U.S. Even more egregious, under the terms of chain immigration, this opens the door for the mother's entire family to legally come to the U.S. This is, to say the least, unethical and should be illegal. But our politicians have sold out the nation they pledged to serve and protect.

- **Entitlements for Illegals:** So, while we have veterans and other U.S. citizens sleeping on the streets, we house Illegal immigrant that are given a variety of entitlements. The intent is to drive the U.S. into bankruptcy, and it is working. Democrats initiated a government shutdown in Fall 2025, demanding billions for undocumented immigrants' healthcare. This must stop.
- **Work Visas for High-Tech Jobs:** If we wanted, we could train Americans for any job. But the corporations would rather give work visas to foreigners because they will work for less. Secondarily, they want us to be ignorant because an educated American citizenry is dangerous. We might just want to stand up and take back our country.
- **Healthcare for Illegals:** Ever wonder why your healthcare insurance is so expensive? It is because when an illegal immigrant needs medical care, they go to the high-priced emergency room, and the U.S. citizens get the privilege of paying the bill. Somebody has to pay. Why not you?
- **Right to Vote in Local Elections:** Beyond the pale! You come to the U.S. illegally, and our politicians are willing to allow you to vote, a privilege that is supposed to be reserved for citizens. Can you guess what they vote for?
- **Sanctuary Cities:** Unbelievable! You came to America illegally. Even if you are a criminal, U.S. politicians in Democrat sanctuary cities will harbor you and give you financial aid. I say again: the plan is to breed crime and to drive America into bankruptcy!

POLITICAL CORRUPTION

- **Stolen Elections:** As discussed, we have not had an honest election since McKinley in 1843. The three wealthiest men in America colluded to get McKinley elected. At that point, the globalist understood that they could select men, groom them, finance them, and place them in any political or public sector position they wished and thereby control the world from the shadows just the way Obama has done in recent years.
- **Lobbyists and Special Interest Groups:** All that need be said is that money buys power and influence.
- **ActBlue and Money Laundering:** A multi-trillion-dollar Democrat money laundering scheme was recently uncovered. Money was used for campaign funds and other illicit projects.

- **Russia Gate:** Whistleblowers will shortly be coming out proving the 2016 presidential election was stolen. Hillary and Obama will be exposed for their part in the crime and may well be charged with treason. Unlawfully elected politicians and judges will be removed, prompting a special election and hopefully the restoration of the republic. The swamp will be drained!
- **Arab Spring and Benghazi:** Whistleblowers will expose that the Arab Spring was intended to destabilize the Middle East and North Africa, and among other things, unleash an army of Muslim refugees into Europe to destabilize it and usher in Sharia Law. This is not unlike the army of illegal immigrants unleashed on the U.S. to destabilize it as well. Hopefully, Hillary's role in the (preventable) Benghazi massacre will be exposed as well.
- **Democracy vs. Republic:** Our founders called Democracy "Mobocracy," likening it to socialism and communism. By contrast, a republic is the only governmental system ever devised to be a government of the people, by the people, for the people. Likewise, it is the only governmental system to protect property rights. America was the world's first republic, and that is what made America so great.
- **Seeding of Manufacturing from the U.S. to China:** When Carter opened trade with China, America was over 200 years old and had a scant $660 billion national debt. Next came the intentionally losing NAFTA trade deal, and America began its climb to its current national debt of over $38 trillion. It was planned that way as a means to collapse America under a mountain of debt. Add in the Iraq war, the '08-housing crisis, and COVID-19, and America teeters on the brink of bankruptcy. All planned.
- **Intentionally Losing Trade Agreements:** Trump's Tariffs are an effort to restore fair trade agreements that were gutted by the intentionally losing NAFTA agreement.
- **Suppression of Patriotism, Christian and Family Values:** The greatness of America was built on the fact that it was united. Knowing this, the globalists have endeavored to undermine patriotism, family, and Christian values, believing that it would cause America to collapse from within.
- **The Patriot Act:** As previously discussed, the intent of the Patriot Act was to create a legal dictatorship and establish a surveillance state.
- **Insider Trading by politicians:** No mystery here. This is one of the chief ways politicians become multi-millionaires!

- **Community Organizing Groups:** They are the boots on the ground that organize protests, riots, and other nefarious activities. For example, Obama wanted same sex marriage, so gay rights organizations organized protests. The fake news outlets covered the protests, and on cue, Obama stepped in and said it is the will of the people, and overnight, it was the law of the land. Then all the sudden we had drag queens reading to our kids and same sex bathrooms in our schools and men in women's sports.
- **Homegrown Terrorist Groups:** This is accomplished through various means: online, in our socialist universities, and MK Ultra programs, etc. Young kids are radicalized. They are often used to commit things like bombings or mass shootings to stir up support for taking our guns.
- **Suppression by Globalist UN - WTO and WHO:** The UN is on record as being a globalist organization committed to open borders and one world government. All of its satellite organizations, such as the WTO and WHO, share their goals and are therefore enemies of sovereign governments the world over. If we want peace and prosperity, they must be dissolved because they are the enemies of humanity.
- **Usurping of Security Agencies:** The U.S. was preparing to enter World War II, and it needed a spy agency and had none. So, they went to the traitorous CFR, and they became the CIA. The rest is history. America's intelligence agencies were compromised from their inception.
- **Orchestration of The Great Depression**: As previously discussed, it was planned and calculated, intending to bankrupt the U.S., which it did in 1933. At that point, the U.S. government was declared to exist in name only, and an army of unelected bureaucrats were imbedded into the government to dismantle America quietly from within.
- **Orchestration of '08 Financial Collapse:** As previously discussed, following 9/11, manufacturing had been outsourced to China, and the stock market had crashed, so the one remaining engine of the U.S. economy was real estate. Obama stepped in and sued Citibank for redlining, creating the predatory lending zero-down, no income verification mortgages. The unqualified buyers were given short-term mortgages (ARMs) set to have interest rate hikes at a set time. All that remained was for the interest rate hikes to go into effect, and an instant real estate crash just as planned. Not enough time to get into it here, but as previously discussed, Clinton and Bush were coconspirators in this treasonous act.

- **Orchestration of Coming Financial Collapse:** It is simple. Create a $38+ trillion national debt, raise interest rates, schedule refinancing of one-third of the debt at high interest rates, and if all goes as planned, the U.S. experiences another bankruptcy. This is the Cliff Notes version. Hopefully, you get enough of the drift to know it is planned to bring down the U.S. because it is the only nation capable of stopping the birth of the globalist one-world dictatorship. There will likely be an assortment of different types of traumatic events that occur at roughly the same time. Call them an insurance policy!
- **No Bail Policy:** Made-to-order chaos. For example, you burn down a business in a peaceful riot, get caught, are booked, and are back on the streets in no time flat, ready for another bonfire. Alternatively, if there is a bond required, it will be provided by the financiers of the barbecue.
- **Defund the Police:** A simple equation. No police, no resistance to criminal activity. It is "Chaos 101."
- **Riots, Looting, and Burning:** Just another name for a peaceful protest!
- **Domestic Terrorism:** How about allowing tens of thousands of military-age men in the country? What harm could there be? But what if they happen to be trained military agents? That would pose a significant national security threat, resembling a Trojan Horse.
- **Black Lives Matter and Antifa:** Nothing but paid protesters and rioters.

DOMESTIC TERRORISM

- **Drug and Human Trafficking**: A favorite tactic of the British. They used it on China in the 1800s when they pacified China by flooding it with Opium. To free the nation, China fought two wars (known as "The Opium Wars"). Ironically, China is using this same tactic on America. Side note: Things got so bad in China that the emperor ordered all the Opium dens raided, and they took all people with an addiction out and killed them. Today, it is Fentanyl and, in the U.S., it kills over 100,000 people a year. The worst part is how it affects the nation. It is a cancer eating away at the soul of the nation. It is a silent war.
- **Illegal Immigration:** Think about it. We have over 20 million unenvied guest and the Democrats expect us to take the food from our children's mouths to feed a host of what may well be an invading army.

- **Sanctuary Cities:** This reminds me of the wild west, where outlaws hid out. It is happening again, except it is the Democrats, and there aren't hundreds of criminals. There are hordes of them filling our towns and streets, turning them into crime and drug-infested hellholes. Just go to what was beautiful San Francisco, and it will make you want to cry. This infestation is killing our soul just like it did in China so long ago.
- **Poverty and Homelessness:** The U.S. is being turned into a squalor as bad as you would see in any third-world country. It has to be stopped, or it will be the end of the United States.
- **Gangs:** Our adversaries are releasing criminals such as murderers, rapists, drug dealers, and gang members into America to create fear within our homes, as stated by Trump, who claims expertise on this issue. It must be stopped.
- **Gun Violence and Gun Control:** Make no mistake. The violence and shootings are intended to justify taking our guns away, and with them our right to defend ourselves from a tyrannical rogue government.

ECOLOGICAL CRISIS

- **Clean Water Crisis:** This is avoidable. But instead, our would-be slave masters are using water as a weapon of war. California farmers have to let their land lie fallow while meltwater from the Cascade Mountains is flushed into the ocean. Reservoirs and catch basins could be built to capture rainwater, but that is a problem because it would solve the crisis.
- **Drying Aquifers:** As previously discussed, our aquifers are drying, signaling a future famine. Yet greedy corporations are allowed to buy millions of acres of farmland for the water rights, take the land out of production, and sell the water to cities in arid regions at 10x profit, and our government does nothing. This is tantamount to mass genocide. It just has not reared its head yet.
- **Potential Famine:** No, not a potential famine. If we keep doing what we are doing, it is a certainty. The result will go a long way toward giving the Elite their dream of a global population of 500 million.
- **Weather Manipulation:** In the 1970s, the U.S. government signed a treaty with Russia agreeing not to use weather manipulation as a weapon of war across borders. During the Vietnam War, under a secret project called "Operation Popeye," the U.S. created manmade monsoons to bog down enemy supply lines. More recently, say in the

Carolinas, where there happens to be a valuable Lithium deposit, there just so happened to be the mother of all hurricanes, causing what I call a land reclamation project.

- **Directed Energy Weapons:** The targets are California forests and historic property in Hawaii; the objective is valuable land not for sale, short of tragic fires driven by high winds and a shortage of water. Call these natural disasters if you will, but I call them "acts of war" committed by greedy men intent on being our slave masters. People who take what they want, no matter the consequences!
- **Chem Trails:** Aerosol poison is administered to deliver slow-acting heavy metals and chemical agents to inconspicuously kill plants, animals, and humans—mass genocide in disguise.
- **Nano-plastic Particles:** Forever chemical agents that kill marine life and get into the food chain. Eventually, they are absorbed into our bodies, even our brains, and slowly kill us. Very little is done to address this crisis because profits are more important than the environment or human life. There will be plenty of time to solve the problem once the useless eaters are removed. The Georgia Guide Stones tell us that the perfect number of us (Useless Eaters) is 500 million, so just short of seven billion of us must meet our maker. But what a utopia they will have when we are gone!
- **Desertification:** Just another way HARRP is used to control us. Want a drought? It can create it. Want a hurricane? No problem. How about an earthquake? Coming up! The options are many, all of them devastating. But no matter, the end justifies the means. Utopia awaits as soon as we are dead!.
- **GMOs:** Just a little genetic tampering. But wait, it may destroy the ecological balance of the planet. No matter whether it is good for the bottom line. We will address the issue after we get rid of the pests.
- **Dying Reefs:** Check out what is happening in Florida. The Reefs are bleaching out and dying. Cause: Rising temperatures. Blame it on climate change. Not so fast. Remember, HAARP raises the temperature to create all those juicy Hurricanes Florida had this year. Don't forget those trillions of nanoplastic particles floating in the ocean. They create a heat sink, raising water temperature. It is just like baking a cake: put in the right ingredients at the right temperature, and you get a natural disaster cloaked in plenty of plausible deniability. For goodness sake—wake up!

- **Declining Marine Life:** I've got an idea. Let's starve those pesky eaters to death. It's easy. The recipe: Overfishing without adequate fish hatcheries to replenish the fish population, add in a few trillion microplastic particles, heat the water, kill the reefs, destroy the food chain, and mission accomplished. We have the technology to cause such ecological tragedies. But we also have the technology to fix the problem. But wait! That would be counterproductive to the endgame objective.

MIND CONTROL

- **Brainwashing:** Imagine being able to reprogram someone's mind so thoroughly that they automatically dismiss any opposing views, regardless of the source. That phenomenon is called "cognitive dissonance." It is what I refer to as "Brainwashing 101."

  Here is how it works: Create a set of circumstances where the person is fed information that is repeated over and over. Deny them any information that contradicts what you are telling them. Even the deepest, darkest lie becomes an irrefutable truth.

  Now think of our federal education system and project head start that gets access to the narrative in our children's brains when they are literally a blank, impressionable slate. Now think about the world we live in. The schools have a script they feed our children; our politicians follow the same script as do the fake news outlets and Hollywood. Hollywood is particularly effective because they catch us with our guards down. After all, it is only entertainment. No, my friend! It is predictive subliminal programming.

  Next, consider the little gadget you and your children can't live without (the phone) and its big brothers (the Internet and ChatGPT). You have just been brainwashed without realizing it. As they say, "Resistance is futile." How can it be otherwise if you are utterly oblivious to what is being done to turn you into a passive puppet?

  Finally, if there are a few people who are immune to this predictive programming, they can be neutralized. Just call them conspiracy theorists, and the fact-checkers call them idiots or worse, liars. That puts the icing on the cake. You have just created an army of submissive slaves scripted to accept your narrative, no matter what it is.

- **Socialist Ideology:** So, given what you just read, perhaps you can understand how, under Hitler, children turned their parents over to the Gestapo to be tortured and killed. Likewise, maybe you can begin to understand that, despite your best efforts, your children grow up believing that socialism is good and capitalism and America are evil. We have to get back control of the narrative. We need your voice to help counter the opposition. Please make your voice heard.

- **Division:** How to turn the mass of humanity against one another. Create a dichotomy. A situation where good is bad and right is wrong. Use that framework to create a narrative where virtually anyone who is even slightly different from you (or your group) can be framed as an enemy. Hopefully, you begin to understand why literally the mass of humanity is at one another's throats!

We only have one enemy. That enemy is a small group of evil men who want to create a one-world dictatorship and are willing to commit mass genocide to achieve their maniacal agenda of world dominance. We are all just pawns in a chess game for world dominance. Just because someone is a different color, race, religion, nationality, economic or political group, or from a different age group, that does not make them enemies. What it does is make you a pawn in a game aimed at dividing humanity. Hence, we actually bring about our own slavery, misery, and death. What are you going to do now that you know the truth?

GLOBAL GENOCIDE

- **Georgia Guide Stones:** These stones declare their agenda of death to the world. Remember, for some unknown reason, they always have to tell us ahead of time what they intend to do to us.
- **False Flag Wars:** Kill tens of millions and create chaos.
- **UN Agenda 21:** The objective is to create the narrative for the climate change agenda and the eventual genocide of most of mankind.
- **COVID-19:** Kill hundreds of millions and, by locking down the world, create enough debt to collapse the world economy, leading to their version of the Great Reset. This happened to create their global dictatorship and the death of 7.5 billion people.
- **Vaccinations:** This causes genetic alterations and suppression of our immune systems, so over time, millions, billions of us could die from a variety of causes while having plausible deniability.
- **Sterility:** Since COVID-19 and the corresponding vaccines were implemented, sterility and miscarriages have skyrocketed. Go figure!

- **Genetic Modifications:** Alter the genetic structure of our foods and beverages to cause significant microbial issues to our health at the molecular level.

WARS FOR PROFIT

War is Big Business. The Elite don't give a damn who is killed or maimed. The more carnage, the more money they make. Likewise, the longer the war last the more money they make. Also, it doesn't matter one bit if the war is justified (or if it is based on a false flag event). Consider the wars listed below. Need I say more?

- World War I
- World War II
- The Vietnam War
- Operation Iraqi Freedom
- Arab Spring

WHAT CAN YOU DO? WHAT WILL YOU DO?

Now that we have an understanding of how our enemy controls the masses through various forms of unconventional warfare, let's explore how their control mechanisms affect us on a more personal level. Specifically, the:

- Impact on the Family and Our Children
- Impact on the Millennials, Generation Z, and Generation Alpha
- Impact on the Elderly

At one point in America, the nuclear family was strong and resilient. America's faith, family, patriotism, and morality were what made America invincible. We were all united around a set of core values.

Growing up in the 50s and 60s, I remember these common observations of our nation. How about you?

- The nuclear family was the core of society.
- Marriage was the norm. There were very few people who just lived together.
- Marriage was between a man and a woman.
- Mom was the caregiver, and Dad was the breadwinner.

- There were very few single mothers.
- Families ate meals together and shared their day with one another.
- Families went to church on Sundays and then spent time together afterward.
- Parents tucked their kids to bed at night with a hug, a kiss, and a prayer.
- Parents raised their children without interference from the government.
- There were dress codes, and piercings and tattoos were frowned on.
- Children played together.
- There were rules, and they were followed.
- It was an era of patriotism, baseball, and apple pie.
- Prayer and the Pledge of Allegiance were in every school.
- Jobs were secure, and a family could live comfortably on one salary.
- People spent quality time with each other instead of being tied to their phones and computers.
- Most people owned a home, and there were relatively few apartments, so there was a real sense of community.
- Mothers and fathers saved and helped their children get a start in life, so they didn't start in debt.
- Children took care of their parents in old age instead of putting them in a nursing home.
- People and relationships had respect for each other's values.

The foundation of society has since been fractured. The globalists have pushed us too far too fast, and we have woken up, and now we will take back our freedom. The FED and the central banking system are being dismantled, and with it their control over humanity!

America is indeed a nation of immigrants, but those who founded America shared something vitally important. They were all seeking the American Dream. They were fleeing oppression from European feudalism, where they were denied the right to own land, or, for that matter, have any rights. The immigrants who founded America were hardworking, self-reliant, and patriotic people willing to assimilate into American culture.

By contrast, the immigrant army of today is made up of people who demand entitlements while waving foreign flags and chanting anti-American slogans. This is an invasion orchestrated by The Globalist intended to collapse America from within.

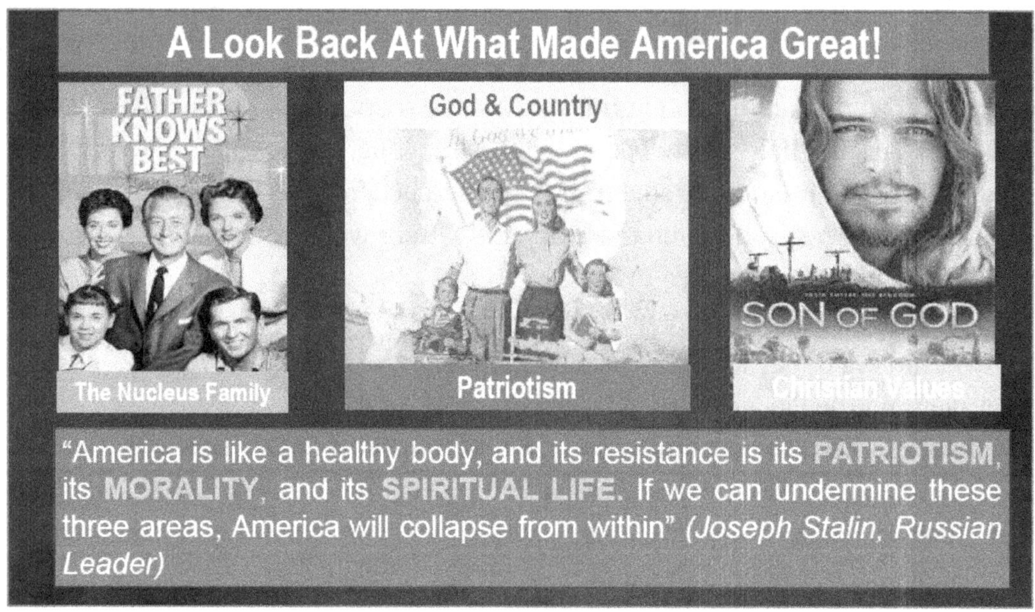

Are you willing to stand up and restore the American heritage for your children and grandchildren?

IMPACT ON THE MILLENIALS, GEN Z, AND GEN ALPHA

My heart goes out to the current generation of young adults. The financial stability that my generation enjoyed is largely not available to your generation. It has been stolen from you by those who would be the masters of us all. Your generation has been denied the simple pleasures my generation took for granted. You are literally slaves without chains.

When I grew up, the average home cost was $23,000. Today it is $400,000. A new car was around $4000. Today, a new car is $30,000 and up. A dollar was worth a dollar, and today it is worth around four cents. Today, the average salary is $62,000. Klaus Schwab said, "*You will own nothing and be happy.*"

That is a lie from the pit of hell. The American dream of home ownership is being intentionally denied this generation. Most first-time homebuyers are priced out, and tens of thousands of homes are being built for rent only. It is slavery without chains, and it is being done intentionally.

THE WORLD IS DEPENDING ON YOU!
YOU CAN MAKE A DIFFERENCE IF YOU STAND UNITED AND SAY "NO" TO YOUR SLAVERY

I want to leave you with a note of encouragement. The global financial system is about to collapse. It has to collapse because the world has reached the point where it can't absorb any more debt. The fiat dollar will collapse and be replaced by a gold-backed currency. All the sudden, the cost of everything, including houses, will revert to 1950-1970 prices.

When this happens, banks and corporations will collapse in mass. When we find out that our elections have been stolen, massive numbers of politicians and government bureaucrats will be removed. If you prepare now for what is coming, you will have amazing opportunities open up to fill the void that is created.

Don't stand idle. Don't be stopped by the fact that your college degree has not prepared you for financial success. It was intended to be that way. Do like your forefathers and rely on yourself. Assess your skills. Ask yourself what you are good at, what you live, what you want, and go after it.

Stop thinking in a limited way. Could you start your own business? The big box stores are crashing, making way for small family businesses. What are you good at? Stand up, be creative, and take control of your life. How can you make a difference? What do you want? What will you no longer tolerate?

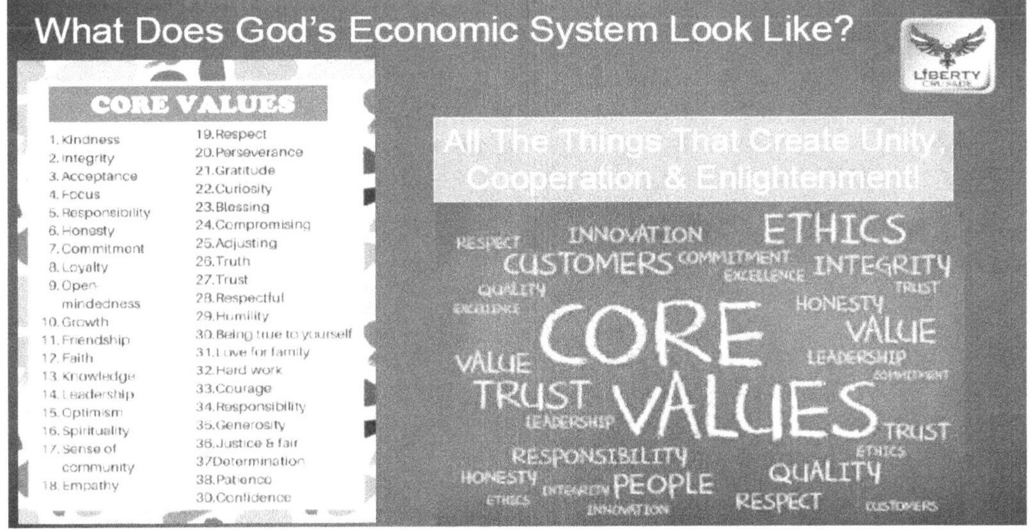

The core values mentioned on the previous slide contain the future that God wants for America and for the world. Change is coming. The system is collapsing. Take advantage of it!

Some of us are in the winter of life, including myself. But we are still fighters! The government has done everything to see that you retire totally dependent on them for social security, Medicare, and other basic needs. But let me offer some words of encouragement as I close this chapter:

- The future is yours for the taking!
- Your future depends on what you do now.
- The next generation is looking to you for leadership. What are you going to do?
- The corporatocracy is on the brink of collapse.
- Trump is taking down the FED and confiscating money from the Elite.
- Just say "No" to your slavery, and they will fall.
- Now is the time. If we stand united, we will soon be free.

The Elite have done everything they could to divide us because they know a nation divided cannot stand. Thanks to Trump, the globalists are backed into a corner, and they are vulnerable. More is happening than you think. If we stand together and make our voices heard, it will make all the difference. Governments and corporations are capitulating and showing signs of falling. Now more than ever is the time for *Restoring the Republic*!

ABOUT THE AUTHOR

As mentioned in the Introduction, author Larry Ballard heard from the Lord after a near-death experience in his young adulthood. Larry received instructions from God for his life's assignment. God told him:

- Read the Quran for context, but study the Bible for guidance.
- Study history because it is a great teacher.
- You will have several accidents, each of which should kill you, but you will walk away unscathed, so you will know you have a guardian assigned to guide and protect you.

Sure enough, after that last word of knowledge, Larry experienced several incidents that could have and should have taken his life. But true to His Word, God spared him from them all. Larry Ballard:

- Fell from a five-story building. As he fell, Larry's foot got caught, and he hung upside down until he was rescued.
- Lacerated his head in a cave accident. At the ER, the doctor swabbed the injury, and the artery burst. Had that happened in the cave, he would have died.
- Was involved in a head-on car accident at 70 miles per hour. Larry managed to jump into the back seat, and the engine ended up where he had been sitting.
- Was in a plane when the engine exploded and caught fire. *The Sioux Falls Newspaper* said it best with their headline: PLANE ENGINE EXPLODES AND CATCHES FIRE, BUT MIRACULOUSLY NO ONE WAS INJURED.

God also told Larry that his jobs would change frequently, each one divinely appointed to teach people something God wanted them to know. And Larry heard God say that he would travel to nations at pivotal moments in time to experience first-hand the events shaping the world. Larry's work experience has included:

- **Being a construction worker, building skyscrapers.** There, Larry worked with Thermite, giving him the knowledge that on 9/11, the towers were brought down by a controlled demolition. Thermite is the only substance in the world capable of bringing down a steel skyscraper. It burns at 4,500 degrees, melting steel like butter.

- **Monsanto Chemical,** where he learned about GMOs
- **Atomic Energy of Canada,** where he learned that energy is a control mechanism. Note: Canada has socialized medicine, which is a form of control and suppression.
- **Twenty-two Years in the medical field,** which helped him see how hospitals and drug companies prioritize profit over cures.
- **CGR Mev Paris, France,** where Larry saw the early formation of the Socialist European Union. While there, he witnessed the enemy's plan for a ten-nation trade block that would control buying and selling. Today, the UN openly promotes this alliance of evil.
- **Real estate broker,** which taught him how the 2008 financial collapse was perpetrated on an unsuspecting public.
- **Involvement in three acquisitions and mergers,** which showed him why perfectly solvent companies were taken over and then broken up and sold off in pieces. This was done to seed trade supremacy from the U.S. to China. The intent forms a hybrid super-capitalist economy controlled by a global elite intent on enslaving humanity. This effort was orchestrated by elements within our own government, with Presidents Nixon and Carter as their pawns.
- **Being in China, during the Tiananmen Square protests,** where Larry witnessed the social contract that the CCP made with the Chinese people, which would lead to their demise. Following the massacre, China was poised for a coup when the CCP promised the people that if they would live under communism, they would be guaranteed full employment and a better standard of living. Today, unemployment is rampant. The Factories are closing, and the people are protesting by the tens of millions because their dream of a better life has turned into an oppressive nightmare.

Throughout his life, God has sent Larry's pre-ordained mentors. God told Larry, "Because your preparation will take decades, I will periodically visit you in the early morning hours to guide you. I will also send mentors to teach you." Over time, this has proven to be true.

The divine appointment that God brought Larry in his darkest hour happened in 2009. The 2008 housing collapse and his divorce cost him a real estate business and $1.85 million.

Naturally, he was devastated and wallowing in pity. But that's when he had a divine appointment that got him back on track.

Larry recalls that it was at a Wednesday night Bible Study when a church member escorted a blind lady in, who asked the pastor to pray for the restoration of her eyesight. The pastor laid hands on her, and her anointing knocked *him* to the floor! When the pastor stood up, he asked the blind lady to pray for those in attendance.

There were only about half a dozen there, and God told Larry to go last. It turned out she was a prophet. She quietly prayed over everyone and gave them a prophecy that was exactly what they needed. But when it was Larry's turn, she blurted out at the top of her lungs, *"It's you! God sent me here to tell you that if you didn't stand up and stop pitying yourself, I am going to give your assignment to someone else!"*

Later, in private, she explained that she had been sent to be Larry's mentor. And for the next three years, until her passing, she taught him how to walk with the LORD.

Don't forget to check out Larry Ballard on *Rumble*, where he is involved in these weekly shows:

- *Liberty Crusade Official*
- *Blessed2Teach*
- *Upfront Front in the Prophetic*

He is also a frequent guest on *Nino's Corner* with David Nino Rodriguez, and *QFS1776*, hosted by Mel Carmine and Dr. Meri Crouley.

Coming in late 2026 is Larry's new book, *LIBERTY CRUSADE: Restoring the Power of the Bible.* It is the historical account of how the people who crucified Christ usurped his throne, controlled who could translate the Bible, and inserted false doctrine in it as a control mechanism. God is releasing the latter-day rain and Harvest of Souls. It is time for the captives to be set free and for the world to experience signs, wonders, and miracles never seen before!